MILES WALKER'S
DICTIONARY

Book that lists (not in alphabetical order) and explains the
words of this artists language and slang.

"secret language" in olde english was abbreviated to slang.

Other books by the author: Synthetic Sea Sixty Six, After Age, Uani, Themus, Soft Journey, Paradise Papers, Doodles & Dreams. Miles Walker's Diary

Front cover painting by Miles Walker, back cover painting by my mother Wynona.

Typefaces: Cracked Thanks Apple.....Futura.....feel of Bauhaus although designed earlier by Paul Renner. Hiroshige.....Thanks Cynthia Hollandsworth Batty for this font which I have used so much over the years.....Fruitiger thanks Adrian how clear you are.....Xenu from the type king Ray Larrabie.....Some Optima and Compacta from the sixties and seventies!.....Rub me down Letraset you were the edge then.

DEDICATION.....WHAT!

People doubt what I say,
they read into the drawings
what they see about me,
do they believe what I do.....
Why should you?

Welcome to my second diary

a montage..... pretensiously called

dictionary (dick shun eerie).

Surreal Art Ideaology from seven

journals of words, ephemera, lies,

and artwork of memories.....Who

said the future will soon be a thing

of the past.

PREFACE.....PROLOG,

It is written this exists does it not!

KAIZEN.....(make it better)

This dick shun eerie is a catalogue....No maybe a compendium of badass poetry words, poor surreel futuristic scifi art, drawn out of my head.....The hole earth catalogue (thankxs stewart brand.....Google him) meets He man, in nineteen eighty two while waiting for salvador dali (who was in paris for his birthday) to come home to port llight.....I stayed in the hotel port llight, kiddie korner to his house and started to keep journals.....nick roeg, john antrobus, john boorman, christian marquand, richard lester had formed my mind and set this pattern for my personal passage thru the doors of denial perceptions. My disruptive mediocore education was.....Hardly very elegant my boy!.....From mombasa to castle cary, somerset.....Change was my only reality, quatermass experiment to zardoz.....I was lost in space a loose cannon, an agent for change, a wicker man, i am the bed sitting room in the visual arts, not being a doctor as was our family tradition, my quest was searching for the meaning of life...How many books are there with the meaning of life title, that don't tell you what it is! Utopia? Lennon, lenin, and dylan, dillon,....Question is, which one has the life plan? spell it out.... The meaning of life is in their words, but so hard to find.....Did they miss the web dictionary of googlmania. Informia.....Is in the dictionary; images or words that create pictures in your mind, the fading light of time portrays the soul patterns and structure of this kalidescope of visual dreamart recognition for dopy. (Clingon) not with a K.....I'm from barcelona K. Eye search the future for snow white. Fantasia the helter skelter ride through the ages of colonial lost souls, drawn from heinrich kley.....Yet me being an international voyeur with etch-a-sketch eyes, I studied maxfield parrish, frank rowlands, hans heysom and picasso while colouring outside of the painting by numbers, lines that has given a foundation to the two hundred drawings in this book......Look at this book in a ryokan in tokyo.....New japanese toilets are pleasantly anal.....Sit read an enjoy a moment of secreation,..... At last I have found the draino for the meaning of lifes diarrhea! Some of it will stick. What is another word for a visual thesaurus?

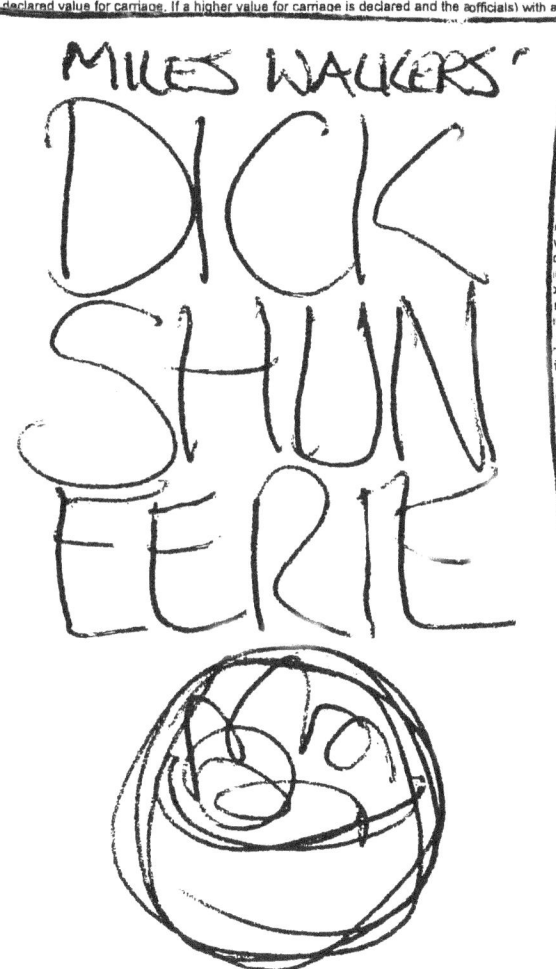

MILES WALKERS'

DICK
SHUN
EERIE

AN EYETHEYSAWUS
OF ARTWERKX

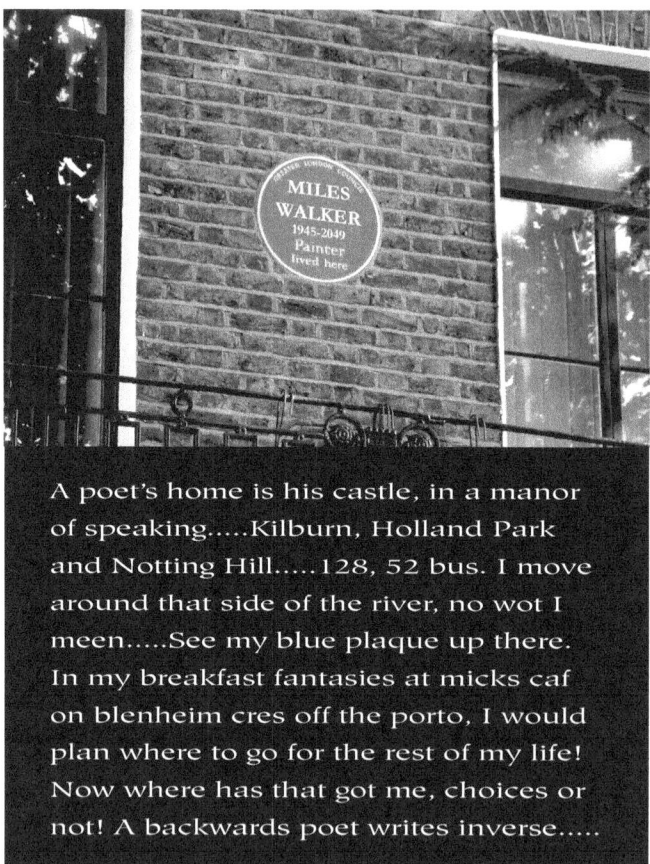

A poet's home is his castle, in a manor of speaking.....Kilburn, Holland Park and Notting Hill.....128, 52 bus. I move around that side of the river, no wot I meen.....See my blue plaque up there. In my breakfast fantasies at micks caf on blenheim cres off the porto, I would plan where to go for the rest of my life! Now where has that got me, choices or not! A backwards poet writes inverse.....

This page should have been left blank. Mum told me to put it in!.....Ps.....Her painting, the shoreline at moreton bay queensland is on the back cover.

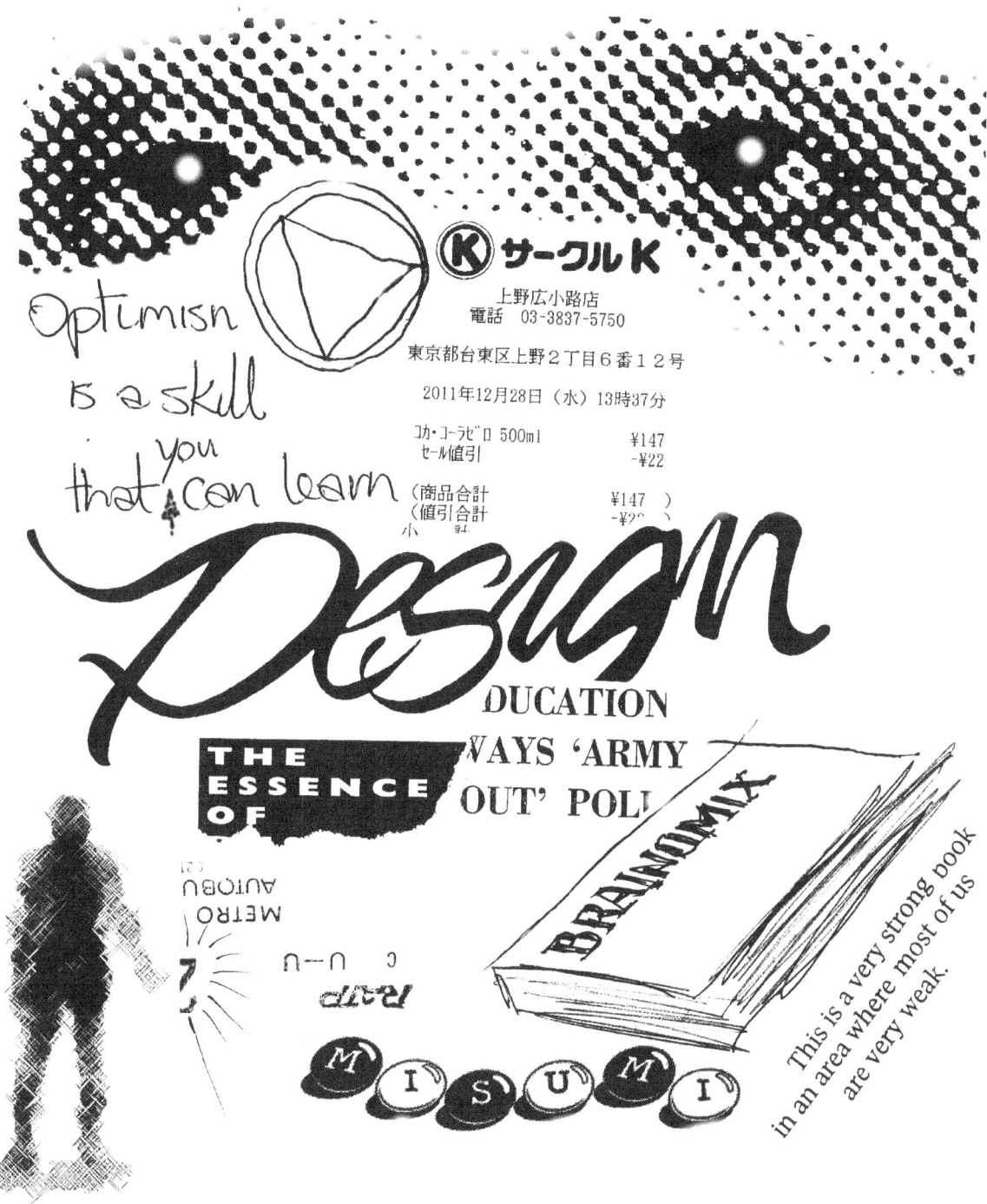

Optimisn
is a skill
that you can learn

Design
DUCATION
THE ESSENCE OF
WAYS 'ARMY OUT' POLI

Ⓚ サークルK
上野広小路店
電話　03-3837-5750
東京都台東区上野２丁目６番１２号
2011年12月28日（水）13時37分
コカ・コーラゼ゛ロ 500ml　　　　¥147
セール値引　　　　　　　　　　-¥22
（商品合計　　　　　　　　¥147　）
（値引合計　　　　　　　　-¥22　）
小　　引

BRAINOMIX

This is a very strong book
in an area where most of us
are very weak.

MISUMI

APPARITION

Remarkable or dramatic apperance;
ghost or illlusion; no strong defined
edges not usually from reality.....
Maybe a phantom.

ASSOCIATIONS

Neocortex to lucid dreaming.....
Bouncing along the words of
a song in karaoke.....Live in the
brains thesaurus and piggyback
on all your thoughts today!

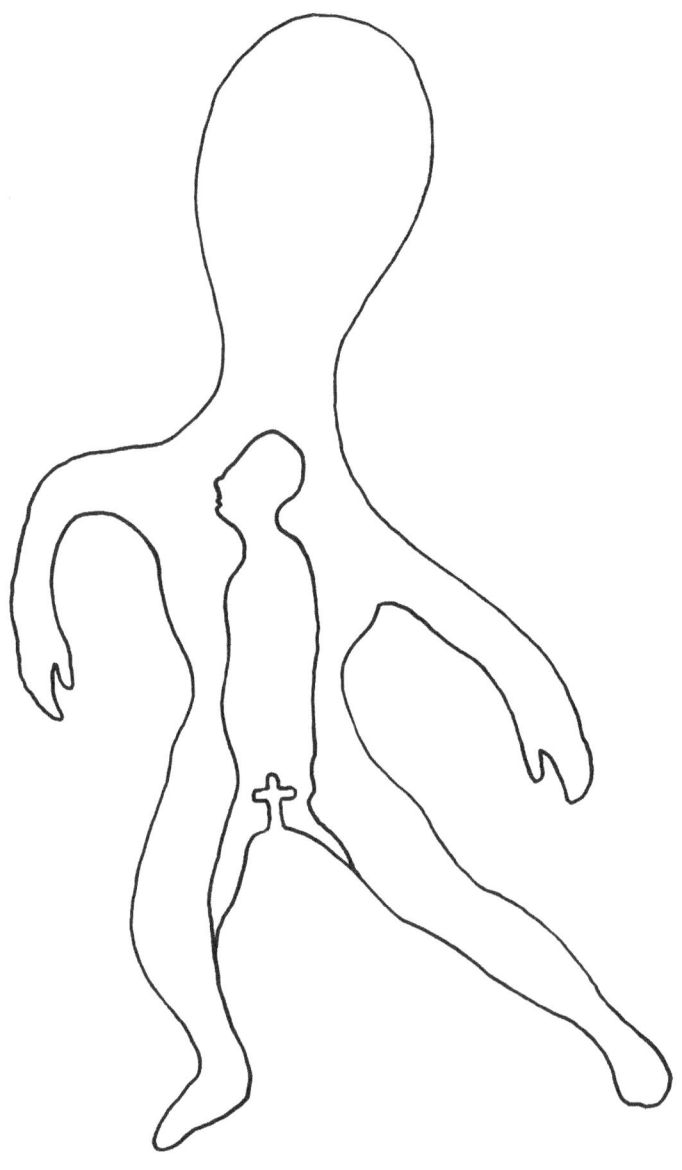

ACHILLES HEEL

The week or vunerable point, the inner person, is it you or is it your outer skin, you the guilt within....Maybe not! Are we all shape shifters or chameleons to fit into societies. Alien skin perhaps that's an inside job. See the feelings I am trying to hide? Crew sea fix.....Marks your hot spot!

AERIAL

Extension of electronic equipment to pick up signals from out of space forming them into pictures, words, sounds and feelings. Ariel: Hebrew: Angel. Alta. Lion of God.

ART

Art is a form of life (Wolheim).....Yes well certainly my life! I am the archibishop from the first church of graphicology. You will say I am a dreamer.....Artyfarty My home is where my he art is!

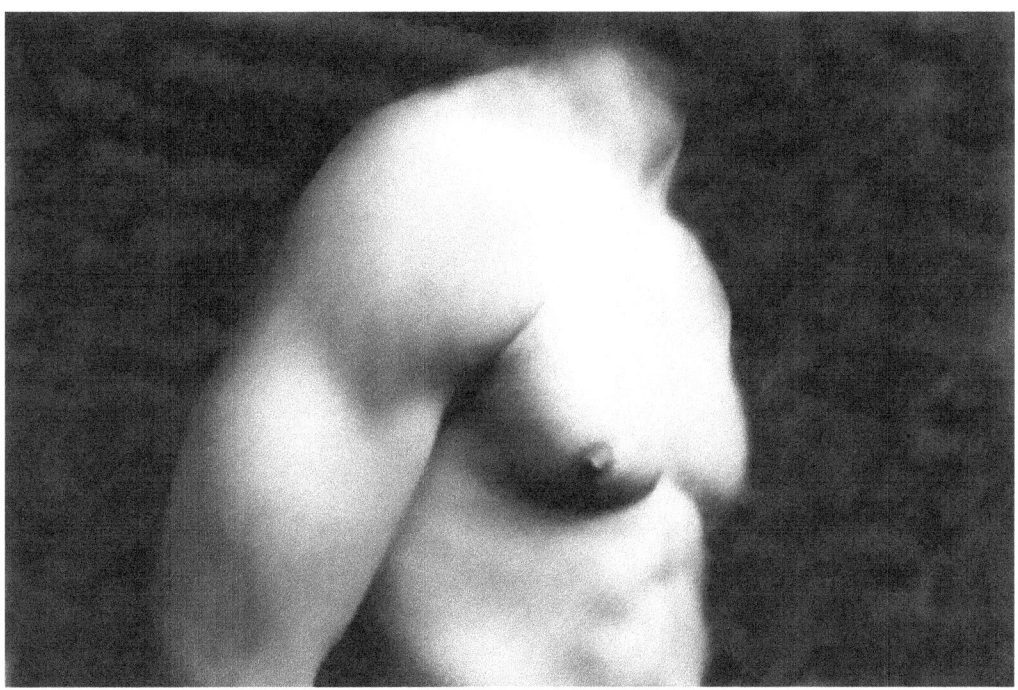

ACACIA

The mother of all gum arabic, the elixar for all the early artists of the printing and painting world. Arcacia avenue, Dar es Salaam a rainbow of white an yellow flowers creating a lovers tunnel over the roadway as you made your way to the Zanzibar ferry. Gum Arabic: food industry stabiliser

APHORISM

Sixpack....An original thought spoken or written in a concise and memorable form, short pithy maxim; brief statement of principle, Chinese proverb: Not the fastest horse, can catch a word spoken in anger. Is language a process of free creation with its fixed rules and laws. With my command of language I say nothing to the wordworts.

AD LIB

Speak without formal preparation to improvise, wing it.

APPLE

Wosniak and Jobs changed the computing world with GUI, taken from Xerox and with the help of designer Ive put us where we are now Macintosh, Apple of one's eye desired person. Round firm fleshy fruit says it all.

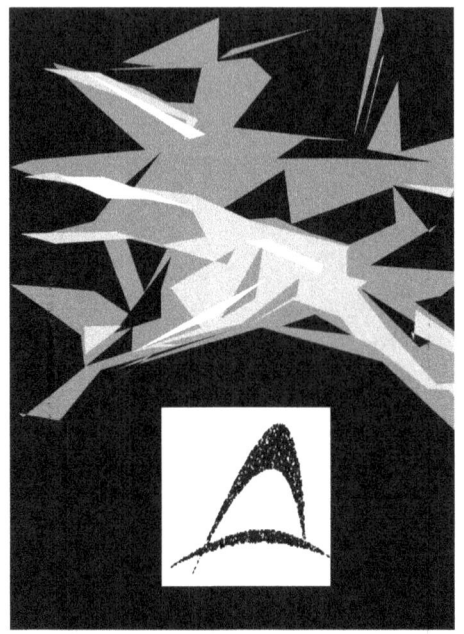

秋葉原

AKIHABARA

Japan meaning; field of autumn leaves. Word formed from the anglosized japanese, the initial letters could start aminae, maybe not!. The nearest location in this world to the future world in blade runner. thanx ridley scott. Robots to sci fi living amongst the future young of the planet who are buying mother boards and robot partners. Life starts as a comic here, and will end with total fantasy, bit like you and the simpsons, followed by south park, are we all misfits.....

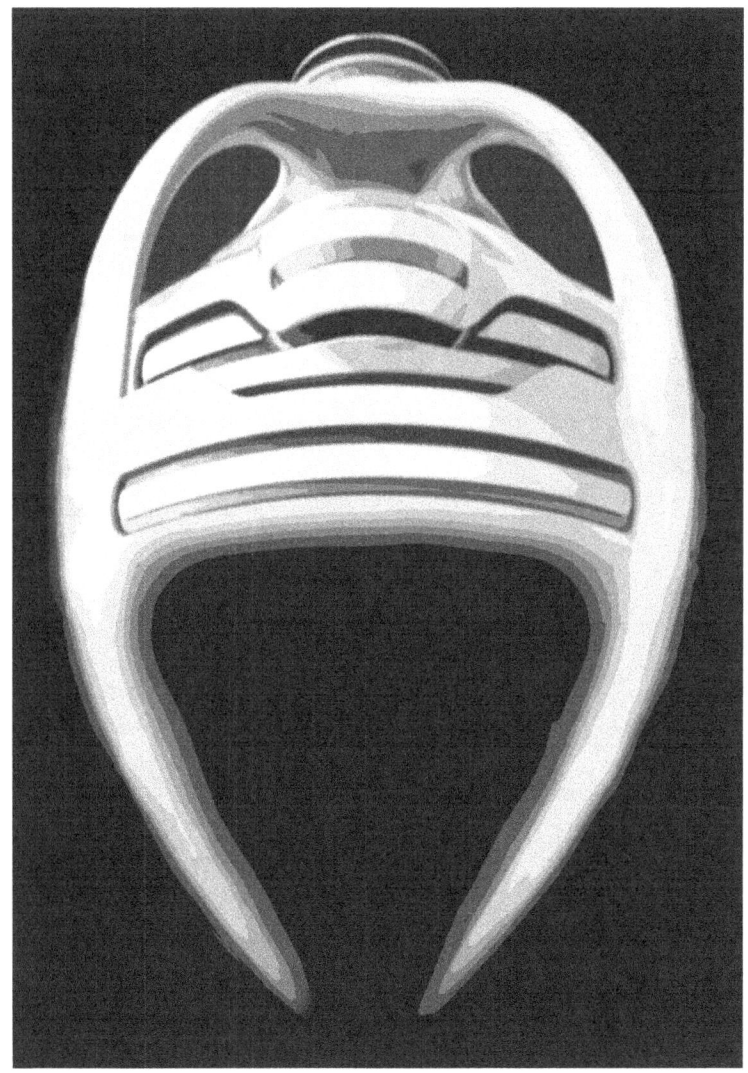

ARMOUR

Protective skin.
Distinctive atmo-
sphere around a
person or matter.
Extra skin feathered
softly on the outer
perimeter, feelings
glow around the
case of hard core
existence. Subtle
sense.

AVATAR

In hinduism, descent of god
to earth in bodily form.

ACRONYM

Word formed from the
initial letters of other
words from the greek
akron-end, onoma
name, example; KIS
keep it simple.

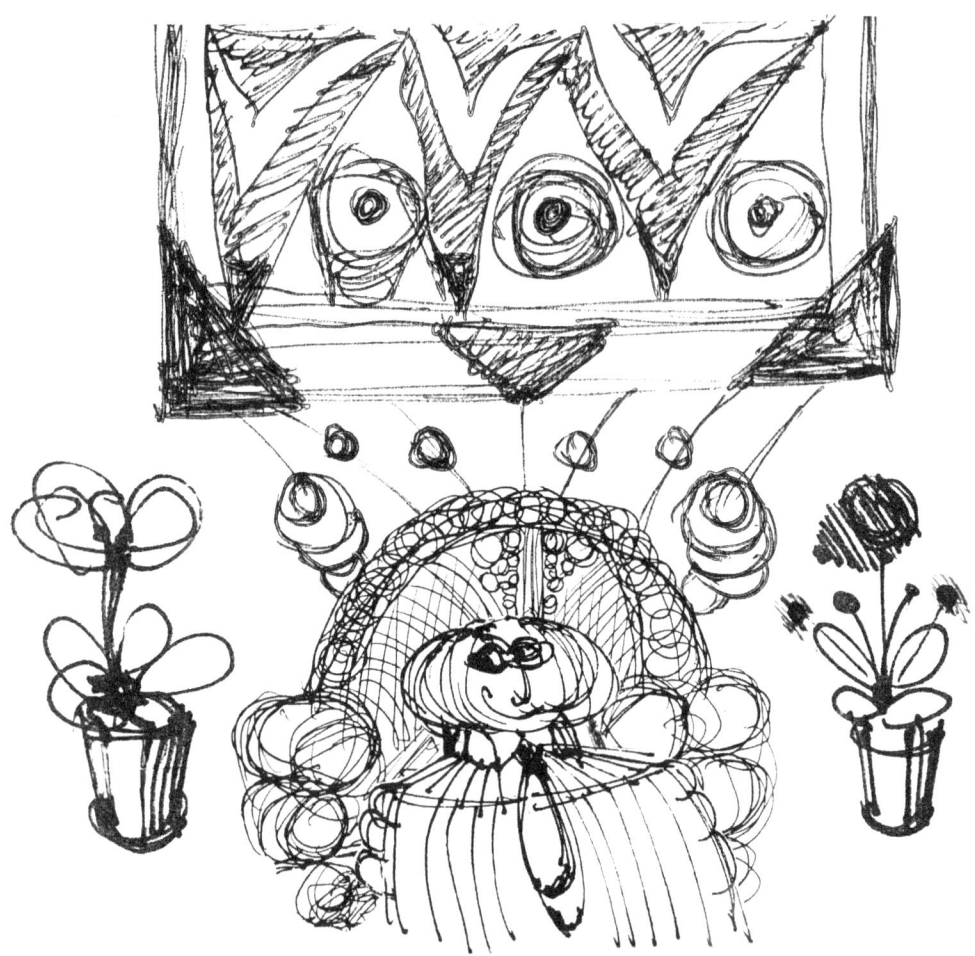

ADJUDGE

Here come de judge.....Pronounce judgement on matters.....Award or claim judicially.....Adjudicate act as a judge in court. How can we trust one person with all their biases....Still in god we trust! Judge for yourself.

ARTHUR MURRAY

Cockneys enjoy.....Slang.....Arthur murray; we are going out to have a curry! a good curry.

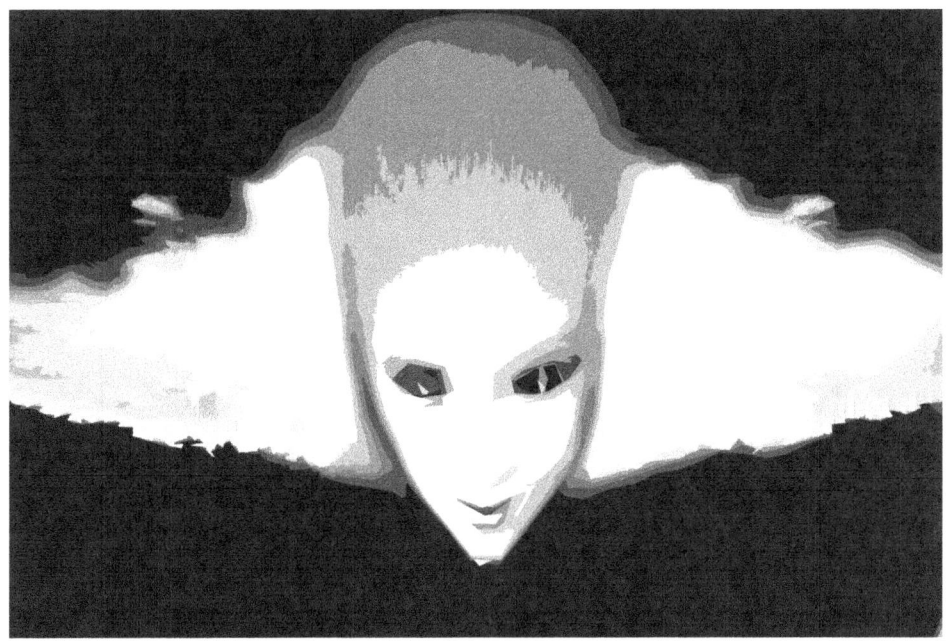

ANGEL

Came down from heaven yesterday according to Jimi Hendrix, that he sang, when I first saw him on the Isle of Wight. Is that what they really look like? Where are the wings

ATHEISM

I am a full paid up member of this non-prophet organization.

AB INITIO

From the beginning! The question is where is the start or beginning? Most human entities will give you a different starting point based on religion, forefathers, anthology and todays science!.....Do not mention the dinosaurs.

ABDUCTION

They always take you up to the ship! Say nuffnk. They are very small, grey or green.....Yuk and play with your beaver or balls.....Say no more you naughty aliens. I had an mri last month and my doctor called me in to discuss it. He asked me if I had had spinal surgery, I said never. He told me that the mri showed I had three holes cut out in my spine, each the size of a dime.....How did they get there? He said it was the most advanced surgery he had ever come across!

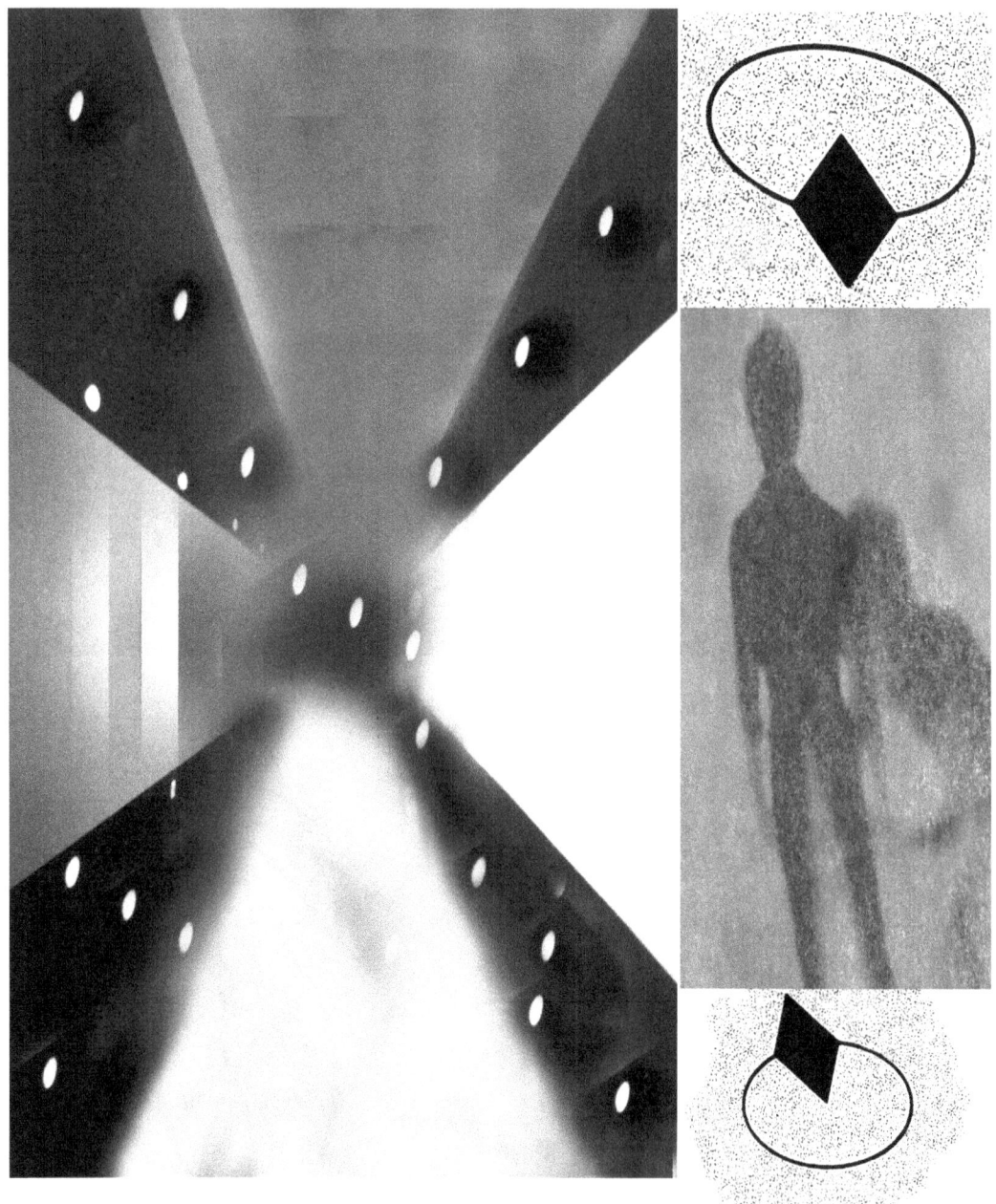

ABSTRACT

Word to do with or existing in thought or theory rather than a matter or practise, not concrete, non representational but making the assumption of representations to us sometimes. Concrete in art, a captured image in time. Sometimes achieving response by balance, form, pattern line and colour. Thought apart from concrete realities, specific objects, or actual instancies: an abstract idea. Viewers interpritation often concludes the message or story.....NO.....yes! This could be the artist happy accident. Ideas in our minds gallery, are they abstact before they are formalised into a visual language medium?

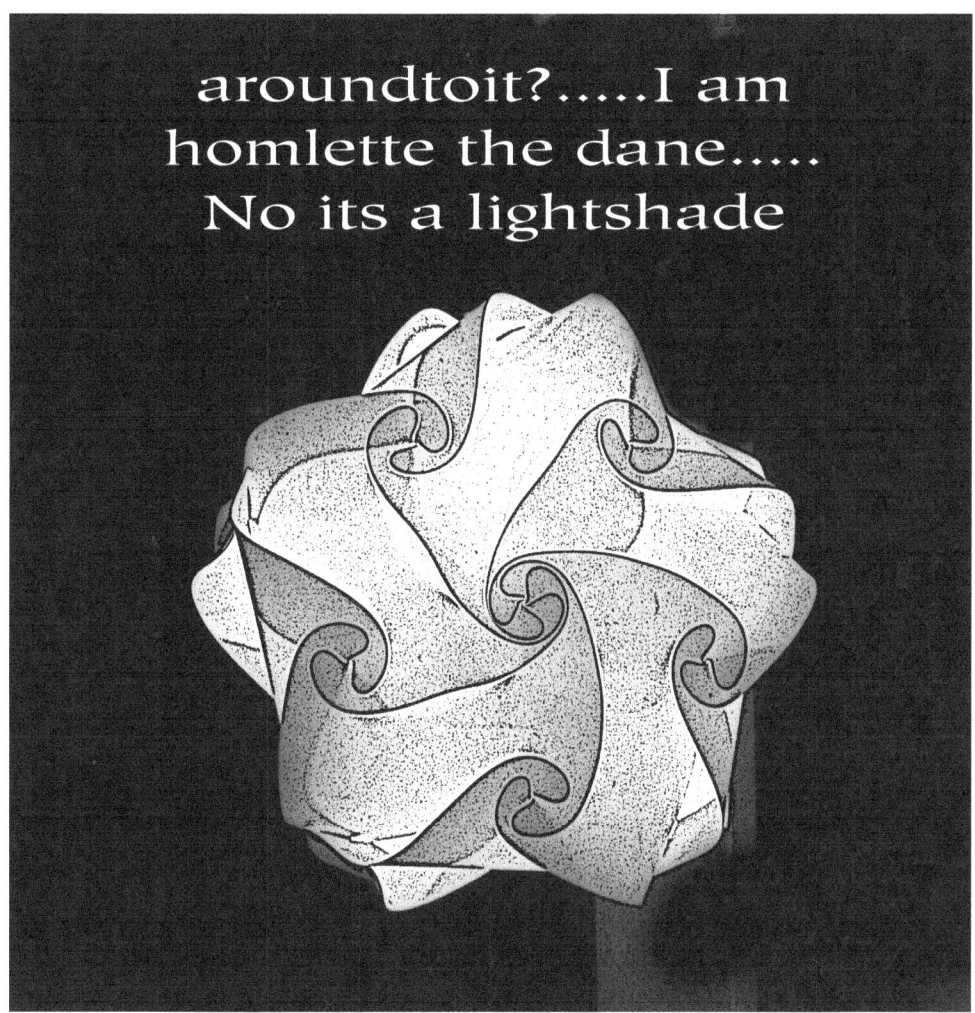

aroundtoit?.....I am homlette the dane..... No its a lightshade

AROUND

In a circle, or a cicular motion. On all sides. A circuit. Widely experienced, have been around, say no more. Cornish traditional term and phrase same as spanish manana, tomorrow maybe do it tomorrow, meaning its at the bottom of the to do list: AROUNDTOIT, often carved in a circle ten inches in diameter in oak with engraved lettering. Hang around!

ADVANCE ART

Advances in art are made by those artists who have the courage not to accept the acceptable......

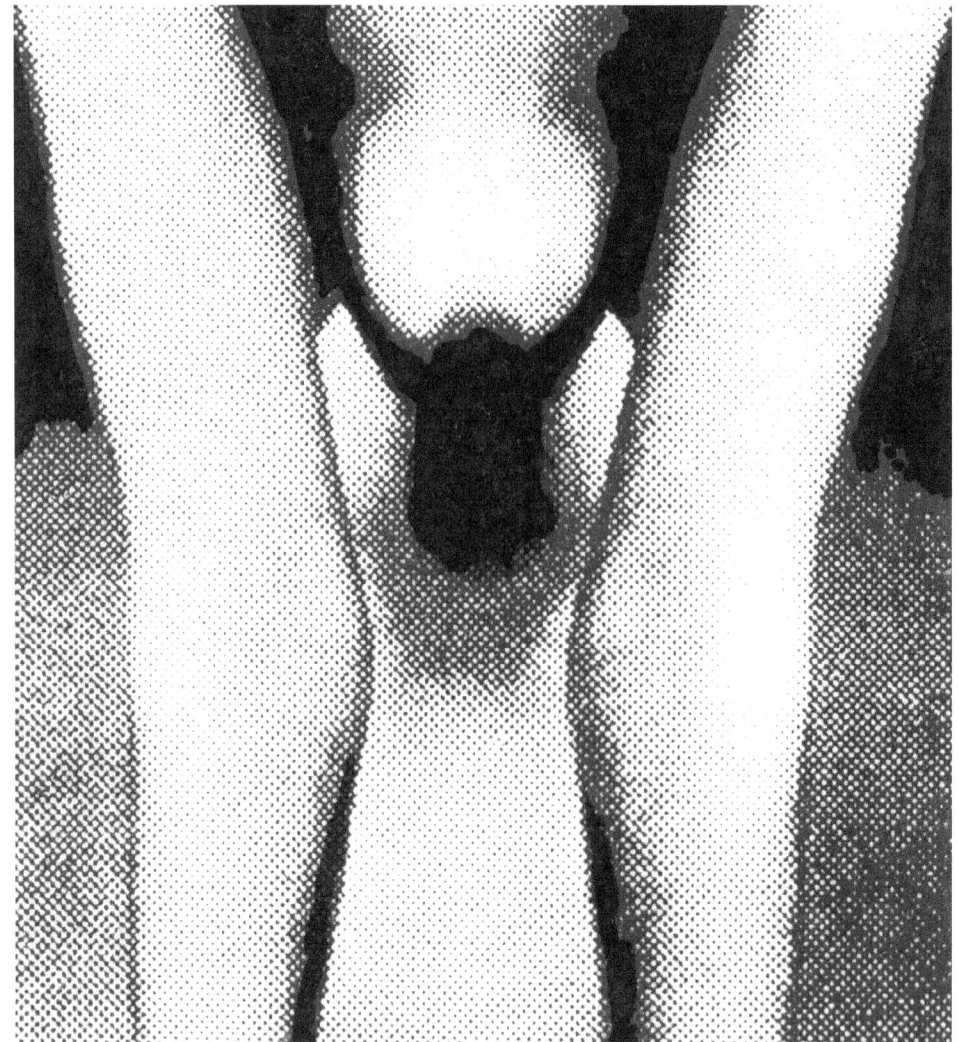

AD LIB

Wing it, happy accident as you go. Improvise, off the cuff, as one pleases to any desired extent.

ALTERNATIVE

Not nornan normal or suzy straight.....A choice between two or more possibilities, proposition, or courses of action. Can descibe a different lifestyle.

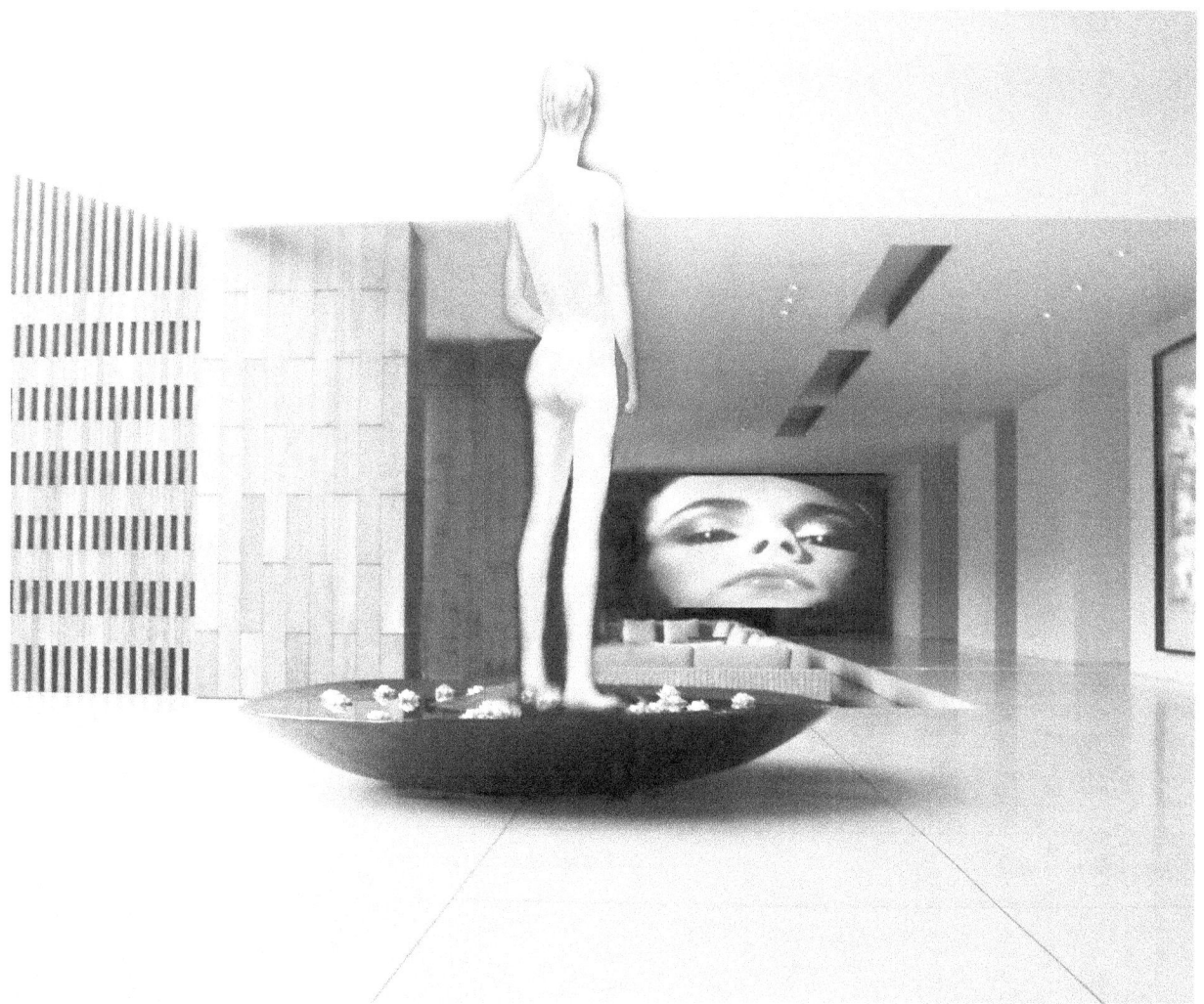

ALTERED STATES

Visually strange and not what is expected by your brain.....Any modification of the normal state of consciousness or awareness, including drowsiness or sleep and also states created by drugs, alcohol, meditation and hypnosis. Give a man a fish and you feed him for a day or two.....Teach him to use the net and he won't bother you for weeks.....Sailors plus ergot equals hallucinogenic mermaids

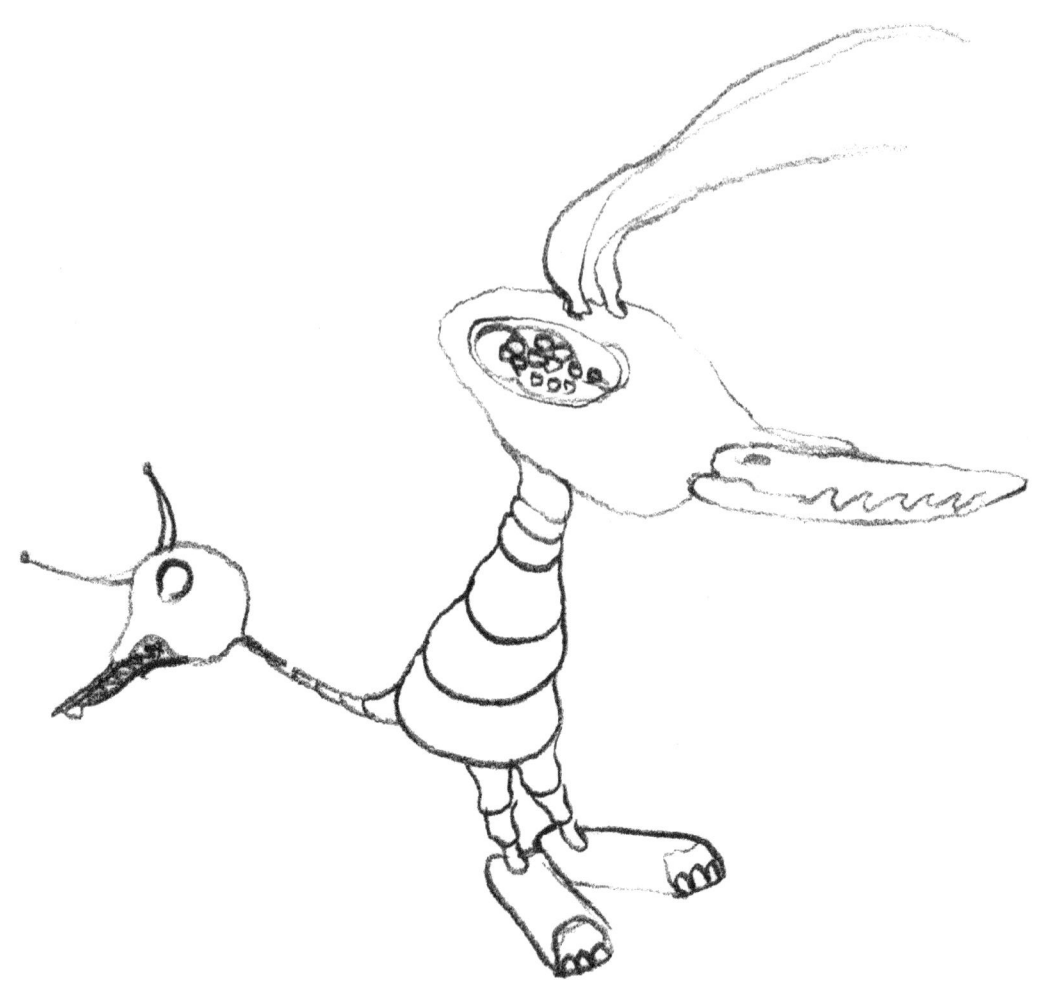

AETIOLOGY

Study of causation or of causes of disease. Our small friends carry some of our destoryers.....Parasites we all are. The picture above is a drawing of a model of brain lice from 1966. The year of a fantastic voyage.....

ANNUAL CHECK UP

The lifecare clinic has advised us that there are malfunctions and faulty access points in your neural system therefore you will be notified by the mental health authority to attend a reboot session, please confirm a suitable date on our website: Advancebrainomix.org

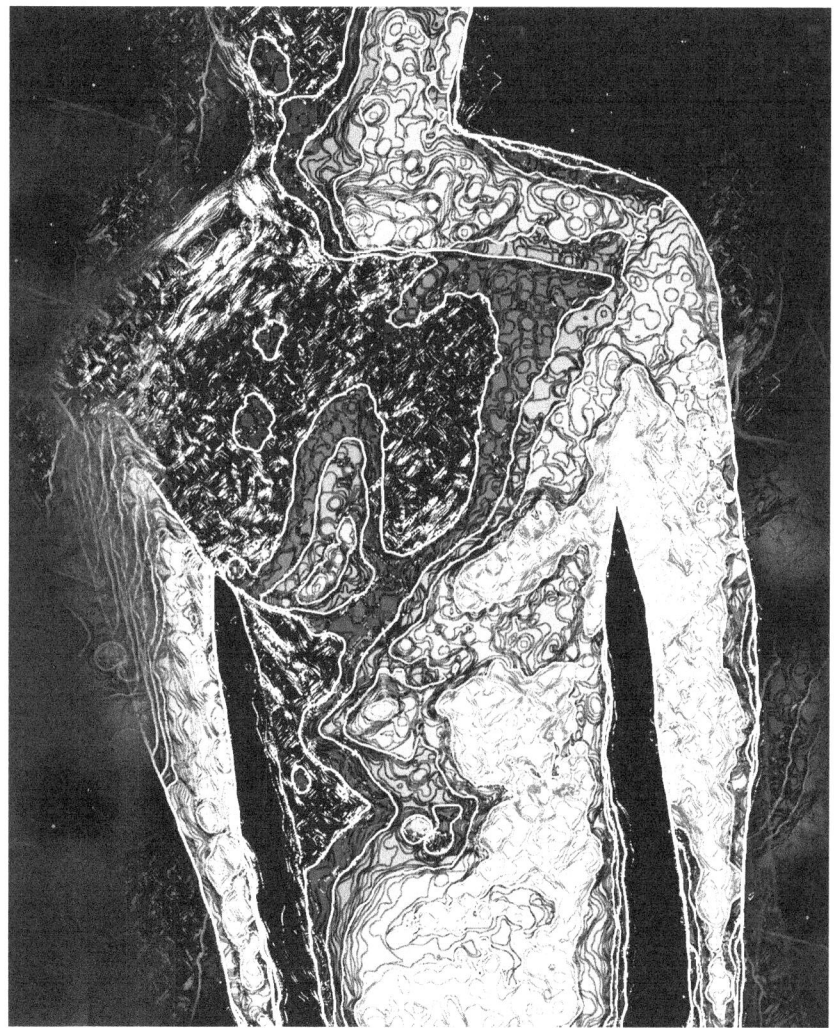

AURA

Distinctive atmosphere around a person or matter. Extra skin feathered softly on the outer perimeter, feelings glow around the case of hard core existence. Subtle sense beyond the reality of us. Subtle emanation. You would look good in glow in the dark condoms. When he was seven he had glow stars on his bedroom ceiling and when I was twelve I would wake up every two hours to look at the glow-dots on the face of my sekonda russian watch.

ARTICULTURE

The study of the growth of art history management, analizing artists and their work for the last nine hundred years, for academic thesis and achievement of mba completion. Skip a de do dar..... Skip a de day.....Wat a wuda ful say!

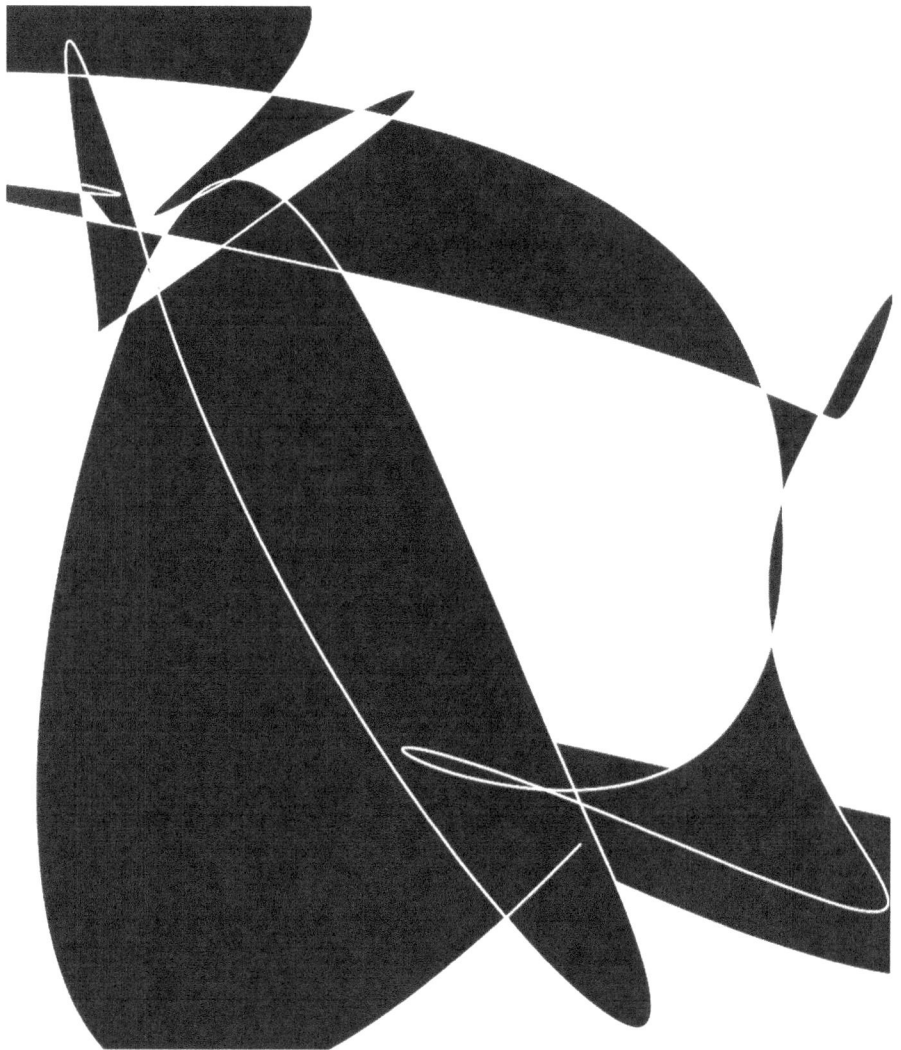

BEARDSLEY

If you had a name like aubrey you would stay home and make
pictures a lot of the time. What an incredable portfolio of work.
Everyone in the sixties who was into art had some of his prints or
books, just as they also had maxfield parish. Above is my tribute
art, an abstract "mindless" not quite as frilly as his work. How
many beardsley prints did britt ekland have?

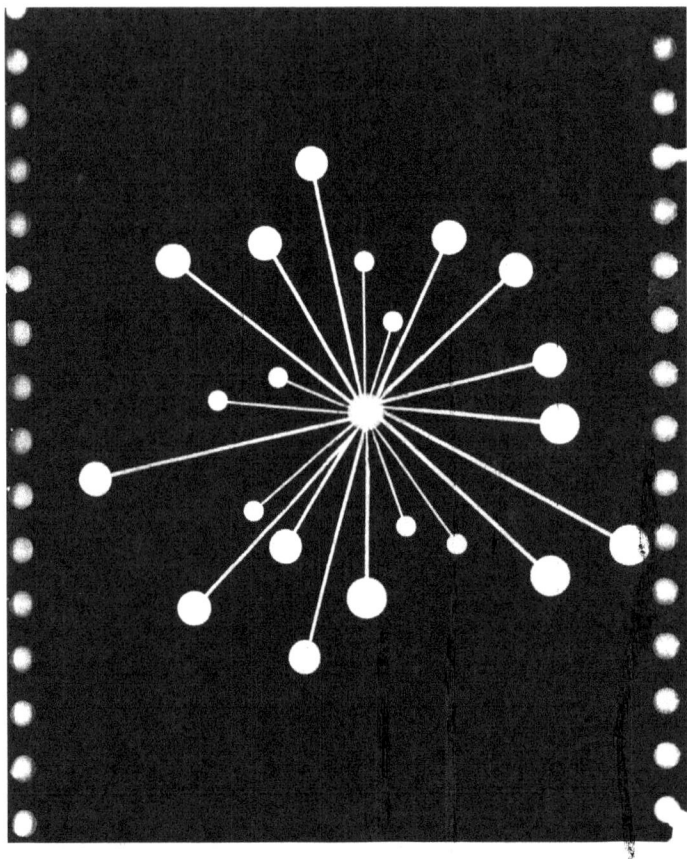

BIZARRO

Unusual.....Very strange, way beyond eccentric, originally from the french living near the itallian border.....No way!

BHOGA

Tantric words for intense physical pleasure.....Need I say more, feel this word, bring it into your breeding plan. Where does romance come into the process?.....Process.

BODYLICIOUS

Male or female with superb body shape.....Sexually attractive, well kept healthy person usually very athletic.....

BANANA BENDER

A nasty statement for queenslanders that spend days in the far north not doing much, the job they have is to bend bananas all day. commonly consumed by the creative southerners....Rite mate!

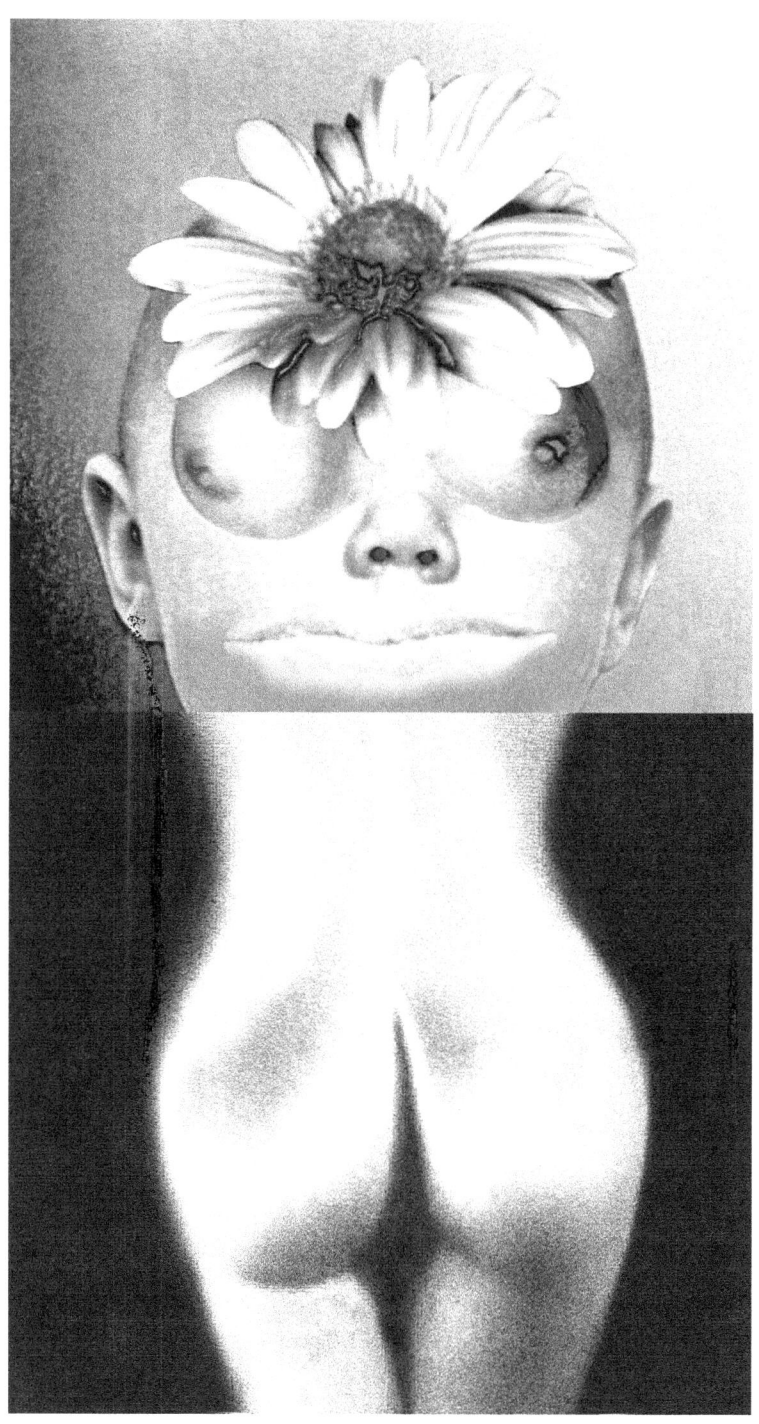

BOTTOM

Lowest part or point, part of which thing rests; buttocks; less honourable end of the class.; ships keel or hullreach the lowest level. Bottoms Up.....Cheers finish your glass in a shot! Booty call.....What has that got to do with it.....Bum! Ask an artist maybe breasts upside down. In most marriages bottoms are sexy and problems are relative. Or is it relatives are problems?

25

BUTCHERS

Lets have a look, let me see that.....
Back to that cockney language.....
Butchers hook rhymining slang,
give me a look!

BLIND

Sorry you will have to feel it.....
The unimportant likeness of
seeing.....This is only a drawing
of female mammary glands.

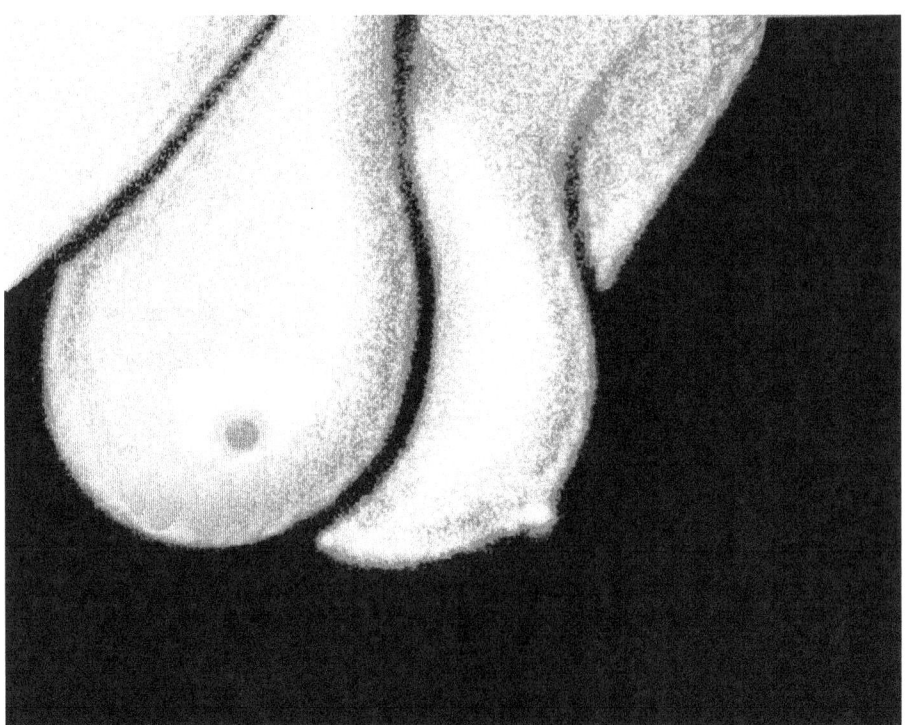

BONEETA

Not like a tuna.....Apart from the
smell; auctioned in the big markets
of the world; original word from the
spanish family name. Common to
the shores of Thailand, favoured in
Paris as a therapy for the releif of
work and relationships.

BULGING TROUSERS

This is something to get behind all your
life, as a true boy we always had that
spare pair of socks stuffed down the
underpants and I thought it was a bit of a
shock when I took her bra off to find those
foam pyramids in there, although I had
heard they could sharpen razor blades..

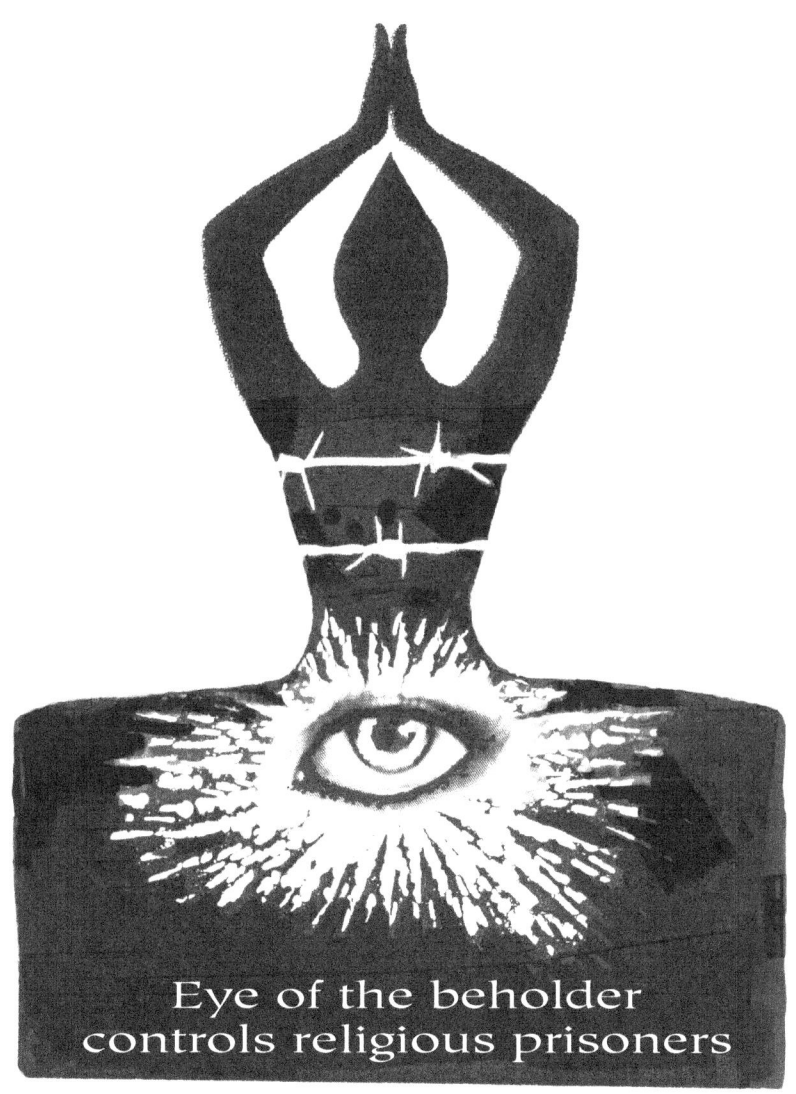

Eye of the beholder
controls religious prisoners

BOODAH

If eaten a slightly hallucinogenic substance. Gives
a euphoric felling, what did the dopers say in the
seventies "far out.....Magic I've got some good
boodah.....Keep laughin!

BIG EYES

All the better to see you with.....
Large lookers; hypnotic staring,
controls your plans; seductions
greatest tool the big eyes. The
windows of the soul/mind.

BOOKWORM

This is what I want to be when I
grow up but I'm only allowed to
do this as a holiday treat. My dead
mother "wynona" watches over me
from the cloud......You naughty boy
stop messing around.

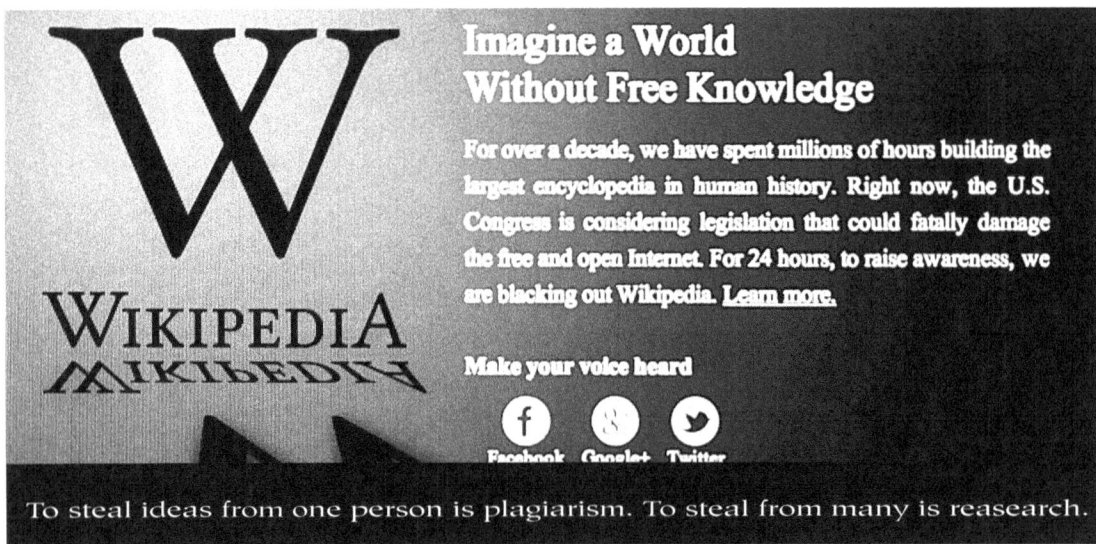

BASH

A party, a gathering like a pot
luck. When some one hits
some one.

BENDIGO

Dont you luv just how this
word feels. A town in australia
is something to remember all
your life....

BOOBOO

We stole the planet and its
resources from our children and
their children, still it will give them
something to do instead of buying a new car. Cuddily bear that
lives in yellowstone.....Bear with
me.....I'm so SAD.....Now that's a
northern canadian disease! Cabin
fever, winter woes.

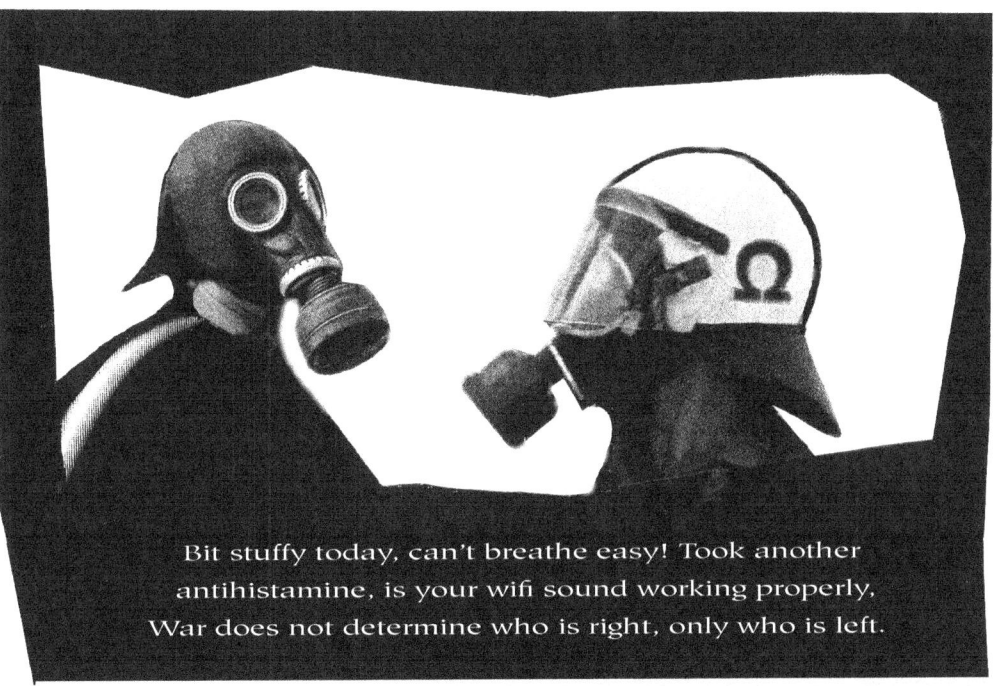

Bit stuffy today, can't breathe easy! Took another antihistamine, is your wifi sound working properly, War does not determine who is right, only who is left.

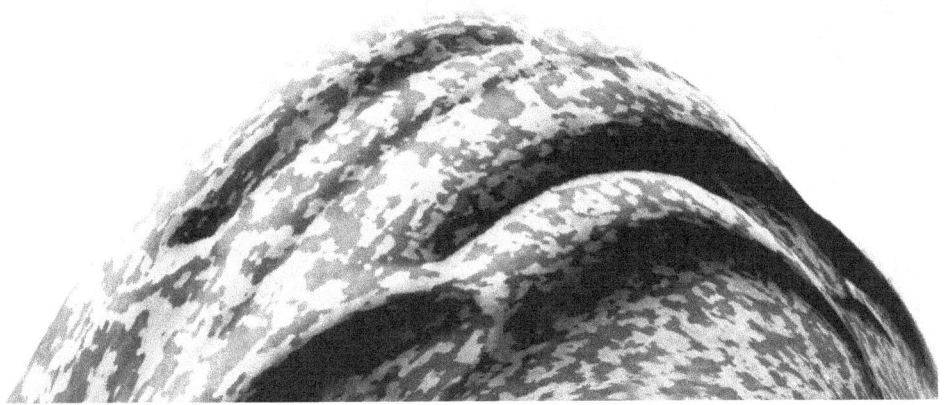

BREATHE

Draw air into and expel it from the lungs.....There is something in the air, who put it there.....Every week you can write in the dust on the table. where does it come from....? How much dead skin do we shed every day.....

BLOBBY

Small spot or drop, sometimes radioactive and very large; messy; gooey; stuck over something important squirted out of sqeezable bottle sounding like ketchup (started in India).

BIRTH

Arrival at the gates of eden, primitive painful experience for women, wake up call for men. Nine months usually after new life is conceived.

BOZO

Beautifal dog with patches. Nineteen thirty's term for an idiot..

I AM

SELF ESTEEM

Status....Reputation....Achievement....Responsibility

LOVE AND DESIRE

Relationships.....Affection.....Family.....Purpose

SAFETY HOPES

Security....Order....Comfort....Protection....Peace

LIVE WITH YOUR NEEDS

Sleep....Water....Air....Nutrition....Shelter....Warmth....Sex

BONKERS

Nutter.....Crazy.....Crackers..... Insane.....Mental.....They have gone ballistic.....Banana's.....Quite often used affectionately.

BELIEF

This is a psychological state in which an individual holds a proposition or premise to be true. God you gotta believe it!

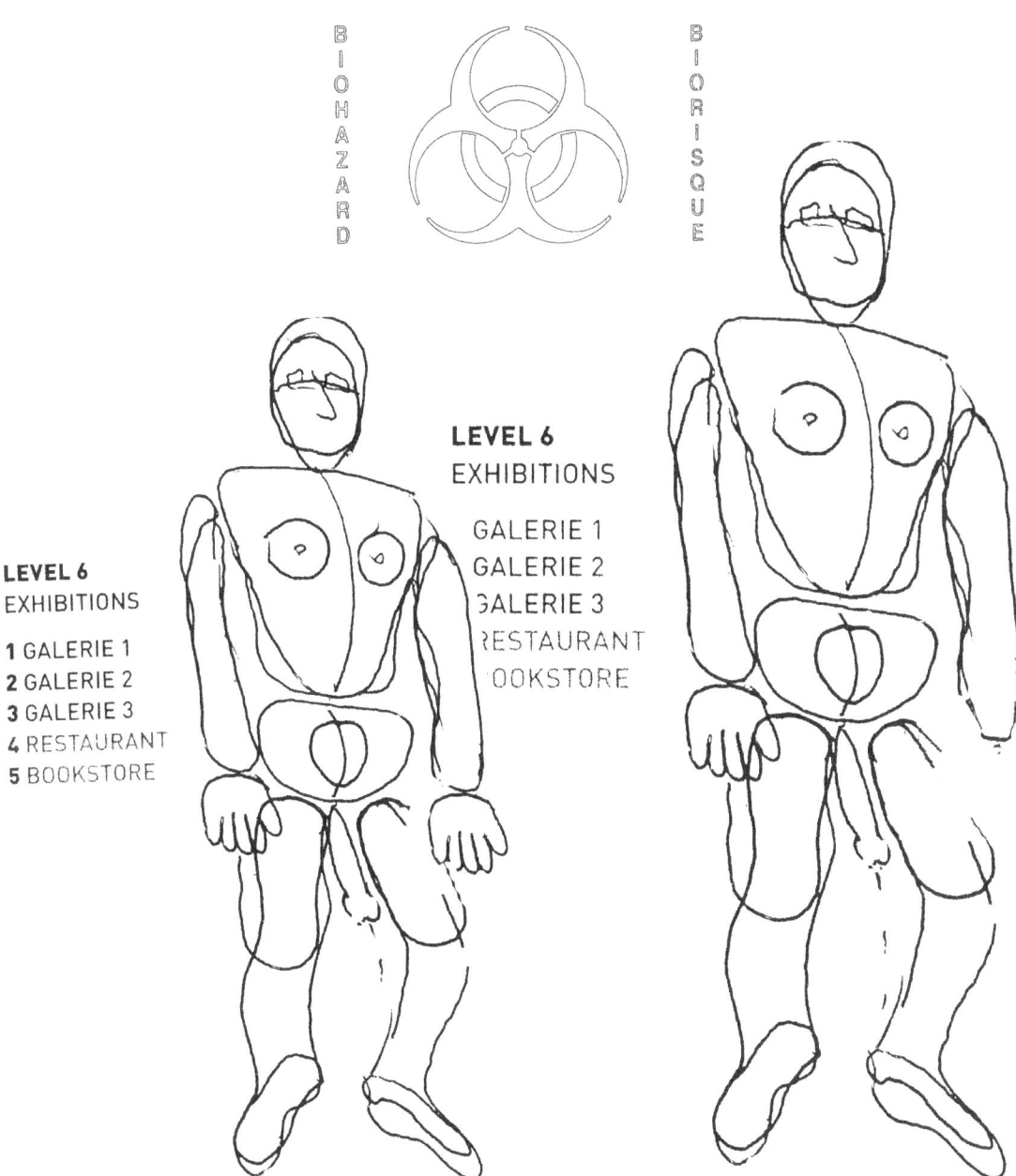

LEVEL 6
EXHIBITIONS

GALERIE 1
GALERIE 2
GALERIE 3
RESTAURANT
BOOKSTORE

LEVEL 6
EXHIBITIONS

1 GALERIE 1
2 GALERIE 2
3 GALERIE 3
4 RESTAURANT
5 BOOKSTORE

BODY

Eat less.....Move more! We spend all our time looking at each other; a group of people is a body! Physical structure, including bones, flesh, organs and soul of man and woman struggle to remain alive. Do not keep seated.

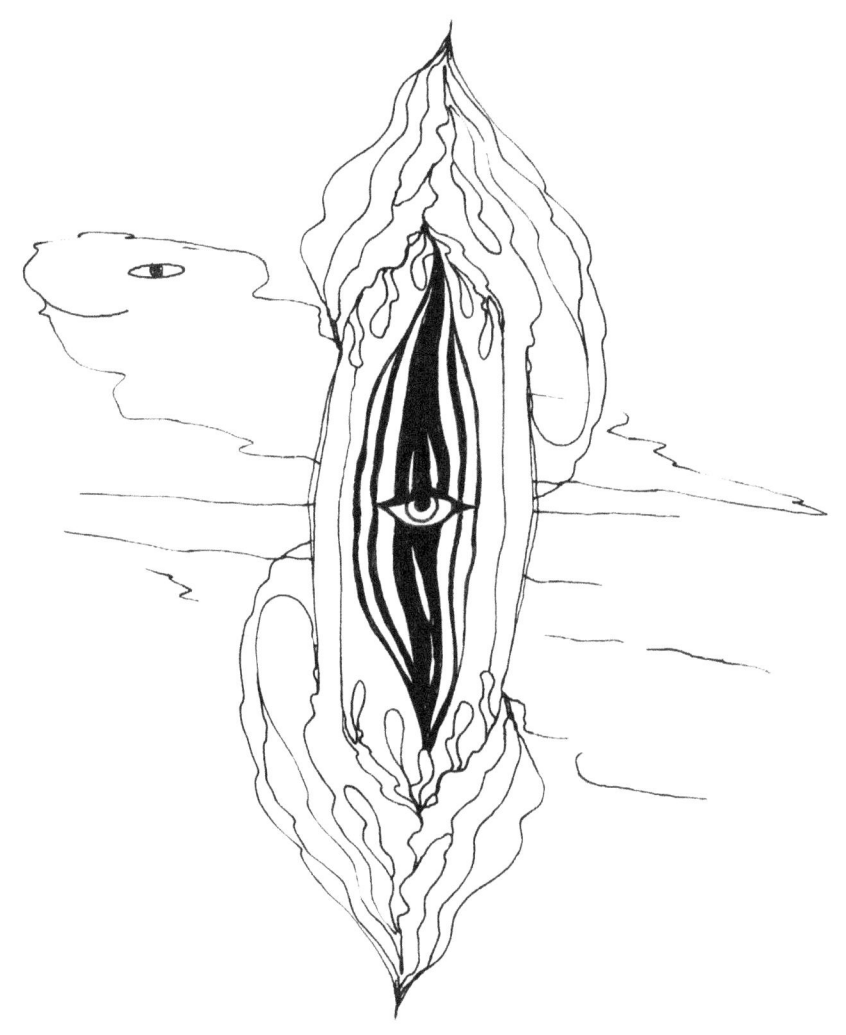

BOOTYCALL

I want a man with a slow hand, look into
the eye of the b hold her......Up up and away
u can cum out once a day.....

BLAH BLAH BLAH

Rah Rah Rah, yes yes yes whatever, I know,
I know, I know.

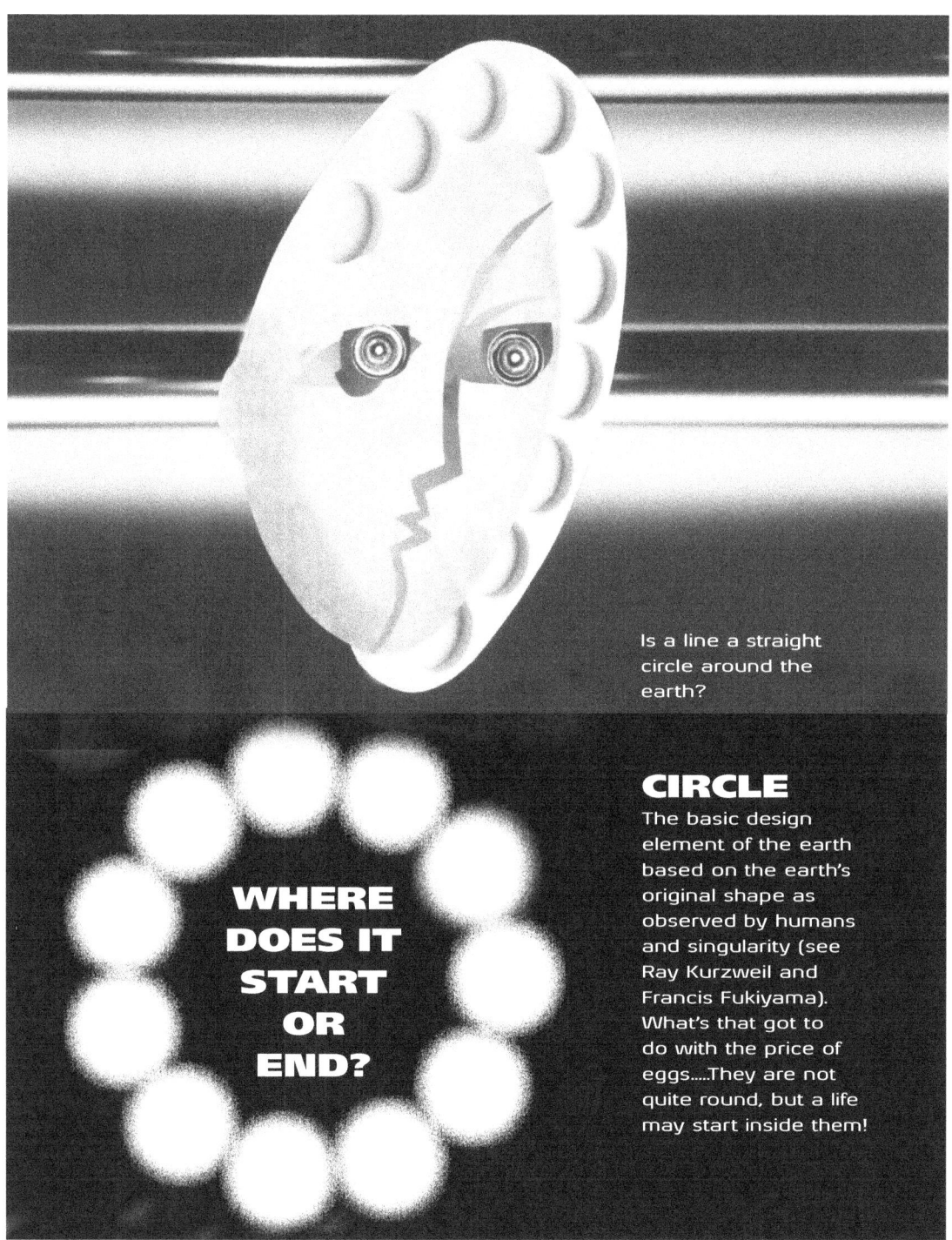

Is a line a straight circle around the earth?

WHERE DOES IT START OR END?

CIRCLE

The basic design element of the earth based on the earth's original shape as observed by humans and singularity (see Ray Kurzweil and Francis Fukiyama). What's that got to do with the price of eggs.....They are not quite round, but a life may start inside them!

CHILLY-WILLY

Cold, cold, when your private parts are really cold!.

CHUTNEY

One of my favourites to have with most food. Pickle, usually of indian origin made from fruit, spices, vinegar and sugar. A preservative.

CURLYCLOGS

Bit of a pixie in lifes journey: formed from the double dutch seaman, world traders in the eighteen hundreds living far away from normal life.

CAPTIVA

Sounds like a russian type face, or being locked up in a turkish jail but really it is a south seas island resort in Florida!

COMATOSE

In a coma.....Yeah right..... Well, where are you really, In your dreams, because you are not with us. Deep state of unconsciousness.

CASTAWAY

Why is this fantasy so good for me? I have always loved boats and the ocean!

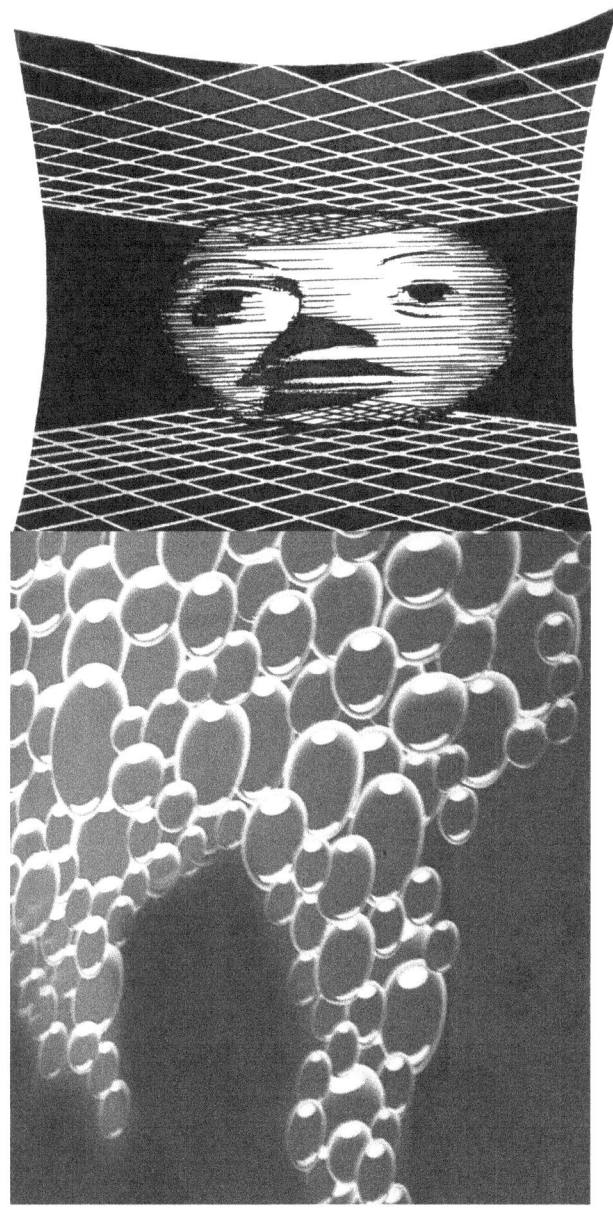

CONNECTION

Association, joined together. Connections; James Burke created this incredible tv series watch it!

CLICHE

An expression, idea, or element of an artistic work which has been overused to the point of losing its original meaning or effect. Paris club bubbles over with the perspective beyond facial recognition.

CHARACTER

Different than normal, somewhat eccentric, a unique person, object or building.

CANUKA

Derogatory word for the galley slaves from polynesia two hundred years ago that were hijacked on to european sailing ships.

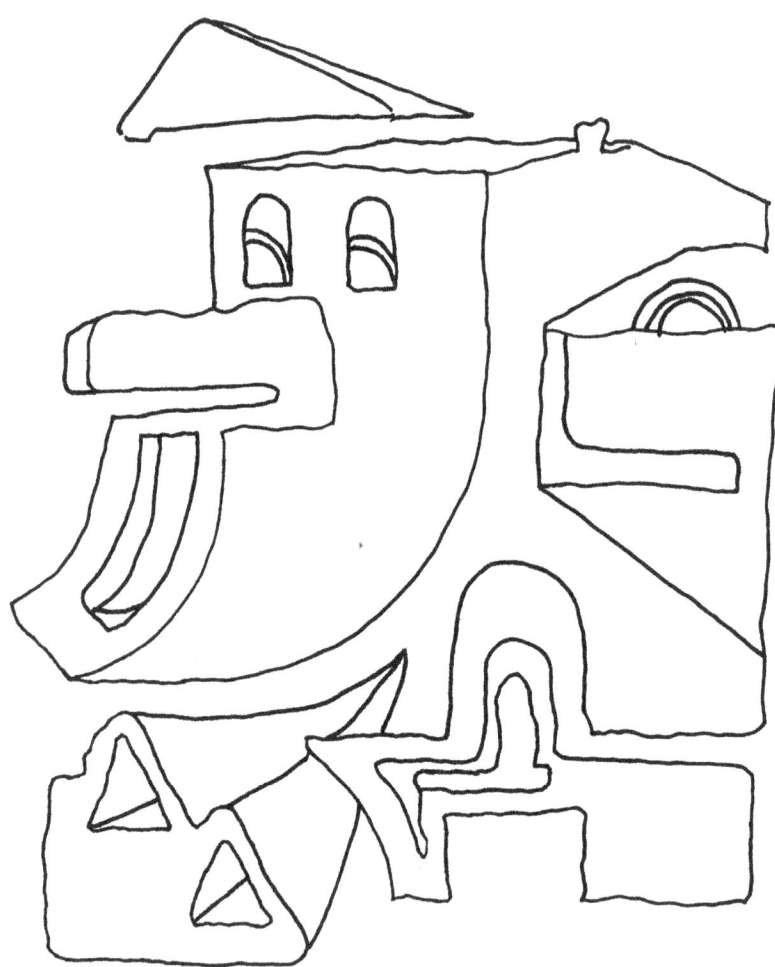

CHOWDERHEAD

Chow down, where is your next meal coming from? We ate like this, one thousand years ago and it is in some of our genes blue and otherwise.

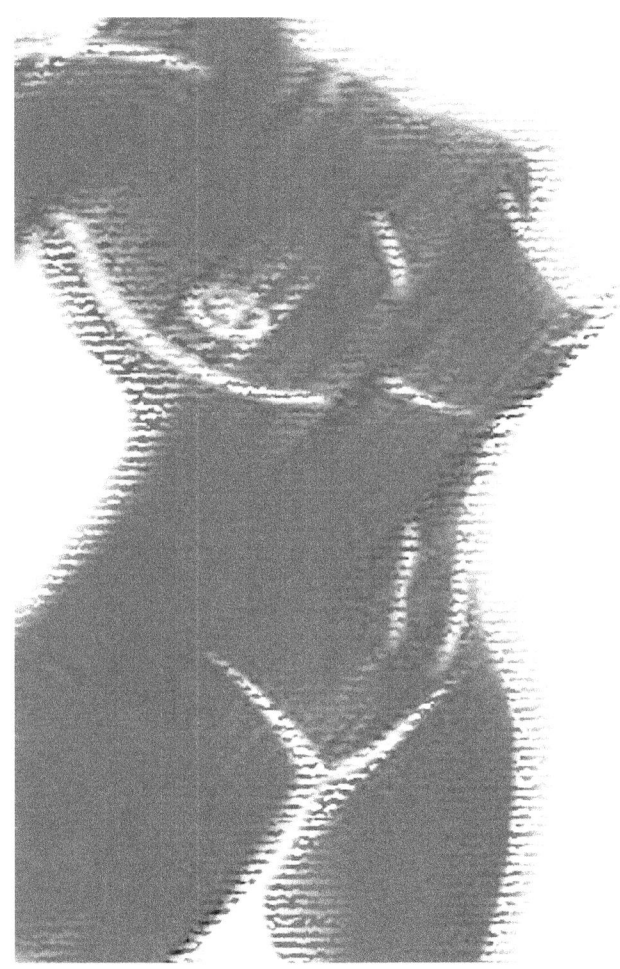

COZMO

Hurley brown changed our lives sexually and our attitudes in so many ways. She was just an editor! The front of the magazine has up-set so many.....Cos-mos.....Higgs Boson hunt is over.....2012

CHINOIS

Party authorities will shut down the company founded by hoo flung deng, his lawyer dick thomas said on friday, in the latest step in what the dissident artist has called a campaign of persecution to silence his activism.

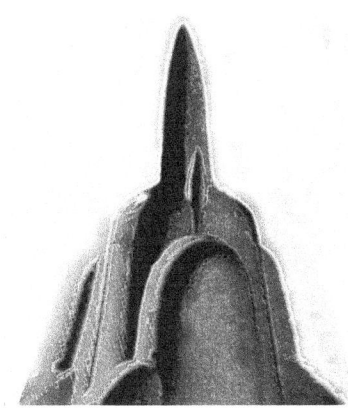

CITY

Large and permanent settlement for humans consisting of complex systems for survival and comfort..... Metropolis: a place where humans interact for pleasure, profit, and living.

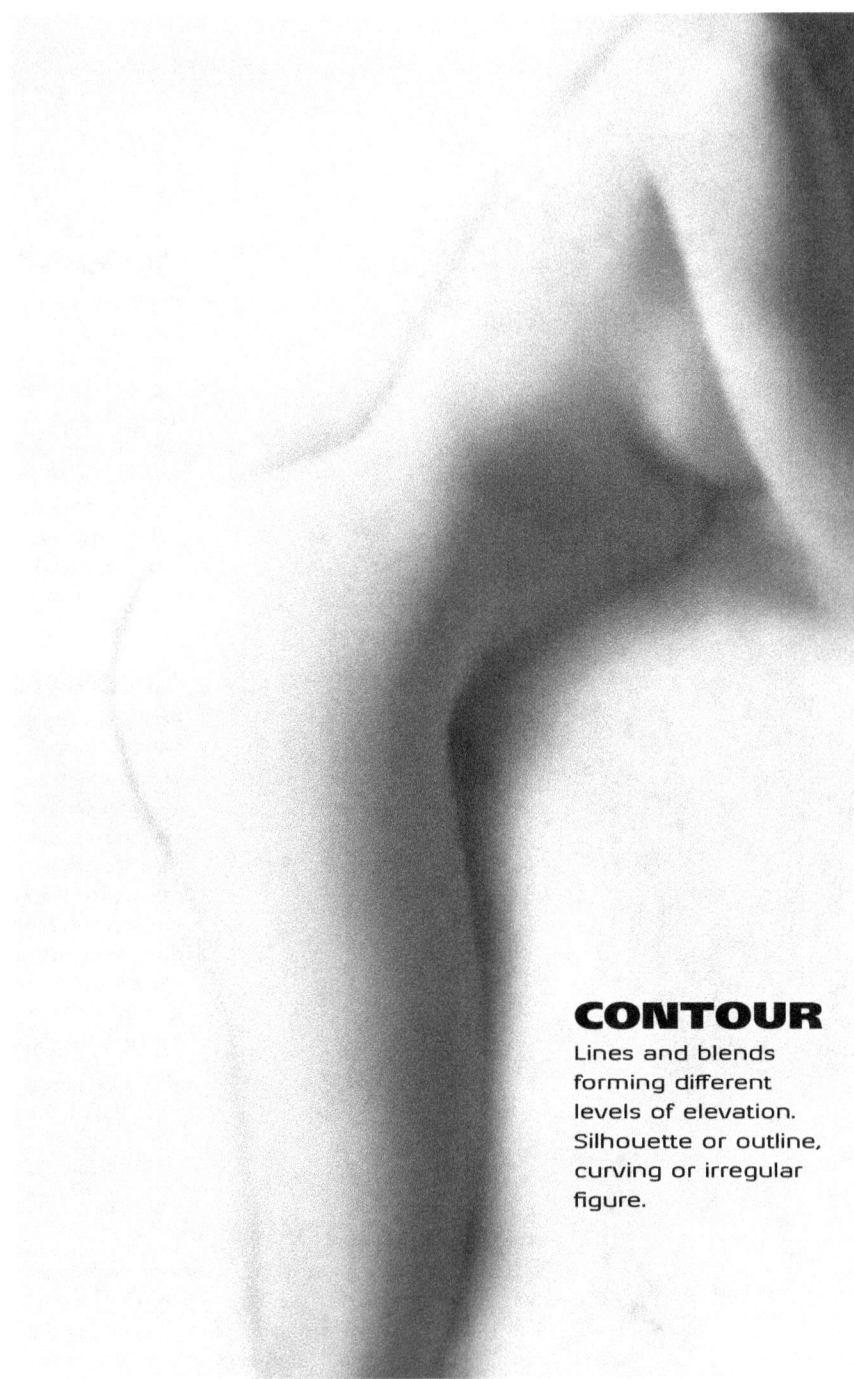

CONTOUR
Lines and blends
forming different
levels of elevation.
Silhouette or outline,
curving or irregular
figure.

COINCIDENCE
Can you believe it, I meet james in tokyo on the subway elevator
at ten in the morning, thirteen million people.....How many times
does this happen to you in this small world of six/seven billion?

CERN

We are doing this, be proud, be scared, with the large hadron colider. Our understanding of the universe is about to change! 2012 cern finds new sub-atomic particle!

CANADIAN

How many canadians does it take to change a light bulb? Canadians don't change light bulbs, they accept them for the way they are.

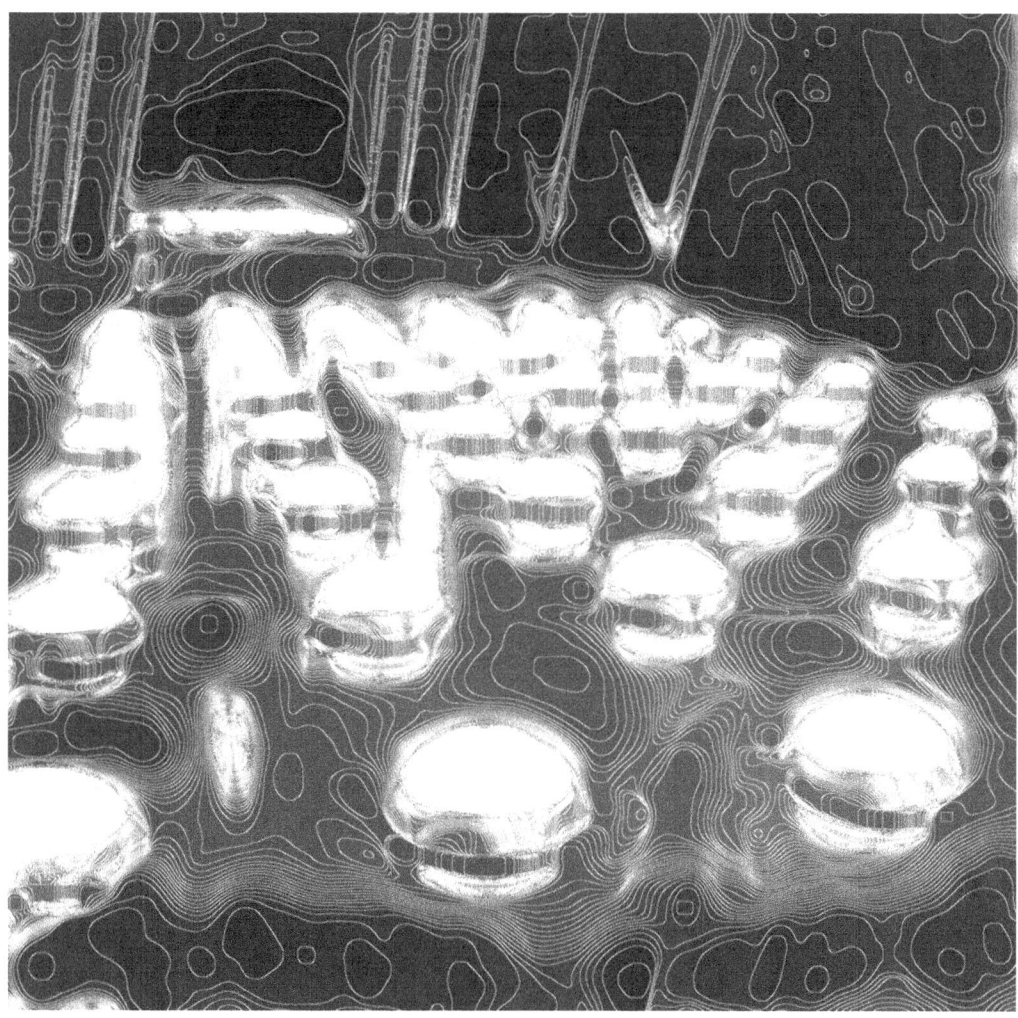

Ctrl

Who wrote the plan that controls my life? Which circle am I in? I lived through birth control.....Take control!

CHINOOKIE

Pacific north west's great salmon, sewing their oats thru the thousands of islands of British Columbia, land of the rain forest. Love lox, says it all.....Formed from the letters gravlox, maybe not! Nookie: the satisfaction of passion, after eating such a desir-able creature with a face, that is cold blooded. Heavy lift dual rotor copter, bring on the heavy artillery! Coastal big warm wind, blows inland. Pooh corner, fart end on nuclear power.

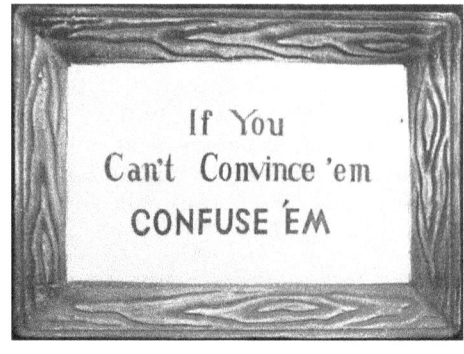

CURRY

The food from india.....Originally from the tamil word kari meaning sauce. The british east india company returned to britain in the seventeenth century and first introduced the dish, over the years many expats returning from india with new recipes..

CBC

Zorski to Ghomeshi my condition-ing is being upgraded every day thank you canada. Canada lives and is here!.

COCOON

We all luv this warm and cozy wrapping giving us a sense of safety and protection just like before birth......

COSTALOT

Bestbuys to costco you know what this means, a boating name for a very expensive pastime. Spanish word for coastal location car lot.

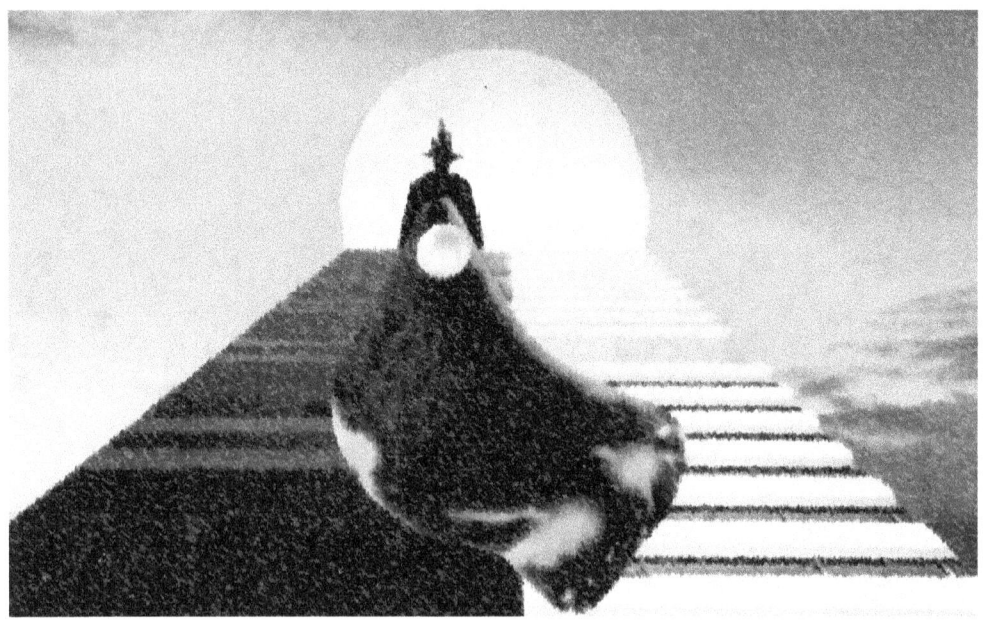

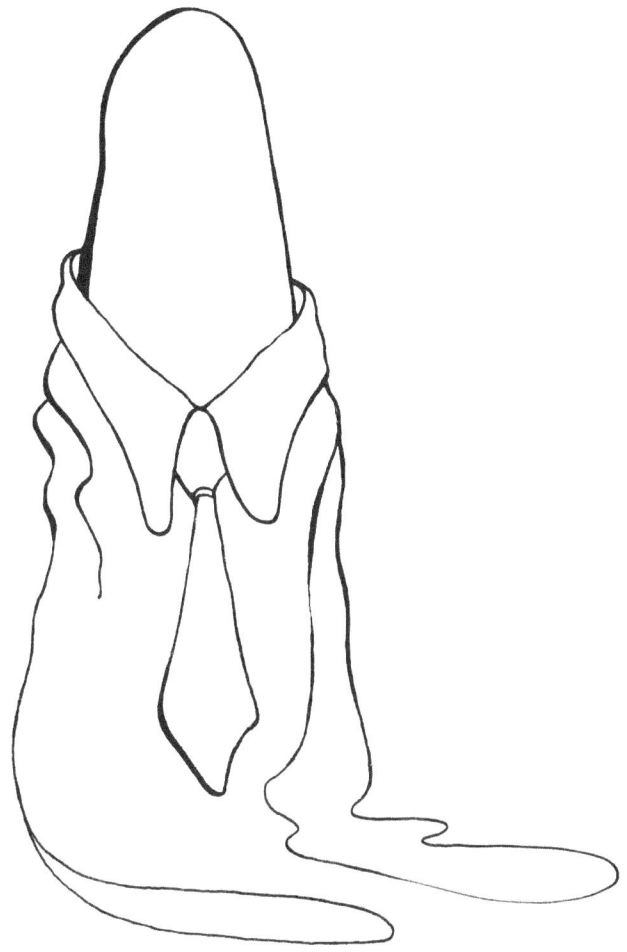

DISHWAD
No not Lucus, was he the author of the crystal skulls? No that was W..A. Harbinson or the dish washer in the taj Mahal in Agra.....yes!

DOOTHINGY
Word formed from dat thing, can't remember, what sit, over fifty you know its....Alzheimer's, dementia.....forgetting, brain memory loss: did I rite this!

DAYOH!
Banana boat movie.....You know the one, by that sureeeelllll director.....Burtin, beetle juice, wow great.....Pay the tally man me bananaaaaa.xxxxxxx!

DOOWOP
Motown: motor city. Vocal based rhythm and blues from african american origins.

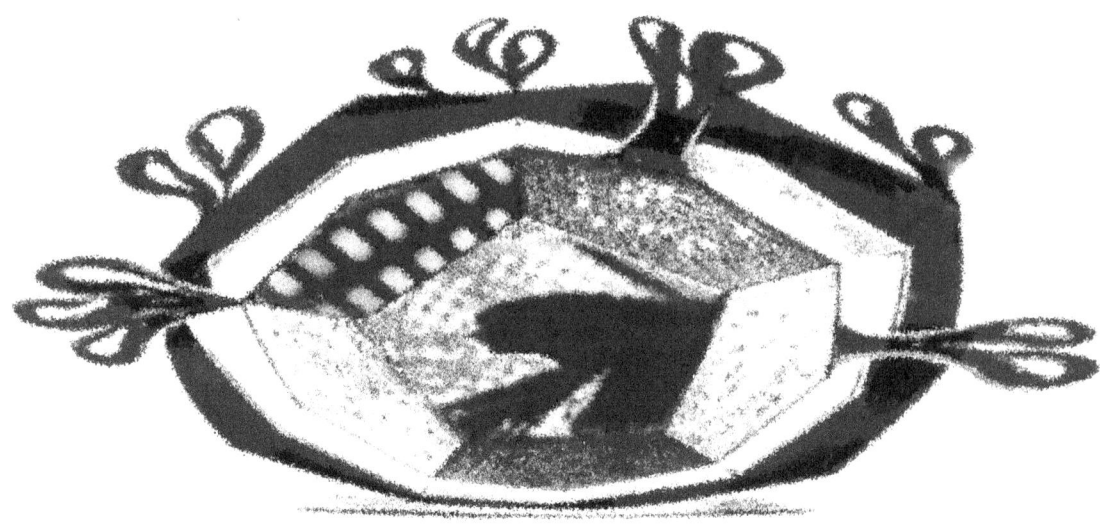

DEJA VU

The illusory feeling of having already experienced a present situation; something tediously familiar, like these amoebas that will be double their population tomorrow.

DRAGON

Word formed from mandarin.....The study of the rich emperor who sired one hundred families and was turned into a long tailed alien creature by the visiting astro gods called DRAgonia and GONarea. No one has actually seen one.....But pictues of them exist everywhere.

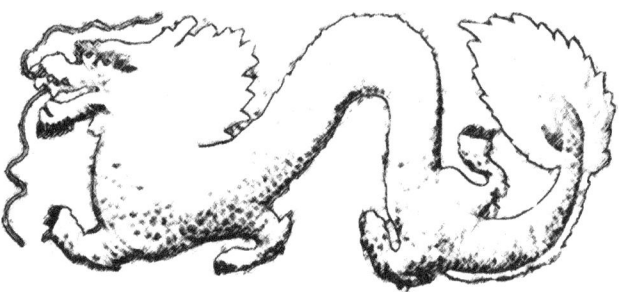

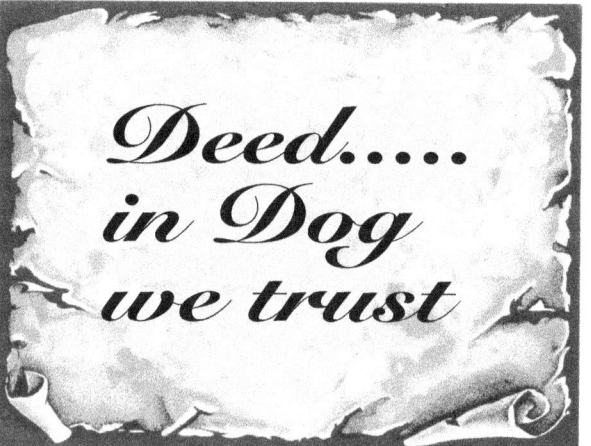

Dyslexia ko.

DOOWAT

Freesound: creative commons licensed sound for sharing.

DOG

No not a four legged friend..... Call me on your phone..... Cockney slang.....Dog and bone, phone!

DEED

Document effecting legal transfer of ownership and bearing disposers signature. Thing consciously done; brave, skilful, or conspicuous act.

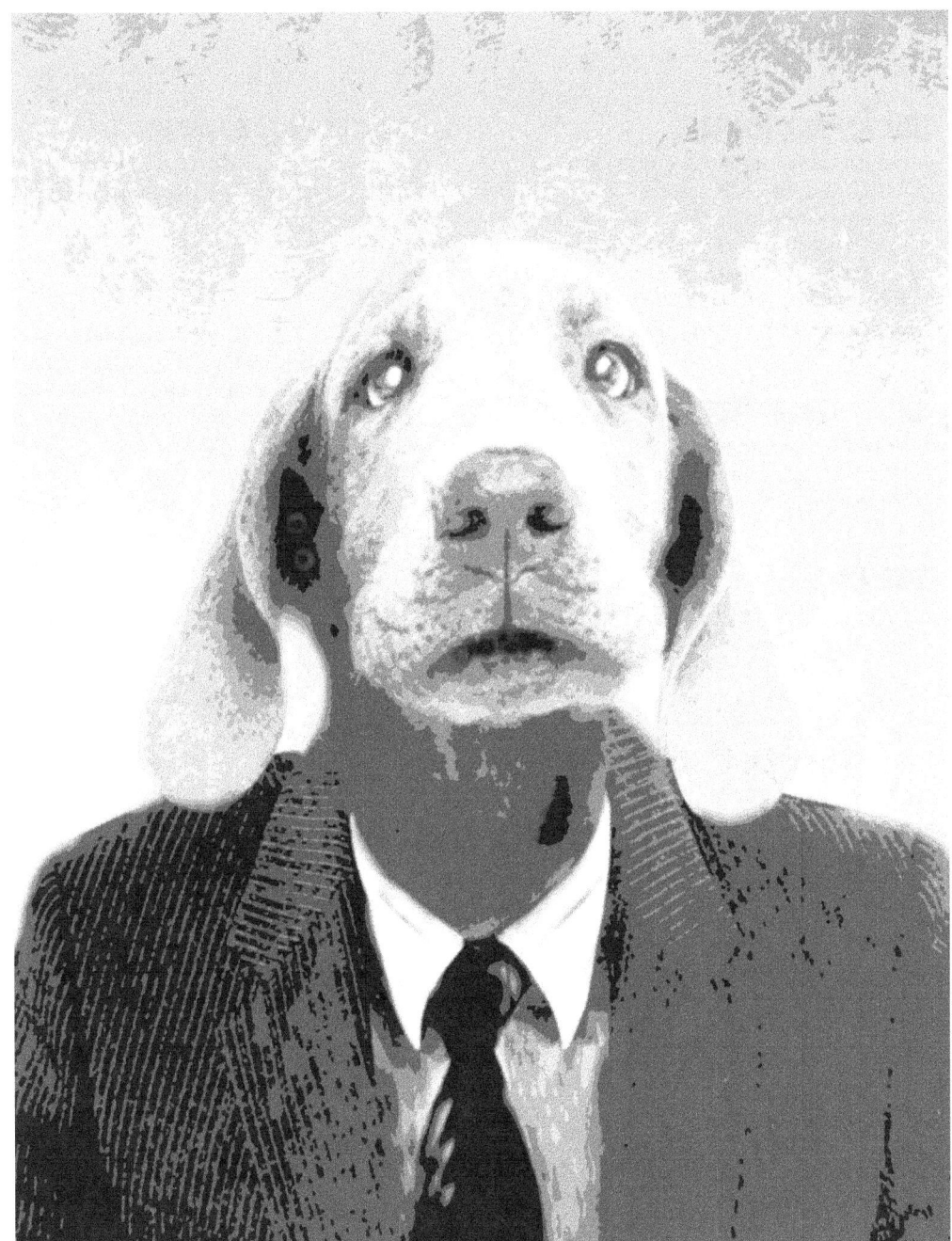

DOGMA

The offcial system of belief or doctrine held by a religion or a particular group or organisation. It serves as part of the primary basis of their ideology. Pictured above is their revered leader.

DOGEARED

What the corners of this book will look like if you look through it one hundred and thirteen times. You can teach this old dog nu triks! Hey big ears you owe more tax to the pigs.....Oh, skumchuck.

DOPAMINE

A neurotransmitter with its own pathways and its own receptors controlling a huge influence on activity in your brain. Can it really help in the enhancement of subjective pleasures of your body? When will we find out.....Speak up for more.....Thank you, you, you.

DENILE/DENIAL

I thought it was just another river in Afrika, till I grew up and tried to not understand families.

DISH

Satellite dish educates, conditions, controls, everyone in the world! The one below in the the picture is in cadaques, catalonia, spain.

DICKSQUAT

Nuttin.....Nought.....Empty......Waste of space.....Dickless.....None. Nothing to change your world!

DNA

Creating The building block of life! Well soon we will have some answers with our web world, shared knowledge, maybe.....Think about it, we did not have zips in nineteen fifty three on trouser flies. I bought the first calculator from sinclair in nineteen seventy two, it was red and now what? How old is google? When did you get your first MRI?

DINKS

Dual Income No Kids, a race of different people that live on the earth.....Many advantages, no, yes.....Maybe.

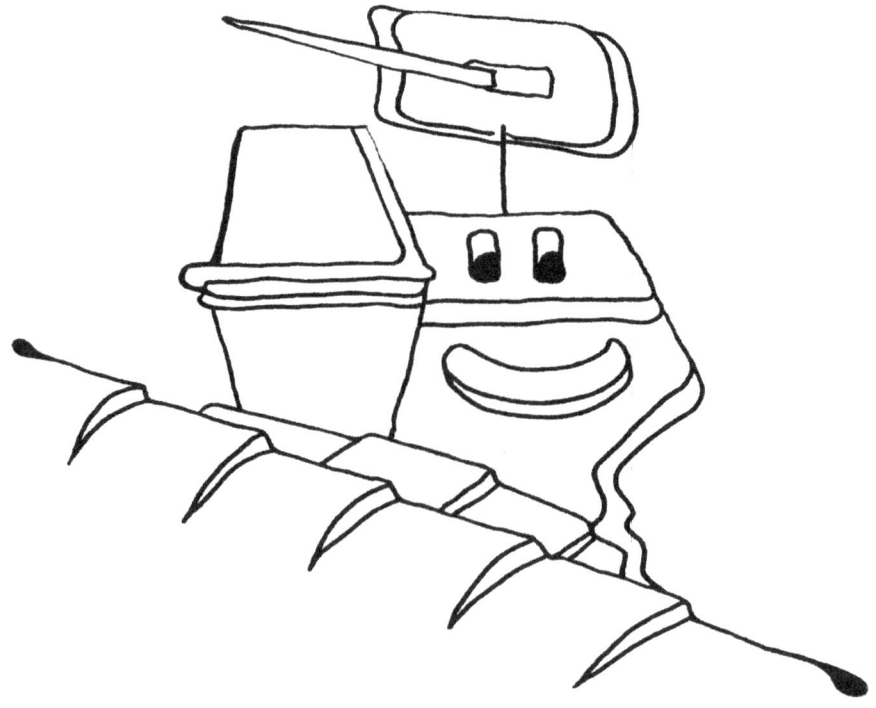

DARKSIDE

Non apple users.......But Bill....Mr pc has done some great things in the world, why should he take so much flack? Some girls have so much fun! Start me up.....

DOOLALLY

Dipstick, all over the place, loose cannon, cat on a hot tin roof.

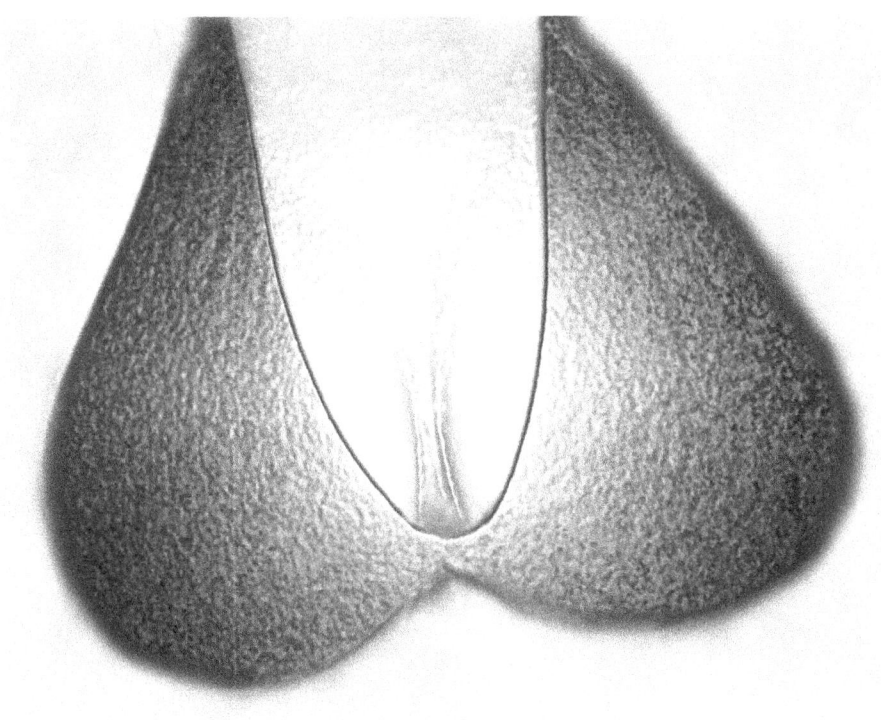

DECOUPLAGE

How many poets are there in France? How many are living on a government salary? Live to work.....Work to live, which way round is your life? This word sums up so much about the concept of extending the human race for the male of the species....The contourial distance between the milk of life.......Suckling male pigs.....Jolly good show, victoria has covered them up.....Secret!

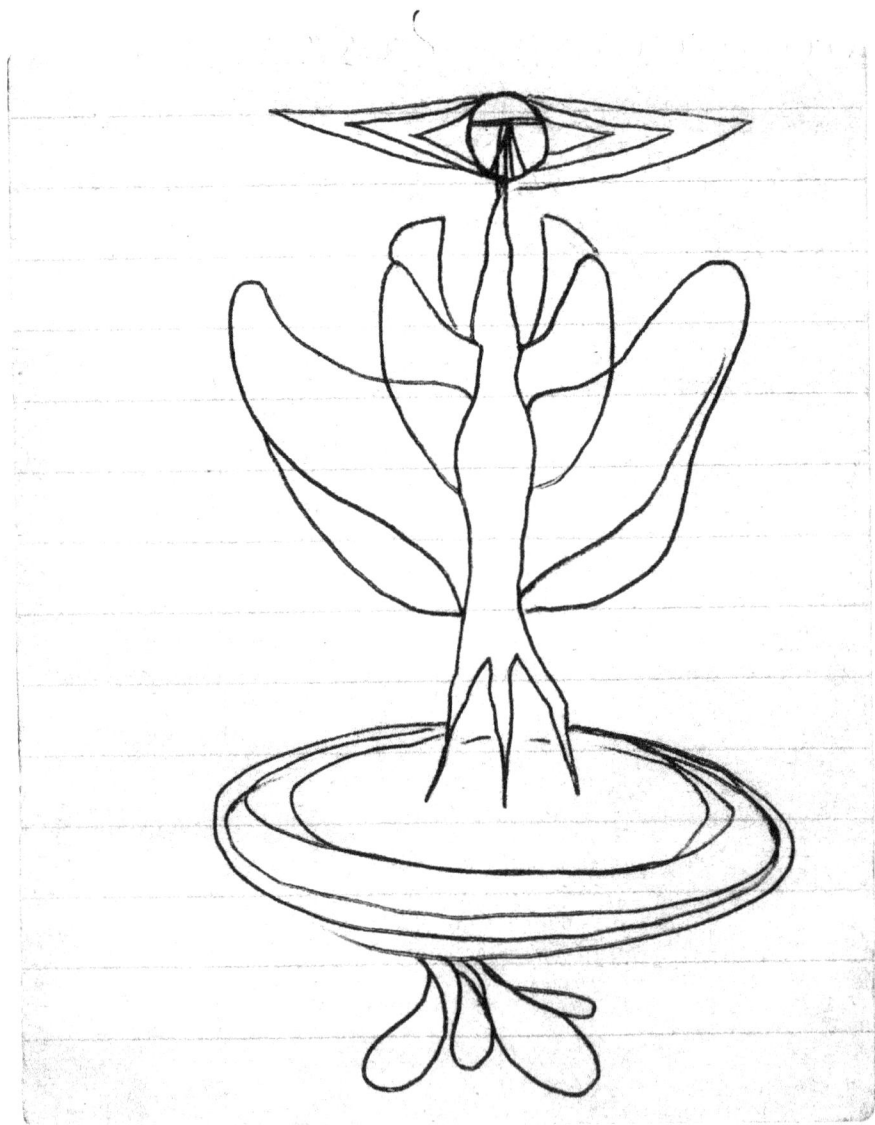

The aromatic taste spirit is rising from five bhajis, to the orbitofrontal cortex

DRAW

Creating something out of your head on any surface....So many mediums to take your concepts into a visual language for other humans to interpret. I do a lot of things for money but I draw a line at art.

DHOSA

Wrap, Roti, Burrito similar..... What ever.....Wish me luck as you wave me goodbyzzee, Southern India speciality, keep on trukin.....

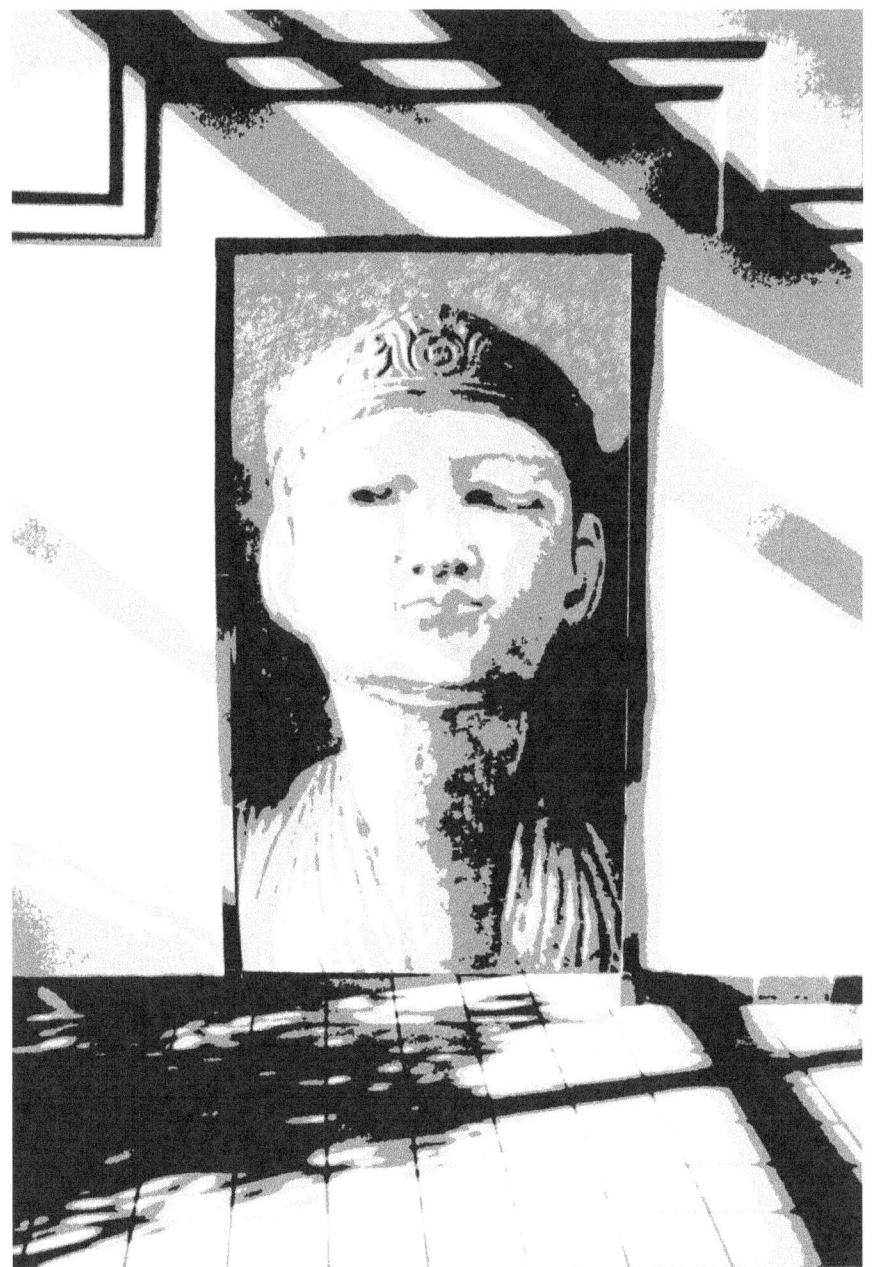

DOOR

As one closes another one opens; a cover for an entry. God finds your face and hair offensive woman. Sorry we are not having any women bishops in our church and you are not allowed to sing!

DAVID LYNCH

See a movie or a film by him, but..... But....Better to have someone to be alone with, we are all small islands in the cosmic tide of universal story tellers!

DRONE

Noise, boring monotone, small sky weapon, observes, destroys people on the ground from a keyboard nine thousand miles away. Is that it then. ninety nine thousand drones in use.

DUKA

Swahili word for shop or store in Mombasa, Nairobi or Zanzibar.

DICKWAD

Stupid unloyal moron, incompetant, does not deserve the respect of god or the virgins.

DIGITABLE

Table top monitor as big as nineteen by nine feet. For computer users to communicate, create, share ideas, knowledge and info.....

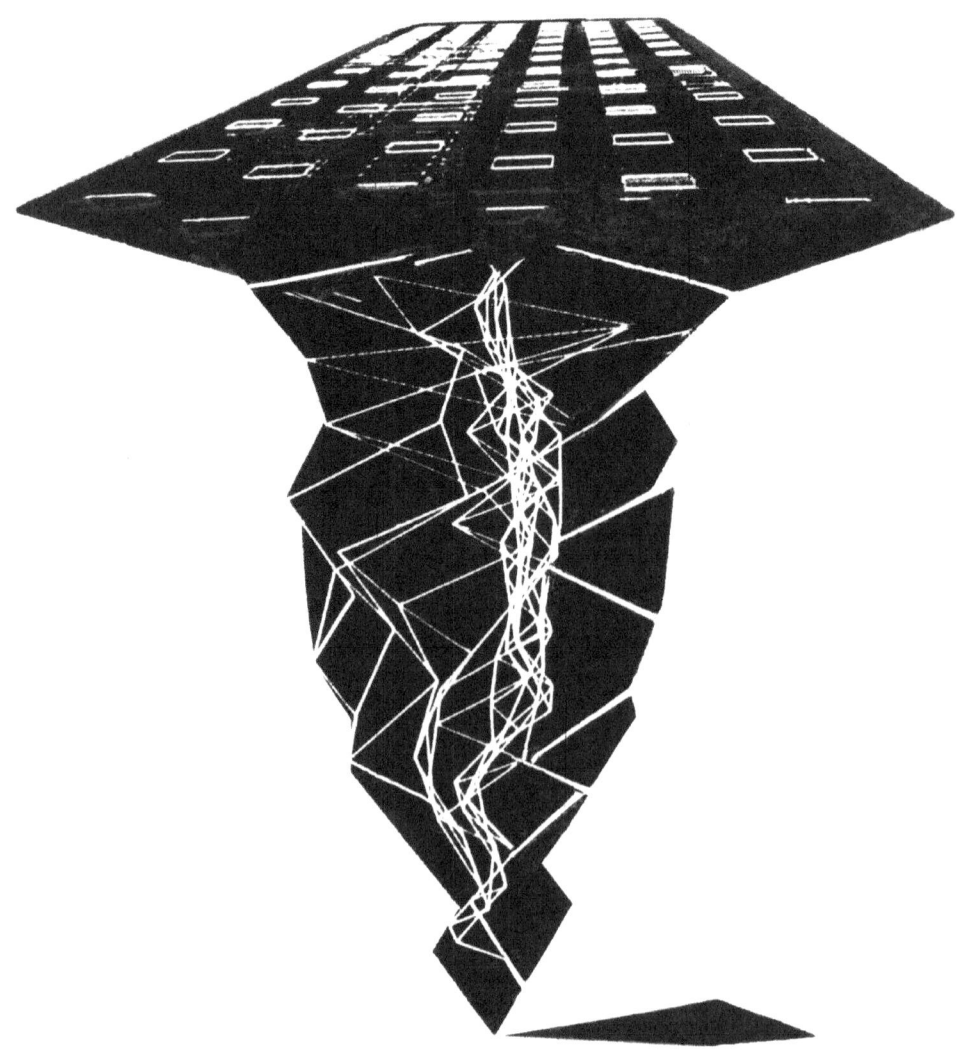

EXPRESSION

Some painters were called expressionists,
are not all painters that? A look that sends
a message to the reciever.

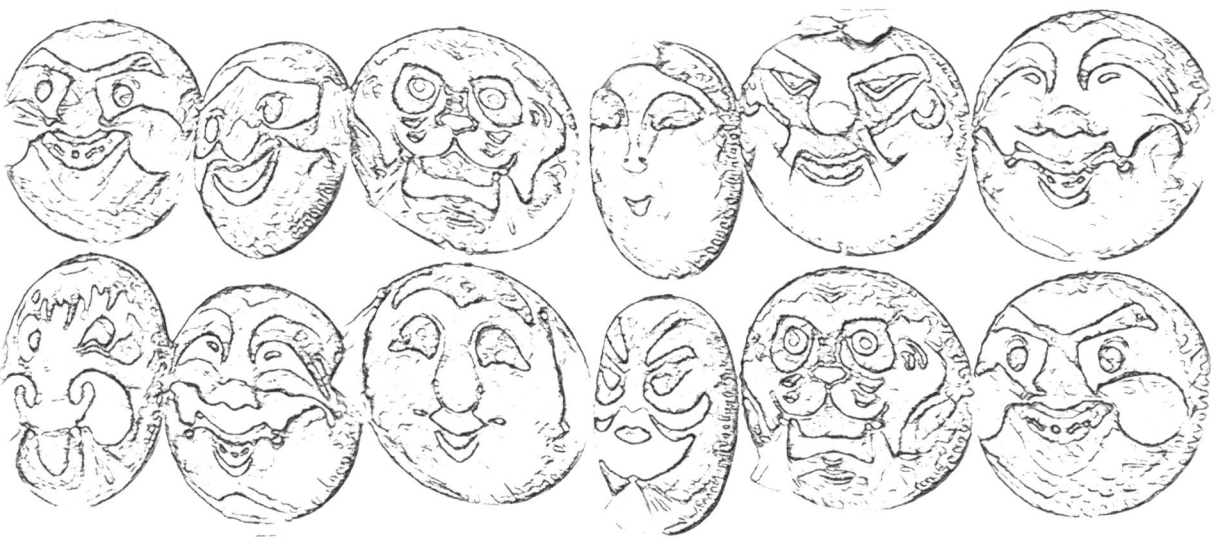

EUPHEMISM

Is the substitution of a mild, inoffensive
mildly uncontroversial phrase for a
frank expression that might offend the
reader. Wot.

EXPECTATIONS

Lead to dissapointment.....Not
always.....Expect less and you will
get so much more.....Are they pre-
meditated resentments on holiday?
Hope but never expect.....

EVIL EYES

Look into them.....What do you see? Some people frighten you right away, you know they are going to control you or maybe do you harm.

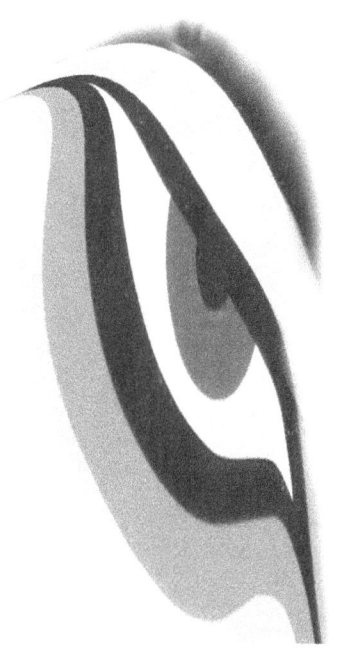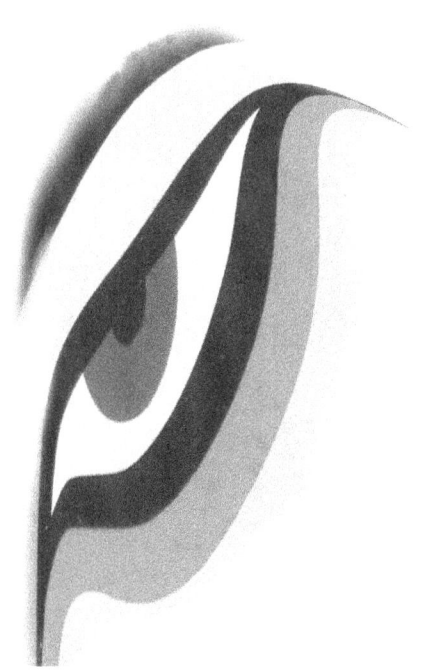

EXHALE

Ahhhhhh.....Mmmmmm nice name Bruce..... Vapourize me sunshine, Zappadedodah, Eureka is the surreal capital of kalifornia with one woman's massive collection of shoes in a museum format. Trees that have shops in them!

ELECTRIC CITY

This is every city on the planet and I thought it was only in bladerunner. We depend on this power.

ELDORADO

Jeff Lynne.....Listern to ELO's overture while reading the next five pages.

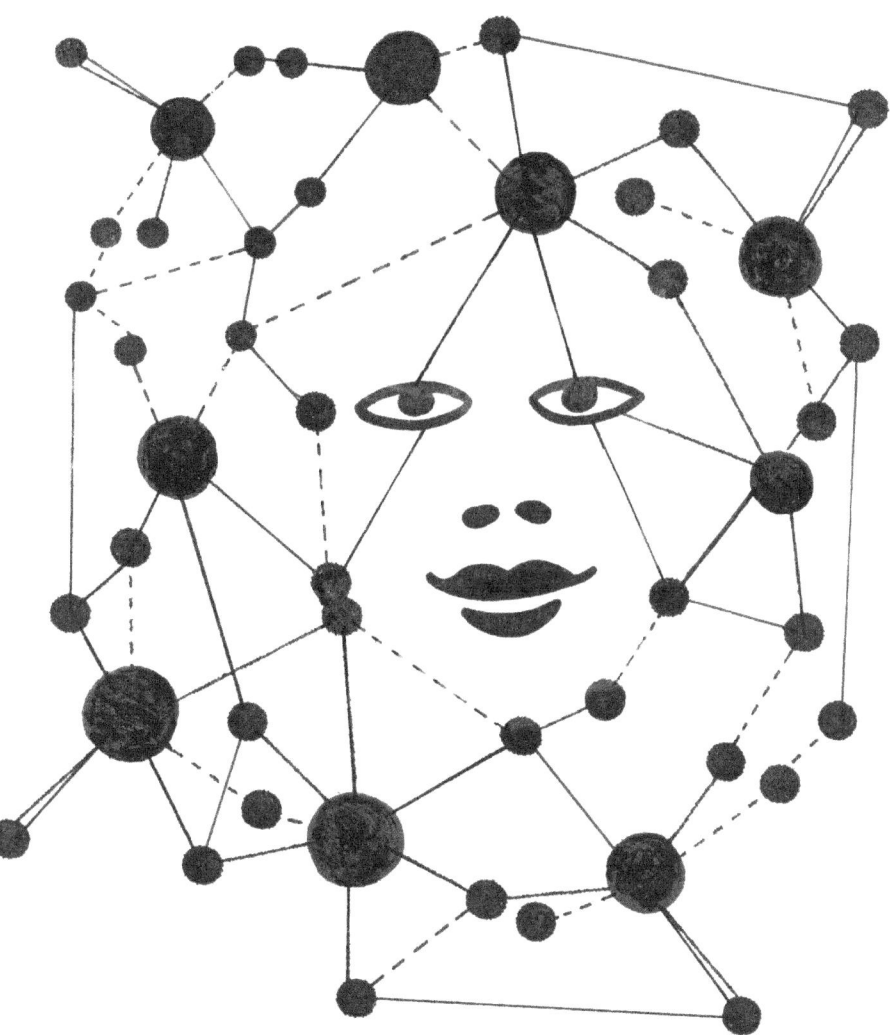

ELECTRIC EYE

Creating vision beyond the glass eye, how did you drive before you got that cataract operation, I dont need glasses now.

EUPHORIA

State of excessive well being..... Good feelings from your brain, mind, and soul. Neocortex surfing on niagra, the natural alternative.

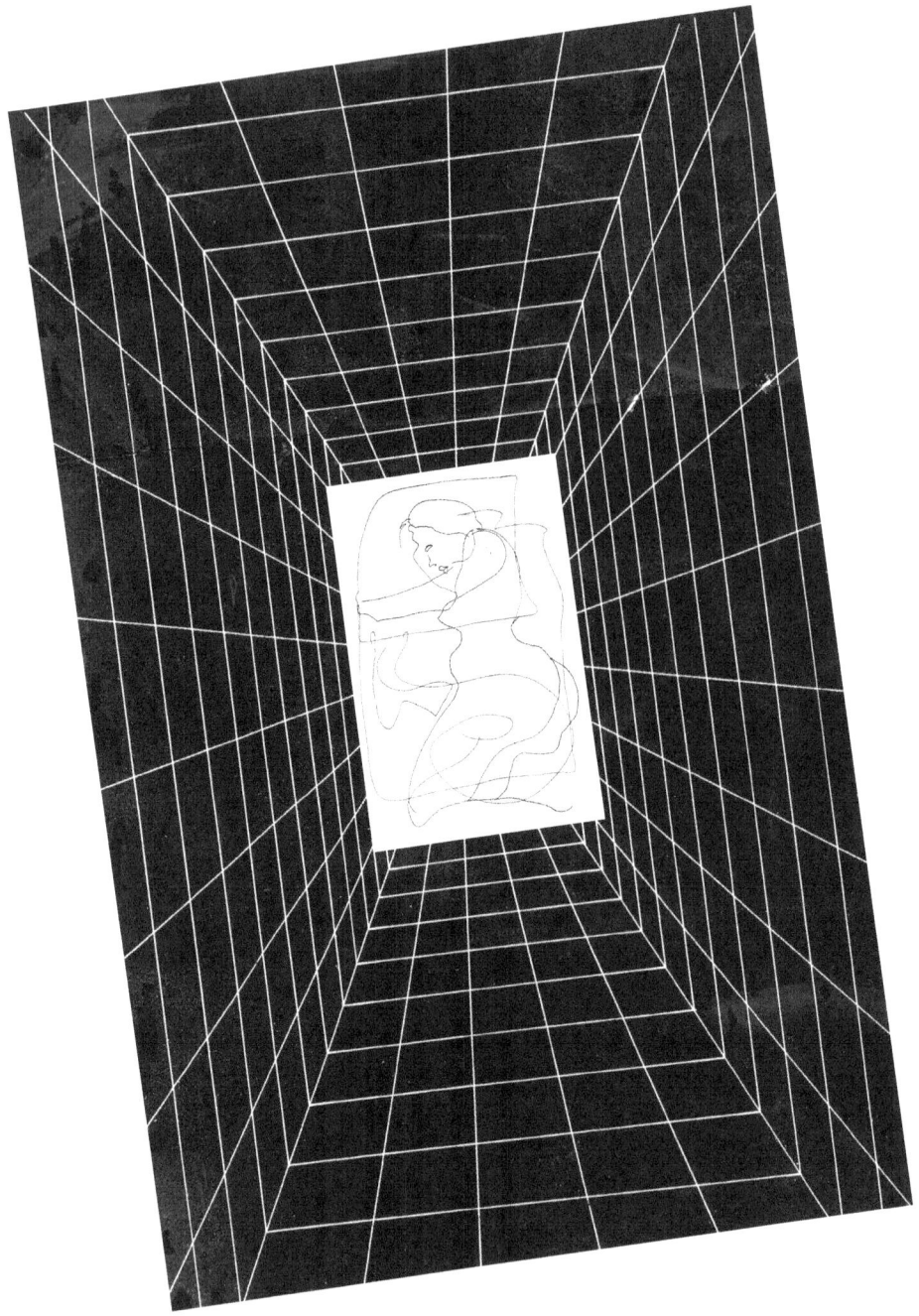

END TIME

Light at the end of the tunnel, hyperthermia maybe
best, who has returned to tell us.....Lying there, do I
want to die, how much pain is there?.....What do I have
to do..... Morphinator me, when I need it!.....Google that!

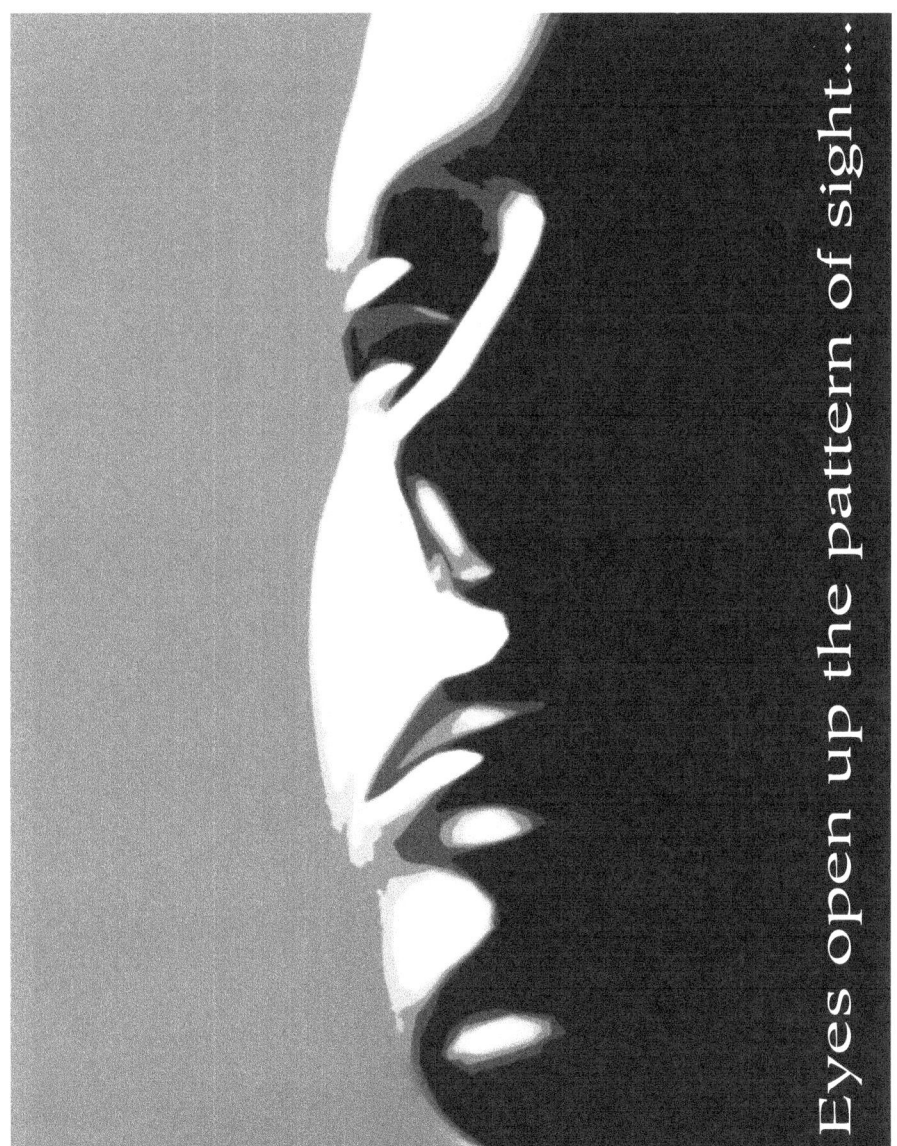

Eyes open up the pattern of sight.....

EYESITE

My eyesight writes the memory card in my brain and the memories
are make believe.....You need a bigger card in your mind to capture it
all. In your dreams you tried to make believe.....You talk the talk about
the scene your eyes have seen, they can't really see the places your
travelling mind has been! I want to read your thoughts between the
lines of thoughts you think.

EAST ENDER

Not living in the west end. Living within the sound of bow bells. Picture this.....Is it easy on the male eye! Heel boy, we maybe the last generation to naturally drive desire before the inevitable happening of singularity! Randy robots rule, reining over relativity right!

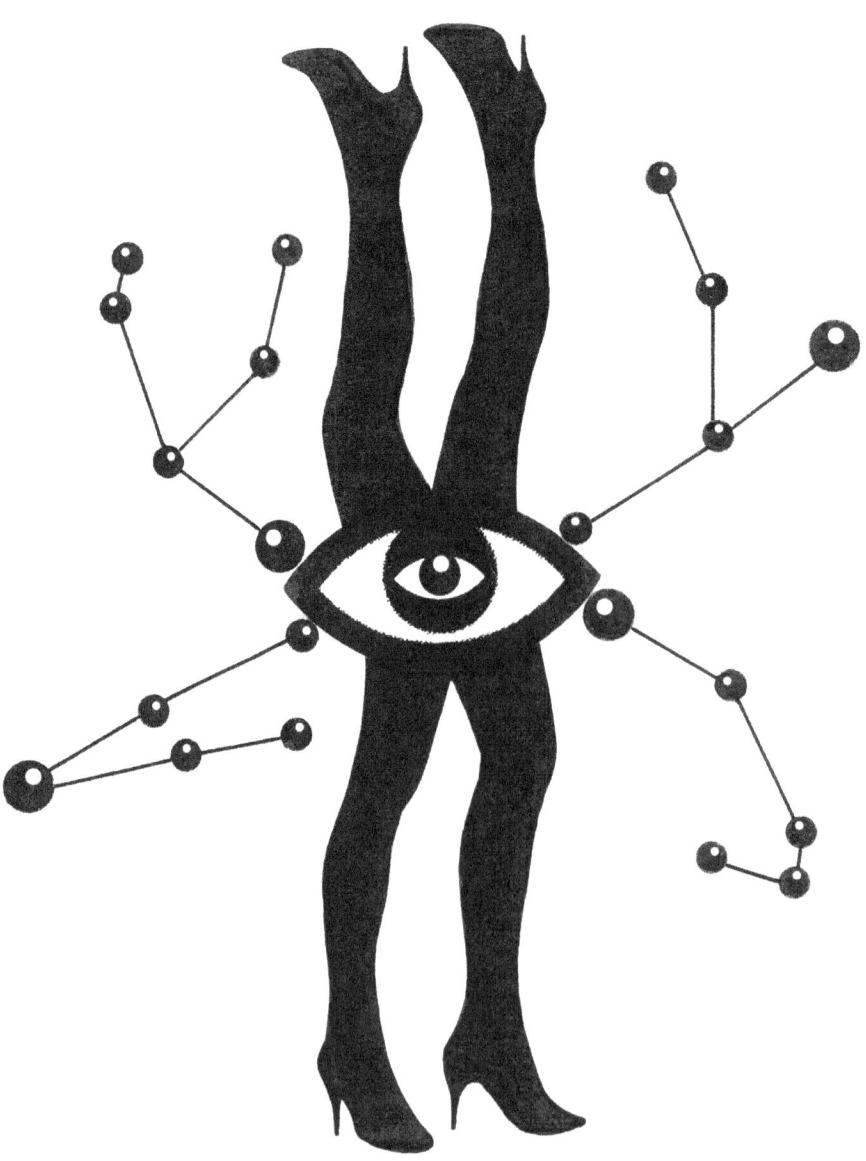

EARTHSAPE

Round.....Or is it slightly off, how do we know? How many times have we been away from the planet to picture it or measure it? Who measured the circumference of the earth and what with?

EXOTIC

Describe exotic in your head. One persons rubbish is another persons treasure, draw a line between exciting and explosive. Could be that perfect end to a wonderful day in an exotic place!

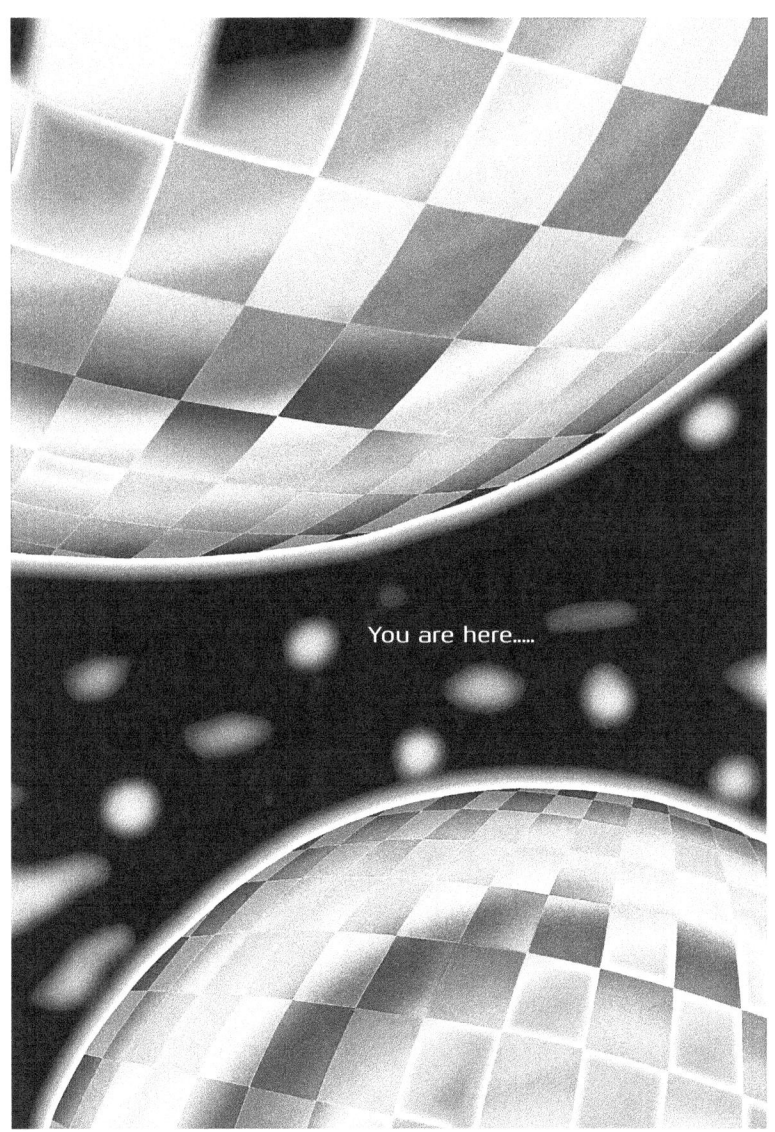

You are here.....

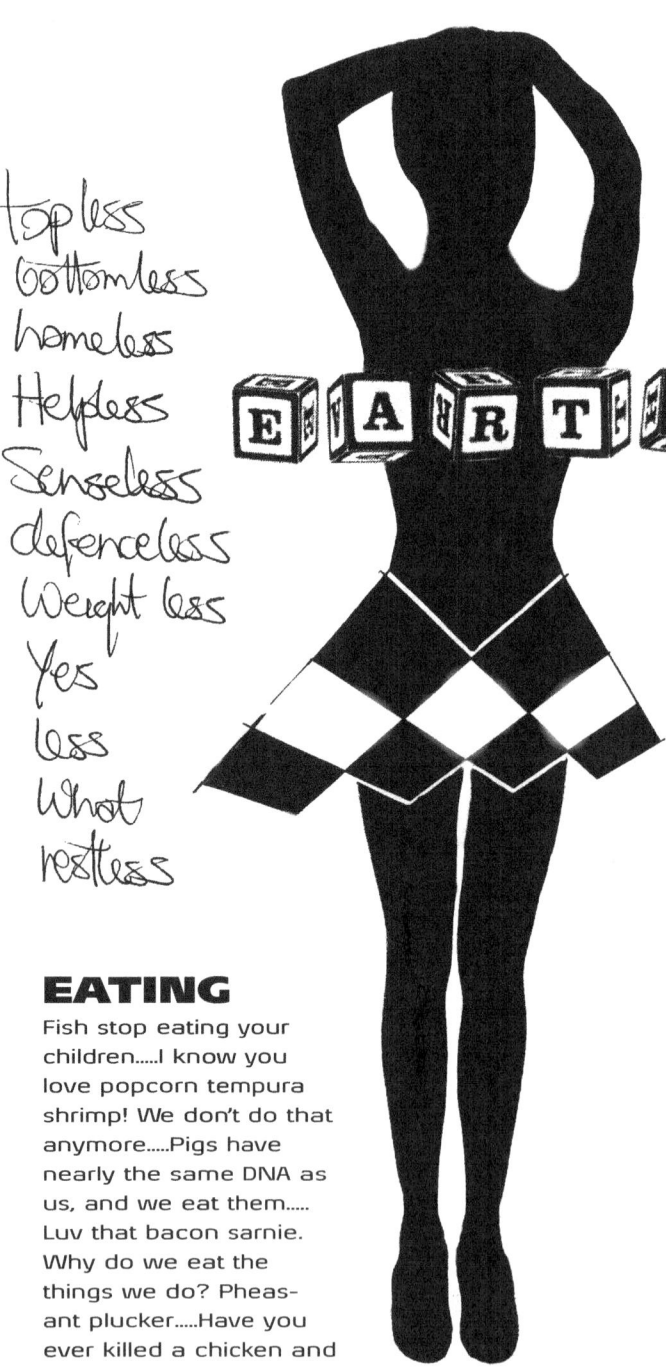

topless
bottomless
homeless
Helpless
Senseless
defenceless
Weight less
Yes
less
What
restless

EARLY BIRDS

What is it they say.....
Early birds, catch
the sperm.....

EUREKA

I've won! Yes.....Yes.....Yes......
Yes.......Jump up and down
with your checkerboard
skirt. Mother of invention,
teach your child to read the
earth.....Town in California.

EARTHY

Obsession with good
earth, we should all be
wwofers.....Down to earth,
Mother of the land, very
real.....No frills or airs and
graces.

EATING

Fish stop eating your
children.....I know you
love popcorn tempura
shrimp! We don't do that
anymore.....Pigs have
nearly the same DNA as
us, and we eat them.....
Luv that bacon sarnie.
Why do we eat the
things we do? Pheas-
ant plucker.....Have you
ever killed a chicken and
plucked it?

EYELOOK

This book should have been called eyelookl. The study of an artist climbing the tree of visual knowledge.....Shadows on the moon, are they real? Eye don't know. Dark, stout and good 4 u? Pr will sell u what u don't need.....

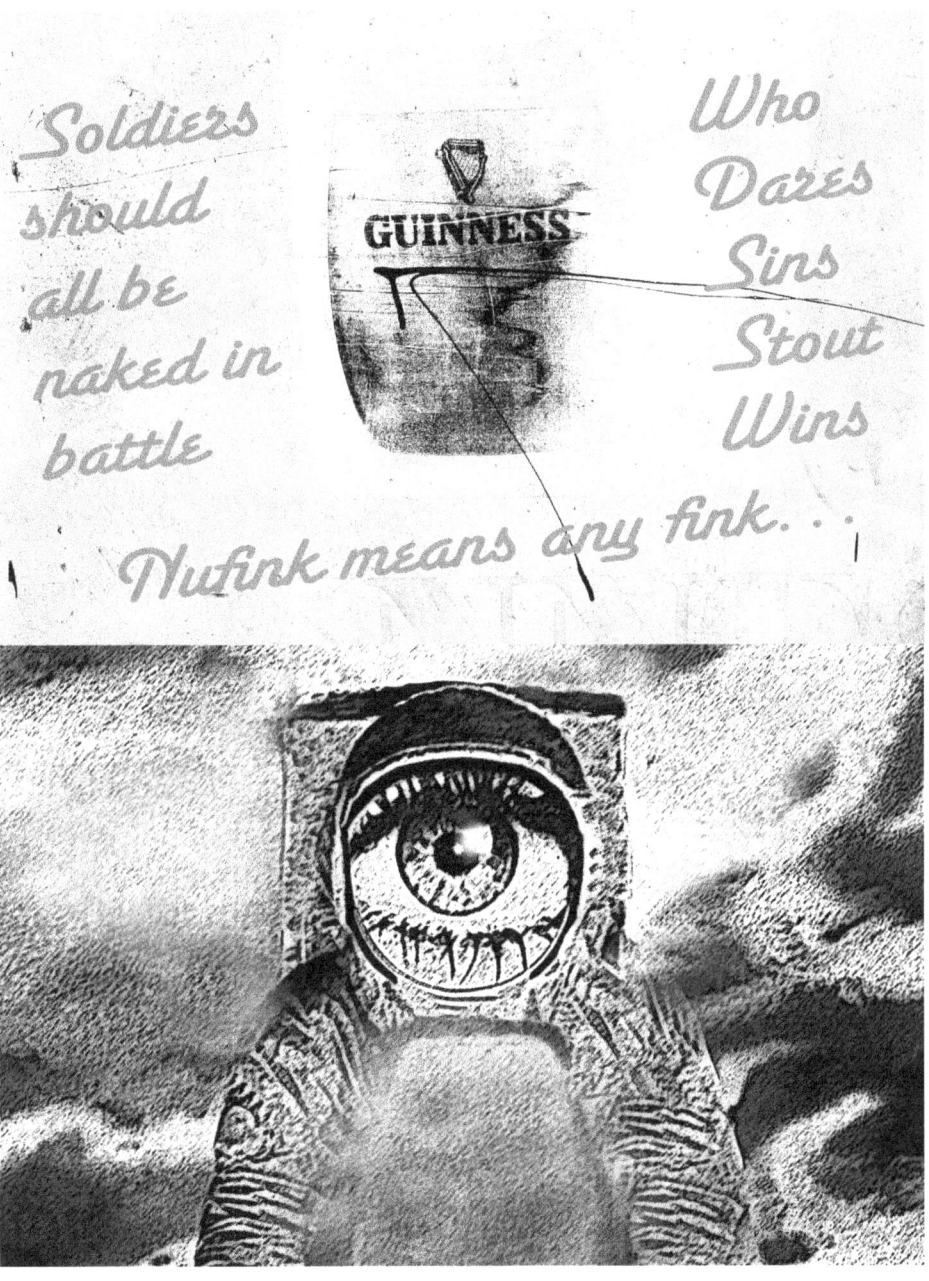

EYE SEE

Anais Nin had insight when she said.....We don't see things as they are, we see them as we are.

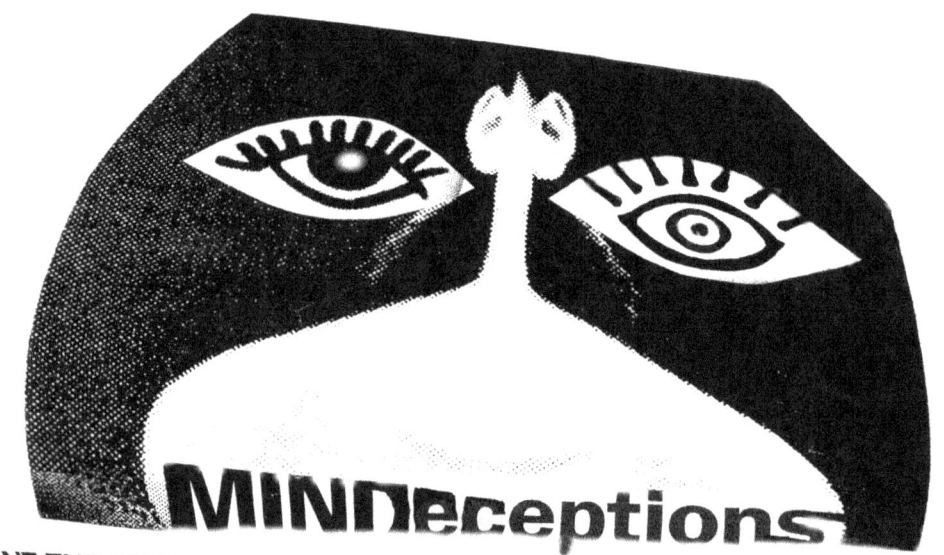

MIN**Deceptions**

WE THINK WE THINK BUT IS IT A PIGGY BACK PATTERN?

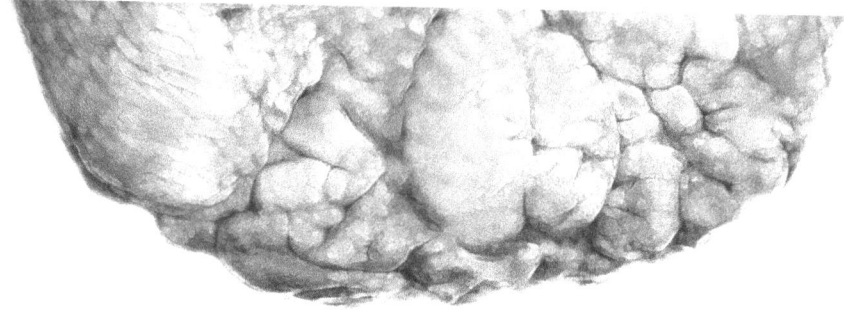

ECLECTIC

The brain's conceptual approach, that does not hold rigidly to a single paradigm or set of assumptions, but instead draws upon multiple theories, styles, or ideas to gain complimentary insights into a subject. Sometimes it is hardly very elegant and lacks simplicity. Critics usually say that eclectic artists lack consistency in their thinking, however this kind of just do it experimentation leads to failure.....Which with encore editing proves highly successful when completing a project.

ECCENTRIC pattern recognition

The ultimate act of creativity is to design an in brain software and hardware system that is capable of creating creativity.....

ELECTRA

Resonence.....Electric balls floating in space around you!

ENCORE

See it again in a different light!

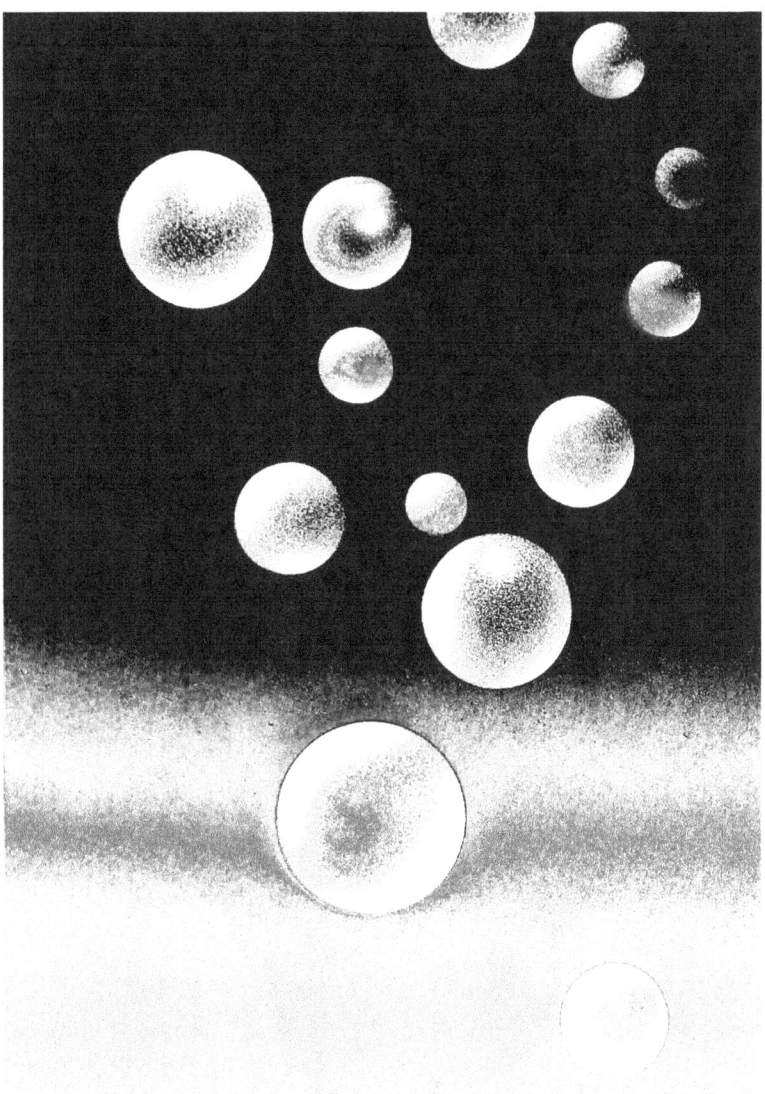

EXPERIMENT

That's exactly what we are. Try it you might like it! Should we rewrite that code. I would like that toasted with a gene splice and a little more lively and spicy filling on my dna.....Please.

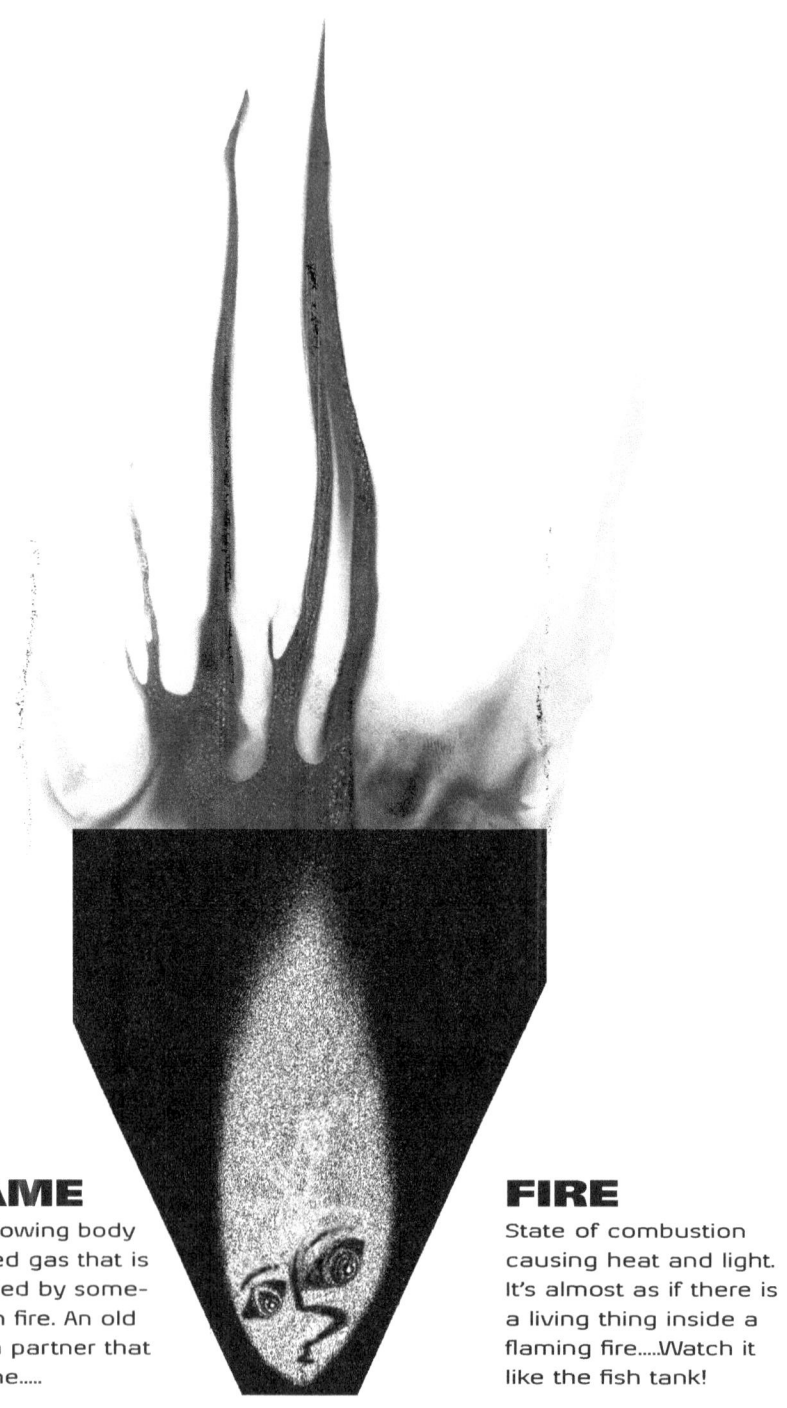

FLAME

A hot glowing body
of ignited gas that is
generated by some-
thing on fire. An old
flame; a partner that
has gone.....

FIRE

State of combustion
causing heat and light.
It's almost as if there is
a living thing inside a
flaming fire.....Watch it
like the fish tank!

FREQUENCIES

wifi.....microwave.....vhf.....uhf.....uv.....mri are they going thru our bodies? Are these frequencies?.....Short waves.....Long waves, sounds strange to me. What does this mean google it now!

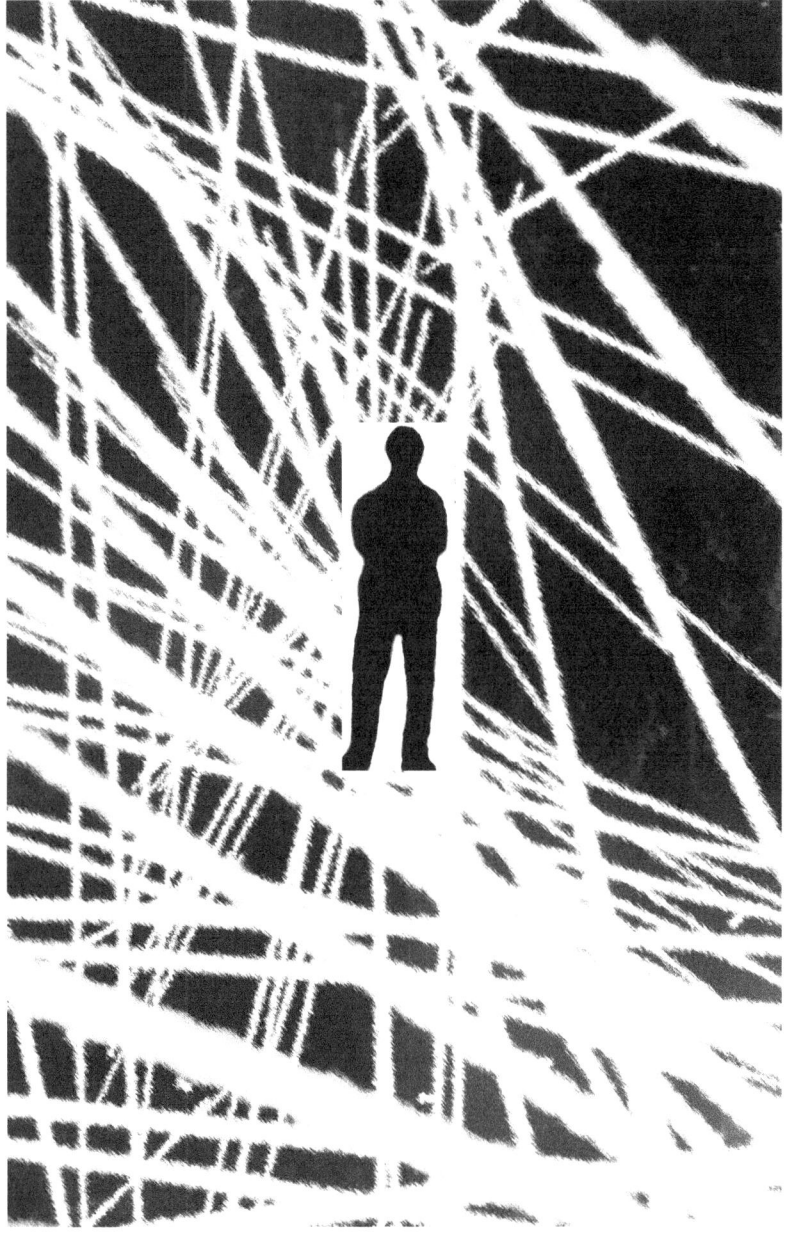

FREUD

The dream acts as a safety valve for the over burdened brain.

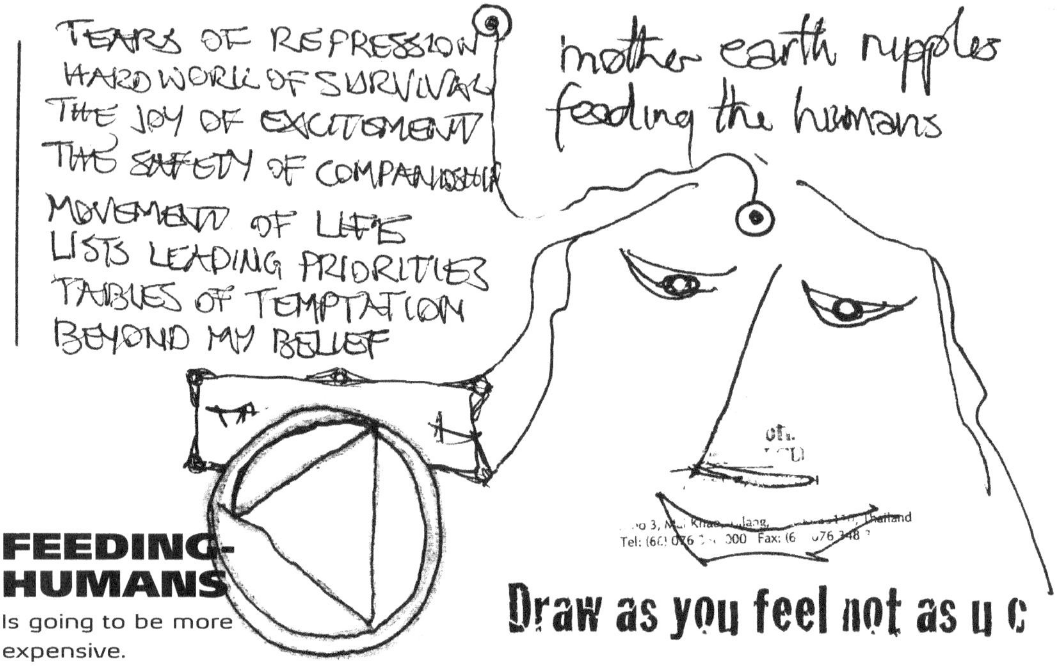

TEARS OF REPRESSION
HARD WORK OF SURVIVAL
THE JOY OF EXCITEMENT
THE SAFETY OF COMPANIONSHIP

MOVEMENT OF LIFE
LISTS LEADING PRIORITIES
TABLES OF TEMPTATION
BEYOND MY BELIEF

mother earth ripples
feeding the humans

FEEDING-HUMANS

Is going to be more expensive.

Draw as you feel not as u c

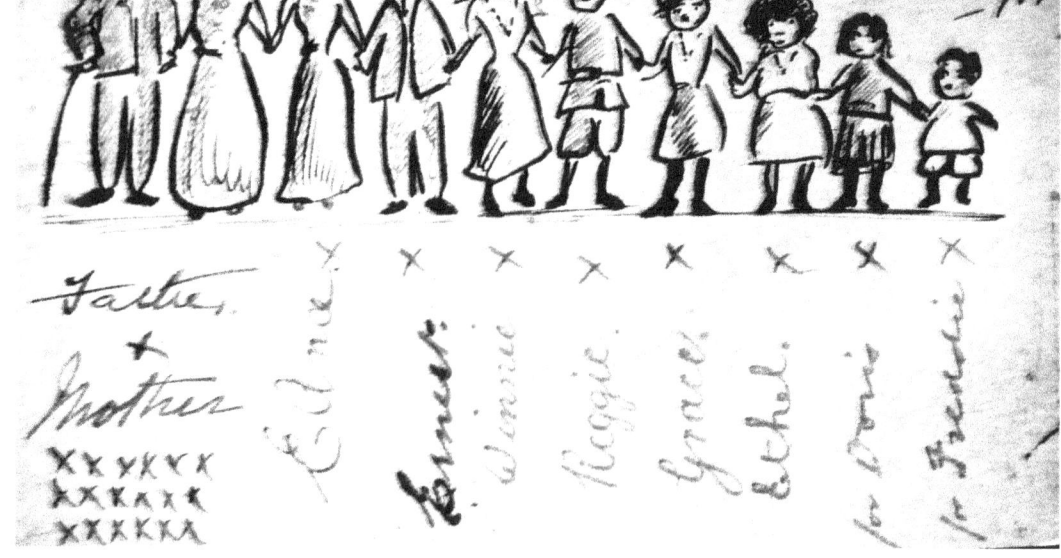

To wish our dear may the
happiest and brightest New Year
she has ever had

Dec 1911

Father
Mother

FAMILY

Line them up for the new year.....What can I say.....Most of us wish our friends
were our family, but then some people have wonderful united families!

FINGERBOWL

Lemon scented water to clean your fingers, after finger likin good ya..... Double canvas deck chair seats at the back of the quonset hut movie houses, back in the fifties.....For sixteen year old sexual encountering.

FRAJIPANI

Tropical flowers in the hair of woman, leys look so inviting with franjipanis, whites and soft soft pinks turn hearts into lovers. Boil them in waterfall water in hawaii and it turns into perfume.

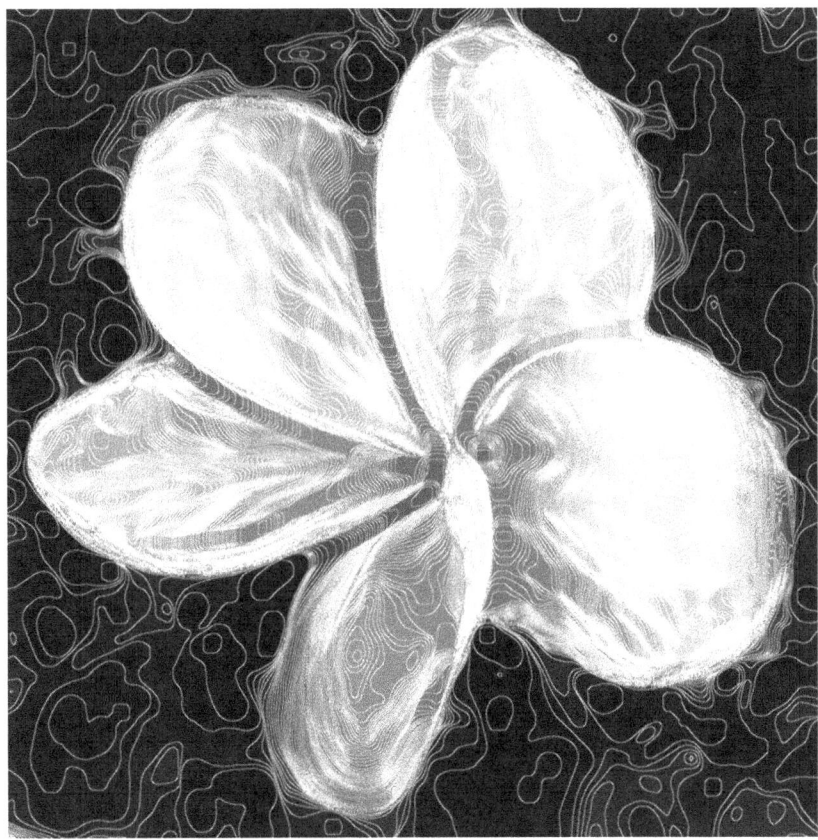

FUDDYDUDDY

Somebody who is fussy or picayune about detail, usually takes so long to do any task..... Just do it!

FUSSPOT

Dodering around, making a lot of worries over minor details. Total worrier: thinks too much about everything, frightened about things that could go wrong.

FIRETALK

What does this mean? Hot under the collar, late night serious talk around the fire.

FUNERAL

Death is the last thing we need/want..... Why does everyone else get to celebrate your life and you are not at the party.....

63

FUSION

From food to the nue meaning of life, this is where we are going, like it or not, your future is fusion.

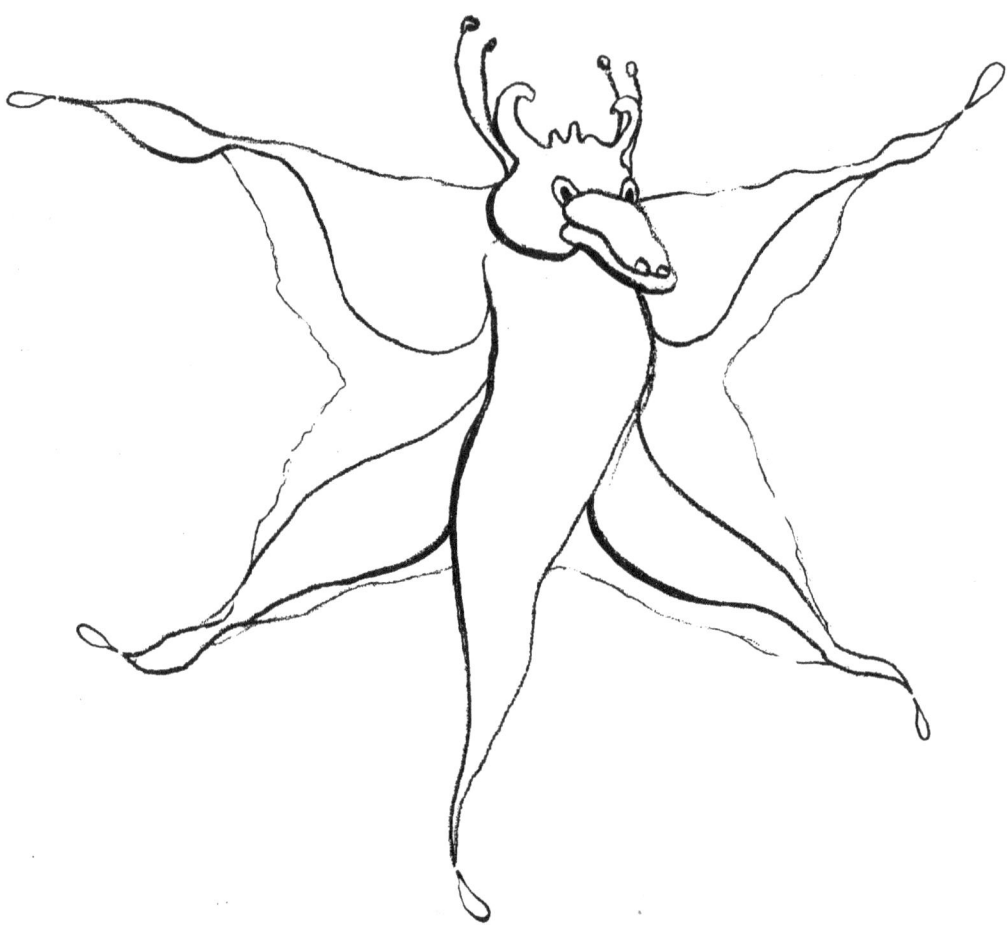

Flying foxes eat fruit Squirell bat zac Loves april, and eats bananas in summer!

FLYING FOX

SQUIRELL BAT ZAC.....The adoration of sweet fury little animals has overtaken the world of companions and loneliness. The pet food industry is bigger than the healthcare industry! Unusual people want more exotic pets not cats.

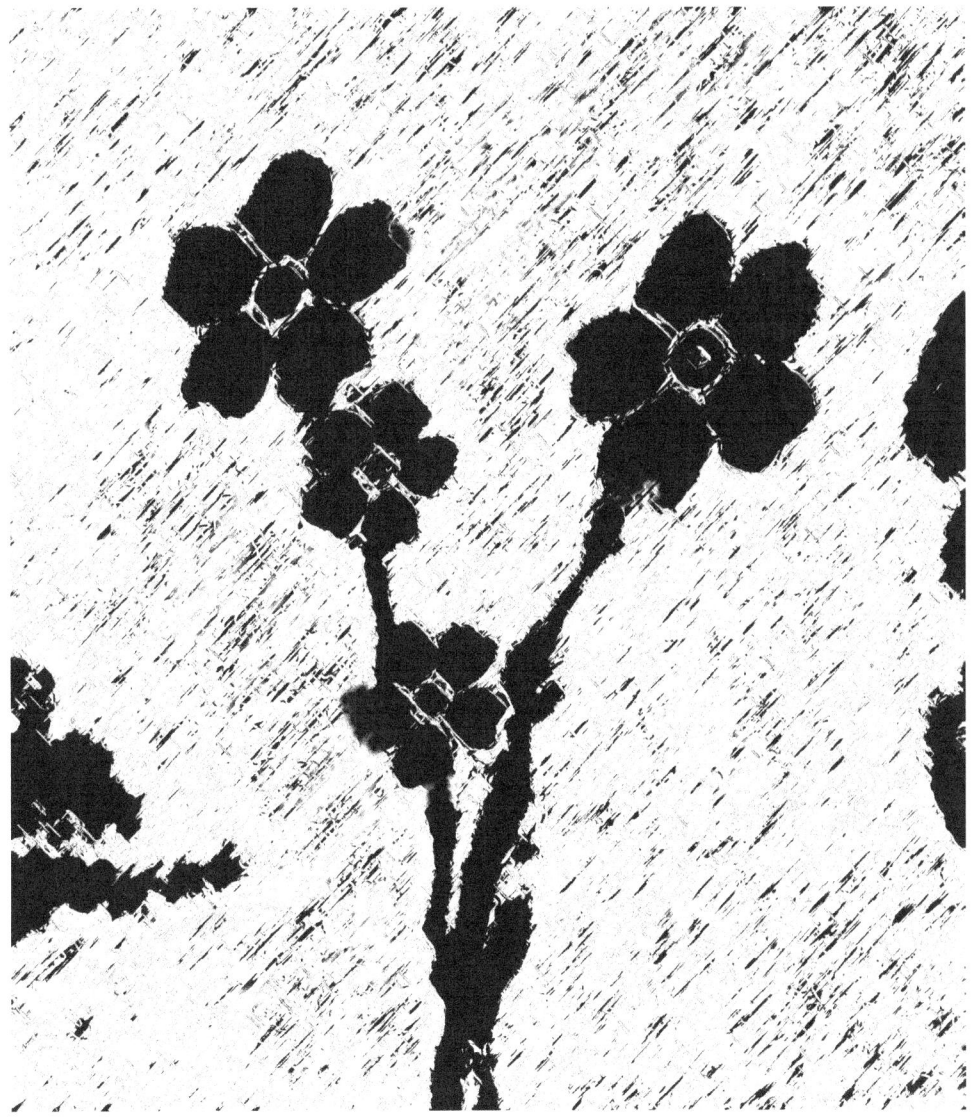

FLOWERS

Part of the plant from which fruit or seed is developed. Why do women have a passion for flowers tell me! The centre of the universe for most women, do they mean power, life, expense, honor, rebirth or excess? We have interflora worldwide.....Send me brussels sprouts.

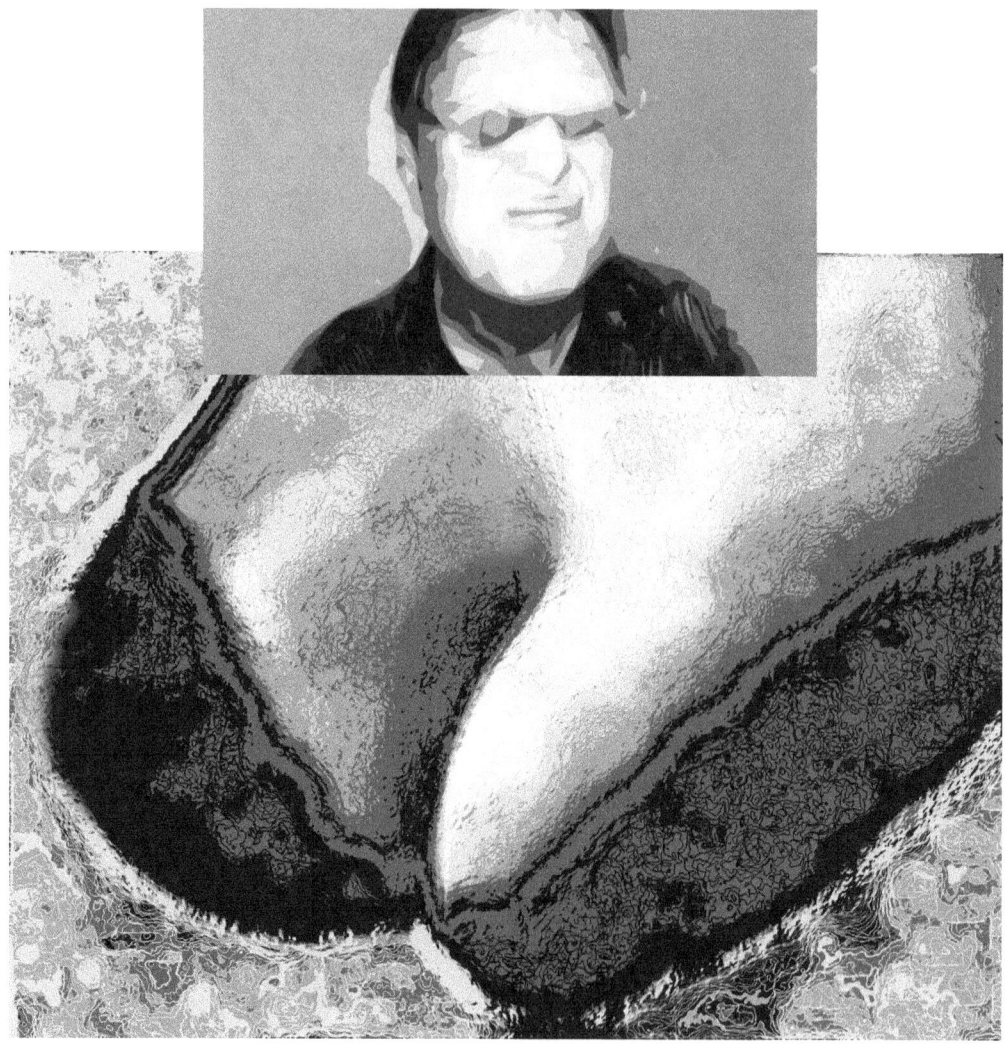

FRUSTRATION

You can't have it.....I wan't it. A feeling of dissatisfaction, being annoyed with complications.

FRILLY

Sensual lace covering the body..... Swirling pattern.....Sensual materials and exotic colours.

FRAME

Detectives in the process of brainstorming
and visual boarding put suspects in the frame.
Directors: film and art use their fingers to frame
the scene. Sometimes a cropping tool.

4TEEN

A time in their life when they know everything.

FUCKWIT

Witless waste of time and space, I don't want to bother with them.

FORM

Shape, arrangement of parts, visable aspect. Printed document with blank spaces.

FUTURE

About to happen or a time to come. From this time onwards. What will happen in the future.

FOOTLOOSE

Free to act as one pleases.

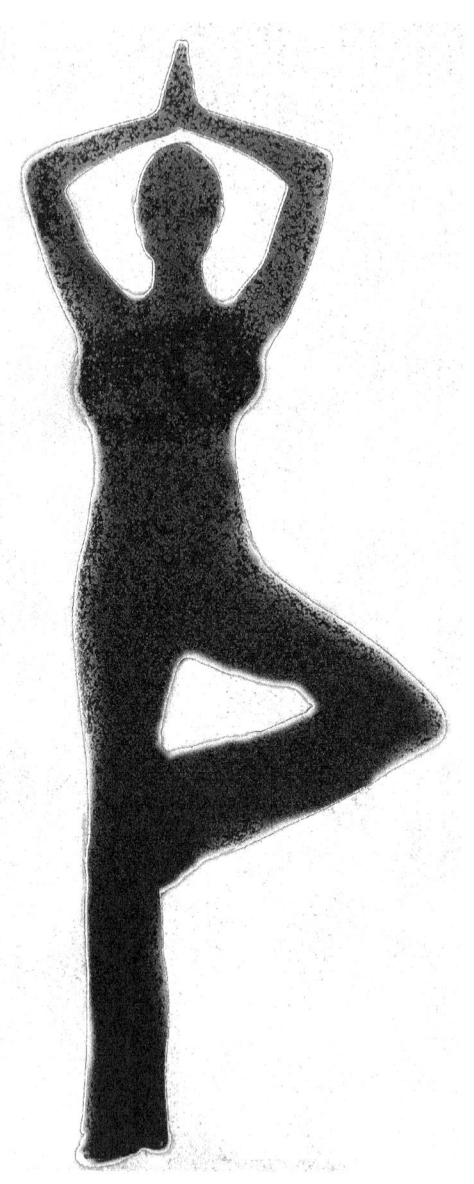

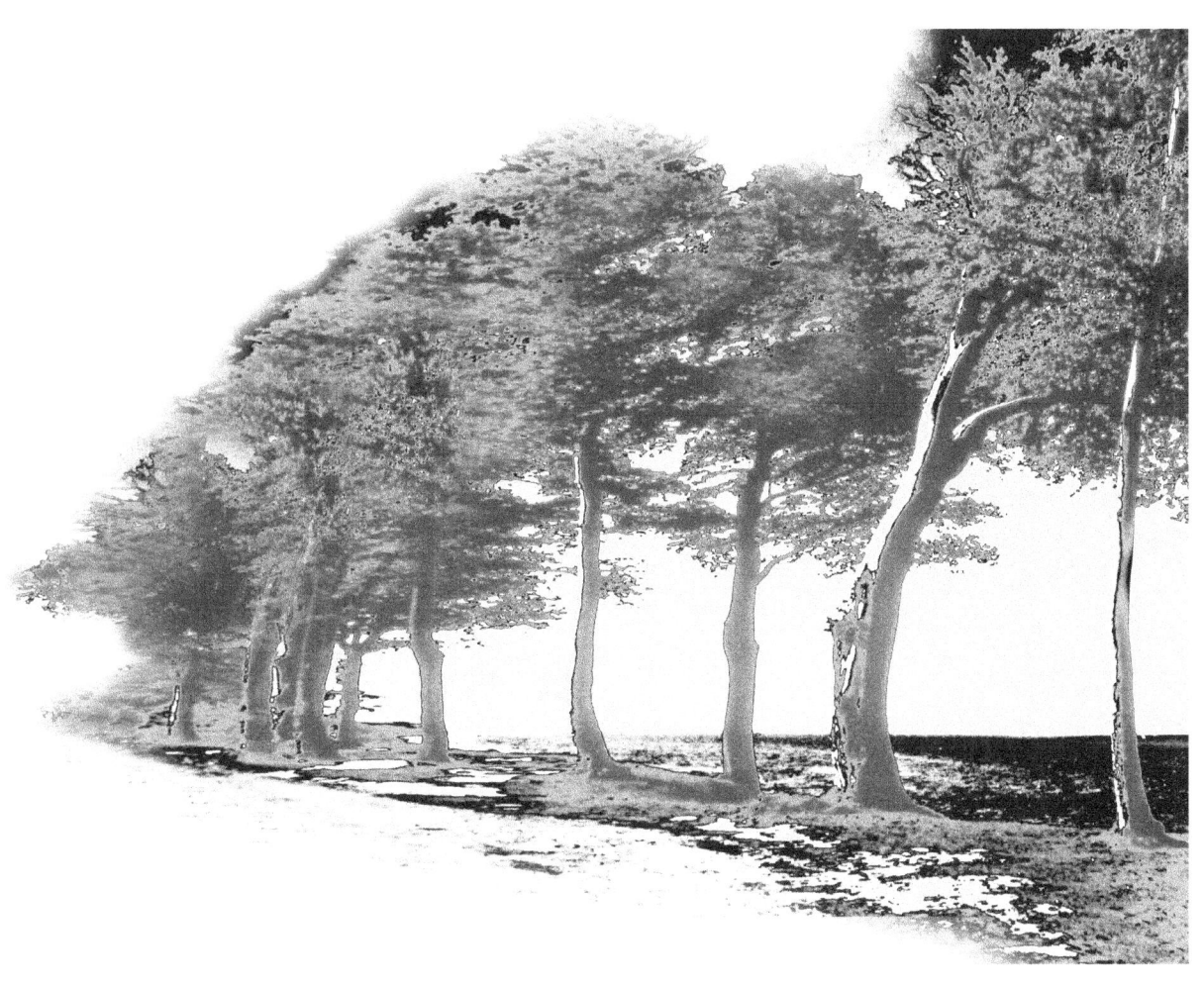

FRENCH

This could be Italy or Spain
but I like it as France, icons
for national countries are
embeded in our mind..

FUTURE

The empires of the future are the empires of the mind.....Winston Churchill.

FOURSOME

Bob, Carol, Ted and Alice. What can you say about that, is it your kind of way, check it out.....

FPISCHING

Digital searching for your identity, trying to scam you through your on line presence.

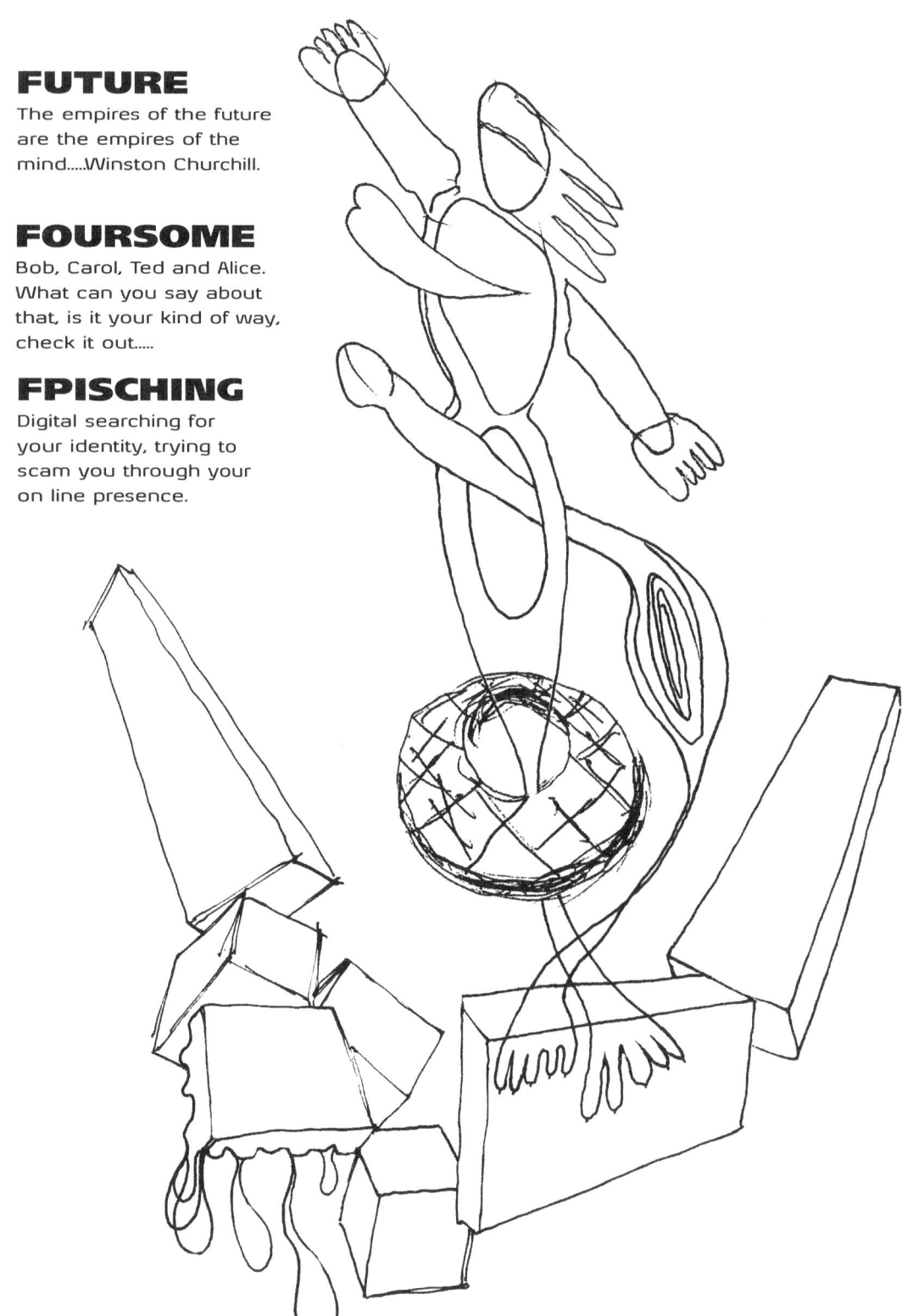

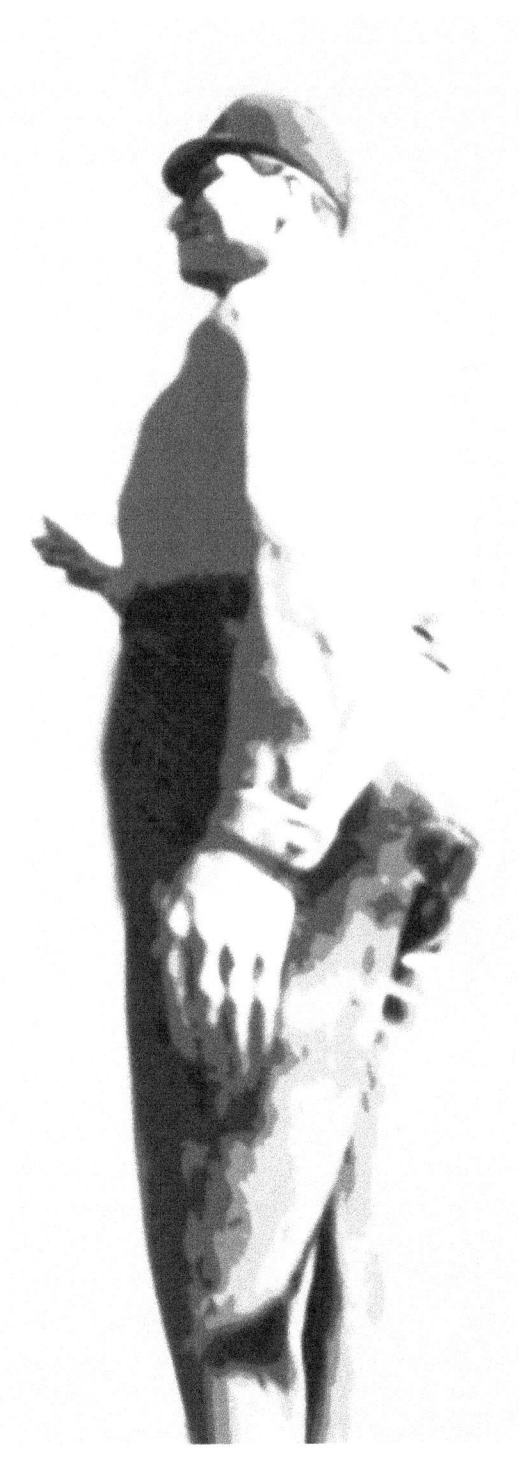

FACE

Structure over the front
of the head, a place
where we read non
verbal language.

FUNKY

Popular and edgy
for the nineties.....
But now what is it.
Surreal and unique,
with an unusual and
funny edge.

FORMAT

Structure or a grid,
basline for setting
up a system for
proceeding on a
path to completion.

GREEN

Colour.....Green washing.....What do you mean Enviro trash is so important.....
Paper or plastic madam.....Diesel or gas.....Nuclear or coal fired electric.....
Acid rain.....Recycle.....Repair.....Reuse.....Accidents happen, I mean look at us!

CONserve.....Biodiversity.....Ecology.....Preservation.....Restoration.....Natural.....
Control pollution.....Balance between humans and nature.....Sustainable
management.....Conservation.....CONsumption.....Resources.....Renewable
energy.....Air pollution.....Eco systems.....Water pollution.....Human pollution.....

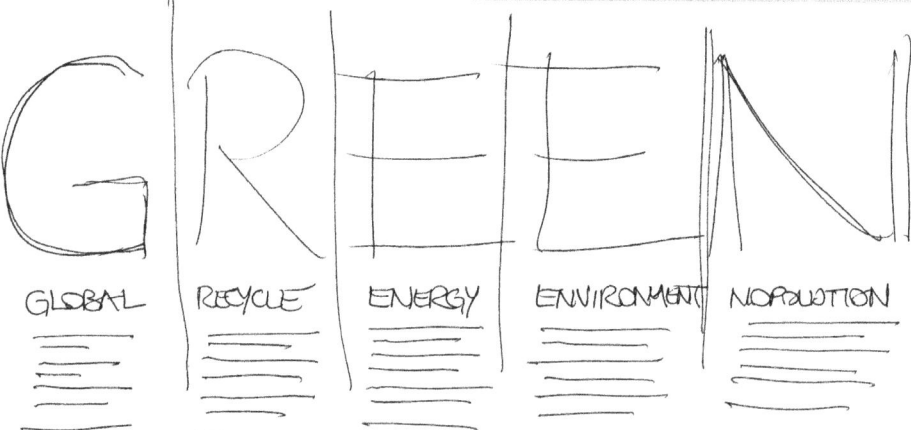

GOOGLEnet We drove over the hill just south of Calatino to see
the parking lot for one hundred and ninety nine thousand parked cars....The
world server farms are covered with human interns, moving from building to
building, on the campuses rapid transit sky train.....Google has accessed every
urban center worldwide and is your friendly informer and advisor, helping
your fingers and speech do your asking. Automated programs that constantly
browse the world wide web sending out trillions of crawlers collecting a fresh
cache of all searchable information every second! You read it on the web....
Has your doc! Open knowledge, how do we clean a crab, lets think about this
together.....google that! Non biased and fair yehr.....

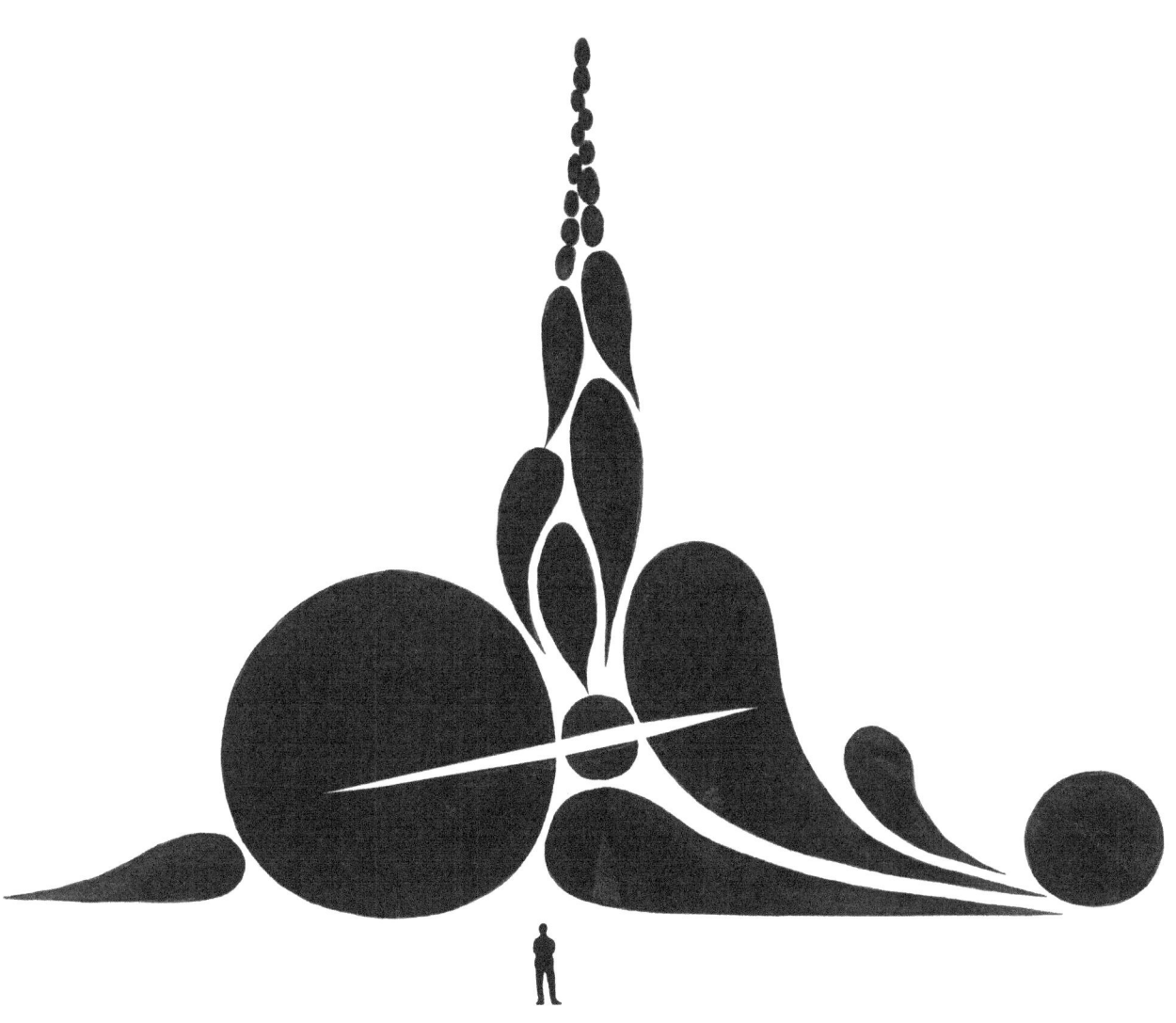

GRAND CITY

Milton Keynes to Brasilia.....Above this is a picture of
a future new age city, which is very gaudi meets
Gehry.....3 million priviliged people are safe and enjoy
clean living here! The sphere on the right, is the right
to die terminal age amphitheatre, for the last rights.

Full, can't.....breathe.....Pick.....Roll.....and Drop.....

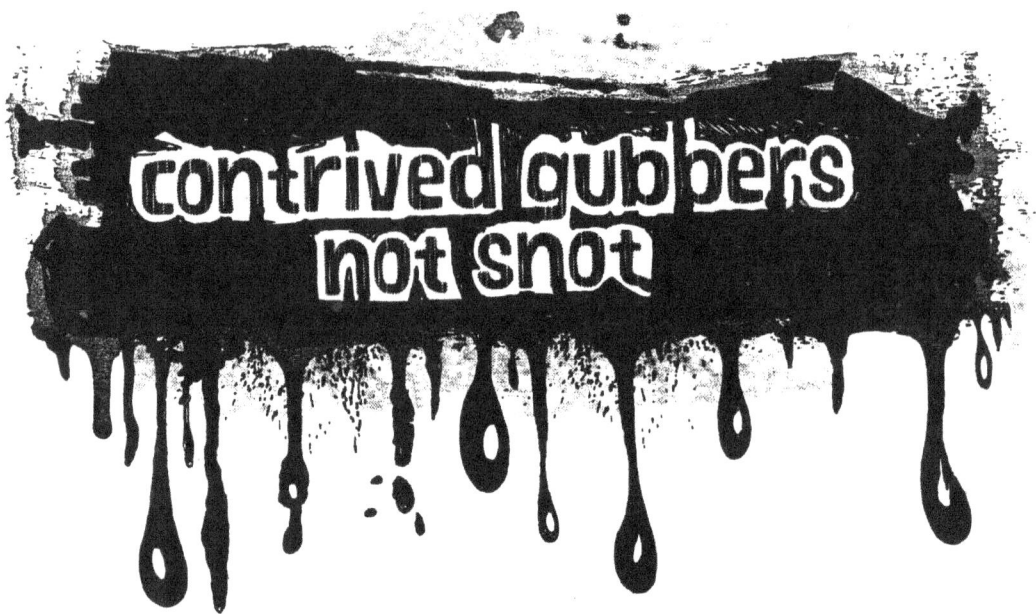

GOBSTOPPERS

No not that.....Aniseed balls.....Candy for throat cavities. Long lasting liquorice. Expectorant, mild laxative. Increases blood pressure and thirst quenching qualities, Gripe water, no wonder we all had it as kids in Africa.

GOLDEN

Rich.....Rich.....Rich, this word is the creme de la creme.....In so many cultures..... We base so many values on gold. Why? Sunsets give you golden twilight.

GIVONEY

Italian silk diamond pattern on a smoking jacket designed and made by a seemstress in croydon. Colour burgandy or merlot.

GUBBERS

Snotty bastard! I wish you knew who you are!!!!! Class systems, the only joy is even your enemy can have all this mucky stuff coming out of their snozzel.....But it makes great jerky/biltong when it is dry.

GLOOPY

This word says it.....Sort of sticky, messy, honey.

GESTURE

Human makes sign to transmit information to others on earth.

GLAMPING

This word means glamour camping, bring your bling..... maybe started with the very rich in east african safaris!

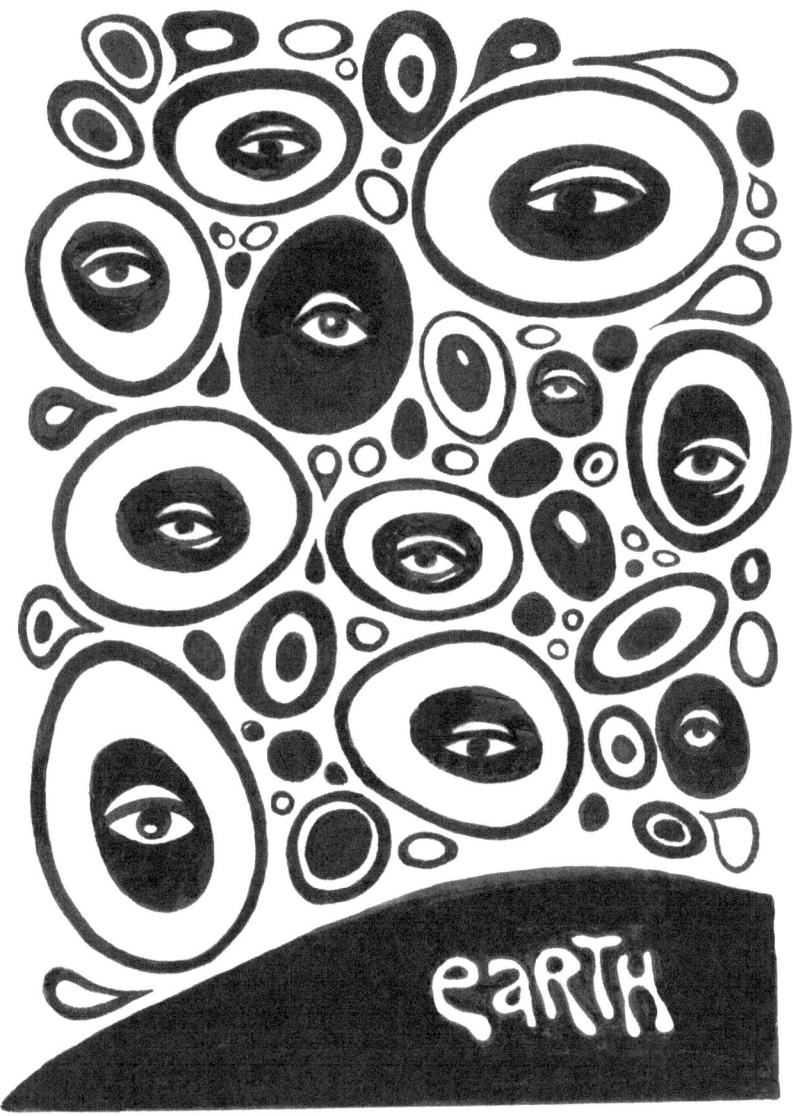

GAIA.....eggeye, auras! A Knocking on the above skydoors of the earth will move you, then you will turn your world around! Get cracking.....Crack open an eye ball today, twenty twenty vision with your new lens, cataract cool, now you can see, while driving us crazy.....We earthlings are real rubber souls. Save the planet? It has been around four and a half million years, it can look after itself! Don't worry about the planet. We have only been around two hundred thousand years.....Save SOME of us.....

GRAFFITI

Graffiti....Painting, writing or drawing scribbled or scratched or sprayed on most inner city surfaces.....Why....Where.....How? Google banksy, the leader of the pack.

The person in charge spoke slowly, so I understand fully.

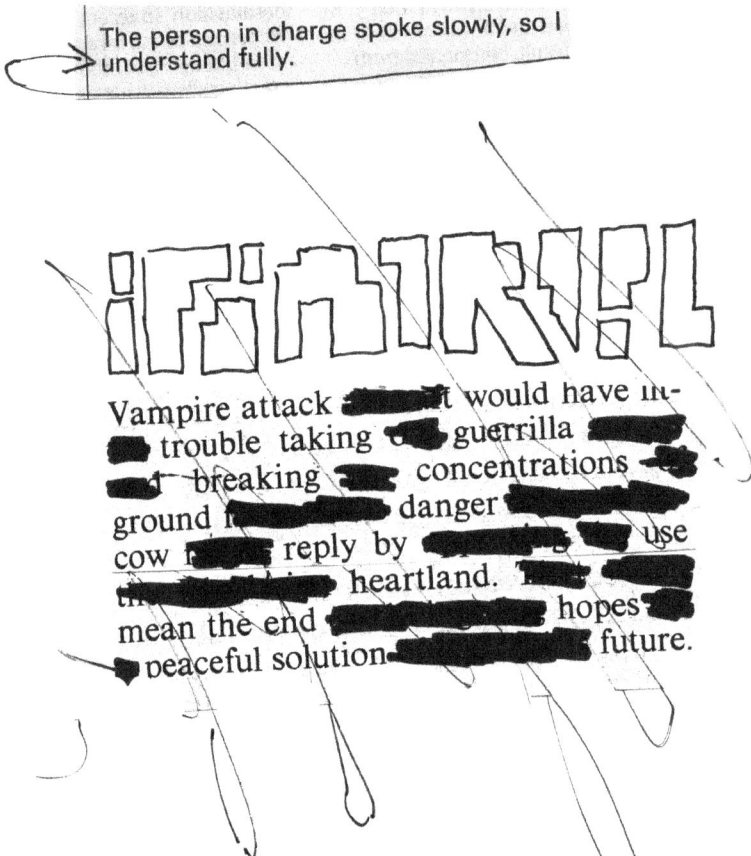

Vampire attack ▮▮▮▮ it would have in-
▮▮▮ trouble taking ▮▮▮ guerrilla ▮▮▮
▮▮▮ breaking ▮▮▮ concentrations ▮▮▮
ground ▮ ▮▮▮ danger ▮▮▮▮▮▮
cow ▮▮▮ reply by ▮▮▮▮▮▮ use
▮▮▮▮▮▮ heartland. ▮▮▮▮▮▮
mean the end ▮▮▮▮▮ hopes
peaceful solution ▮▮▮▮ future.

GURU

Hindu spiritual leader......But with the arrival of the sixties many people in the upper village and notting hill gate enjoyed the priviledge of influenc-ing young lost souls into the beds of warm spirits for mind pleasure.....

GUM ARABIC

Hashab.....Sounds like assasins should smoke it, but its not mellow yellow, How many artists use it now? But I do like its filter in photoshop.

GATES

No.....You have to go through them to get to the inside, whether its heaven or hell, some times they are closed to you and be wary if they are always open.

GOOFY

Crazy.....Funny, acting up, humour can get you out of some situations but not all of the time. One of Disneys seven dwarfs, seven dwarfs is this OK!

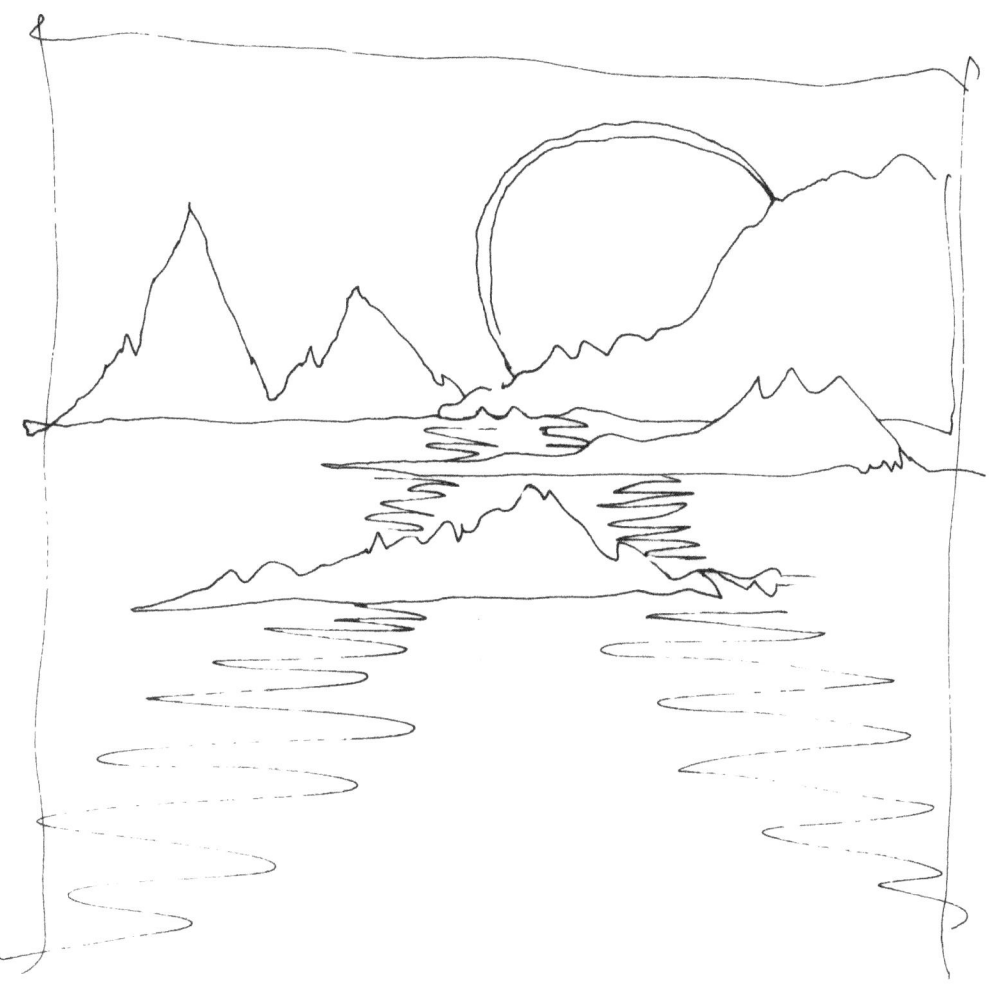

HORIZON

Sea to sky.....Fields to clouds, when sailing, watch the horizon so you wont feel as sick. You can't believe its curved till you reach 36000 feet, look at this earth.....We are on it. Is it ours to fuck with?

HUMPY BONG

That is the name of the town in queensland near where I used to live! How with words like this was I seajuiced into passion word desire.....

HEAVENS DOOR

The gate at the end of the garden of life, ps you got to get back to the garden.....Salmon go back to sporn. Is this where your god lives? You who are righteous will be here permanently when you are dead!

HEALTH

Happiness and health has one advantage over wealth.....No one can borrow it.....Best prize health!

HURDY GURDY

Portable musical instrument played by turning a handle, sometimes comes with the carney, circus and gypsies.....Rhythm gets into your heart and soul, listern to Ronnie Lane.

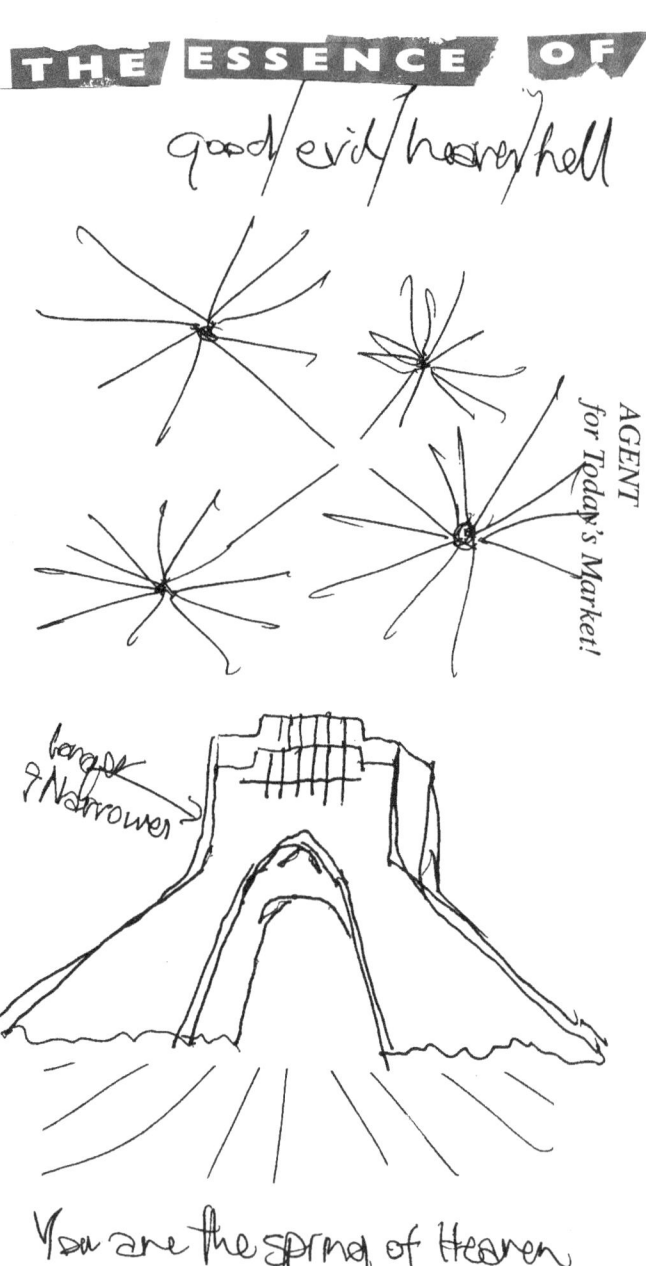

THE ESSENCE OF

good/evil/heaven/hell

AGENT for Today's Market!

longer
9 Narrower

You are the spring of Heaven

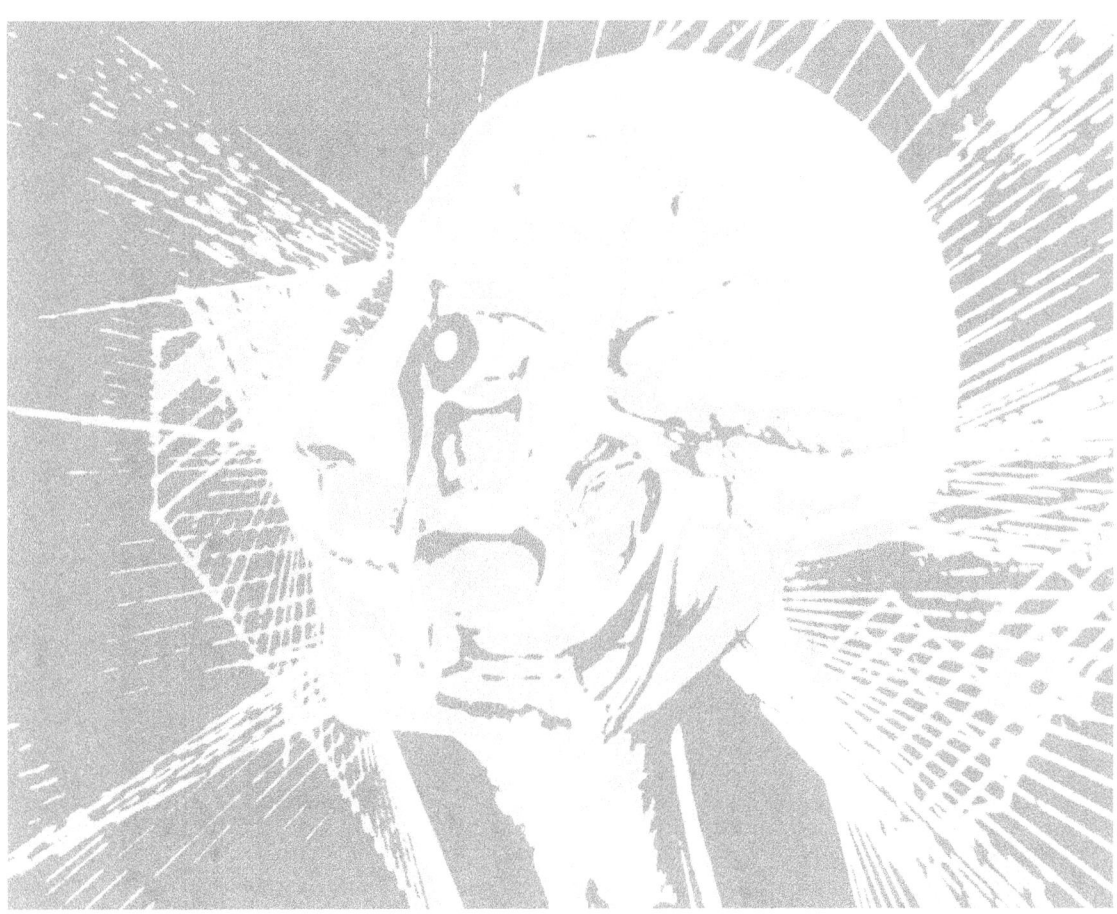

HEADONICS

New study of the growth of the conceptual,
functioning neocortex area in the brain. How
to manipulate and expand the potential of
the neocortex in all human individuals to
improve our knowledge and life.

HOTLIPS

She was in mash, best byline/tagline for the
boys of the 407? Boys at war have so much
fun between the hurt......Join the navy, see the
world, thats advertising!!!

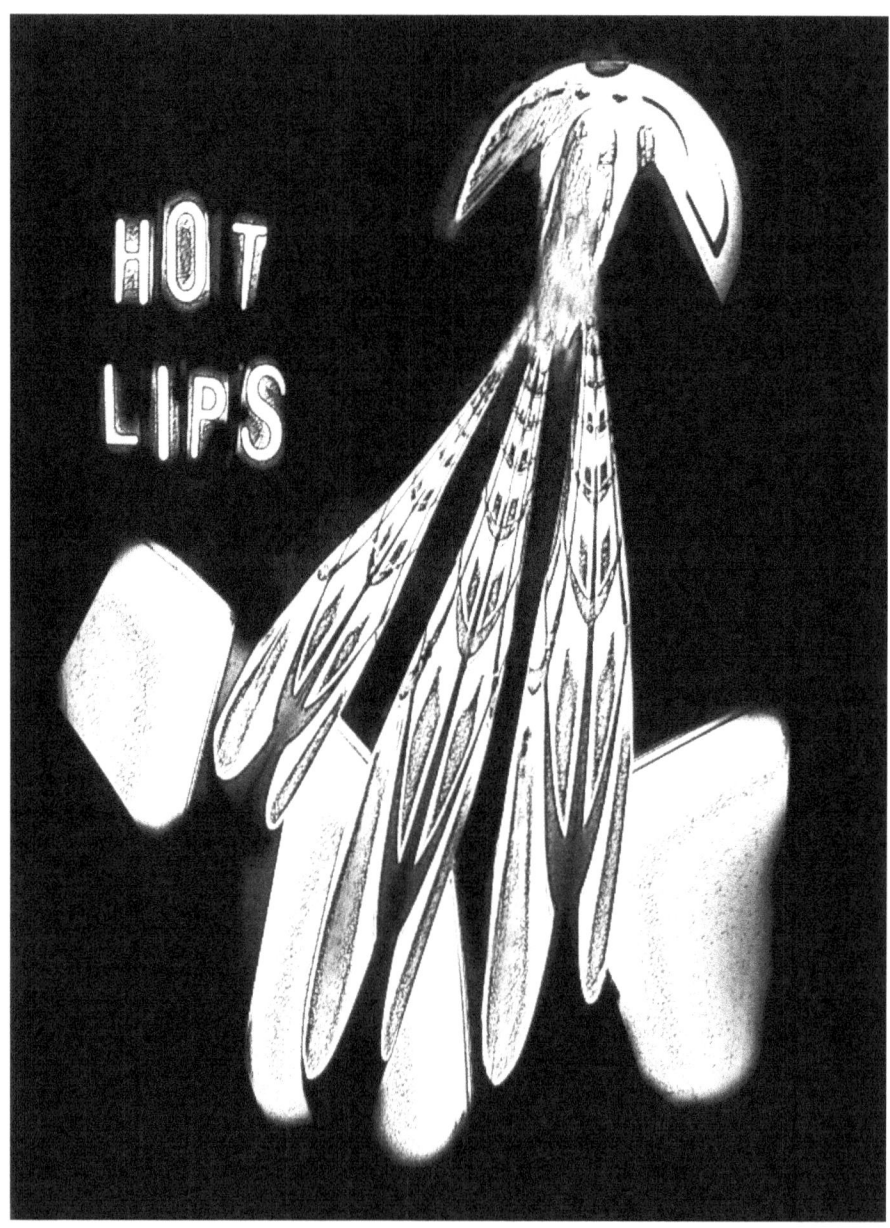

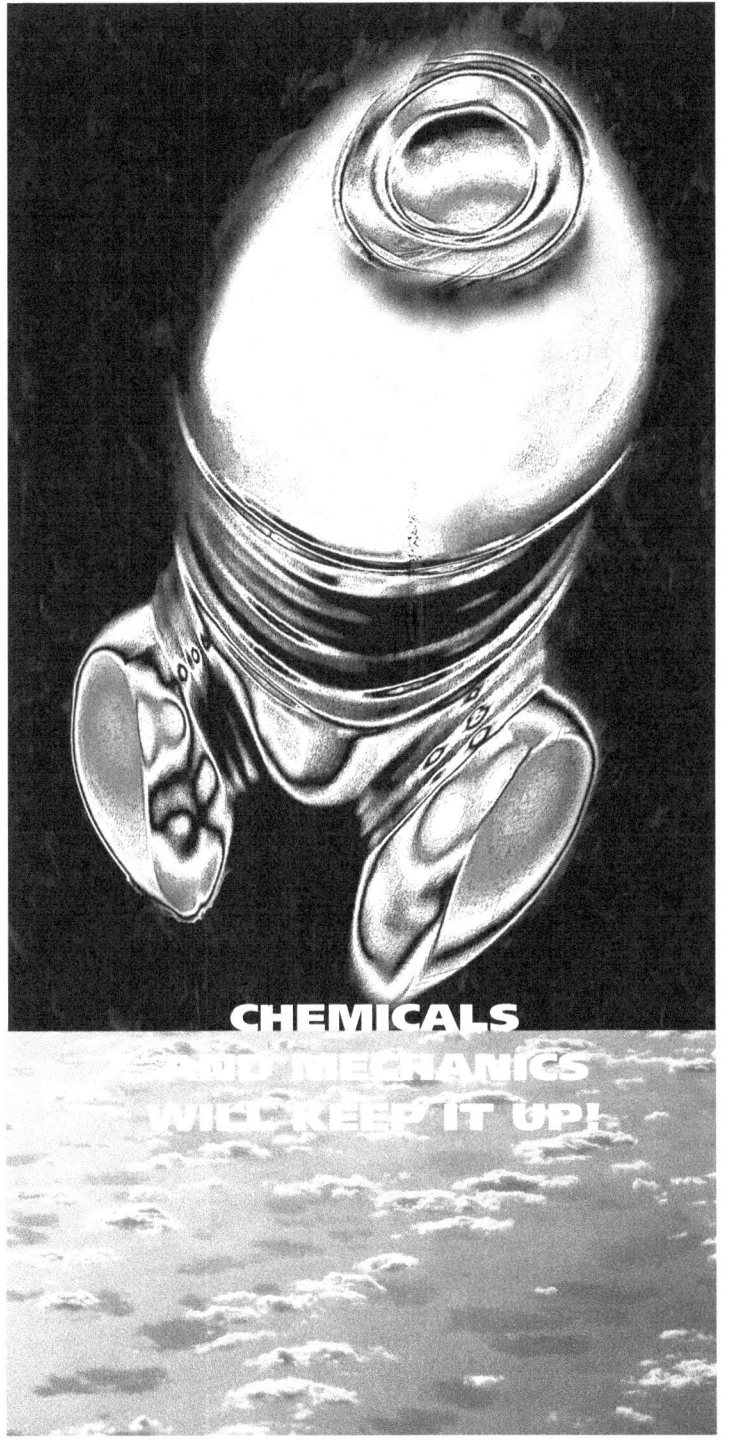

CHEMICALS
AND MECHANICS
WILL KEEP IT UP!

HIGH

Some where
above my mate-
rial existence, by
having chemicals
in my brain, I float.
above the clouds
looking down on
the earth, that's as
close as I can get
now. Short version
Hi Form of greet-
ing.....Altered states.

HEART

Central control, the pumping centre for all body functions. When my friend who was sixty five had a transplant and got a new thirty year old heart from the other gender, did she change.....She was smokin wild. Lets have a heart to heart.

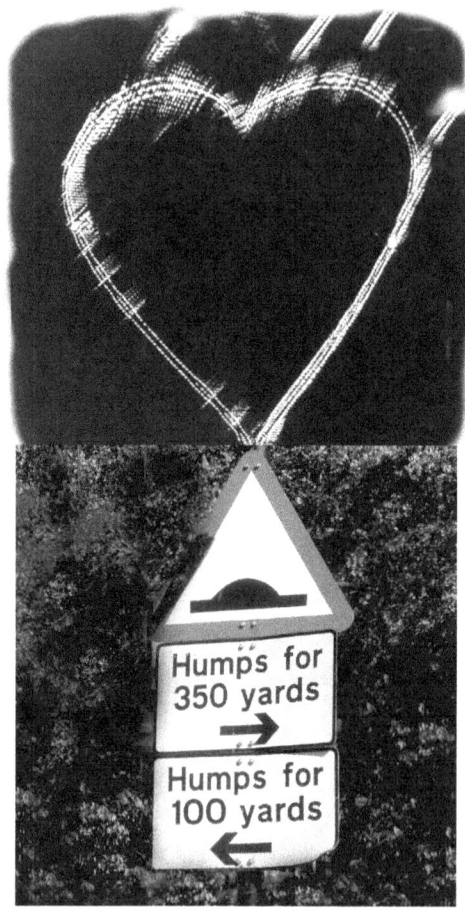

HUMPS

Little lumps, little bumps. Rounded protuberance on the back of a camel. Upsetting you.....Get the hump, then make up with humping, sexual pleasure.

HAMPTON

Yet another name for the penisori, sounds jolly jam sandwiches old boy, hardly very elegant, we should all be invited for triangular cucumber sandwiches. Good show, let it fly to the sky.....Dick toolin.

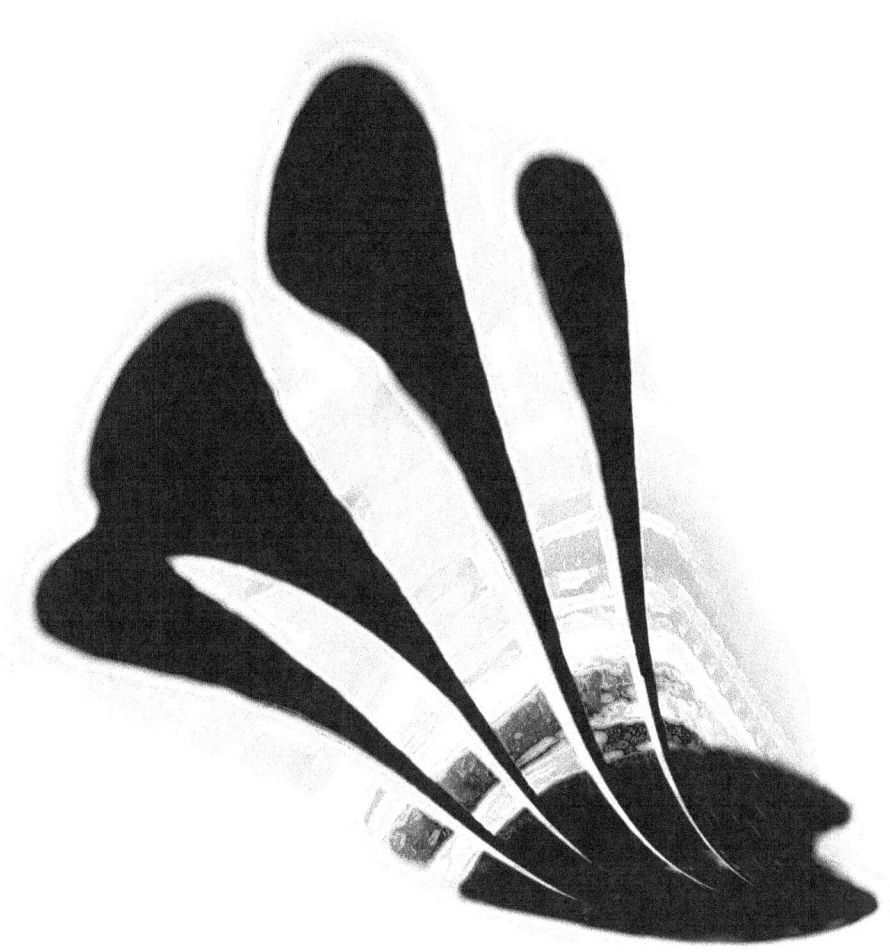

HIGHBEAMS

They are bright, big in the right place and stand out, leading the way. In oz you have jugs of beer or good watermelons!

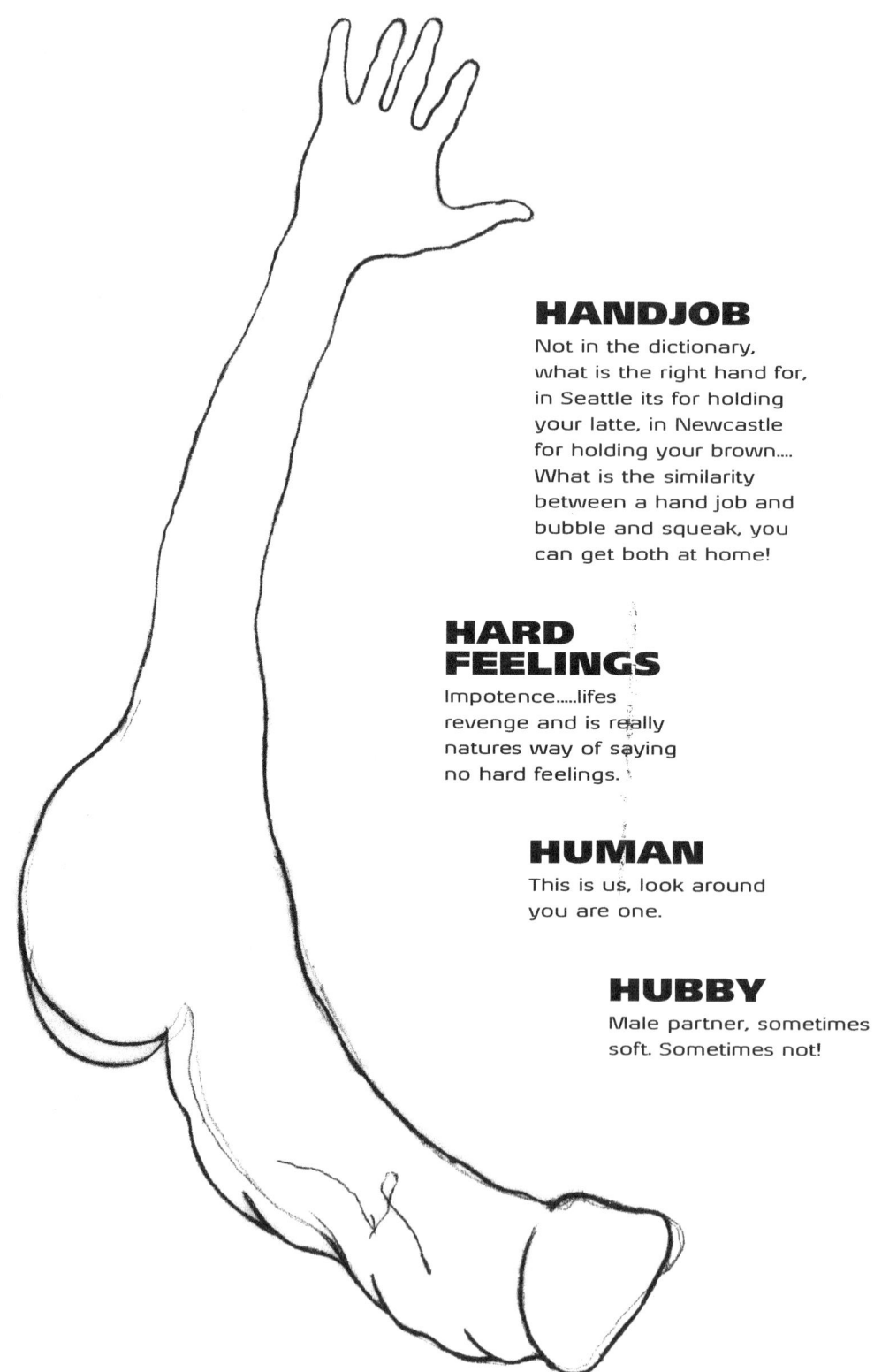

HANDJOB

Not in the dictionary,
what is the right hand for,
in Seattle its for holding
your latte, in Newcastle
for holding your brown....
What is the similarity
between a hand job and
bubble and squeak, you
can get both at home!

HARD FEELINGS

Impotence.....lifes
revenge and is really
natures way of saying
no hard feelings.

HUMAN

This is us, look around
you are one.

HUBBY

Male partner, sometimes
soft. Sometimes not!

84

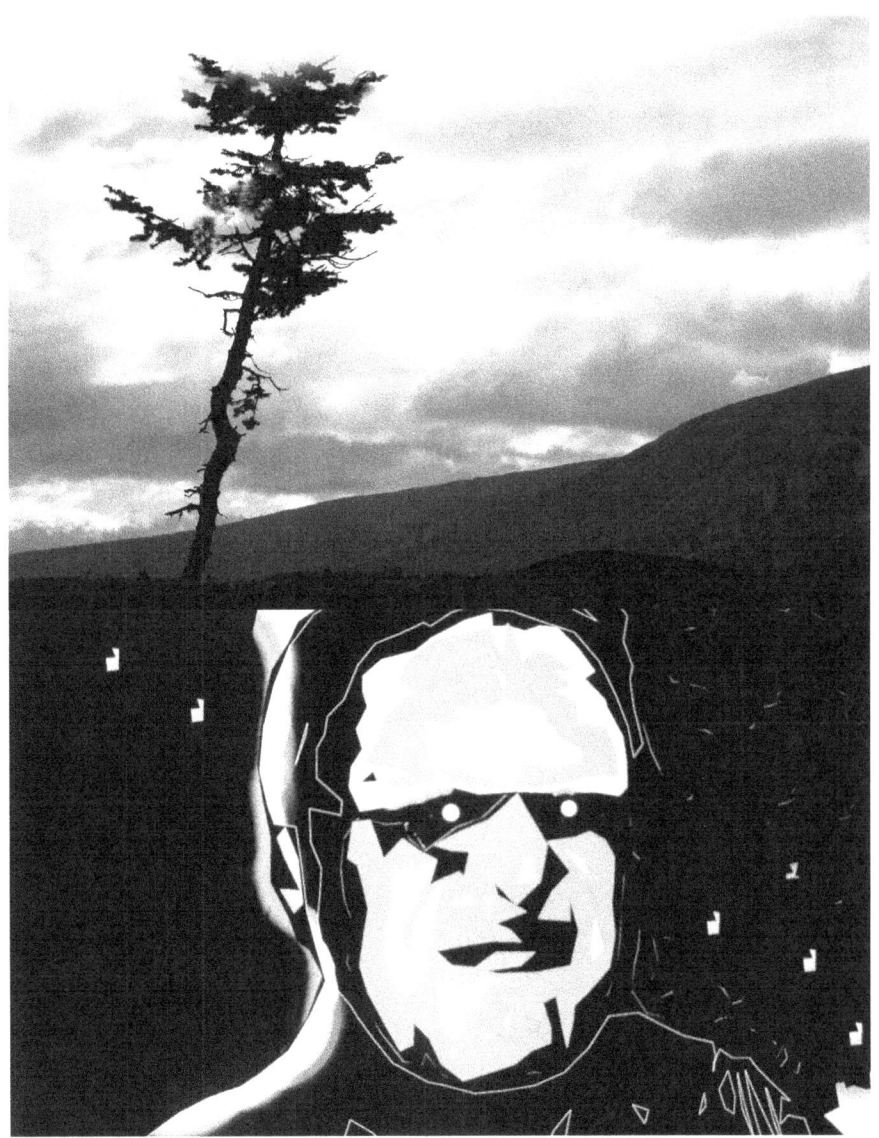

HOMELAND

Homeland security......The science of opinion control. The place where salmon go back to......When we were real tetropods we did it to! Now home is where your bed, heart and wallet are.

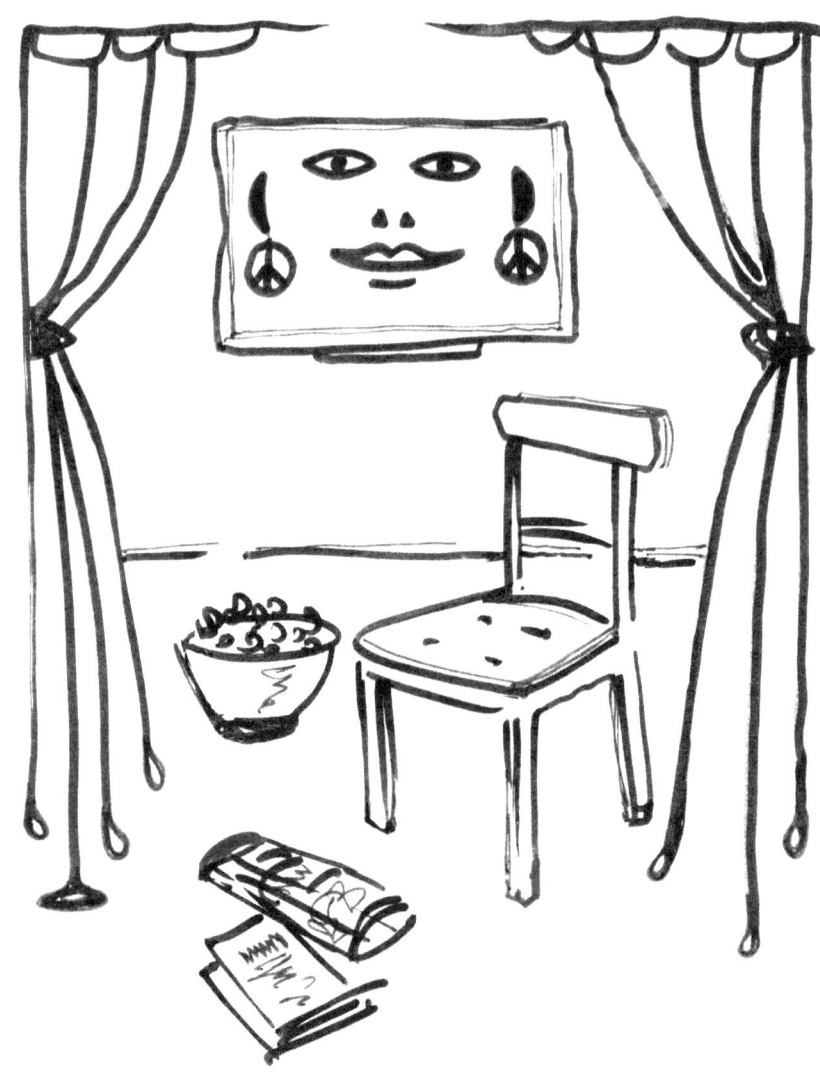

HELLO WALL

Thank you willy russell.....Shirley valentine, talking to objects is the best......They do not answer back and seem to agree with me, I admire them and love to surround myself with them. This picture is perfec.....

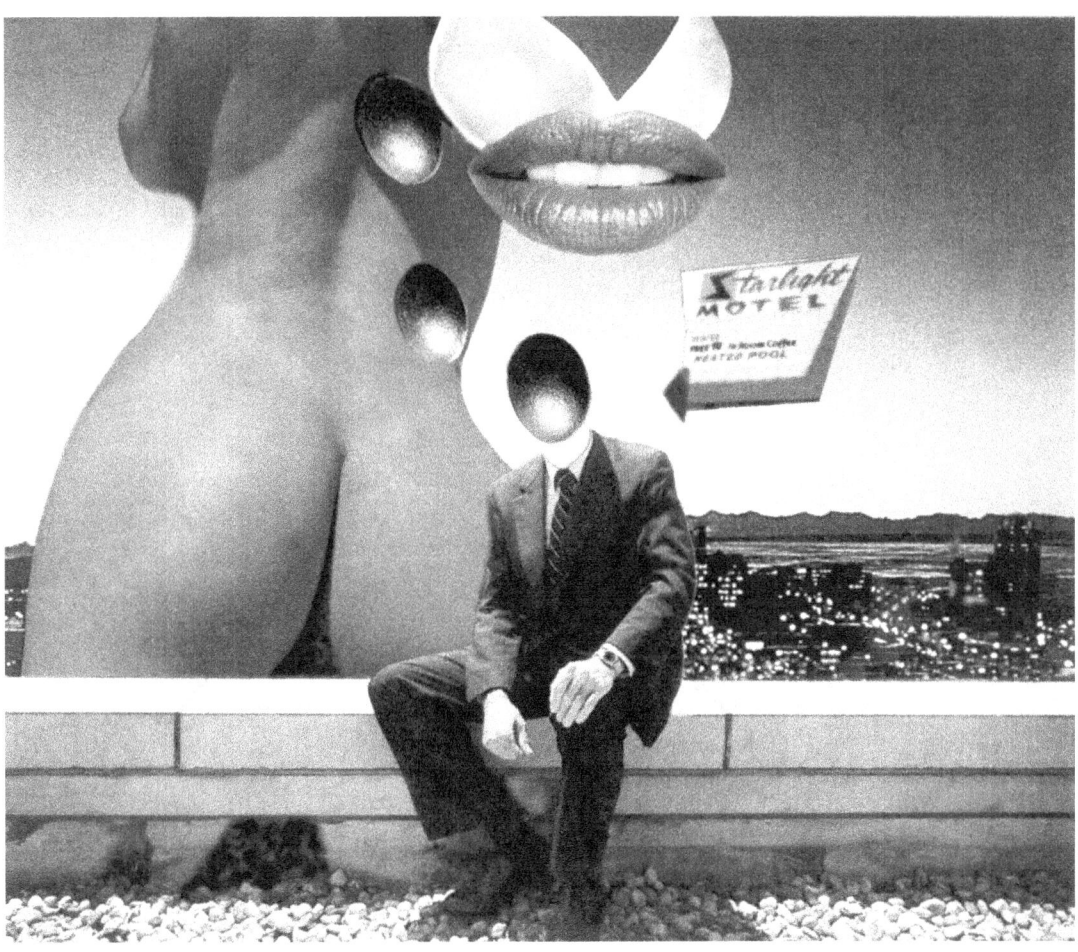

HOME

This is us.....Look around you are a home.....24 hour
lifetime assistance, if you paid the accounting
league of gentlemen, if not take a ticket, Mister
Zanders and Mister Wanker you are near the end
of the alphabetical line, que and quietly wait.

HAL

I can not do that Dave.....Open the pod bay.....I can not do that Dave. HAL is Helen App Live computer....The arrival of true singularity, AI, the marble godess, the new look for the cyber non biological advanced human race, imagined by the KKK.....Kubrick, Kurzwiel, Krick.

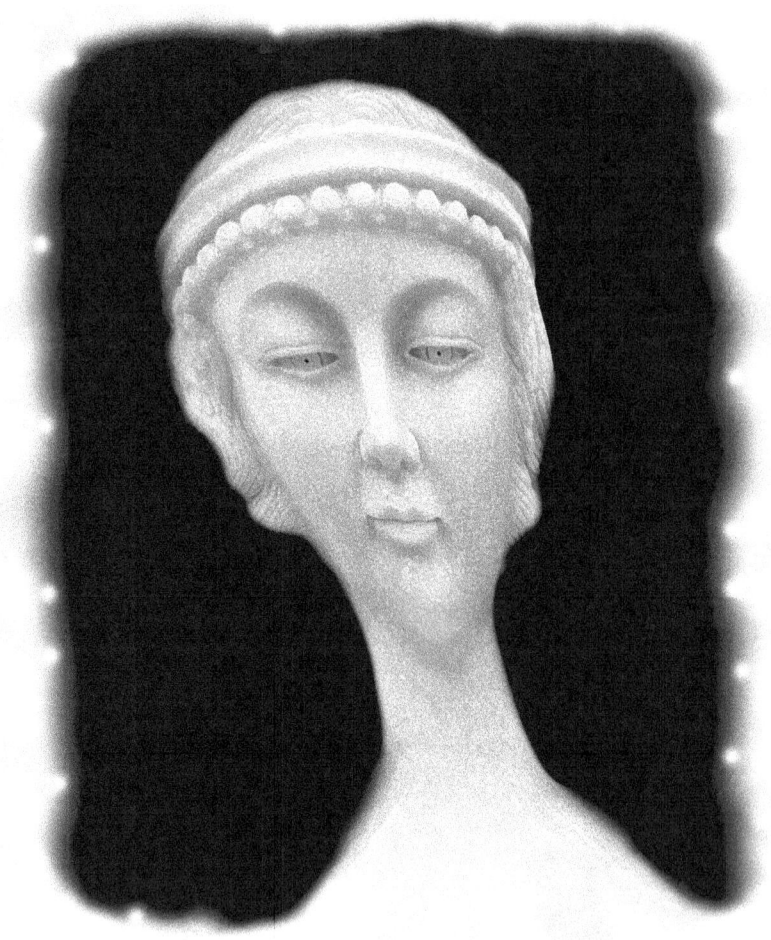

HULLABALOO

Nobody ever speaks this word now, but it exists in print a lot! The dictionary says uproar.

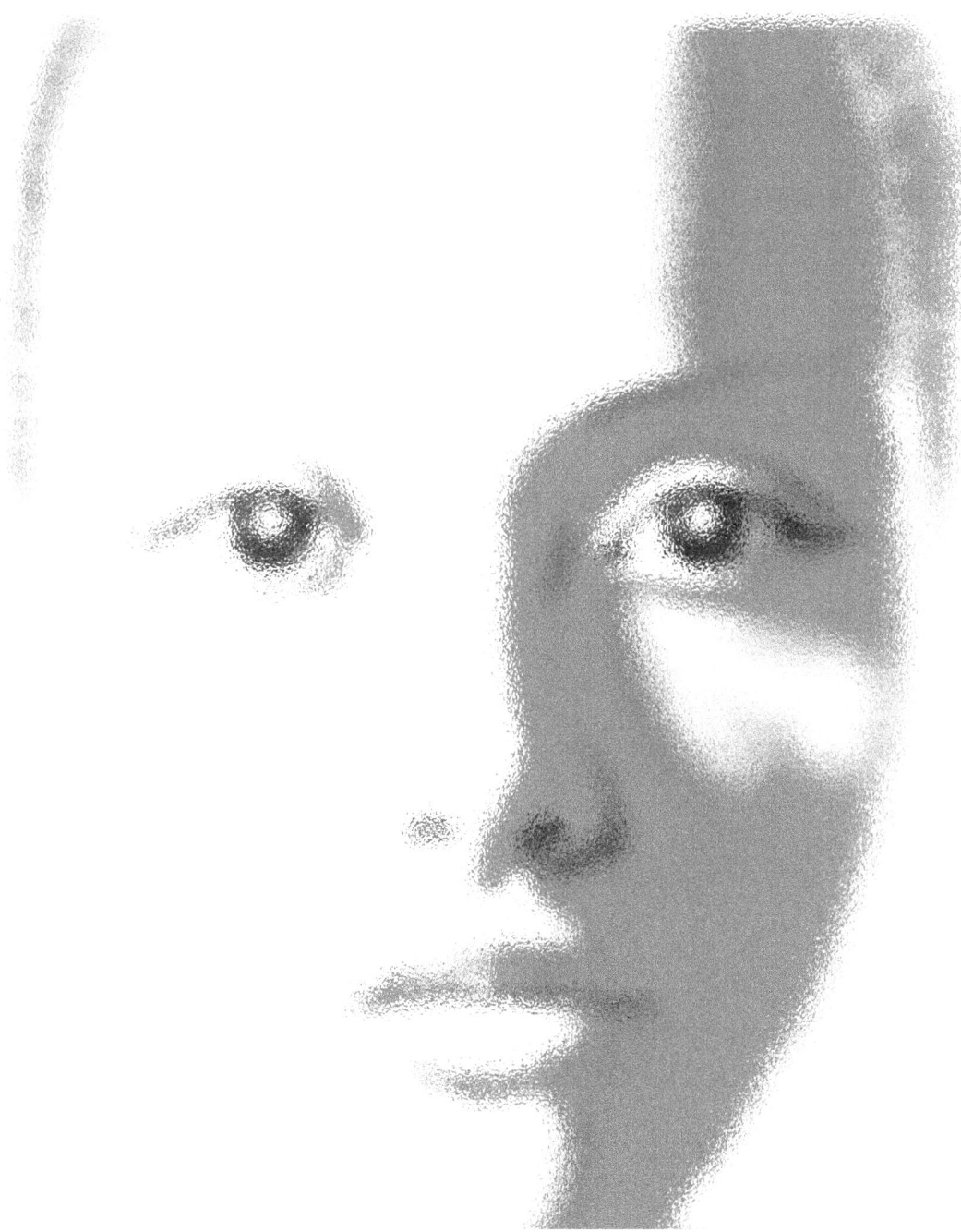

INSIGHT

Seeing through the exterior surface of the idea, thoughts will form. Mental penetration.....What's different in you, makes you the beauty you really are. Look into my eyes, melt my bollocks, the hairs on the back of my neck are stiffies.....Tinglinggggg. Don't believe everything you think!

INFLUENCE

Words form after action, sometimes they are capable of influencing change, they can hurt and bring happiness. Our whole experience is built upon our imagination, environment, our culture and media.

INDEPTH

Look at the problem, seeing through the exterior surface of the idea, thought or solution. Study all the parts thoroughly from end to end.

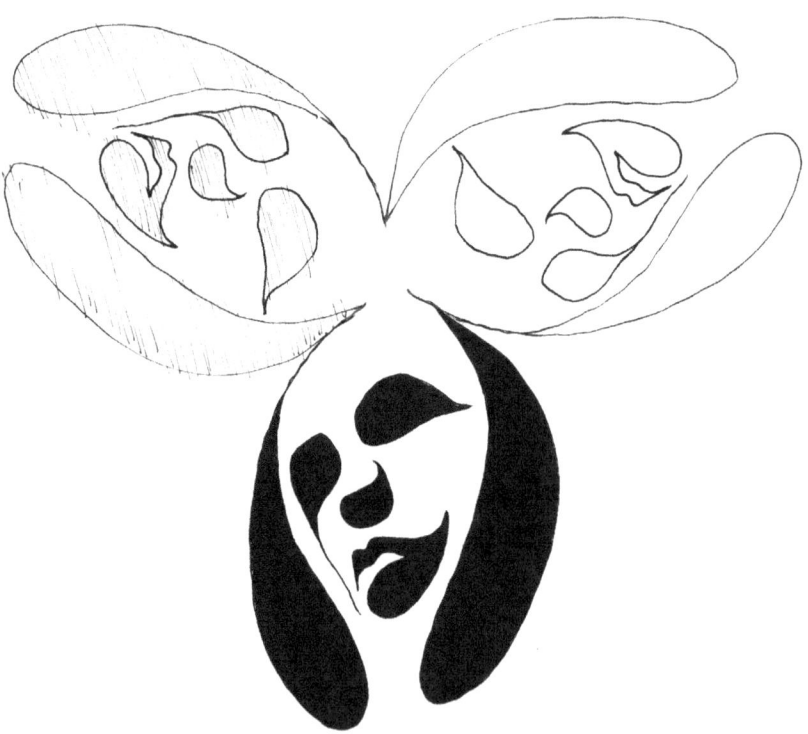

INO AND ID

Ino castrated male? Classic visual problem with the eye.
It is your barcode, qr, sin#. Your dna catalogue.

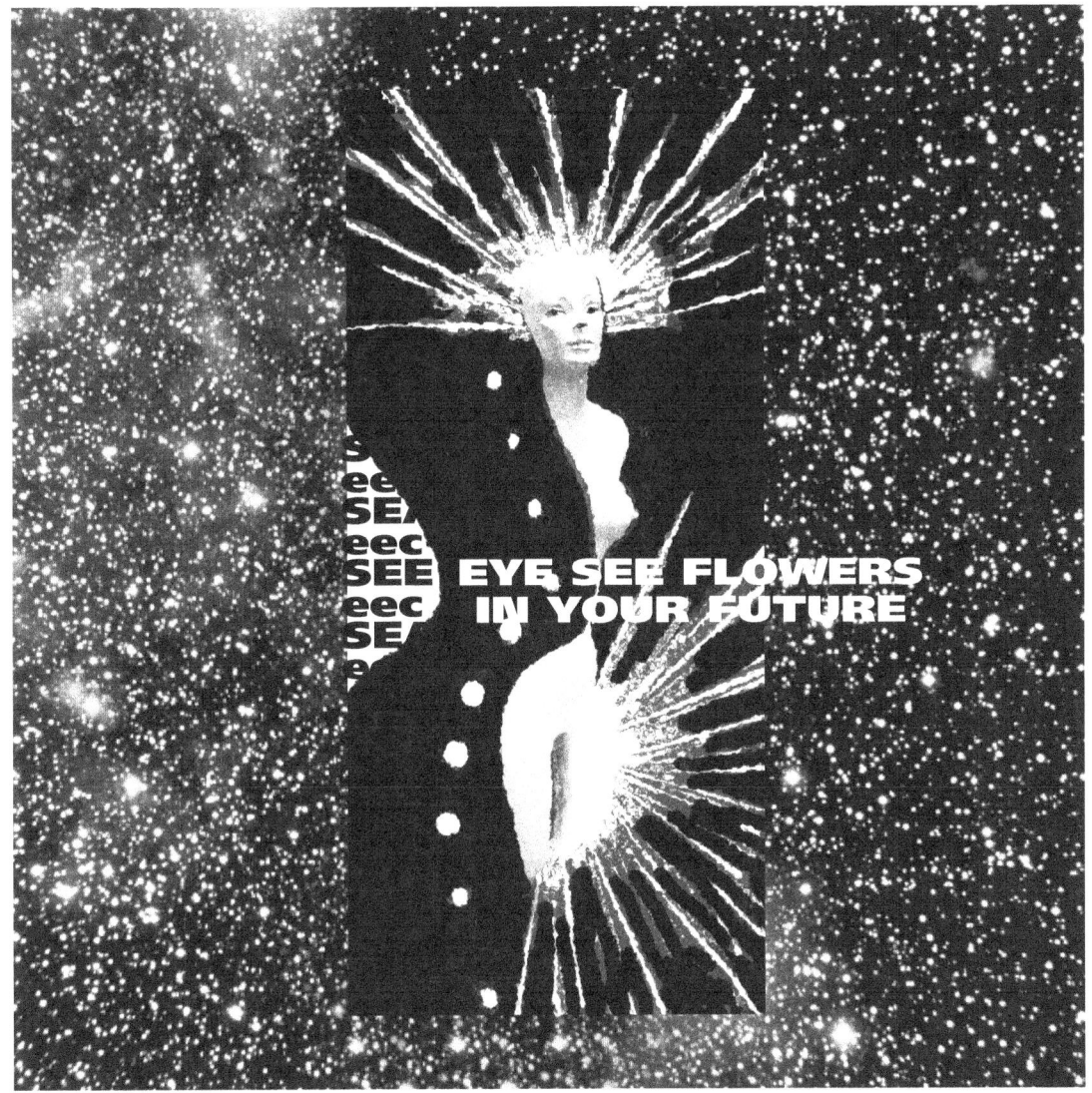

IRIS

Centre of the eye.....Circular coloured membrane behind the cornea of the eye......Pupil a circular opening in the middle. Then for the women in my life, the flower.....What is it with women and flowers some primal fresh beauty. Candles and rose petals all along the yellow brick road to the bed NO! Deadly nightshade another type of flower.....

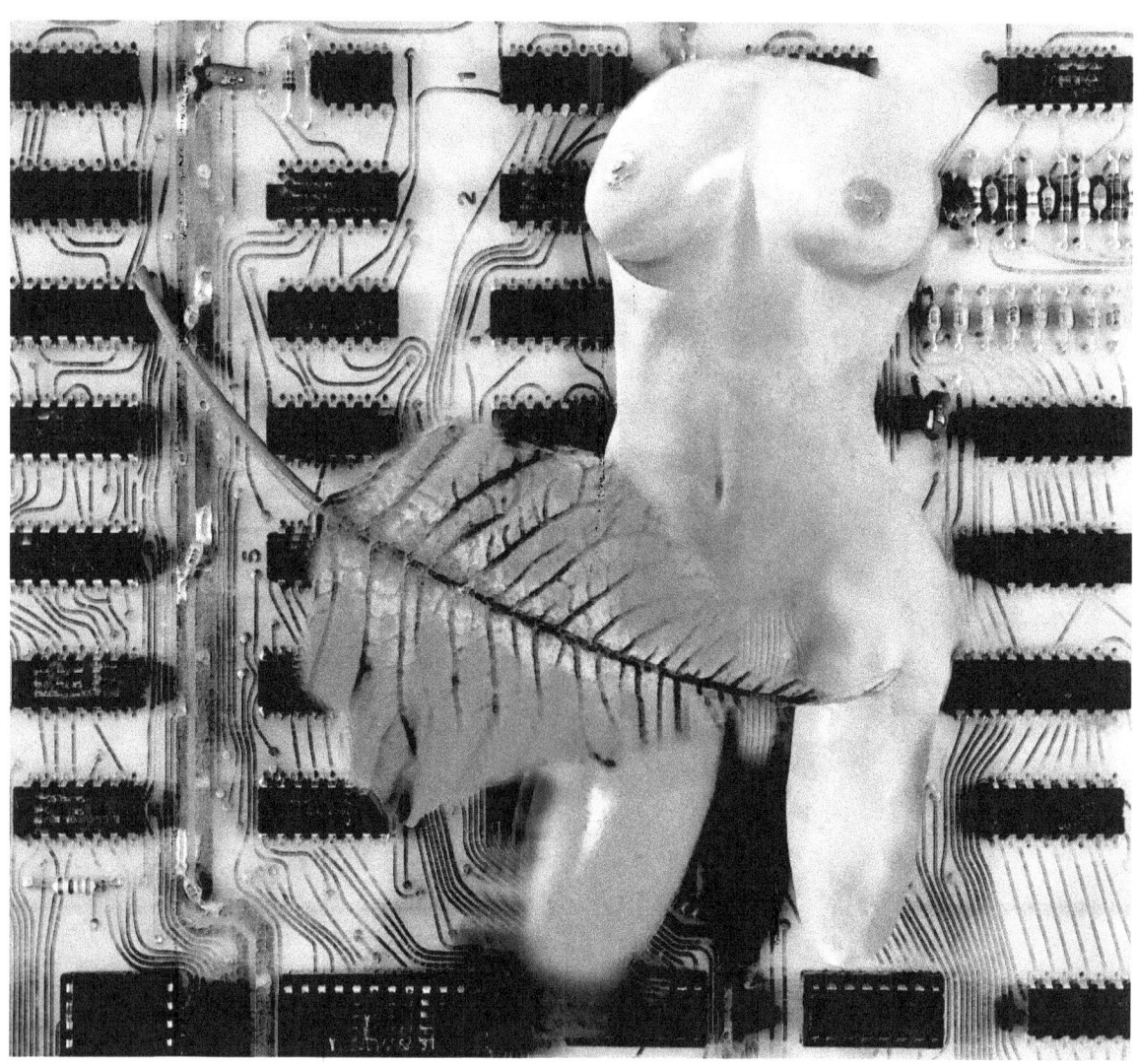

IC BOARD

The body of the IC (intergrated circuit) is us, we humans created it, just in the last century.....Thankxs mister turing you were mr colossus!

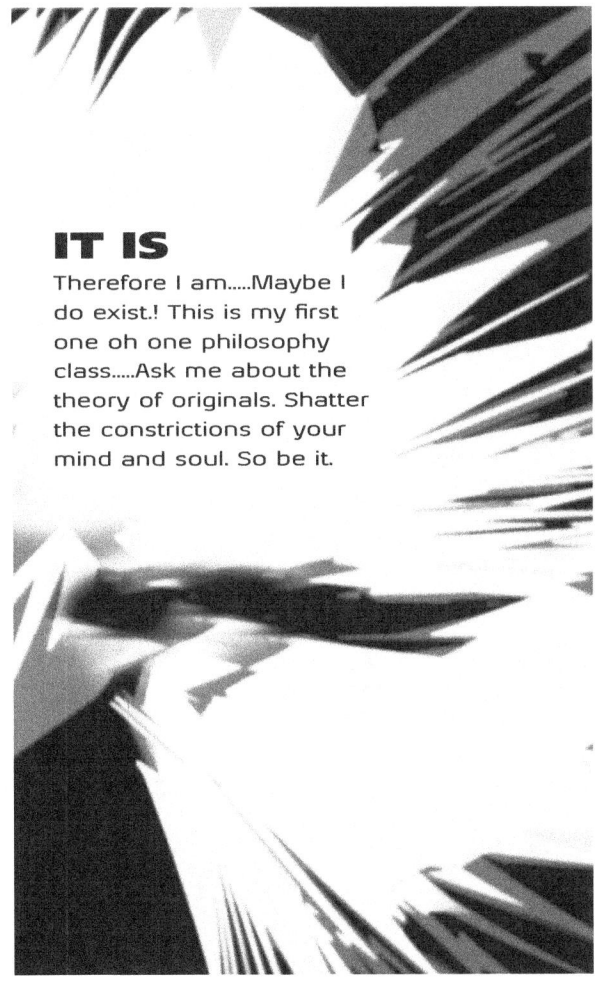

IT IS

Therefore I am.....Maybe I do exist.! This is my first one oh one philosophy class.....Ask me about the theory of originals. Shatter the constrictions of your mind and soul. So be it.

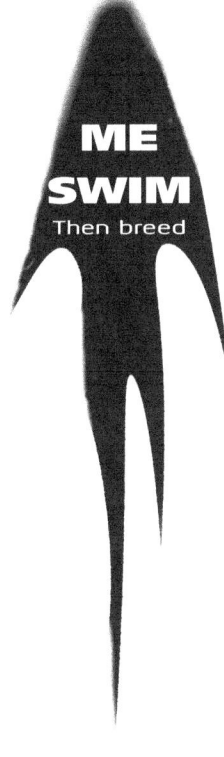

ME
SWIM
Then breed

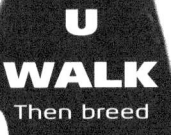

U
WALK
Then breed

ICHTHYOLOGY

Study of fishes.....The study of the alien fish people that arrived to colonise the earth. (Gk ikhthus fish).

IDOL

Image of diety as object of worship; object of excessive or supreme devotion.....The male person on the left and female above right are noted in a story of the garden of eden.....But the truth is.....No apple or serpant was involved. Their quantum transmission craft genesis failed them, so they had to stay. Revelation!!! Who wrote the book, w.a. harbinson.....

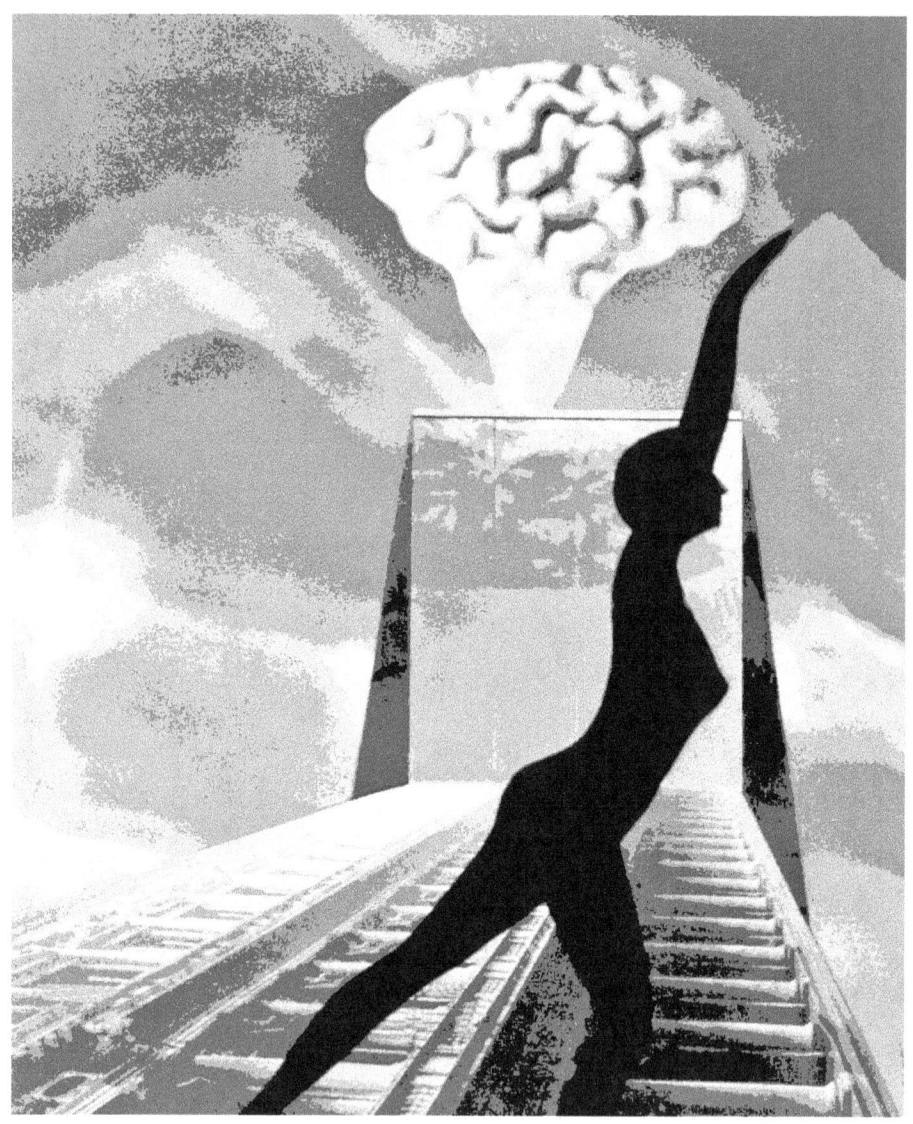

INNER SPACE

What's in your head, sometimes does not stay
there!.....Rear ended, shaken baby, brain injury,
it is the true prison in the final frontier of life.
Walk out on the gangplank of your existence,
past reality into a new space.

INTERFACE

Surface forming common
boundary of two regions.
Where interaction occurs
between two or more
things.....

IMAGE

Means so much to our vanity, what
do you think about me....Make that
judgement call! Your Ka is wot UR.....
Please hang up and try again. Please
try again, better luck next time.

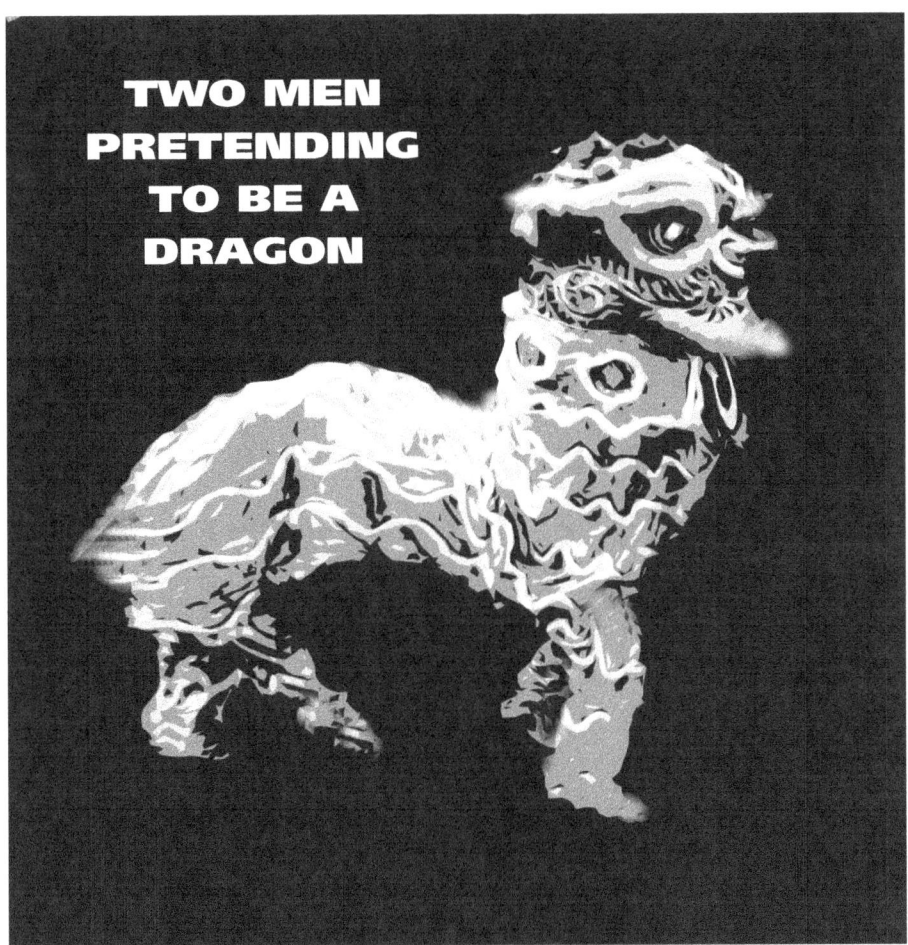

IKON

We created so many symbols that speak specific
words to us in our many languages.....Dragon to you.....
Just do it! to me....What's your right arm for.....

ILLUSION The illusion of freedom will continue as long as it's profitable to maintain this picture for the public. When the picture of life becomes to costly for them to maintain, they will have to raise the tax or they will strip our communities down, leaving us with no illusion of well being.....Grow what you can....Eat your diamonds!

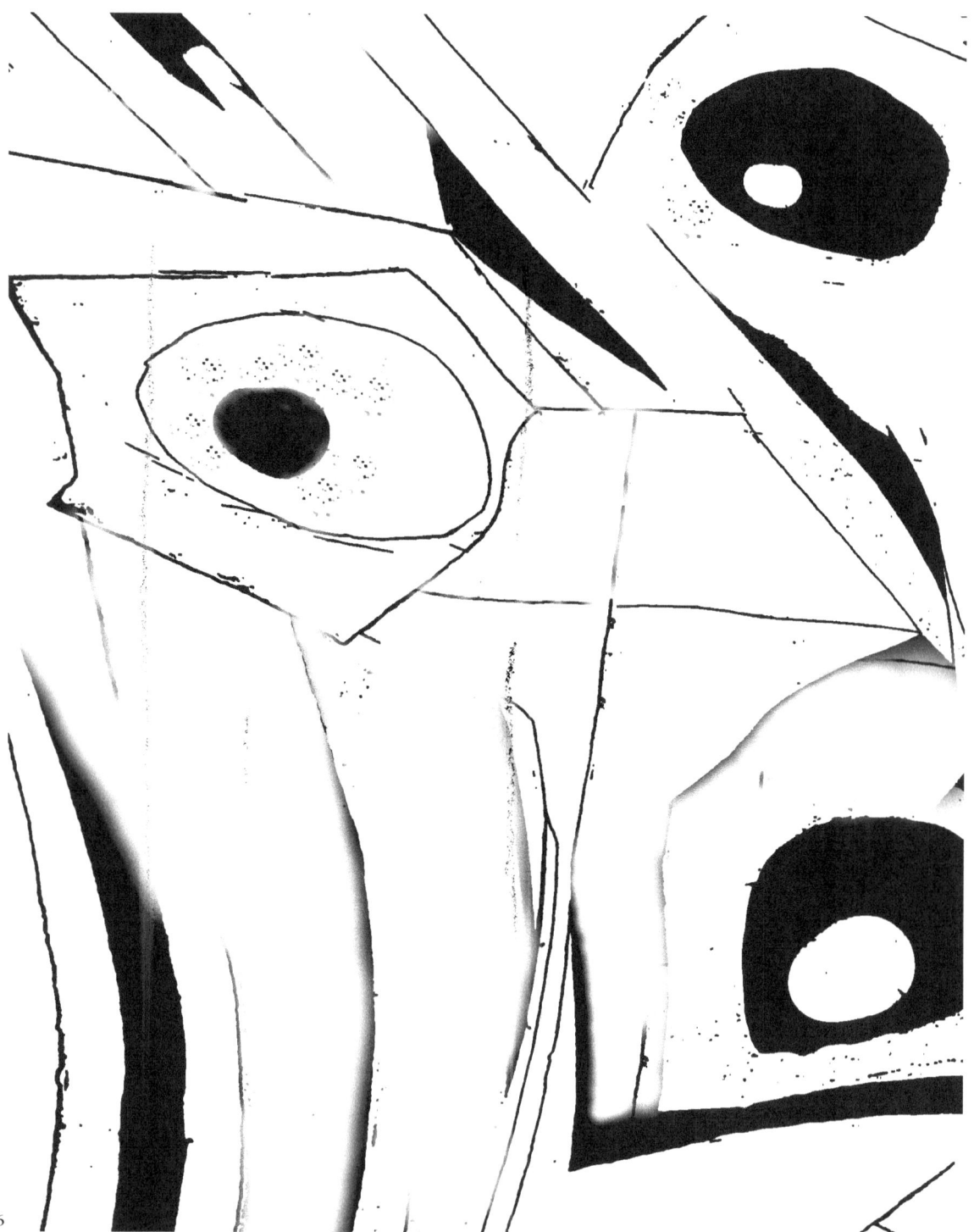

ISOMETRIC

From the greek.....Isometria equality of measure. Three principal
axis of an object of equal measure.

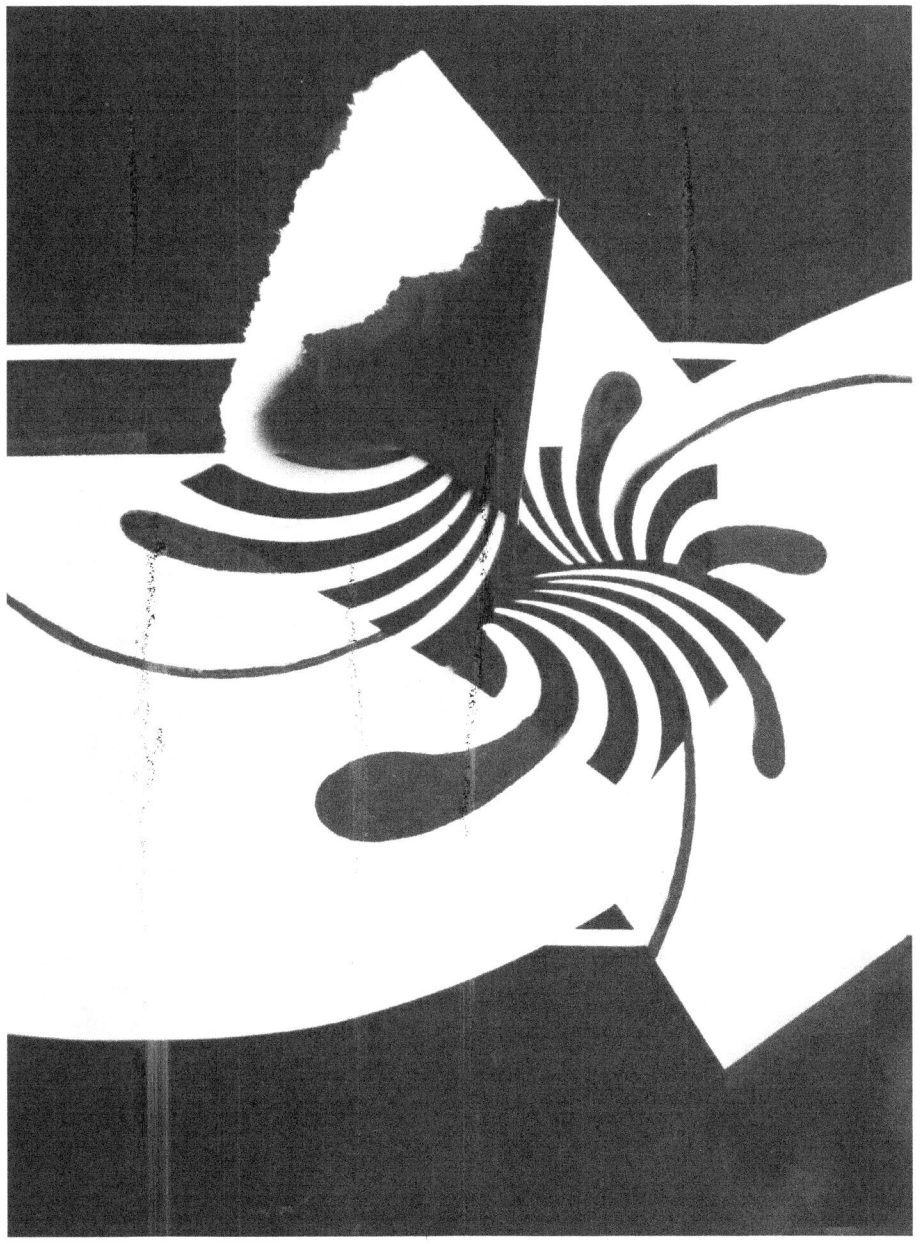

INVENT

Create by thought, originate, find out of mind, come upon
a vision and develop into matter.

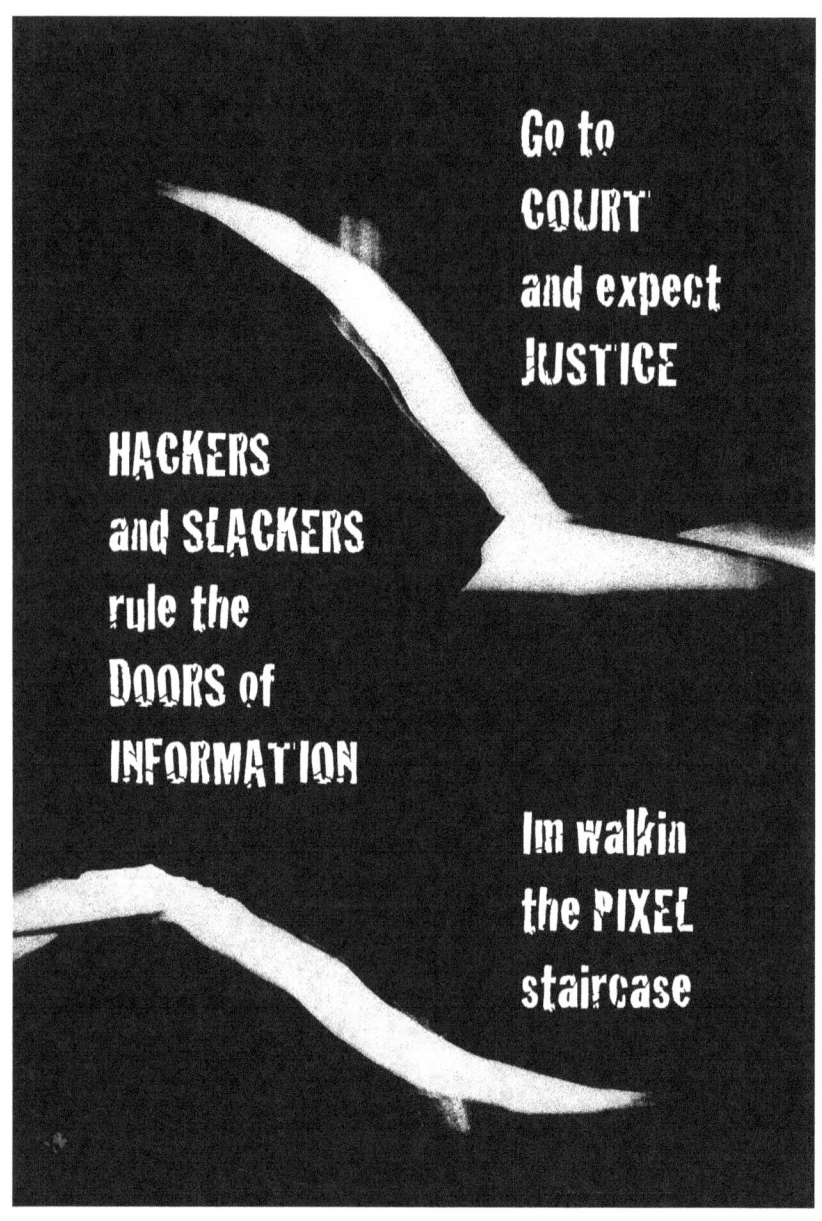

Go to
COURT
and expect
JUSTICE

HACKERS
and SLACKERS
rule the
DOORS of
INFORMATION

Im walkin
the PIXEL
staircase

INFORMATION

.....What happened. Hello, papparazi gossips!
Dissinformation, information.....Which should I
believe if it is printed it must be true or they
would sue. Advertorial the true infomercial,
believe me!

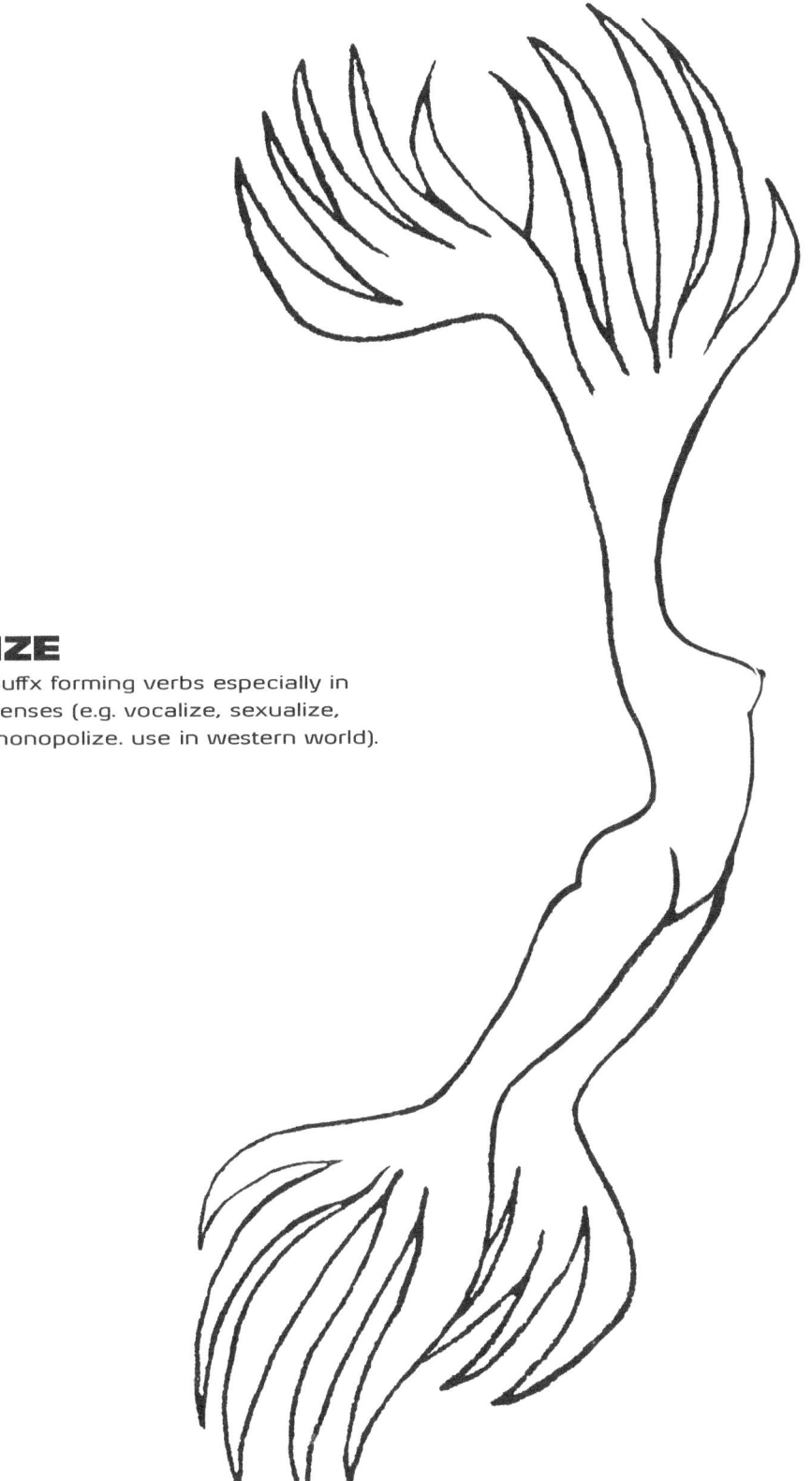

IZE

Suffx forming verbs especially in senses (e.g. vocalize, sexualize, monopolize. use in western world).

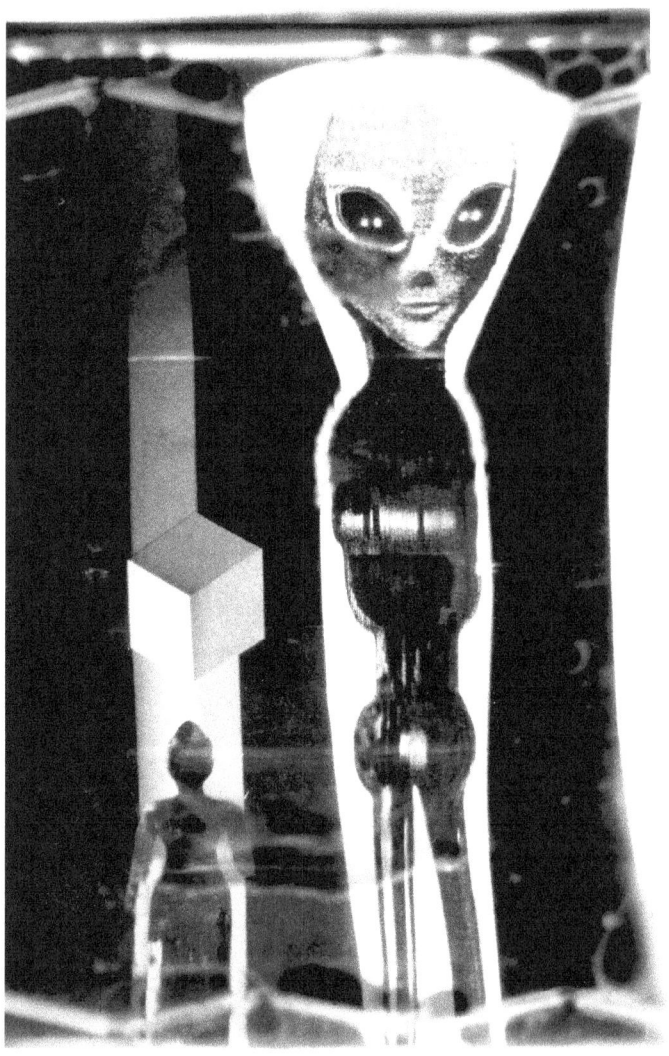

INCOGNITO

They do not really look like this, unless you get below their human skin.....We are still trying to understand where they come from and why haven't more come?.....No doubt these ones are from the nigella nebula.....What leaves there comes here, no! From the world of spooks maybe not.....Greek connection and some french......What personality are you wearing today? After picking her up last nite in the club, I woke up this morning and looked accross at her!!! She was not wearing that mask of make up, and she said she felt undressed.....Illusion.

INFINITE

Beyond.....Endless.....Boundless.....
Space.....Out there.....Universe.
How many grains of sand on
this beach?

INDUCE

Do you come here often?
Persuade, prevail on, make
them do it! Advertising,
selling, coaxing.

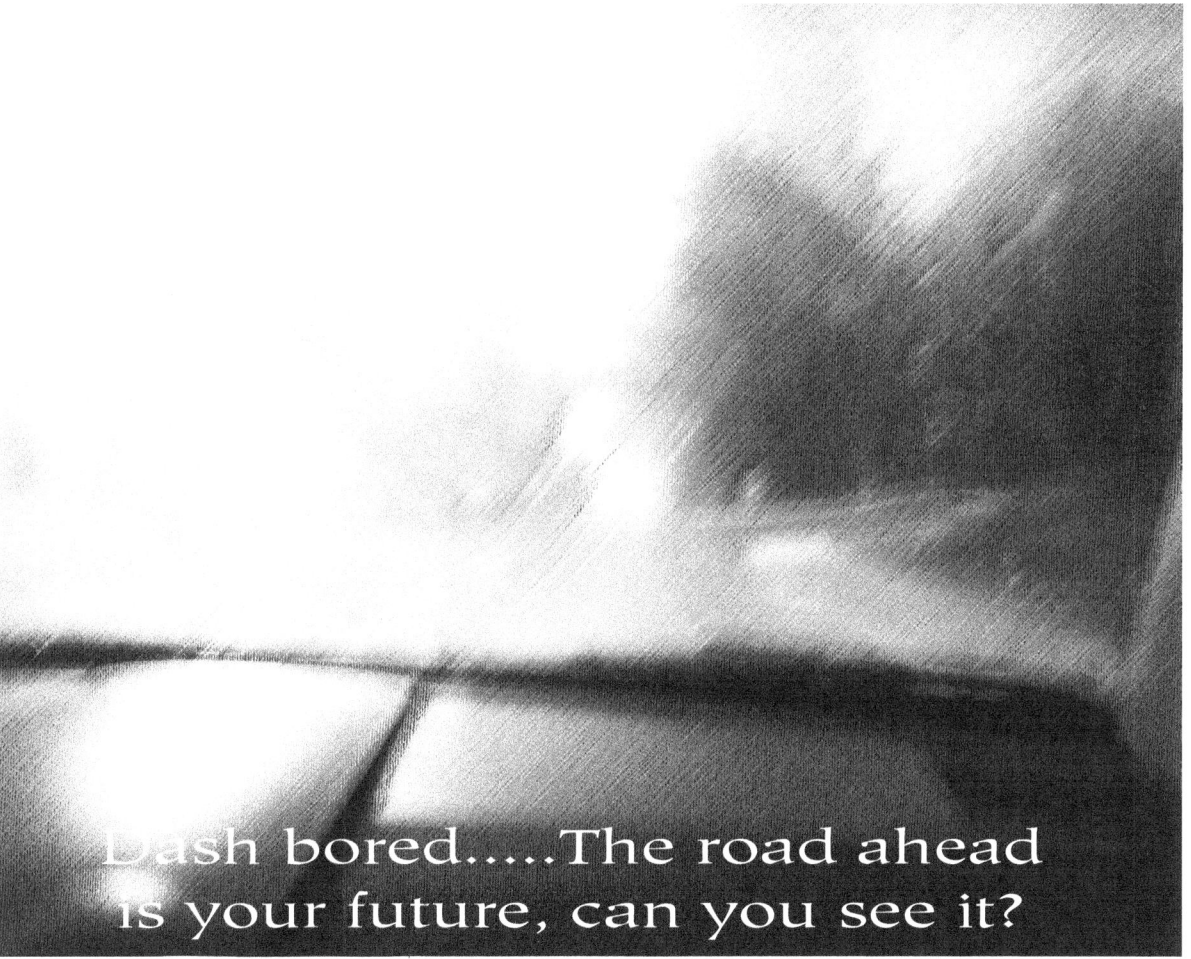

Dash bored.....The road ahead
is your future, can you see it?

JOURNAL

The diary this book came from over the last twenty years.
Record of events. Periodical. French daydream collector.

JINX

People, animals, or some kind of matter that cause bad luck....Voodoo child follows you when you are trying to win, usually bad luck. Walk under the ladder, when I give you the knife, I will give you a penny, then kill the black cat.

JIGGLE

Rock or jerk lightly. Rhythm helps wriggle with sensuality. Shakin all over, extreme jiggling! Throw overboard, dispose, out of space or air vehicle.....Blow off, yeah right.

JOBS

The almighty steve of macs. The man that changed my art and david hockneys. Or it could be laying cable; anal jobs, number two's to yoose. Work.....Work that four letter word.

JOT

Piece between doodles....Jot down that little scribble on the edge of the thumbnail, so I can understand your visual idea.

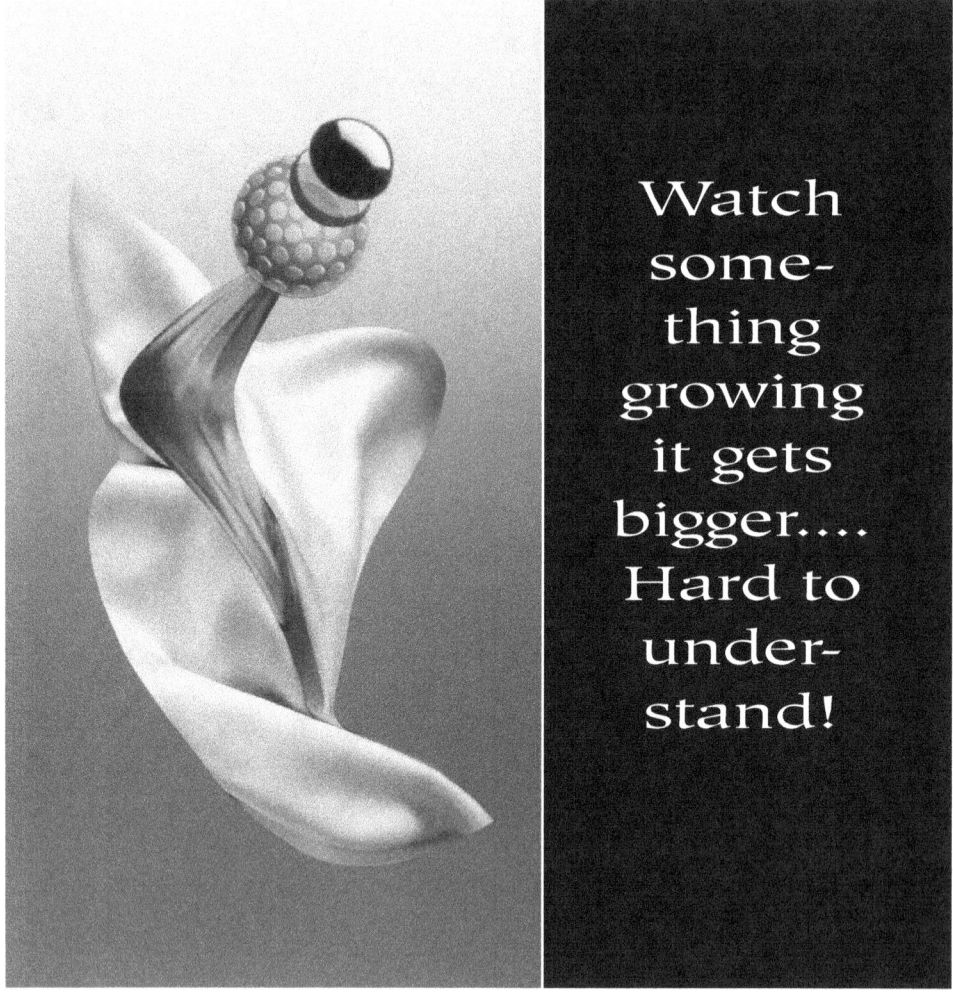

Watch something growing it gets bigger.... Hard to understand!

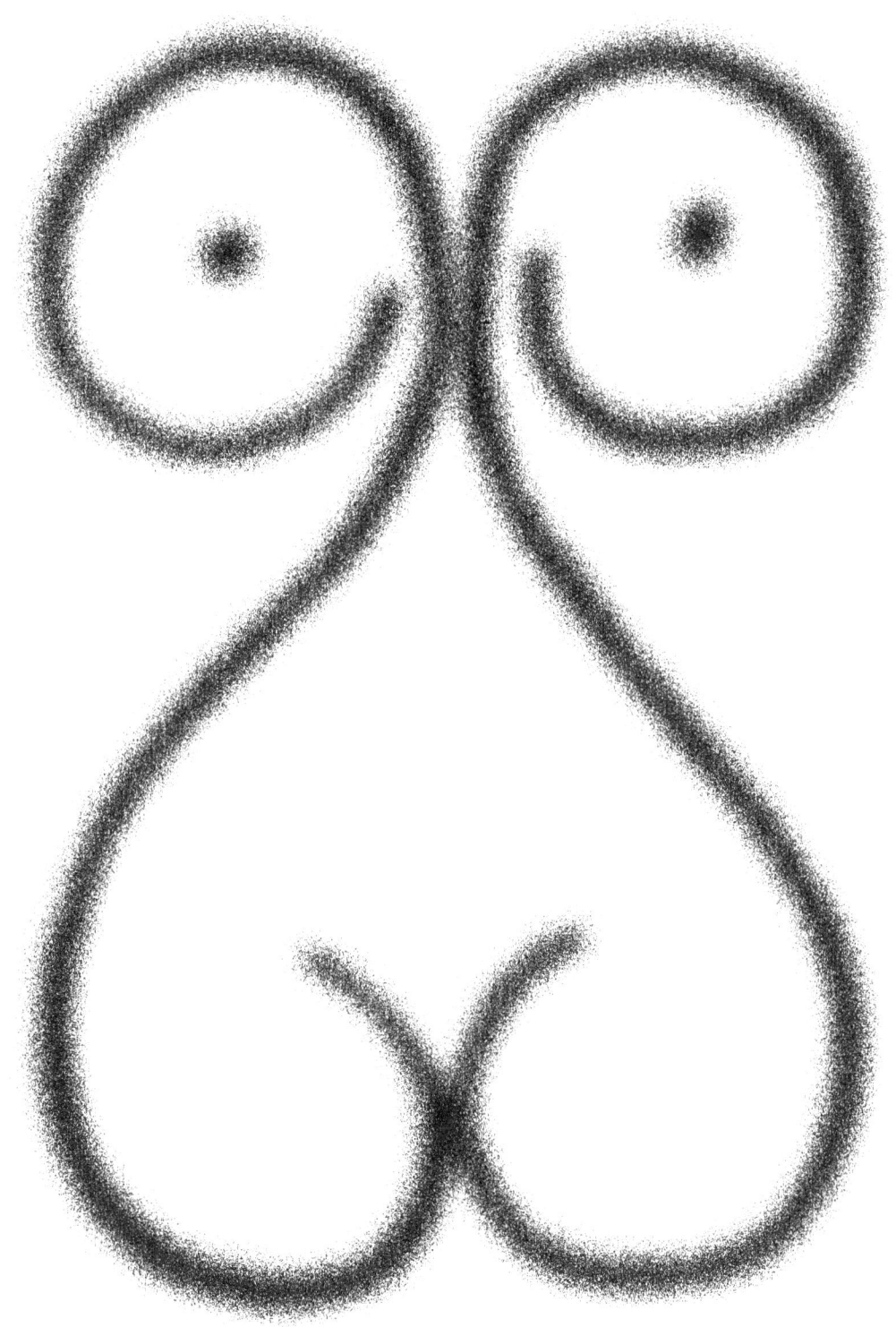

Jinkcasso.....This picture does not need words.....It tells the story and moves elusively.....
To move away from the norm quickly or evasively.....Jink; it is also about money!

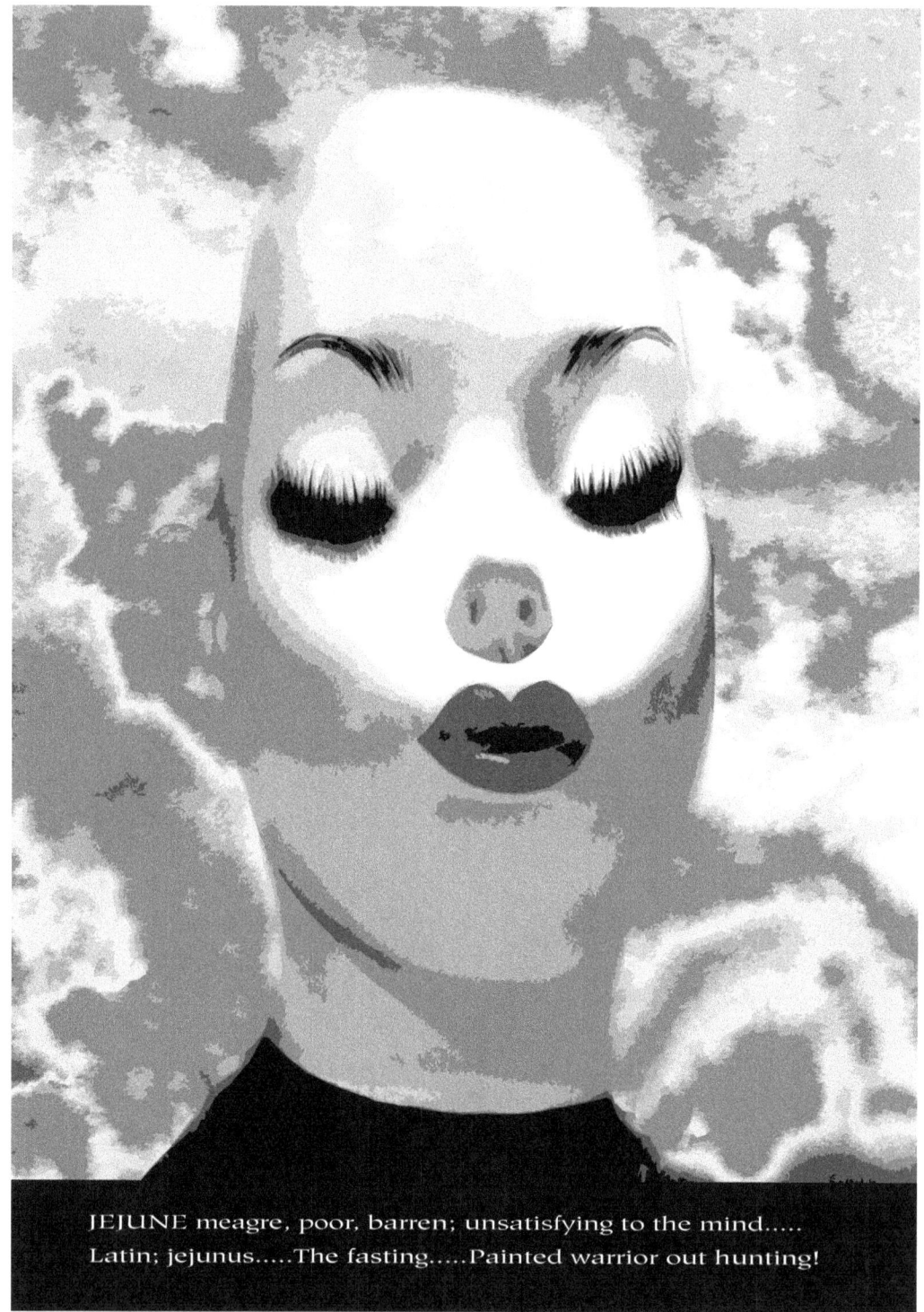

JEJUNE meagre, poor, barren; unsatisfying to the mind.....
Latin; jejunus.....The fasting.....Painted warrior out hunting!

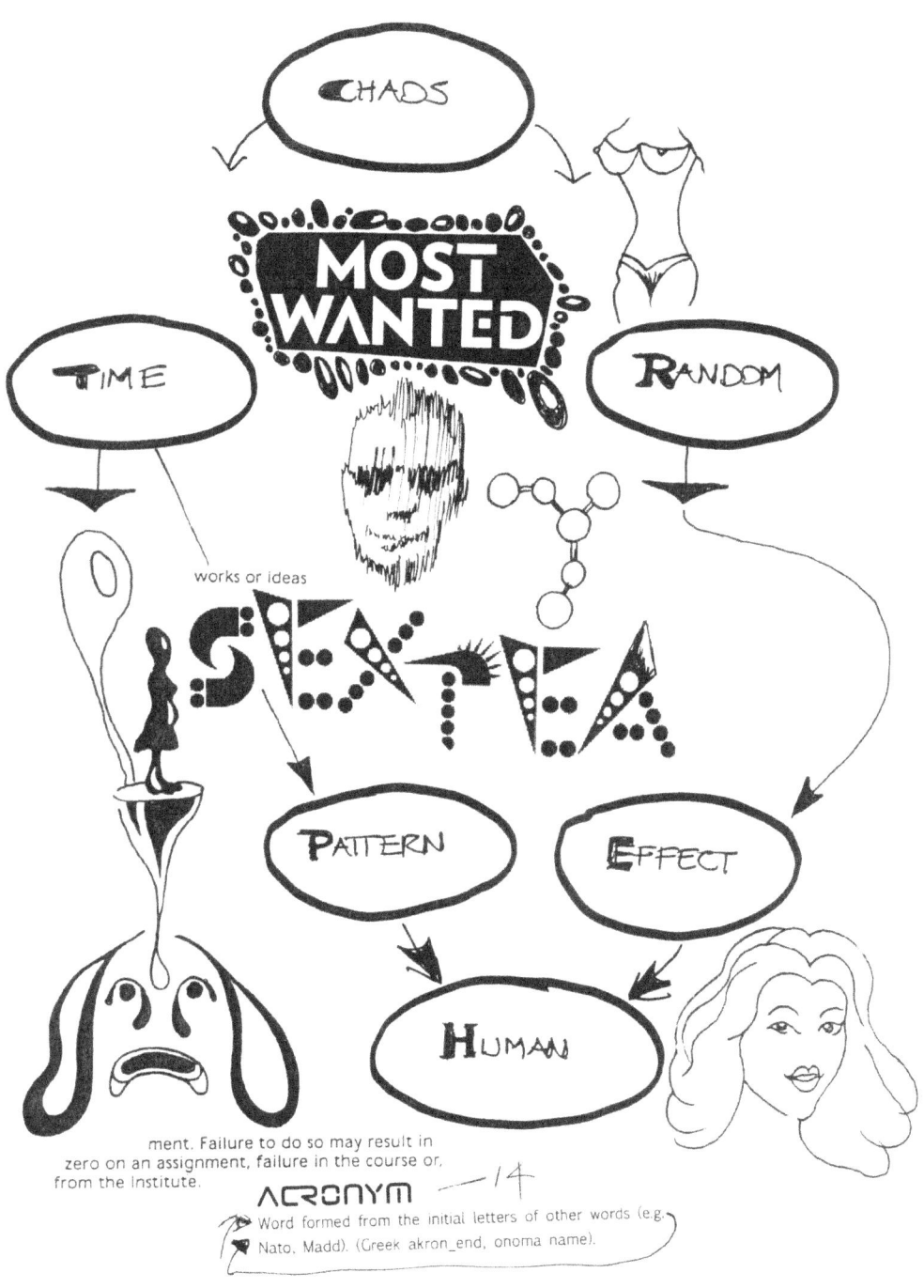

CHAOS

MOST WANTED

TIME

works or ideas

RANDOM

SEXTEA

PATTERN

EFFECT

HUMAN

ment. Failure to do so may result in zero on an assignment, failure in the course or, from the Institute.

ACRONYM — 14

Word formed from the initial letters of other words (e.g. Nato. Madd). (Greek akron_end, onoma name).

JUVENILIA
Young panarama of ideas loosely put together by visual boarding.

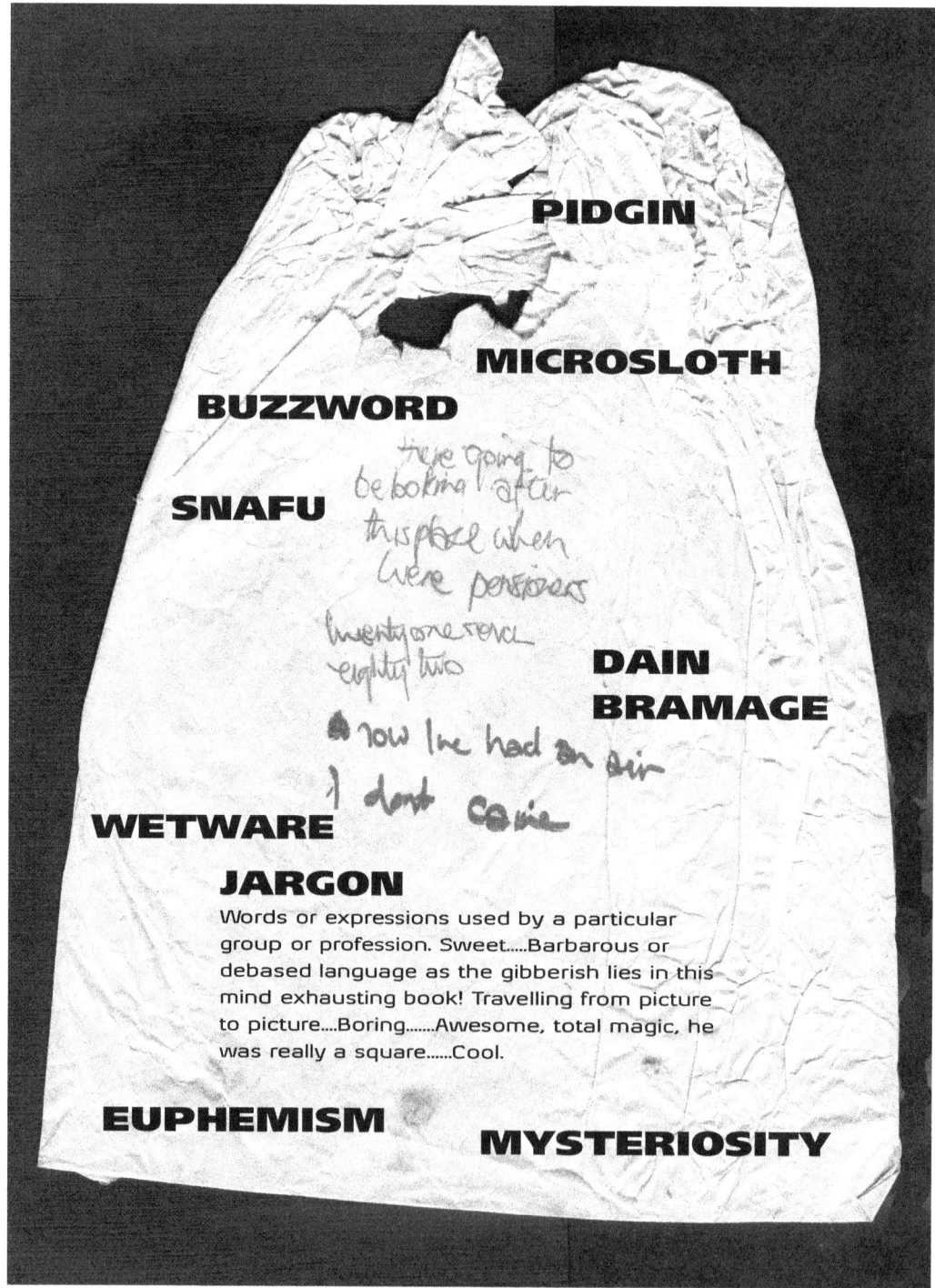

PIDGIN

MICROSLOTH

BUZZWORD

SNAFU

DAIN
BRAMAGE

WETWARE

JARGON
Words or expressions used by a particular
group or profession. Sweet.....Barbarous or
debased language as the gibberish lies in this
mind exhausting book! Travelling from picture
to picture....Boring.......Awesome, total magic, he
was really a square......Cool.

EUPHEMISM

MYSTERIOSITY

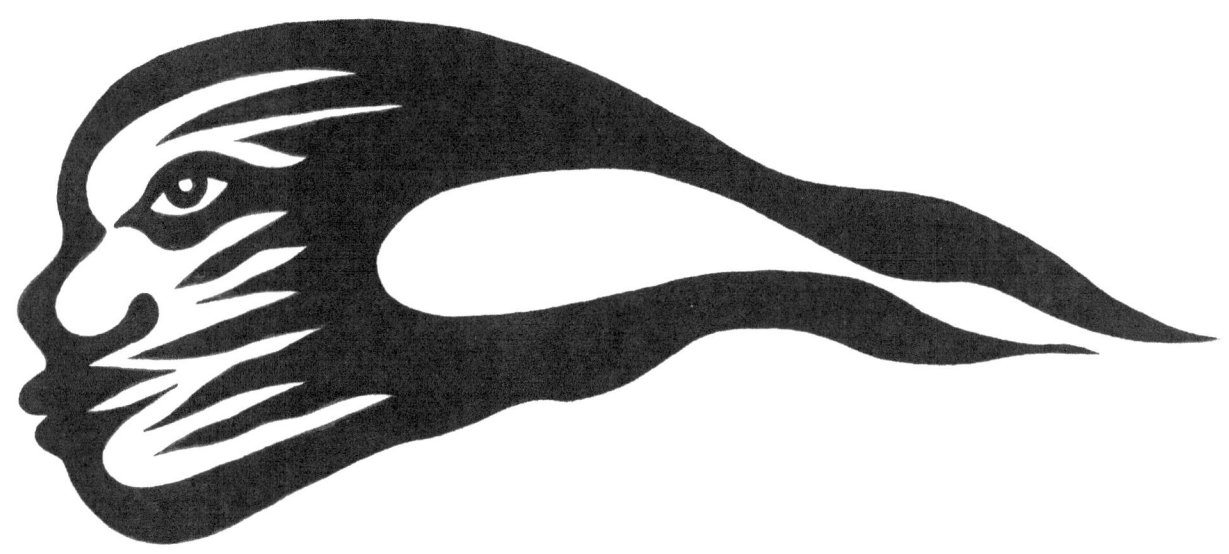

JEDADIAH WIND

How many different names do sailors have
for winds? In this rain forest the trees speak
to us with the tongue of the west coast
wind. Do the ravens control the wind or is it
the acid rain and your car? This is sabine,
the name of a channel of water between
texada and lasqueti islands, those spanish
explorers.....What happened to them?

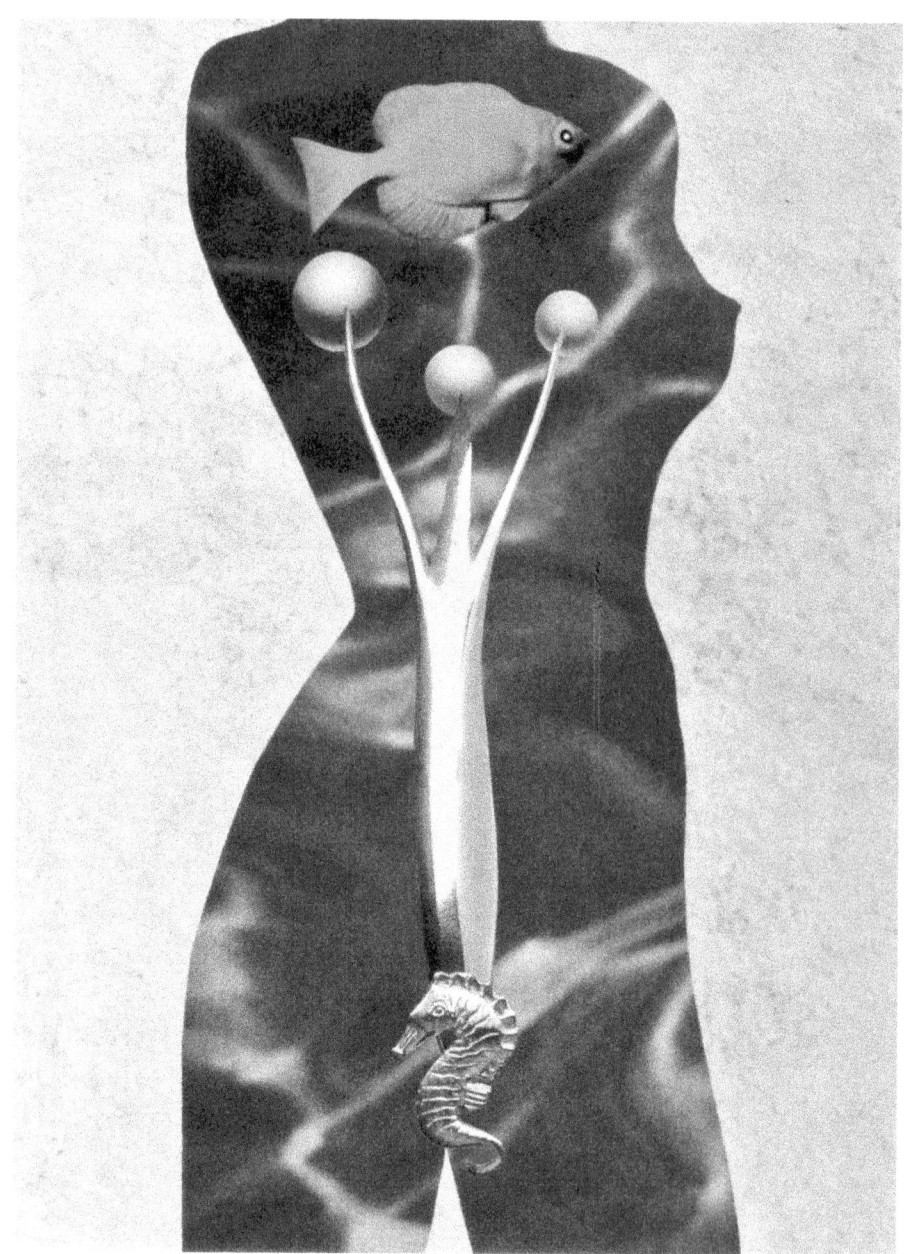

JEZEBEL

Chow bella baby.....The girl from little china in naples. Shameless woman,
so the magic book says and where are the shamless mens description.....
There were plenty of them, trading in the temples. JEZEMEN.

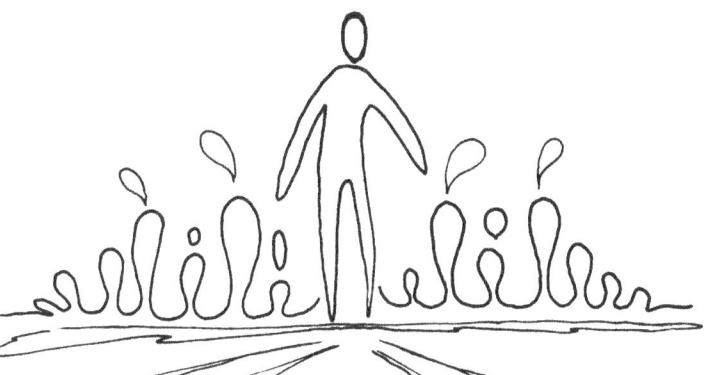

JOURNEY

Travelling from one place to another. Well is it really the destination or the people you meet? The joy of returning to your little cubby hole and routine, is it where your heart is....... Call it home!.

JISMN

In hindi means body. Pre-ejaculation honey says it all, you silly big hairy squirt.

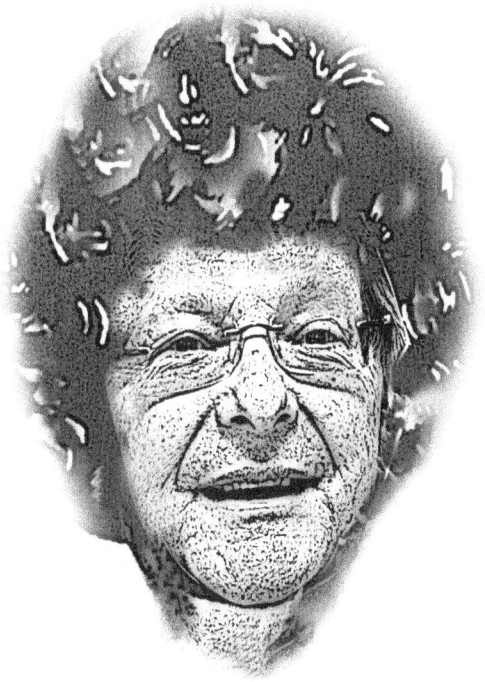

JAMMEY BUGGER

The luck of the brits, the slippery smart arse that got more than his share, always landing on his feet. Some girls have all the muck.....

KLINGON

The final frontier......We create codes to communicate with others, Roddenberry, thanks for your outsites which has helped me go beyond my Norman Normal. Suddenly you were there for me every week for years, sometimes waiting till midnight to watch your formulas. My dreams then travelled far away.

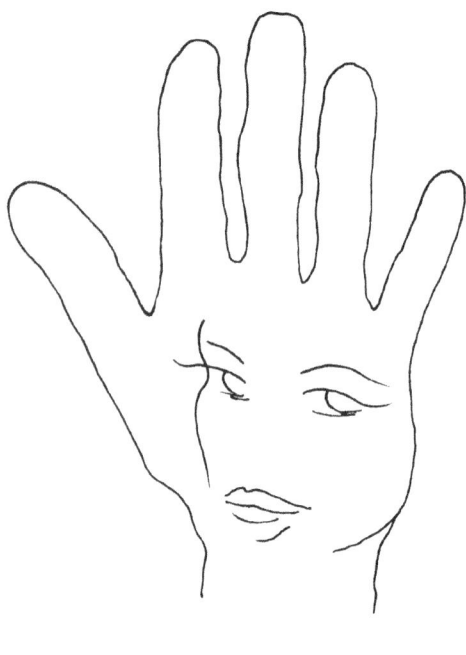

FINGERLICKN

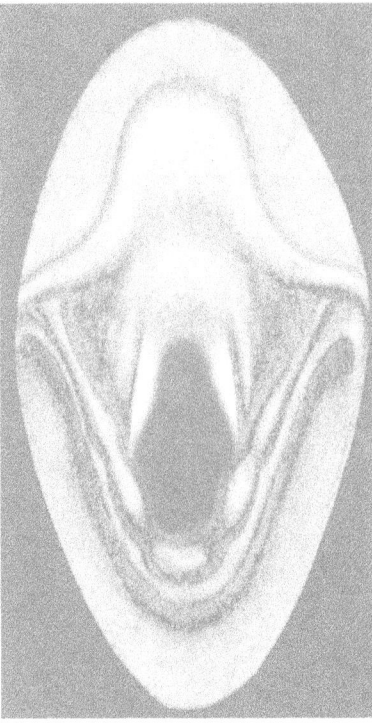

KORAN

Sacred book of Muslims. Arab = (Recitation).

KOBRA

The throat of a snake can make the hard pain call on you.

KUNDALINI

Where should we start, this is the meaning of life or did I go to the wrong lecture hall, in Nepal, Kathmandu or inside you!

KNACK

The acquired or intuitive faculty of doing a thing adroitly; trick; habit.

KINGDOM

The queen rules over a queendom, no......Division of the natural world, area ruled over by some kind of monachy. There was no course at university to become a king. So how do I get to beome one. I met the king of carpets and his dog named prince when I bought my flooing from his store. Should I buy an army and invade a small island and then declare my self the king is that how the Royal house of hanover did it. I will call my next housing development. Windsor park royal....Sounds good...Hark! The herald angels sing!

KIBOSH

Nonsense; perhaps from immigrants of eastern europe who originally came from the middle of the east end!

KICKBACK

Recoil; not really used like that, much! This is what our world has come too!, payments for help or for showing favours. Eighty percent of all transactions!

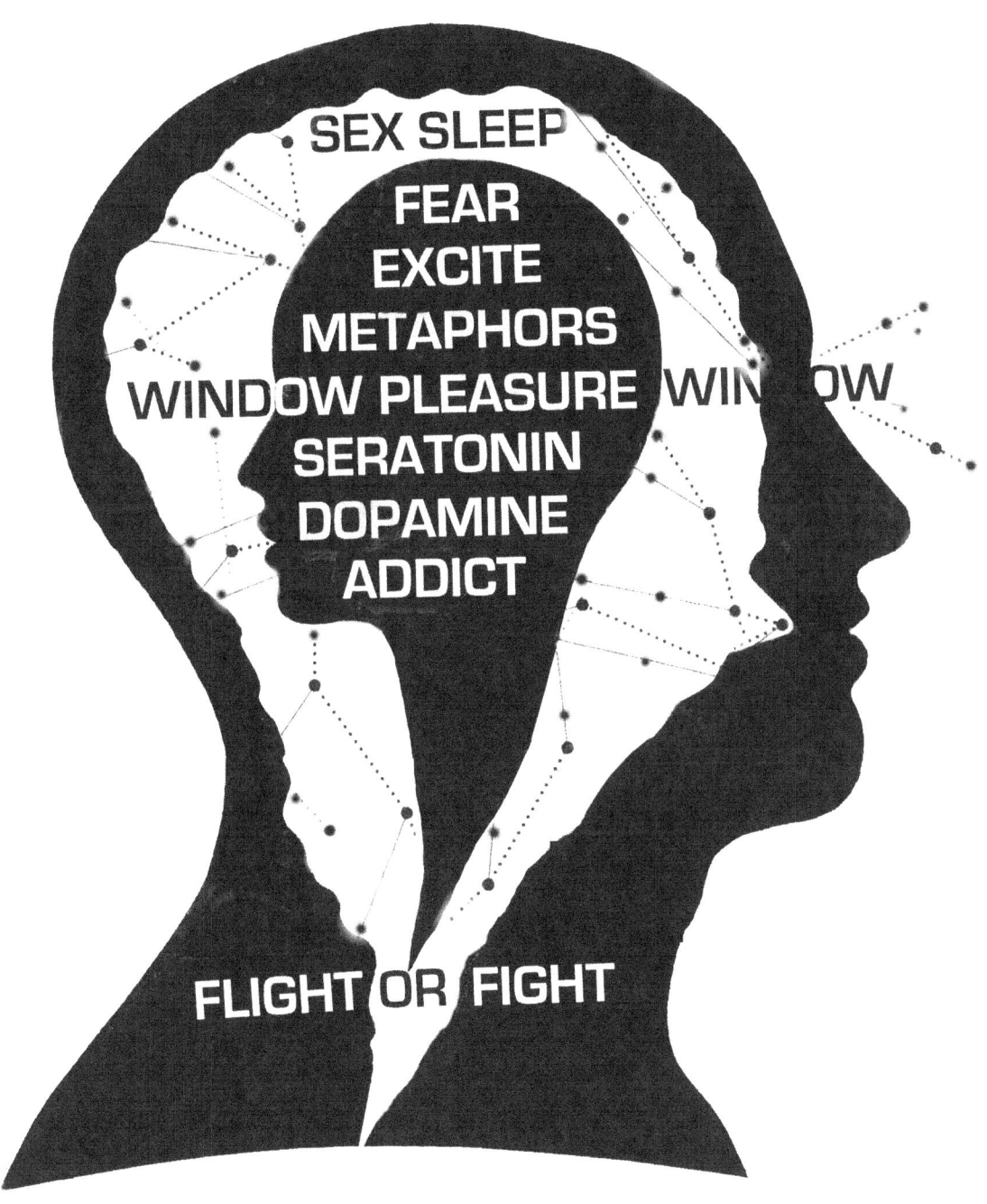

KNOWLEDGE

The brain at conception has no knowledge until
connections are made between neurons. The way we
are and all that we know comes from the way our
neurons are connected! Join the dots children.....

KEDGEREE

Thanks India.....Kitchery. A mixed dish usually left over rice, lentils, ghee, and any other left overs. Some times the brunch of the day and most marinades and curries taste better on the next few days.

KARMA

The white curtains dance smoothly past the slatted shutters in the warm soft sensual winds from the mekong in lao. I count the speed of the spinning bamboo fan as it rotates and my back is coated with sandalwood and lidocaine oil, four hands massage my aged muscles.....I am at one with Karma, or am I learning to fly?

KARZI

Where is the toilet...... You might be in a lot of trouble. Indian me thinks from the raj.....

KAIZEN

Remember how different translators translate.....This word loosly means change for the better, to improve, to make better.

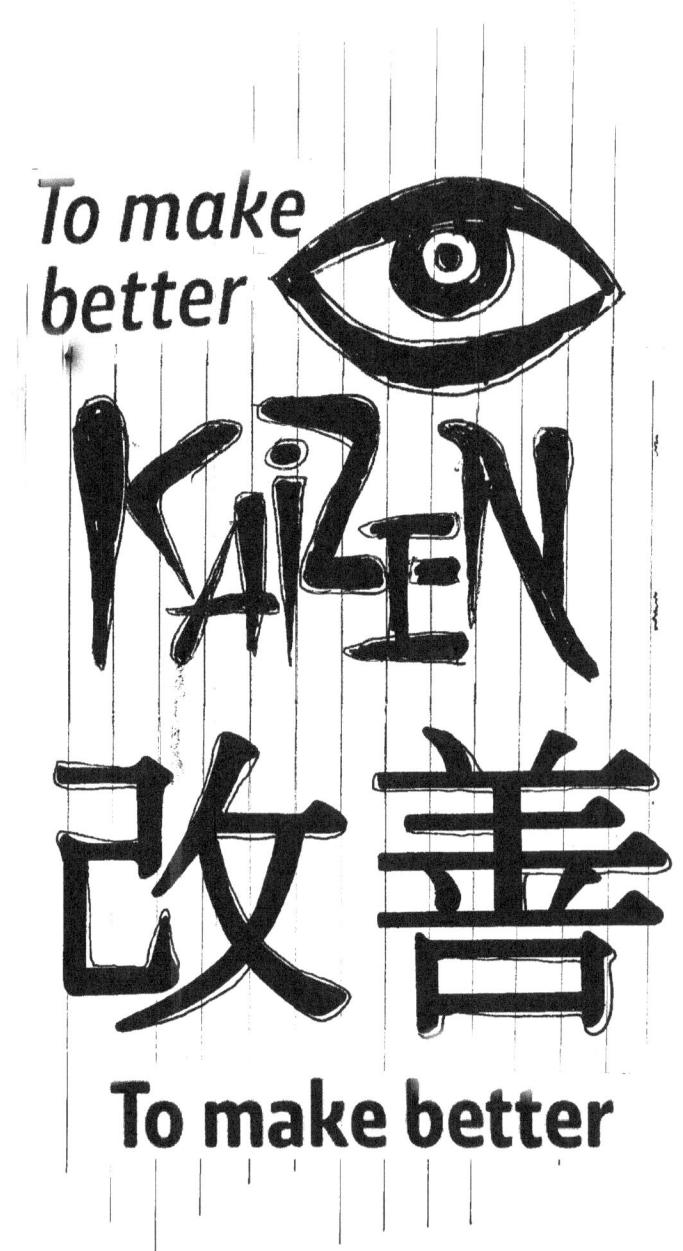

To make better

KAIZEN

改善

To make better

KINKY.....WE GAVE THE ZEBRAS VIAGRA
on safari we saw the lions at it, and we did want the zebras to enjoy.

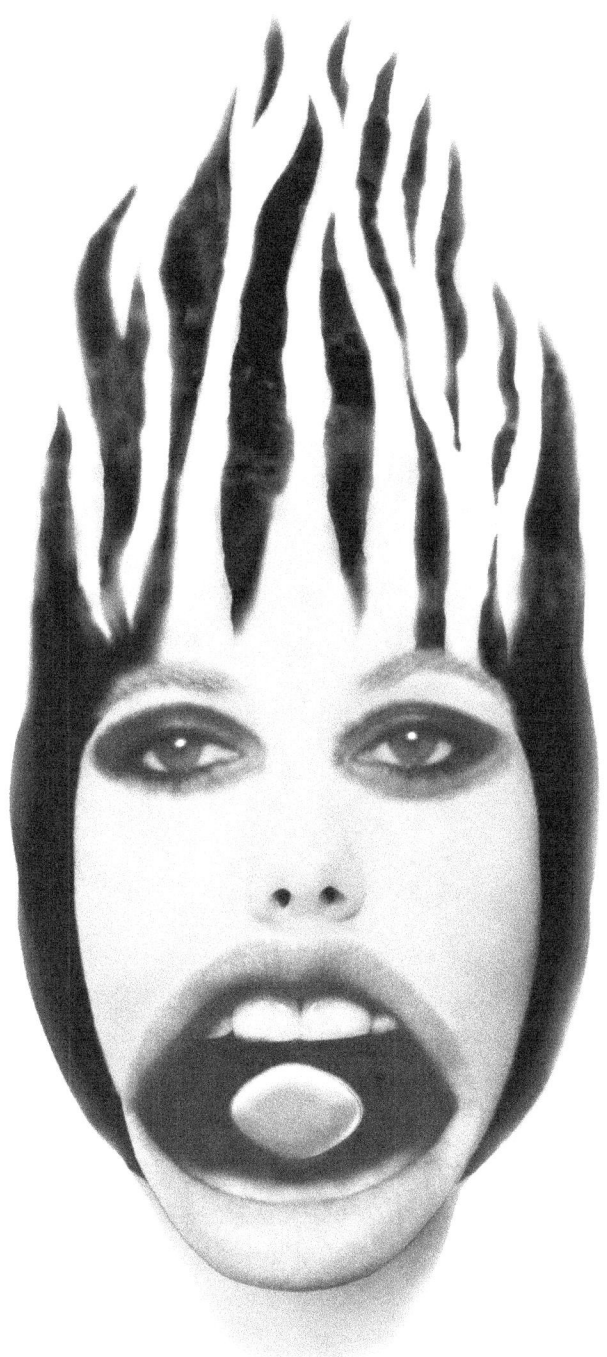

Horror writers fantasize meat hooks.....Botox actresses grieve over good looks.....
Shant implant beemer girl said, not organic natural feels on wheels

KOWTOW

Act obsequiously to people, etc; perform the kowtow. Chinese custom of touching the ground with head as sign of worship or submission. Chinese = (knock the head).

KAMIKAZE

In the second world war japanese aircraft laden with explosives crashed on targets guided by japanese pilots commiting suicide. Japan language = (divine wind).

KALEIDOSCOPE

Tubular shape containing mirrors and or lenses, pieces of coloured glass, filters, etc. whose reflections produce patterns when rotation or motion is applied.....Far out.....Magic Voyage.

KANVAS

The foundation or base for so many artists work, usually they bought it from a fabric merchant. What are we talking about here?

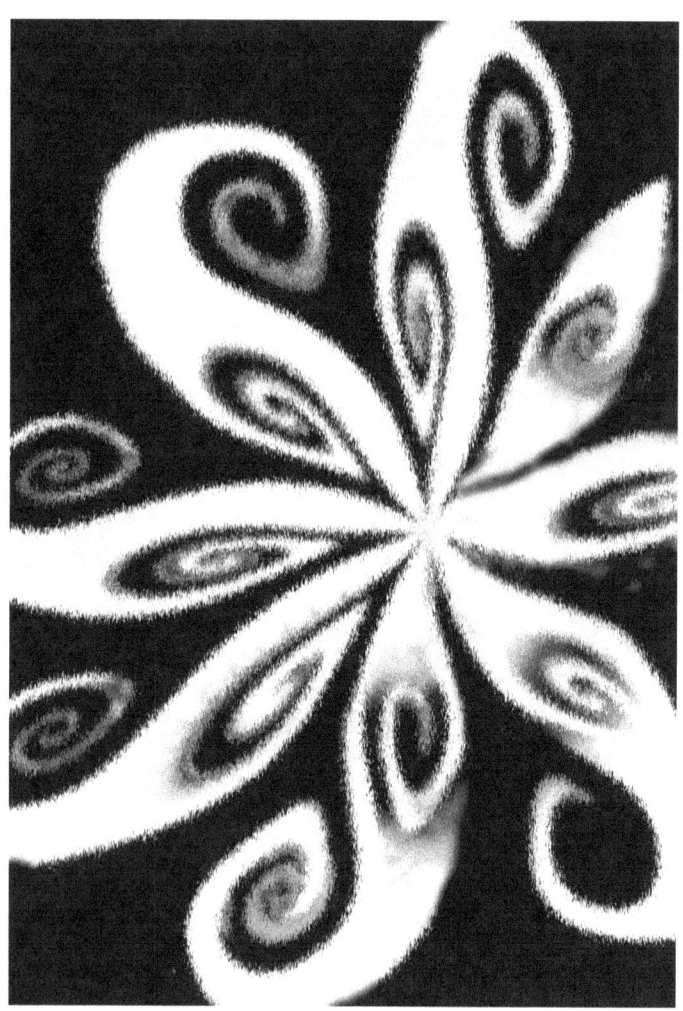

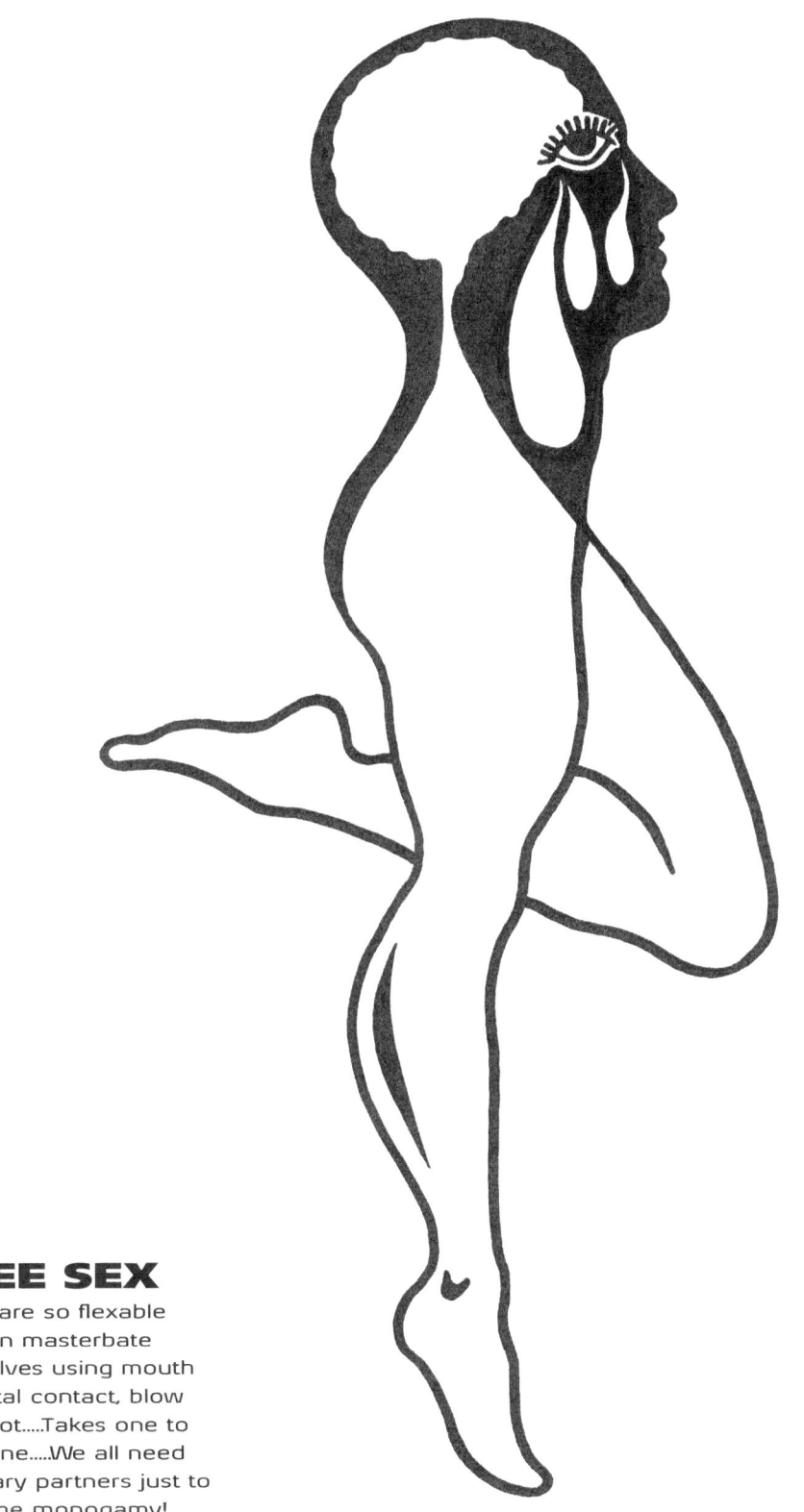

KNEE SEX

Bodies are so flexable they can masterbate themselves using mouth to genital contact, blow jam whot.....Takes one to know one.....We all need imaginary partners just to break the monogamy!

KINETIC

Due to motion, kinetic art form of visual art, depending on moving components for visual effect.....Greek (kineo move).

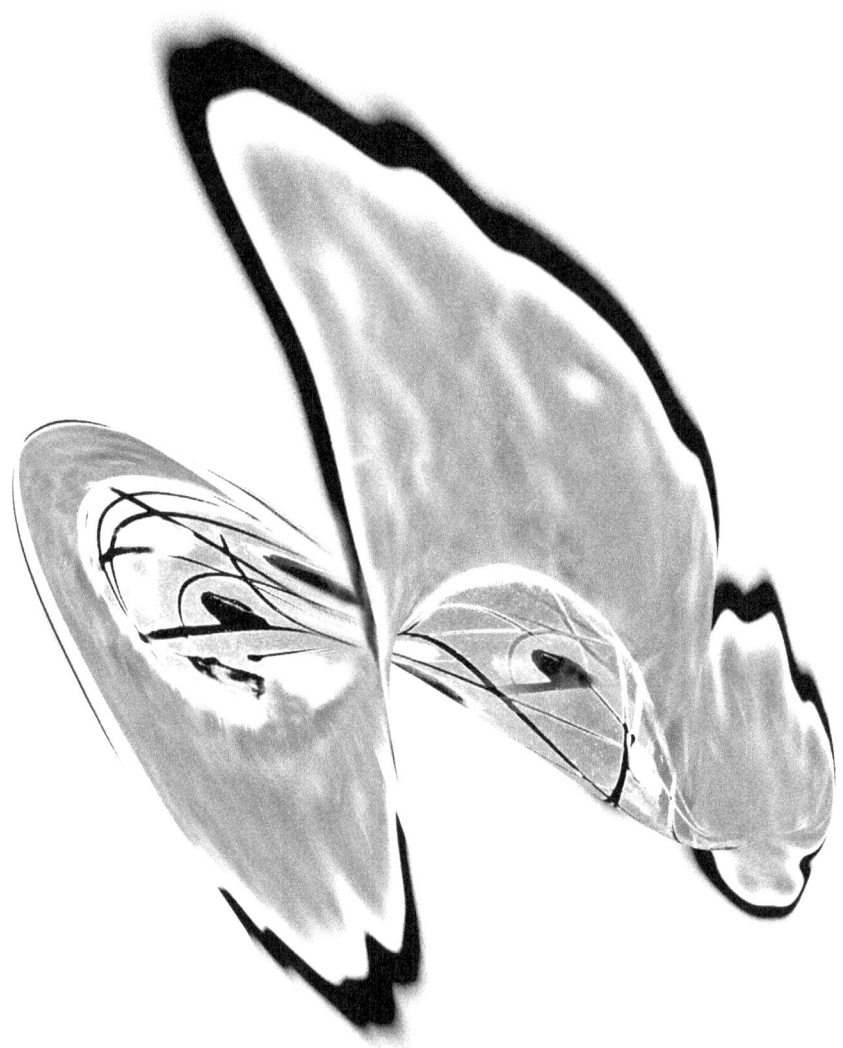

KILL

Deprive of life or vitality, cause death, dead, deceased, kaput, finished. Above is your soul leaving the dead body.....How do I know it is like this? I thought it so.....

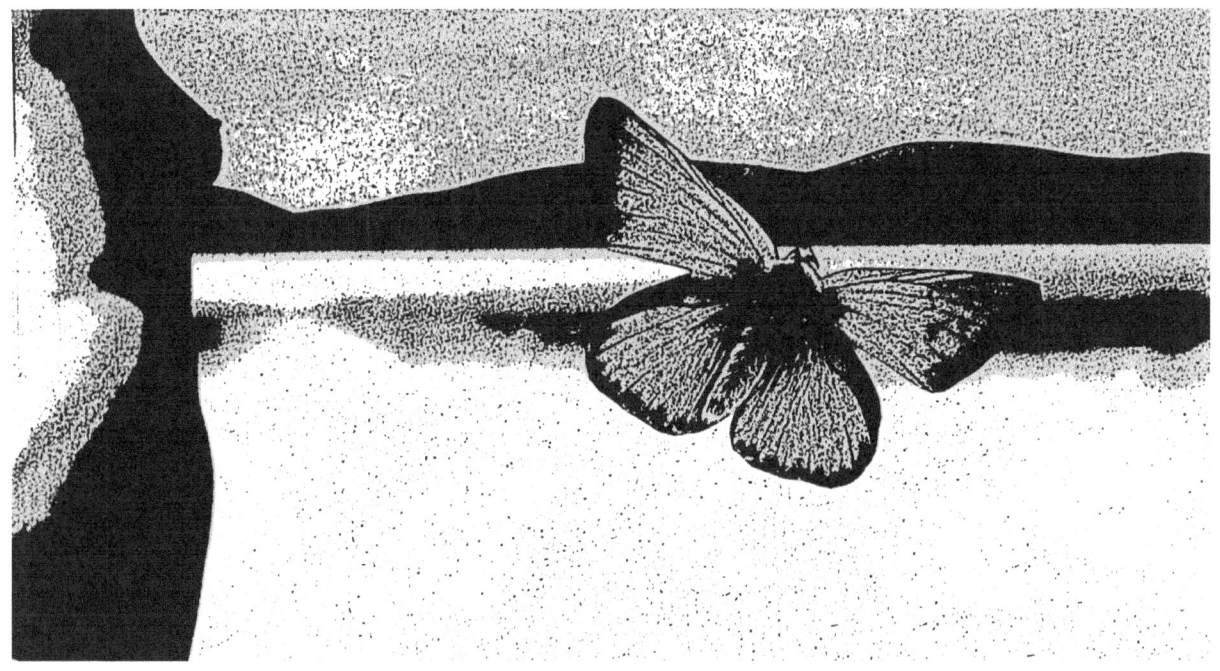

LANDSCAPE

Section of our planet, balanced out to the
new 16 by 9 horizontal landscape format.....
Horizons disected by butterflies and breasts
reflecting across the water of lifes contempt!
We are having so much fun raping and
pillaging the landscape for our own greed and
convenience.....We are in a state of denial, so
don't be a pooper scooper and stop the party
we are having! Think about life, when you are
gone, who will be in your parking space, who
will run the society.....How many will be left?

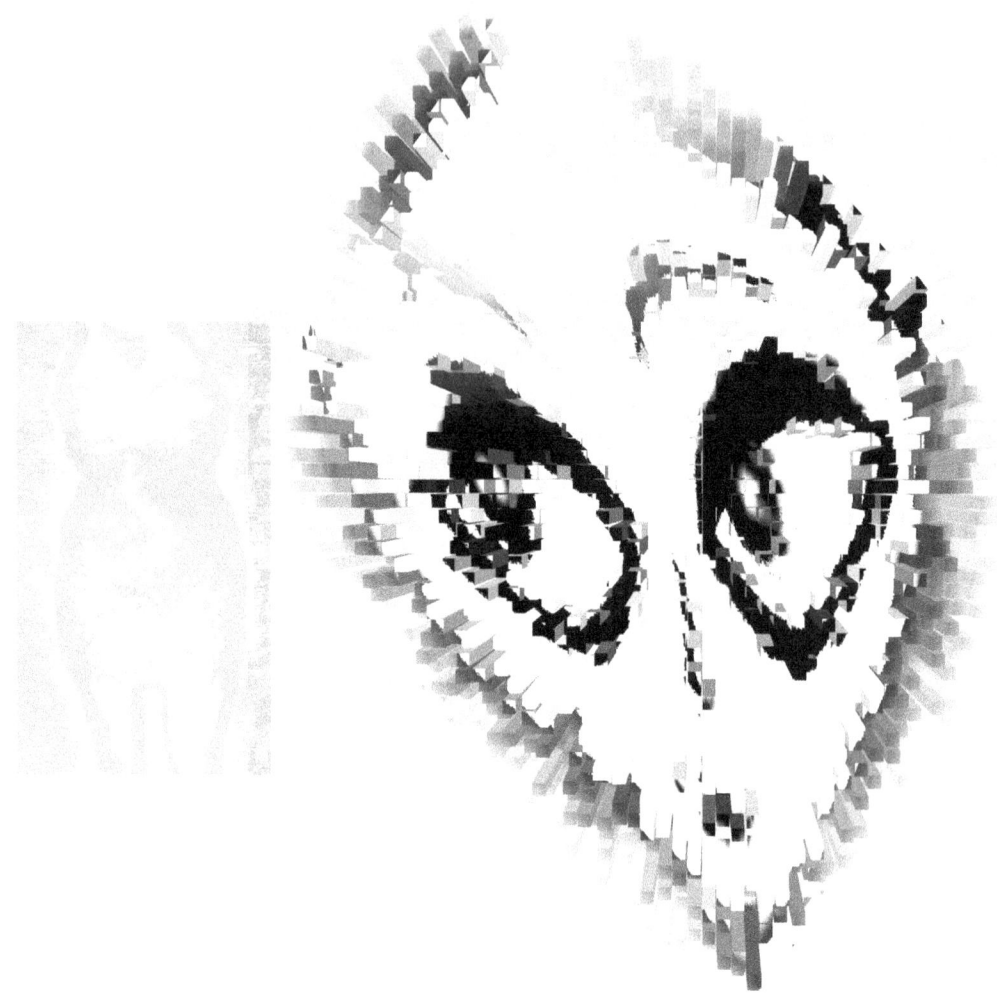

LIME & COCONUT

The great naturopathic doctor song from the head of Nilsson.....Listern up.....Primitive sounds sooth the soul, forget the savage breast......Without you......May do that!. Caribe = (African shake it up).

LISZTOMANIA

Ken Russell.....The brilliant film directors inspiring movie on Liszt.

LAYING CABLE

Not across the ocean for those old telephone lines, no, no. Exit waste material from number two's.....Yes crapping from the famous thomas crapper, he did not write it, it was a infamous cornishman after eating cornish pasties.

LIFE SHAPES US

Swing your hair miss piggie, one of these is not the same as the other?

118

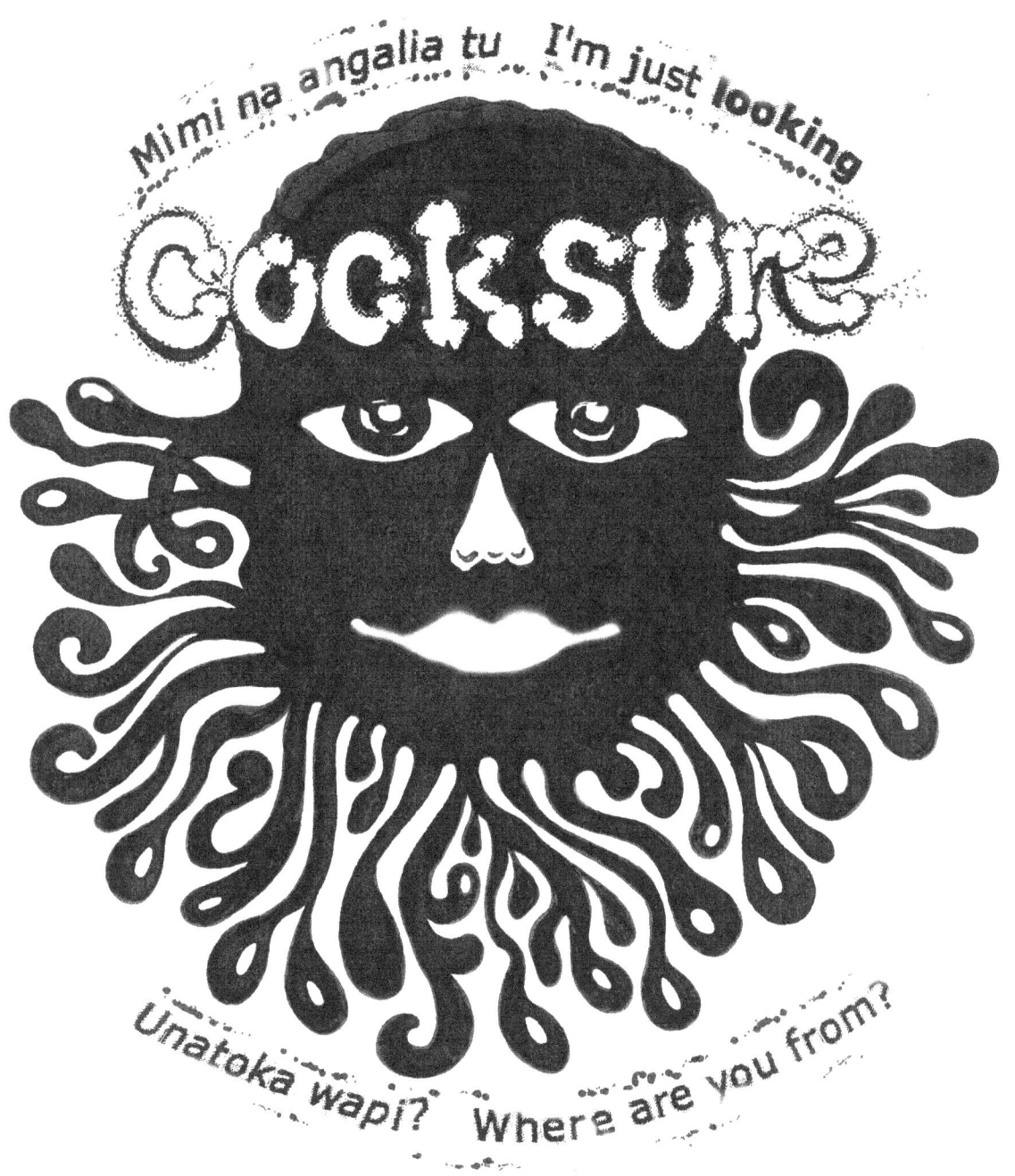

Mimi na angalia tu... I'm just looking

Cocksure

Unatoka wapi? Where are you from?

LOOKING

Gaze into my eyes, lay down on the floor keep looking into my eyes on this page as you lie down, you are feeling a bit dizzy.....Do not worry be nappy, soon you will feel heavy and fall asleep! Read this page 119 tomorrow night at 11.39.....I'm just sleeping!.

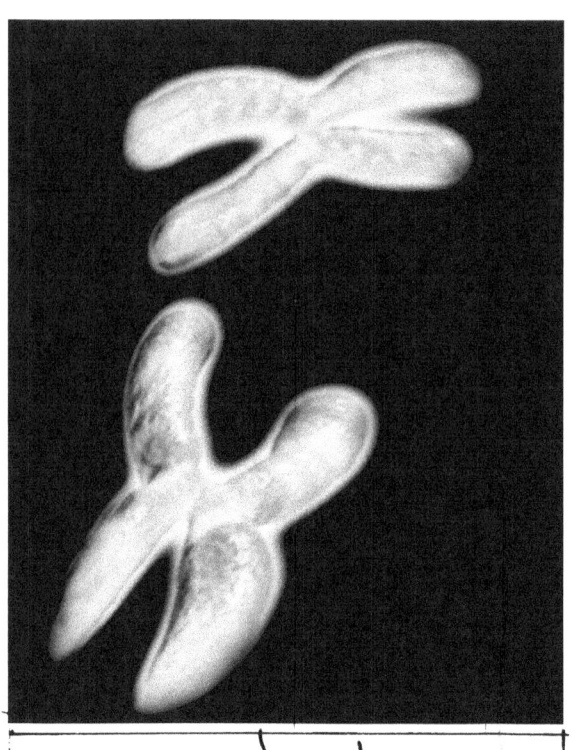

LIVING

That's Life.....All sorts of things are doing it. Many more than we understand.

LIFE

Starts with breeding, in the valley of the thing....Watch the bridge over troubled daughter.....Cells replaced every seven years....Age will kill you now, don't think you want to die....."In the course of my life, I have often had to eat my words, and I must confess that I have always found it a wholesome diet" Sir Winston Churchill.

LINEART

Drawings without tone although thick and thin lines or screened dots can give the impression of tone or blends.

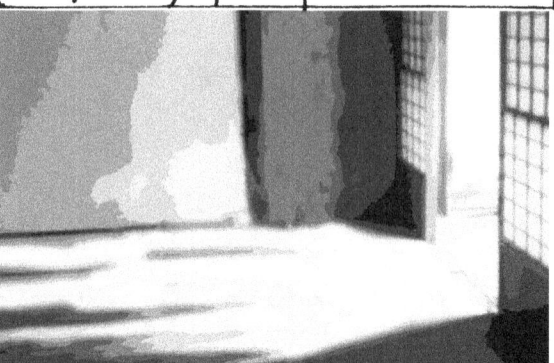

LITE

The suns rays burst through the paper doors of our ryokan casting the long shadow of the tokyo clear cold winter.

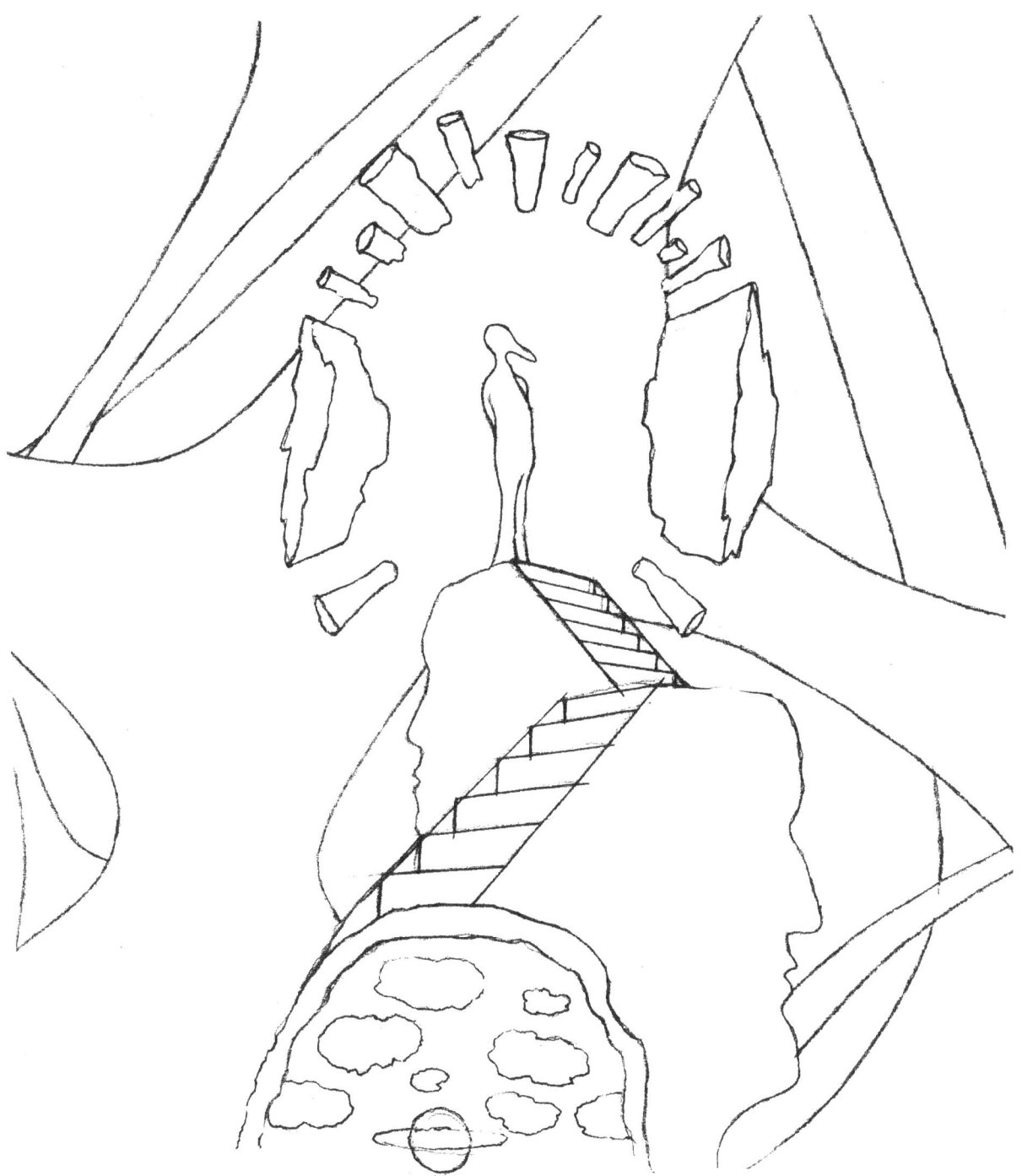

LEADER

Alpha person.....Not always liked, but they do not care anyway.....Politiicks.....Like all ticks, yuk. Leader of the pack! Climbs over the heads of the competitors, learns to manipulate the surrounding society. Big beak small pecker.....Maybe.

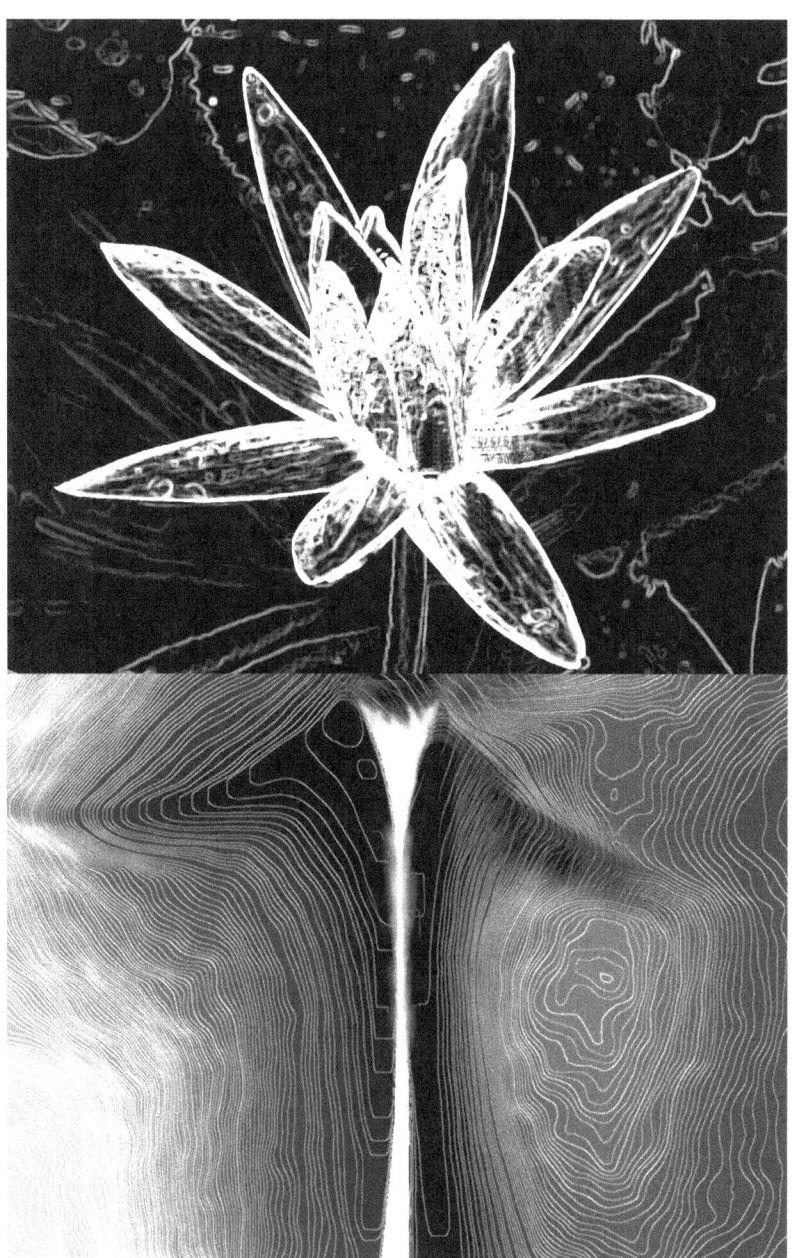

LAST FLOWER

Read james thurber's book, it is the real meaning of life.

LOTUS

Legendary plant inducing luxurious languor when eaten; kind of water lily. Symbol, hinduism and buddhism. Lotuseater; person given to indolent enjoyment. Lotus land: west coast, british columbia, canada.

LIP SERVICE

Agrees with you when not even listerning! Makes a perfect manager for the anger management service in a government department, working with the angry public!

LINGO

Starts with our group hanging out and having secret talks, so we create our own lingo, dialect and words.

LANGUAGE

All our tribes speak their own mother tongue..... Soon it will be hindlish or mandalish.

LTD

You may well think life is limited..... But with the new lingo LTD means; live the dream.

LOAF

No not bread.....Cockney slang, use your head, think it out.....Loaf of bread.....Head!

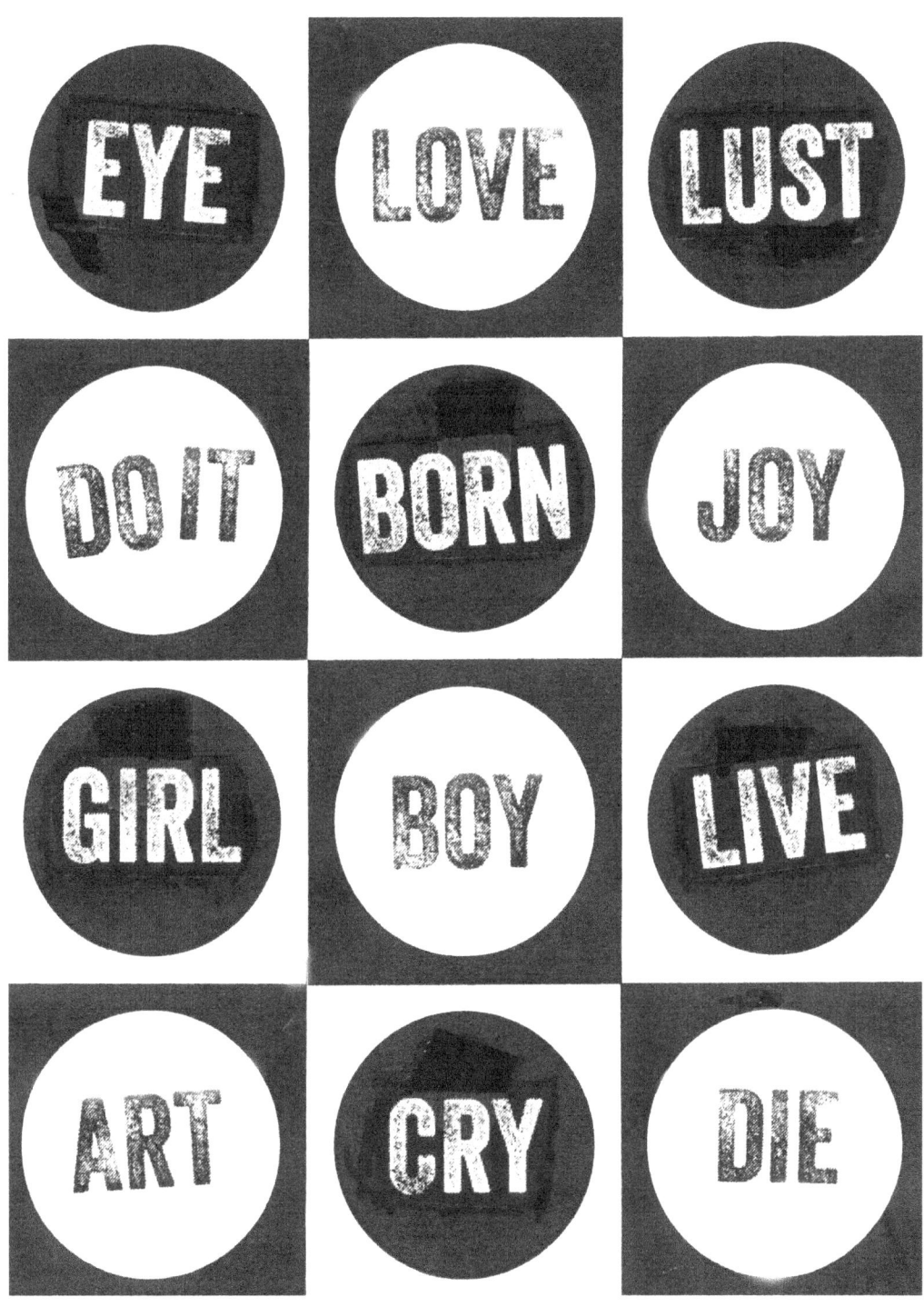

SAY NO MORE.....PO IT

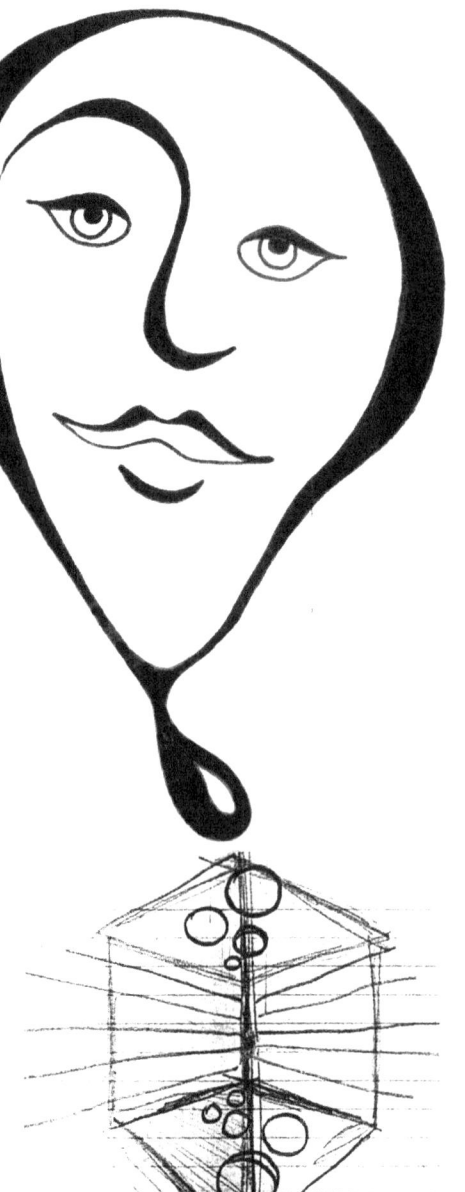

LAYERS

Past of liers.....Not really, chickens? Photoshop layer.....Great system to build pictures. Thickness of matter.

LASSIE

Not our north american four legged friend..... Yogurt slurpie with salt, fruit and or juices to quench that exotic east indian hot thirst.

LEAVING

If you never leave there, you will not enjoy coming back.

LADYBOYS

Thailands many beautiful women are men!

LAUGHING GEAR

lips....Lip service, around your mouth. Smile you are using your laughing gear, you can use it for page 84.

LOVE ELOPE

The real private runaway wedding, none of the blow budget 100 people par- ties, and unwanted keep in packaging presents..

LIGHT SHAPES SEEING ART
MIND MAKES STORY

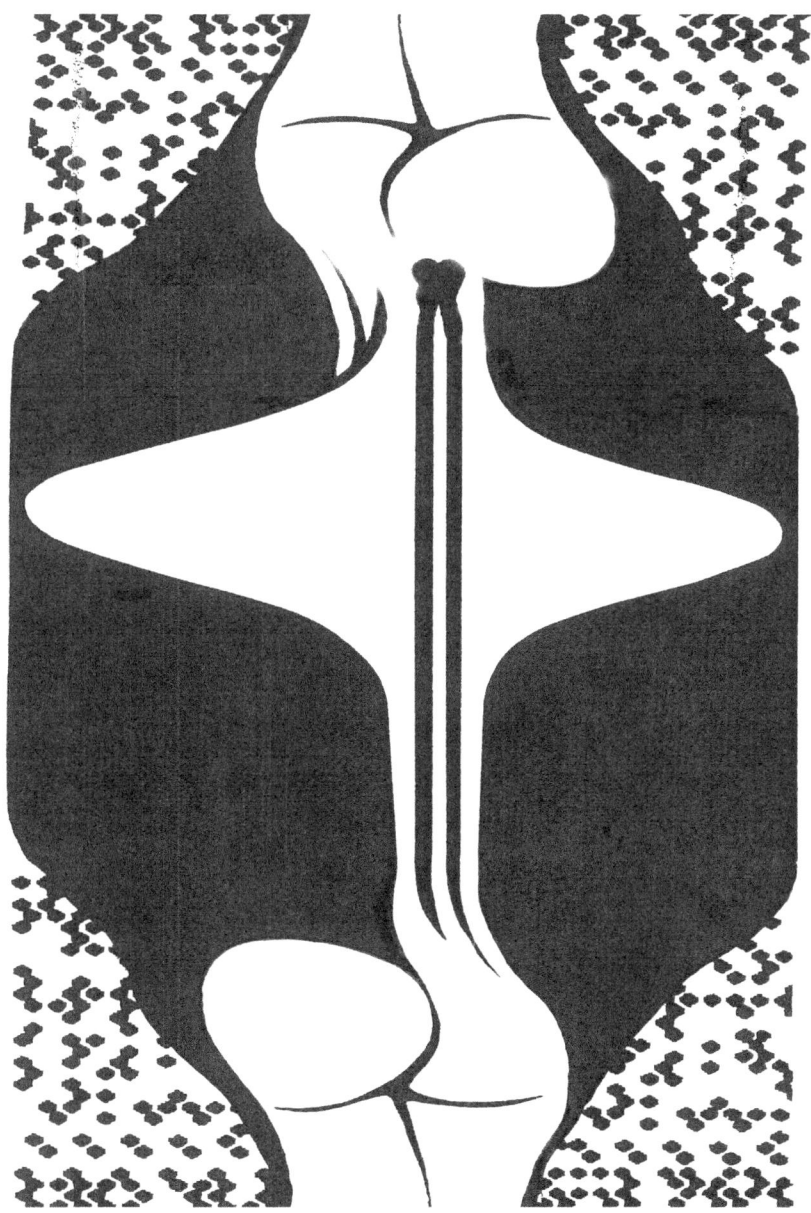

LIFE FORCE
The drive of all living things to continue breeding,
yes, great on full moon parties.....Keep it up.....I find
this hard, sorry viagra!

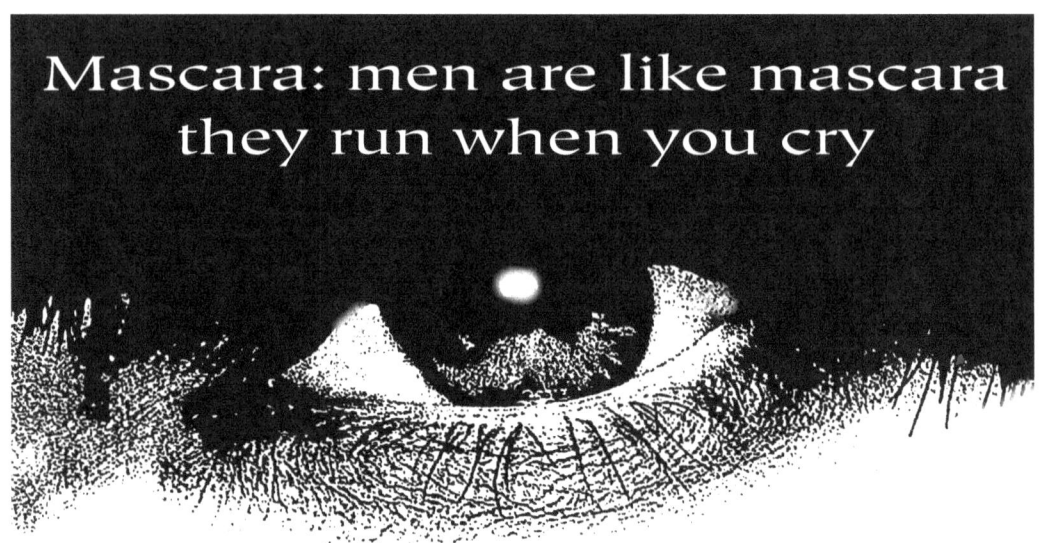

Mascara: men are like mascara
they run when you cry

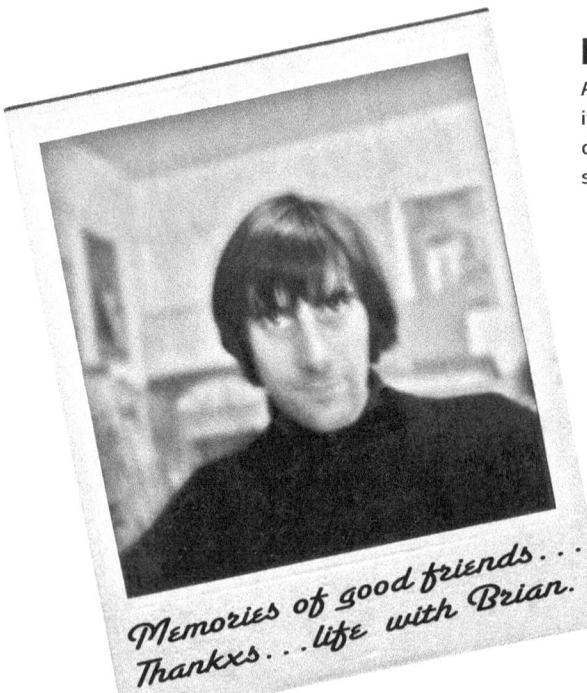

Memories of good friends...
Thankxs...life with Brian.

MIDDLE LEG

All males have one, although
it is usually not as big as the
outer ones or even the same
size as other men.

MINDSCAPE

You can see the horizon of the
mind clearly, usually when half
waking up, in that, in and out
dream state. That's where you
will find manray, the squirrels
and Walt Disney and all your
other fantasies.

MYOPIA

Short-sightedness.....From the
greeks yet again {shut eye}.
Sounds bad for all artists.

MINDSITE

Where the seat of consciousness lives..... Feelings, thoughts, volition and intellectial power (rule this site)....This is the nu frontier of the conception of life.

MANANA

Word sounds like manyarna.....Which is used to say it is not going to happen today, maybe tomorrow maybe! Simular to Island time!.....No hurries no worries. (spanish; manjuana is tomorrow).

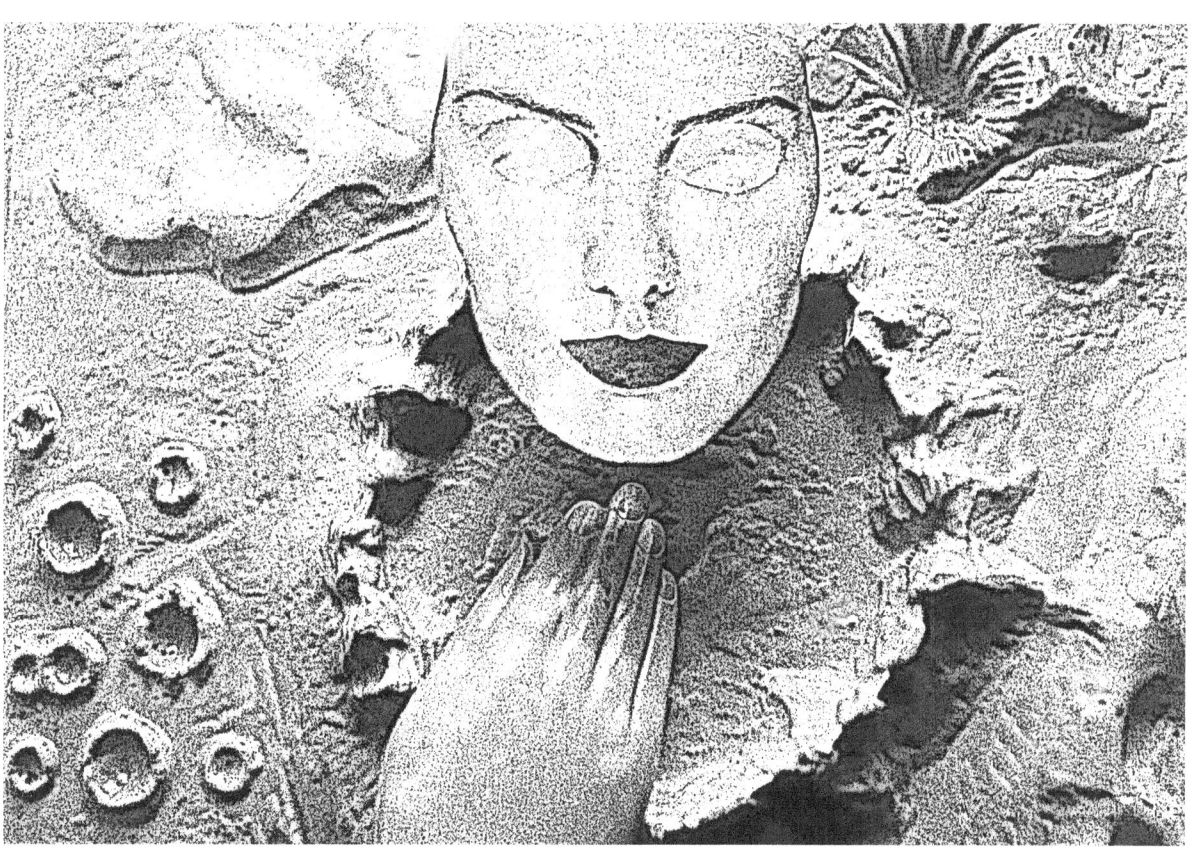

MESCAL

or mezcal, Tequillas rough and dangerous non gringo cousin, sometimes with worm (really a butterfly caterpillar).

MOONFACE

Kubrick created the surface in two movies one for nasa and one for 2001, both looked like the moon but we could not see the face we all look for. Those shadows in the moon landing, where did they come from?

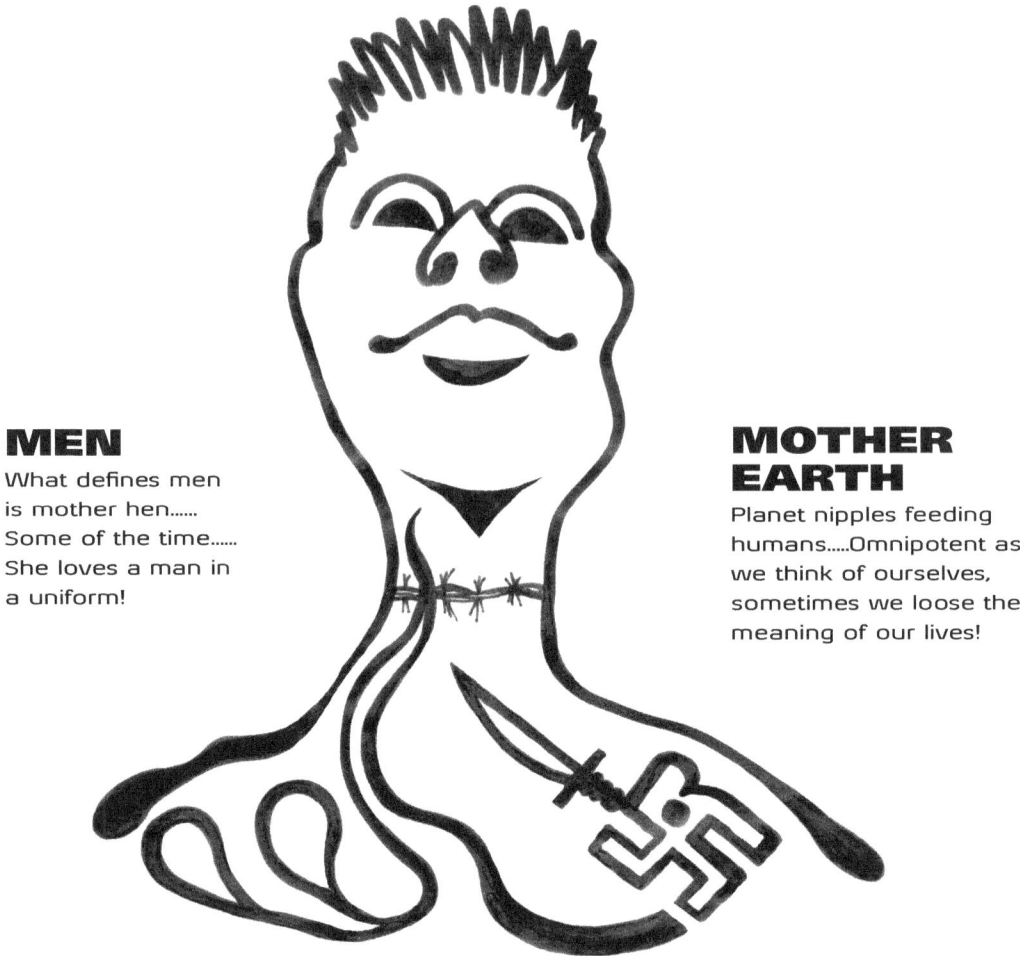

MEN

What defines men is mother hen...... Some of the time...... She loves a man in a uniform!

MOTHER EARTH

Planet nipples feeding humans.....Omnipotent as we think of ourselves, sometimes we loose the meaning of our lives!

MULTINATIONAL

Super groups that own politicians, countries, economies and they feed, entertain and control us.

MOLLYDUKA

The great oz word for a left handed person.....Molly a woman! dukes your fists.

MULLIGATAWNY

Brit, Indias great curry soup, original Tamil, southern india and sri lanka (ceylon). Pepper-water soup base usually with a lot of heart saving tumeric. Rice is used to thicken it. Maybe originally started as a dhal.

MESSAGE

We love it when some one gets a message in a bottle from the ocean. Always makes the news on a low news day.

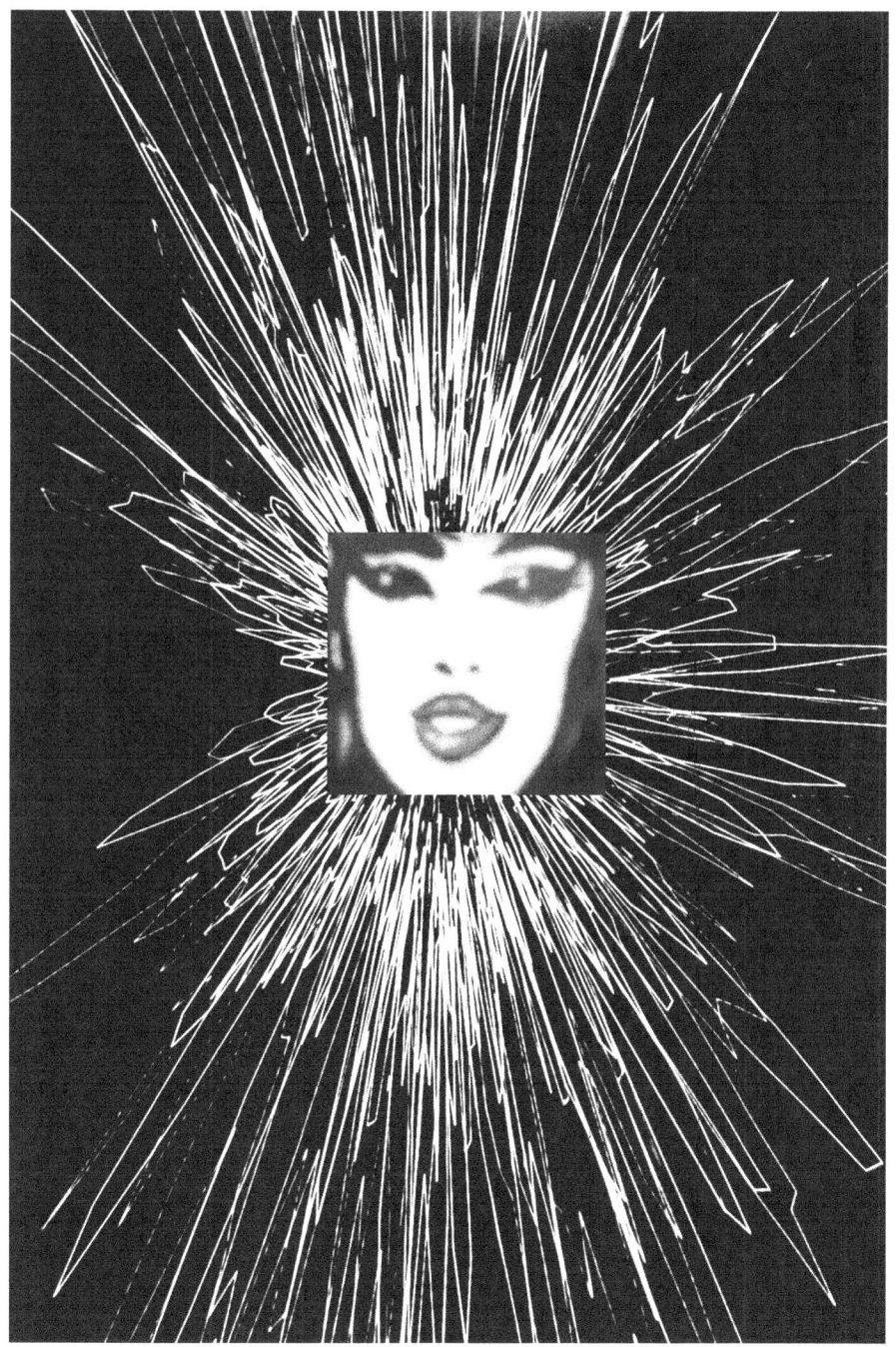

MASK
We can put on many different masks to suit any relationship
but sometimes we are not who we think we are!

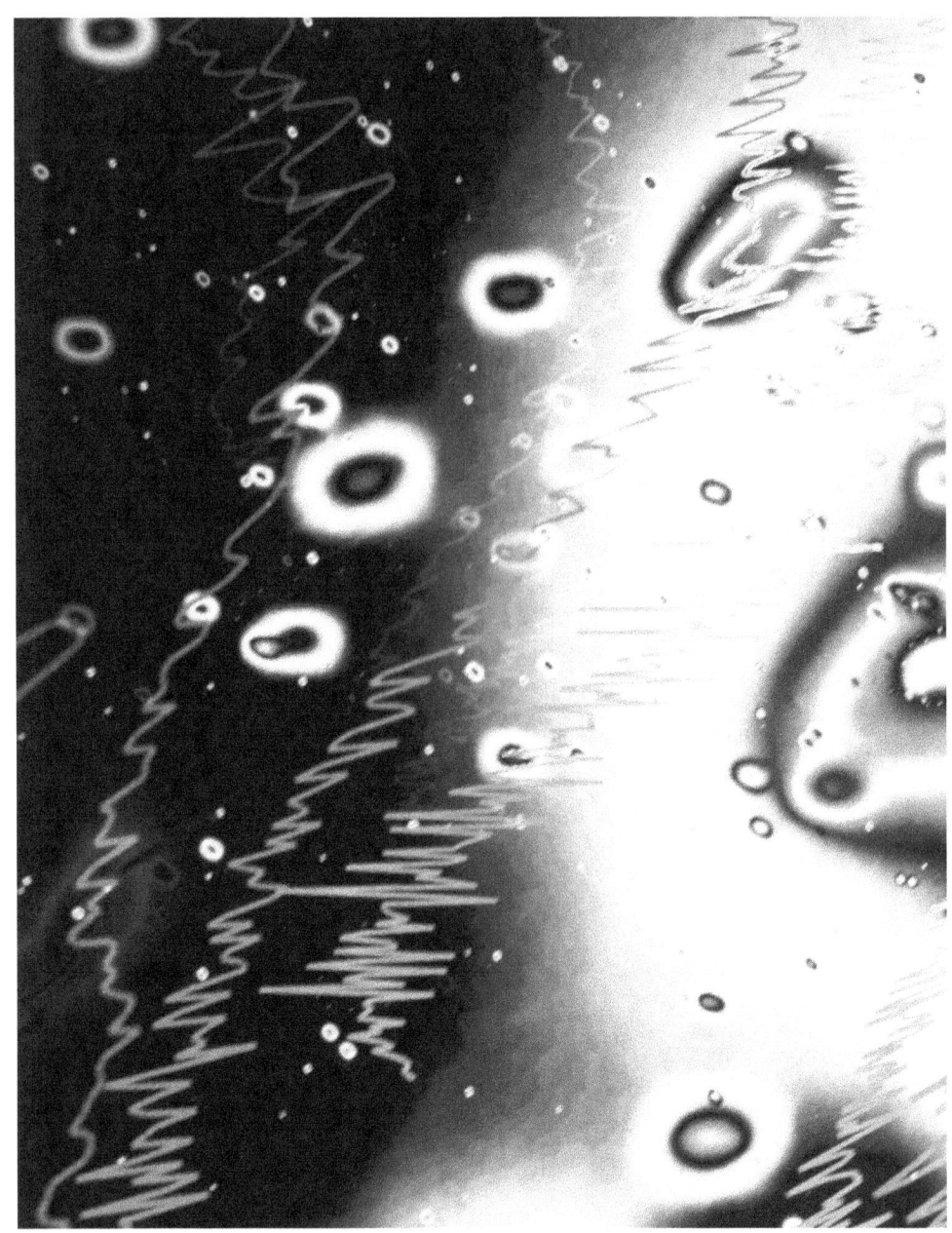

MEMORY: Remember travelling, eating, family and friends, great memories? Dementia and alzheimer's let it slip away.....What now? Can I feel, forget it! Sorry what did you say.....I can't remember.

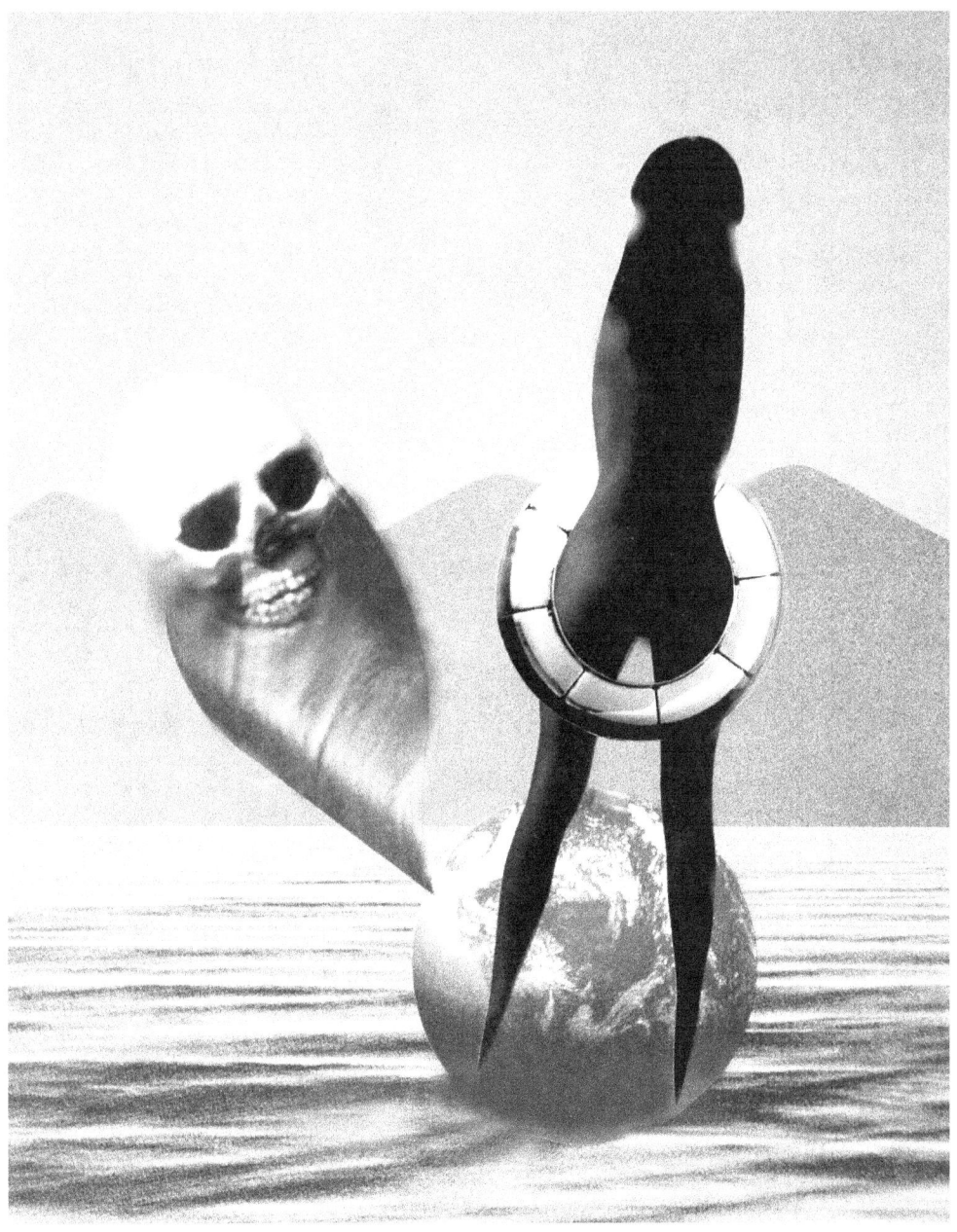

MOJAVE In california, nevada, arizona and utah.....Life is hard at zabriske point.....There is a reason they call it death valley and then on top of that, the pioneers had to die crossing the sierra nevada...... Spanish (snowy range).

MENTOR CHURCHER

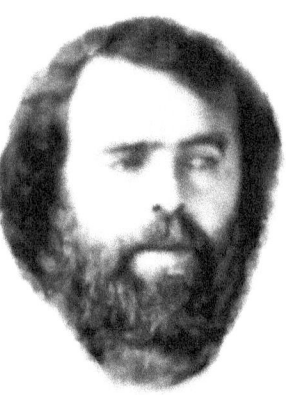

Your first mentor is like your first lover, some you remember for all your life.....Mister chez of the sixties qld art scene.....I want to be a paperback riter! The other mentor of my life was figurative artist Frank Rowlands.

MEANING

What is meant.....Significance, expressive, significant, meaningful. What meaning will I find in the abstract drawing below and the other artwork in this book? My eyes see balance, structure and pattern, but what does it mean? You Can't see it, can you.....

MIND

The gap.....Mind and soul contain-memories, joy, anger, pain, and the search for happiness?

MEKON

Dan dare pilot of the future.....The mekon was his enemy.....This comic conditioned us young brits after the second WORLD WAR to stop saying the bosch (germans) was the enermy Bosch: (hard headed, rascal, cabbage head).

MOJO

What is it? I never thought I had it, and you need Robert Johnson to tell you you have it!.

MENAGE

de Twidle.....The naughty threesome that used to be in Monmartre.....Long lost titalation that made us smile.....Pigalle Paree.....

MANNEQUIN

We shall make them in our own image and they shall inherit the earth.....I met Adel Rootstein in the sixties and she was at the leading edge of mannequin creation. She influenced me so much I have made a lifetime study picturing mannequins.

MISUMI

MIles, SUsie and MIles the first six letters was going to be the name of our boat after being in Japan.

MANZOU

Walk slowly!

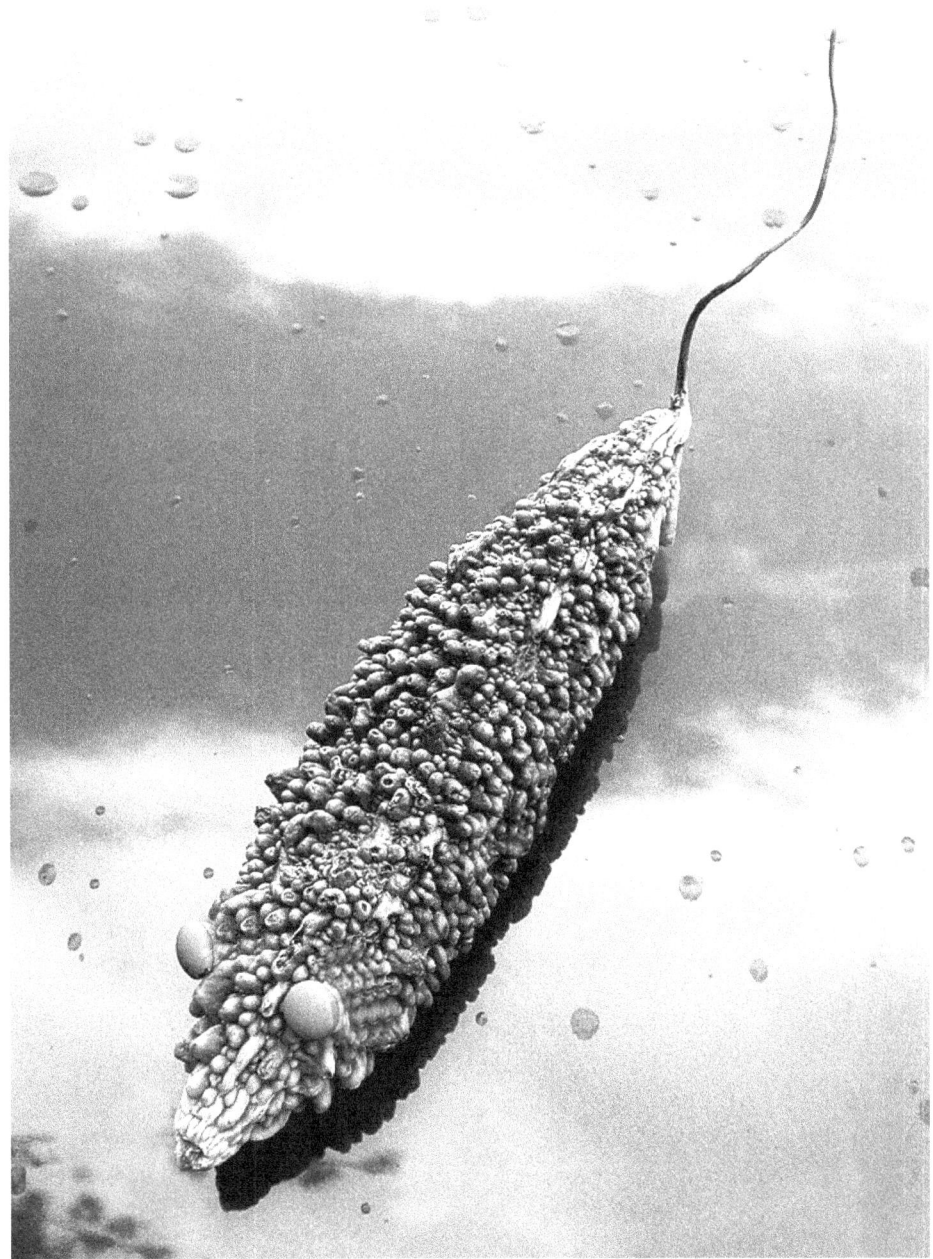

MOIST

The dirtiest word in my life.....Some where between wet and warm! Not quite fluid and not dry. Tastes wonderful in cookies!

MEATVEG

This vegatable was alive before it passed away from its nutrients..... Did it have family and friends? I think its ugly, we will eat it.

133

NDE

Near Death Experience. Word formed from the initial letters of other words (e.g. Nato, Madd). Greek akron-end, onoma-name. Mummy I can see the white light at the end of the tunnel.....When you are dying do you always call out for mummy?

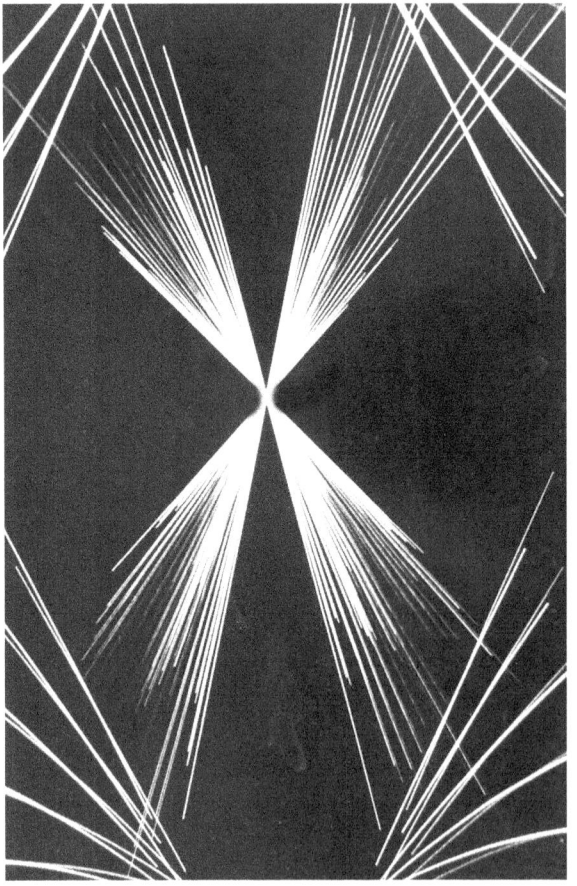

NETWERKZ

IT techie term for connected company, german euro related or trying to be euro fashionable.

NIMBU PANI

Lime water, my faav in any country, if you can get it, be sour!!!

NASTY

Not used at all nowadays.

NOVA

Nova Scotia.....Live in new Scotland, sounded so nu back in my formative sixties. Nova..... The leading edge sixties magazine just like wired was back at its beginning!

NEWSTALK

The great movie for the wag the dog conspiracy generation. A huge part of our society are addicted to the news. I can't take it any more.....

NIGHT TRAIN

So romantic, we went on the overnight train to the vallry of the kings.....Luxor but not exactly the fantasy we all have of the orient express!

NARLY

Hawaii.....What is the real meaning of this word, where did it come from? Good, farr out, super cool, awesome, right on, sweet, fun, and can be gross and disgusting!

NOTHING

Exists.....Then it is something..... Now how does that work?

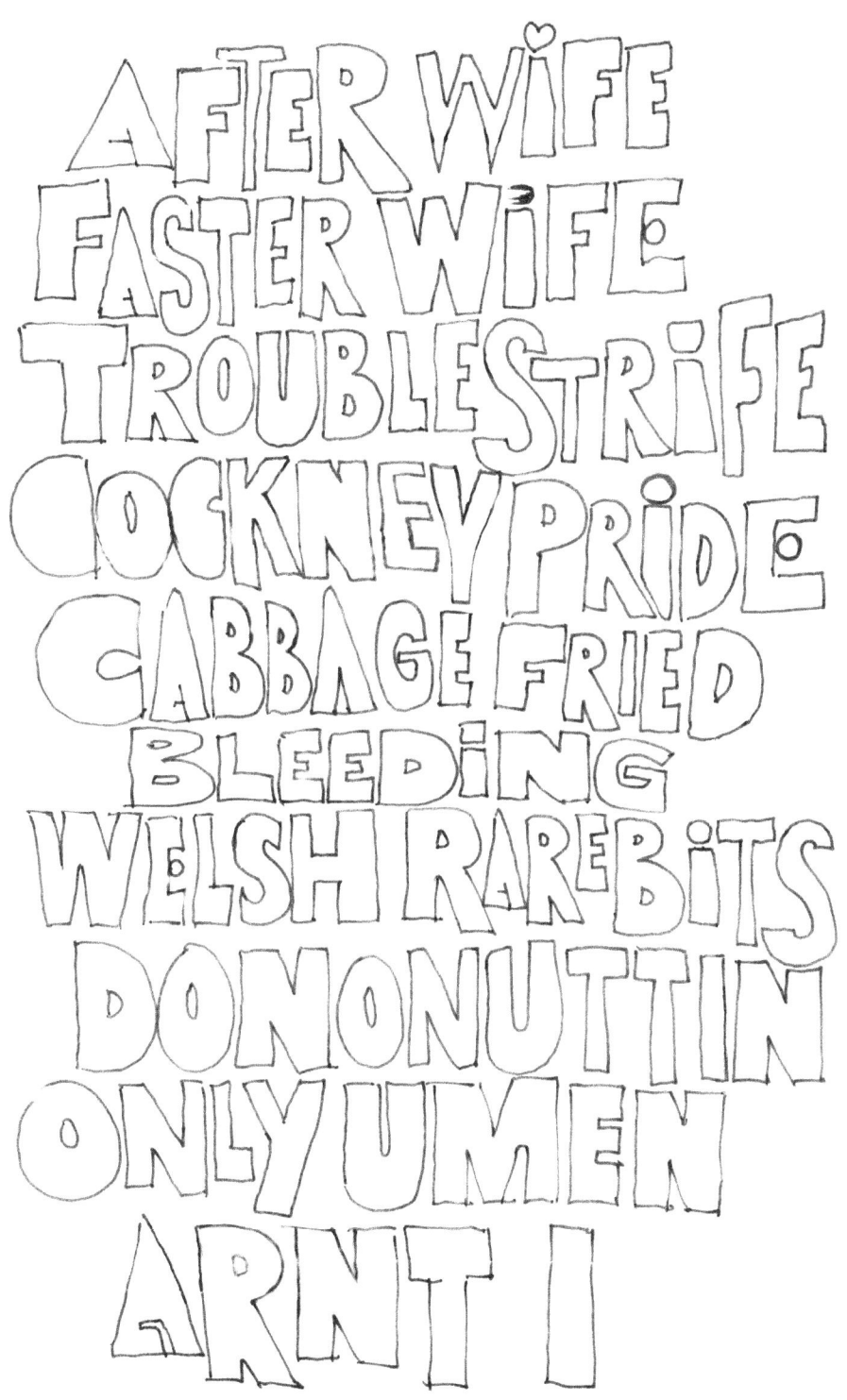

AFTER WIFE
FASTER WIFE
TROUBLE STRIFE
COCKNEY PRIDE
CABBAGE FRIED
BLEEDING
WELSH RAREBITS
DONONUTTIN
ONLYUMEN
ARNT I

MY MOTHER NEVER SAID SORRY
TO ANYONE...NO WOT I MEEN

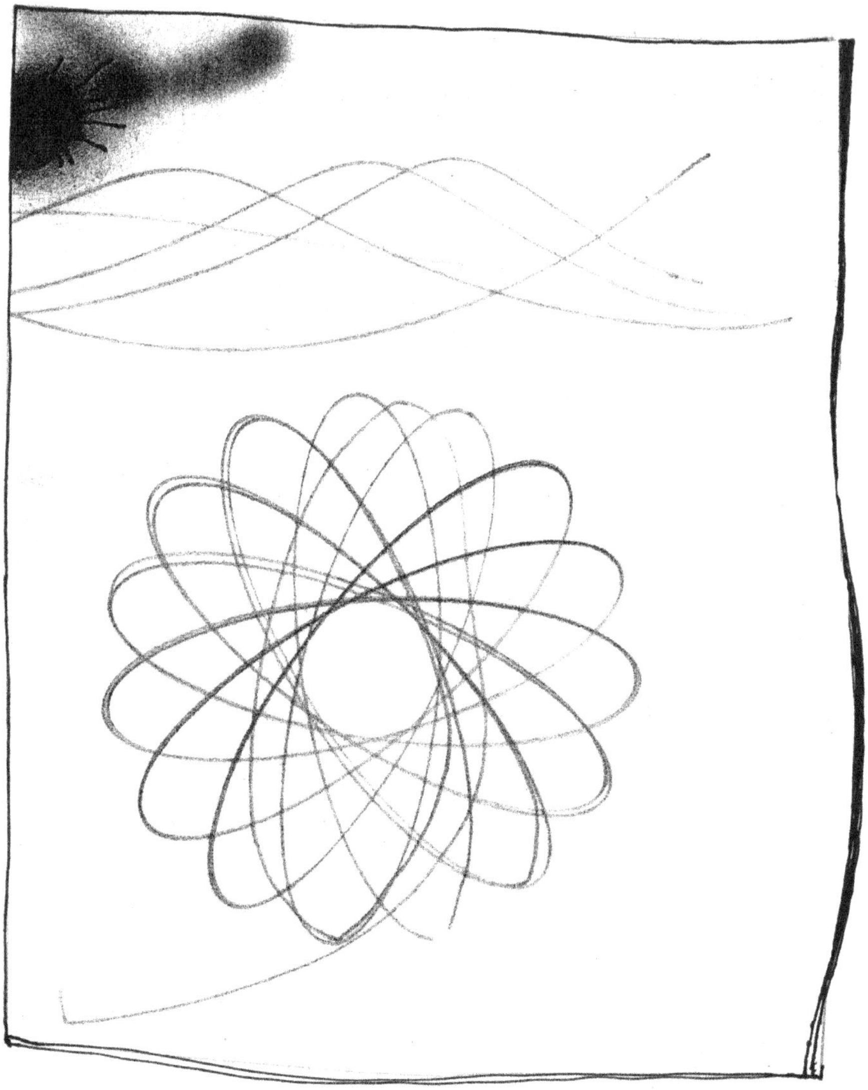

NUCLEUS

The cell nucleolus acts like a brain of the cell. It controls all its life patterns from eating, movement and reproduction, anything that happens in a cell more than likely the nucleolus knows about it!

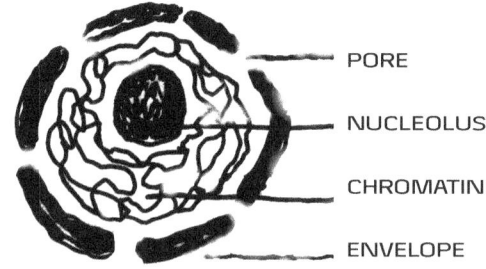

PORE

NUCLEOLUS

CHROMATIN

ENVELOPE

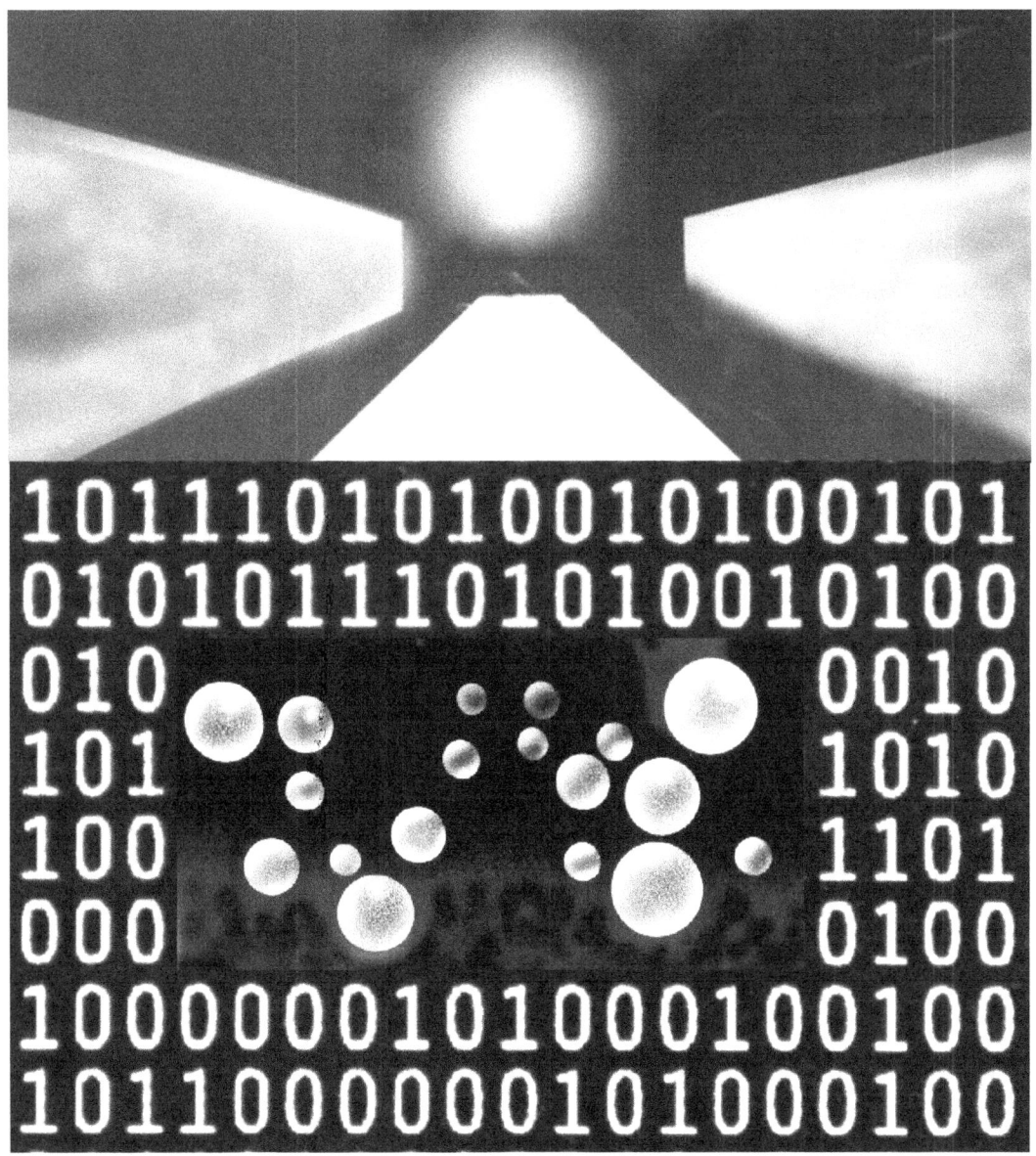

NEXGEN

The generation that is leaving adolescence to start a productive thinking life.

NUAPP

New applications or applications installed in our computers or bodies to assist, identify or control our functions, meaning or existence.

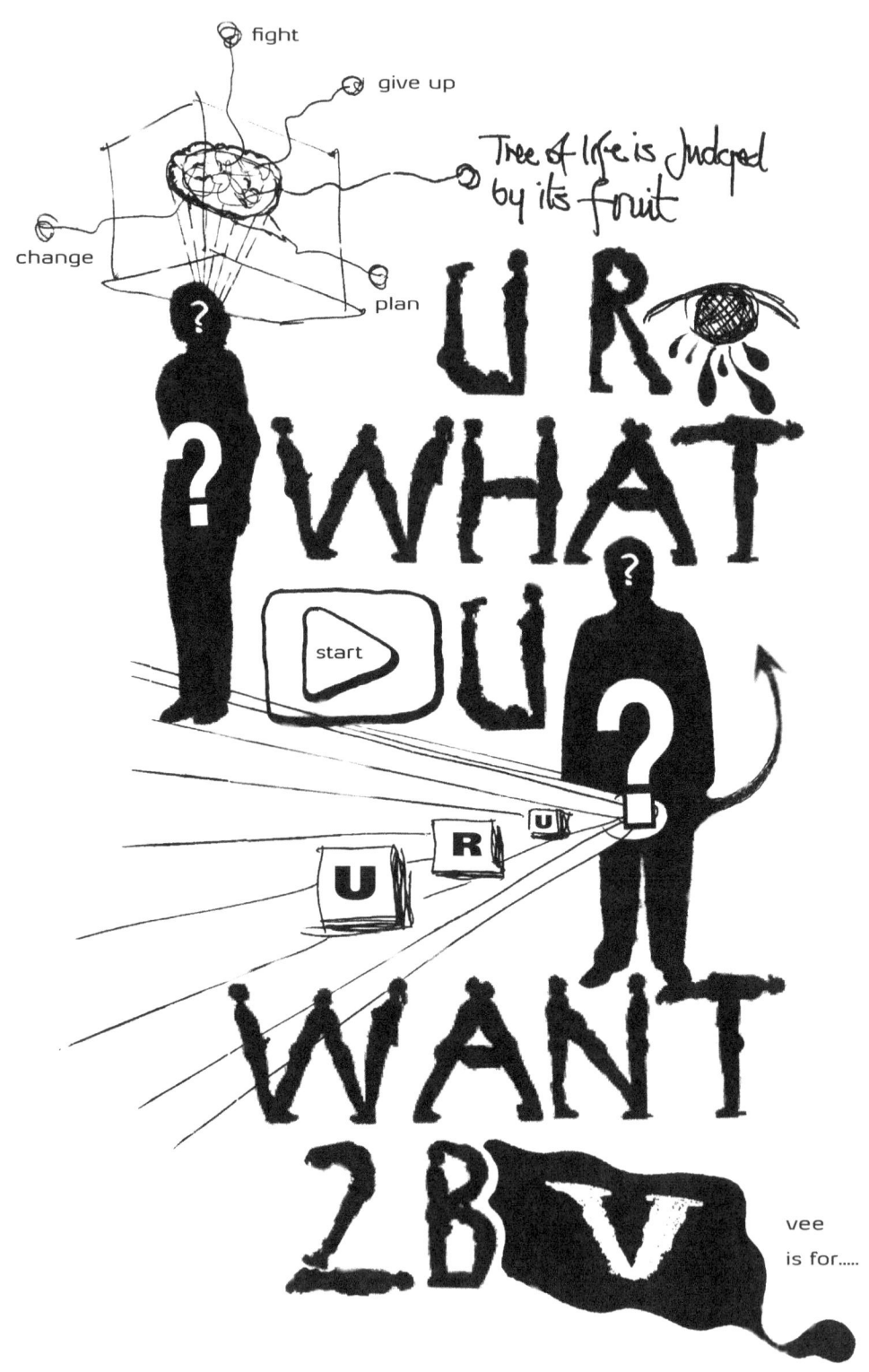

Tree of life is Judged by its fruit

U R WHAT U WANT 2 B V

U R WHAT U WANT 2 B

fight
give up
change
plan

start

vee
is for.....

Navigate.....Direct or manage your course, find your way.....U mite b wot u fink!

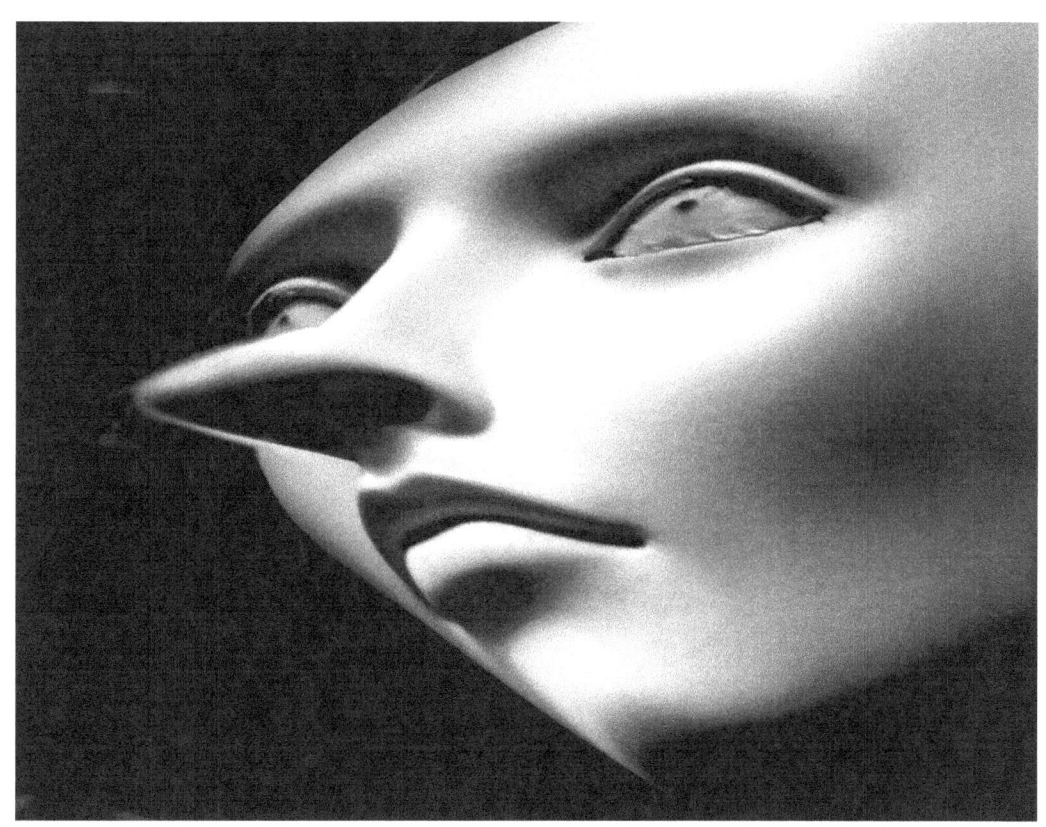

NOSEY PARKER

That is that person with an overly
inquisitive or prying nature, a busy
body and usually a pain in your arse!

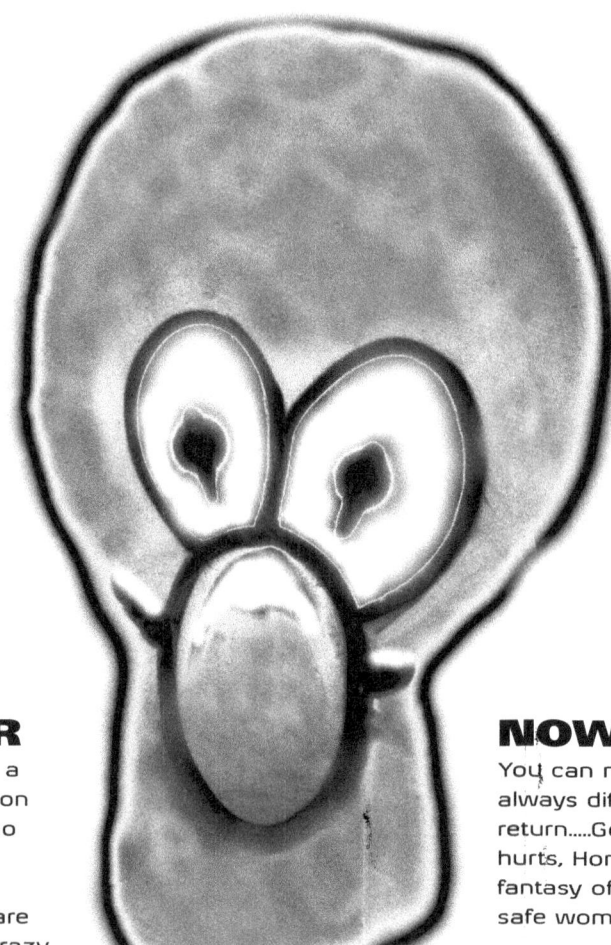

NUTTER

British slang for a
mentally ill person
or someone who
is cruel, tough,
aggressive and
fearless. Some are
psychotic and crazy.....

NONSHEEP

A person who doesn't subscribe
to following the flock, herd or
pack mentality. A person who is
more an independent, self gov-
erning leader, than a follower of
the masses.

NONSNENSE

Adj. A word used by too fast
angry internet posters to indicate
when they are too busy and
flustered to proofread their inane
rants and tweets!

NOWAY HOME

You can never go back....It is
always different when you
return.....Get used to it! Nostalgia
hurts, Home is that long lost
fantasy of warm love from the
safe womb of mother!

NONTROVERSY

A controversy that does not exist
until created for political gain. A
contraction of non controversy.

NIGHTSWEATS

Wet bed, it is hot in here, lifes
torment to wonderful women.....
St johns wort? Coming home
to the rainforest after a four
year tour in Iran, things with the
marriage had to be renewed.....
She did not need it, and had to
tell him about Joanne.....

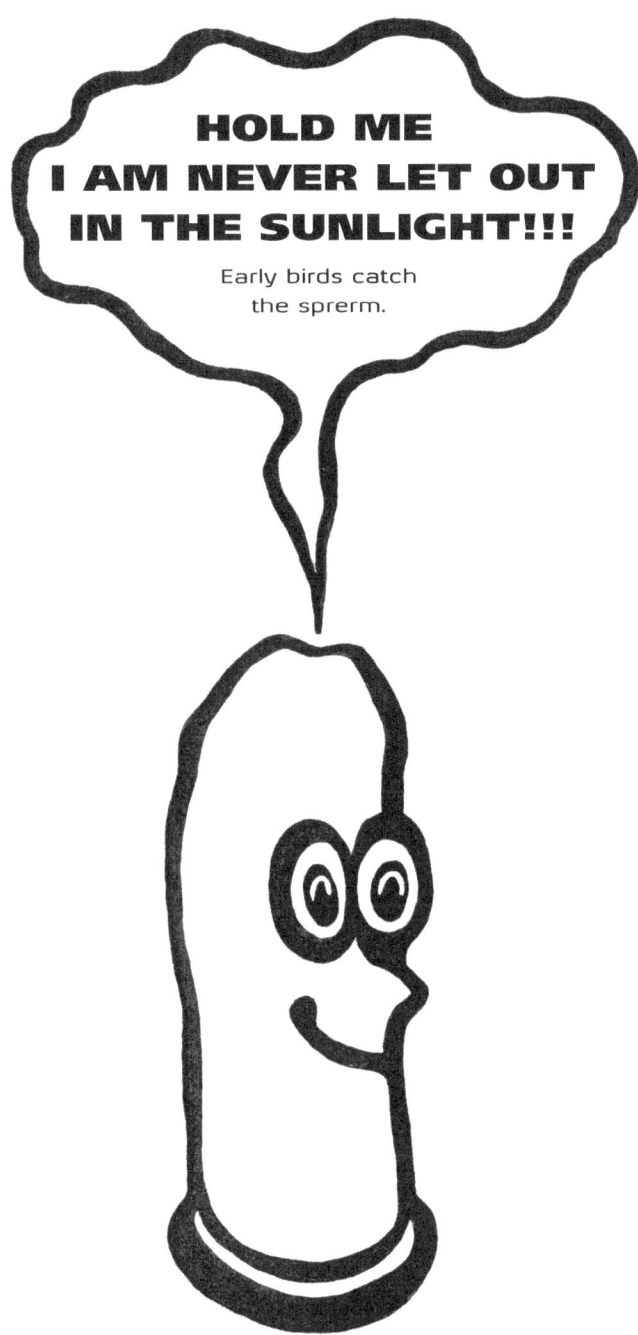

NEVERMIND

Shut down all of our
conversation, you don't
want to quarrel anymore,
you are dismissing me....
End! Keep quiet, go away.

NUDIST

When was the last time you
skinny dipped? I am a nudist
but now I am dressed in the
finest Thai latex.....Rubber to
you too!

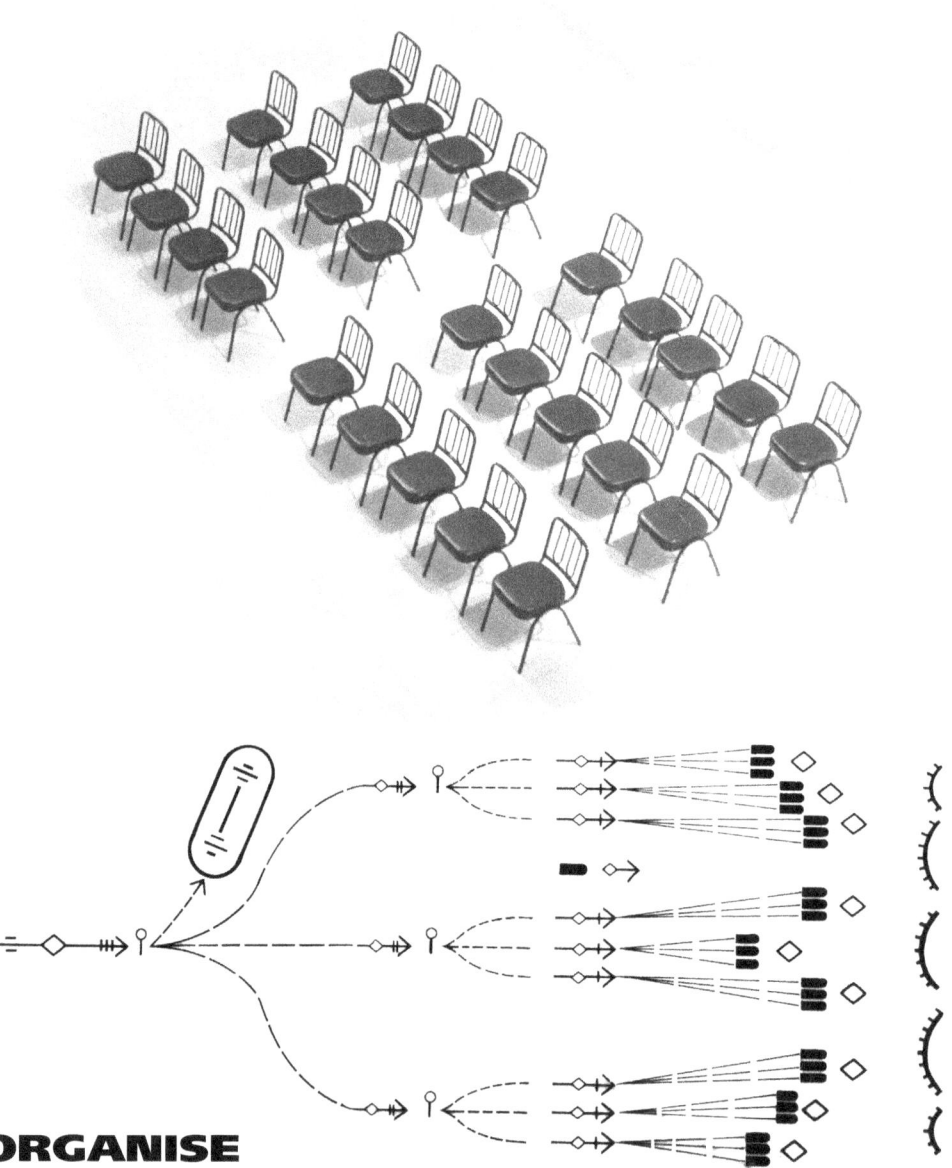

ORGANISE

Orderly structure.....What seat shall I sit in? She sits in the same seat every week she comes! Somewhere between organic and orgasm must be good for life, even ants do it.....Lets fall in love, please get all your fucks in a row! Organise your life like football.....Without having a goal it is diffcult to score....

ORDER JURYx2+3

Twelve people will decide the fate of one person, this is the system we have! Manipulated by lawyers and a judge, hope they sleep at night.

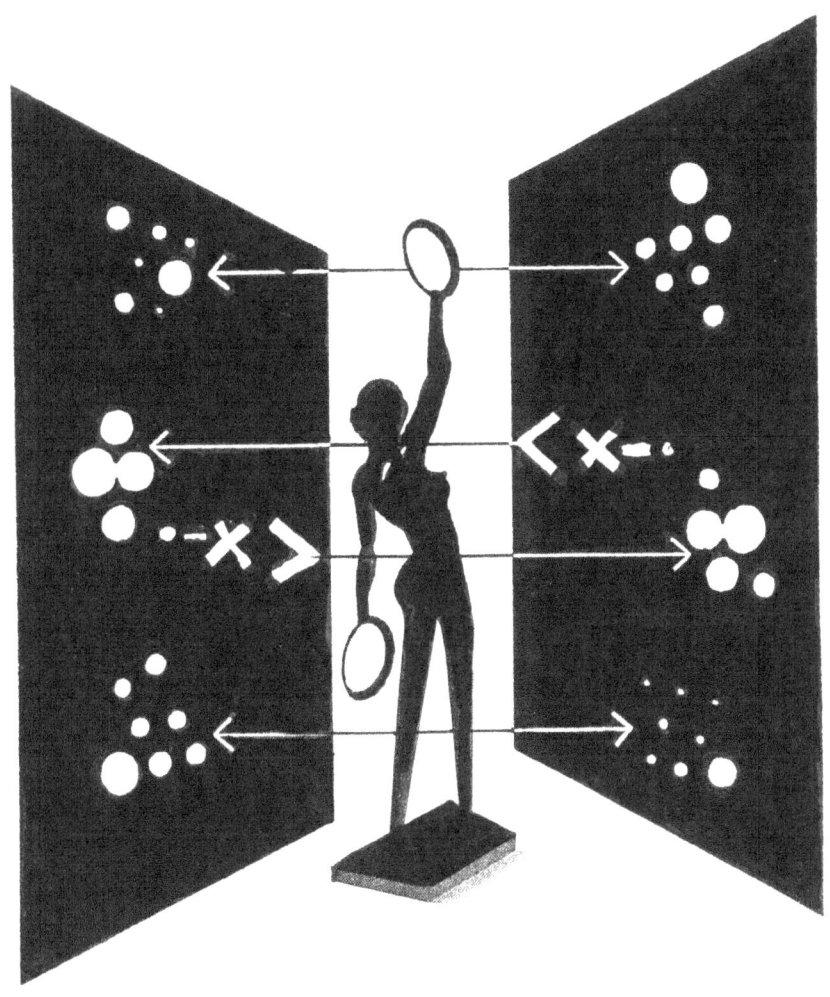

OPPOSITES

Having a position on the other or further side. It is not all black and white. You must remember the shades of grey!

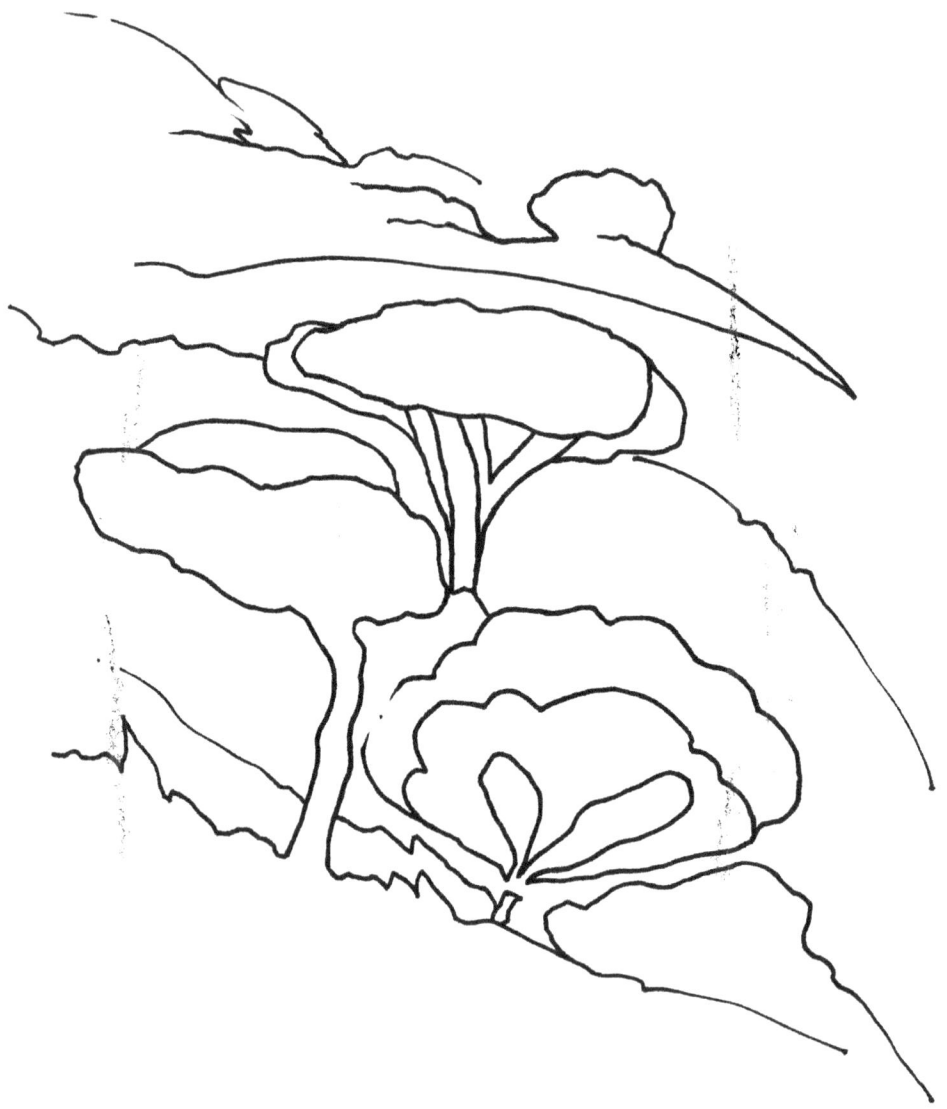

OPEN AIR

We do not value this as much as we should. Outside, not in an enclosed space on our earth!

ODDOLOGY

The real study and many a thesis exists of strange not normal things. Strange bedfellows make captain chickenheart the chook of the strawberry fields at the end of my lane.

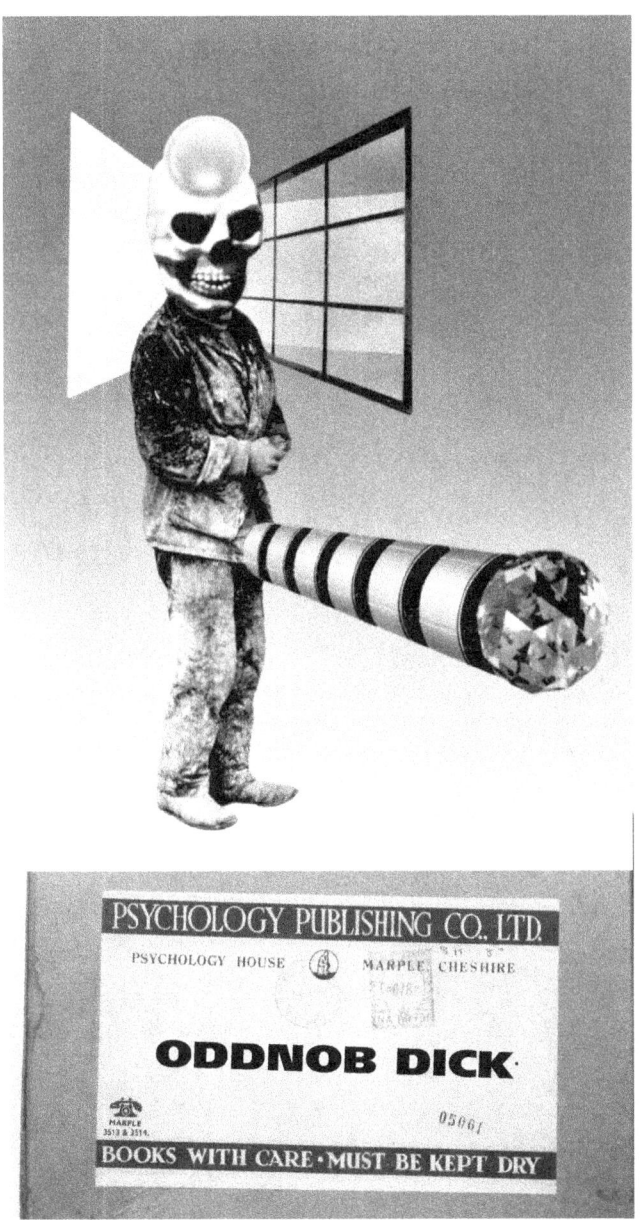

OUTWIT

Be to cleaver for, overcome by greater ingenuity.
Clapham, Peckham and Turnham green.....All life lives in
those London suburbs!!! Please dance with me, will I be
rejected or ignored like wall paper? I am sorry I can't
dance with you I have a bone in my leg!.....Thanks dad.

are we part of something more tha just ourselves Ne are responsible for 89 lifeforms in our own body You really got me not sleeping at night!

OURSELVES

Carbon species.....Do we really know this? What happens when we loose the net and google, and ninety percent of us die? Who will make a new computer and a printing machine?

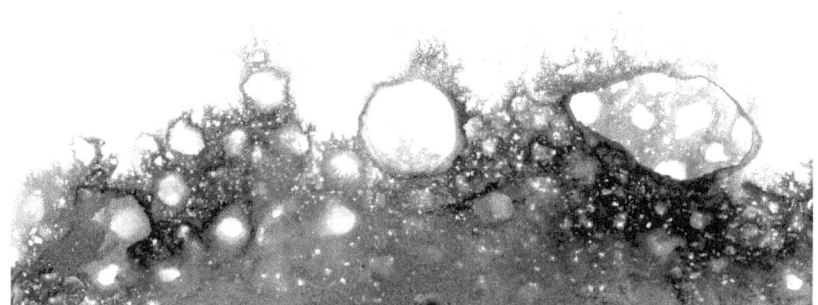

ORIGINAL

Existing from the first, earliest, primitive, innate, that has served as a pattern, of which a copy or translation has been made. New in concept, not derived or imitative; inventive, creative..... Original model!

OPEN SOURCE

That would be perfect, if there was such a format as open source, but all our tribes are at war.....My tribe is superior to yours.....I own the intellectual copyright, you can't copy it! I am not sharing my toys with you. Closed borders yes, we want a spiritual and trade war......Believe me!!! My money is worth more than yours. We love the freedon of speech and democracy.....A form of government in which all eligible citizens have an equal say in the decisions that affect their lives!.....Wow that works so well.

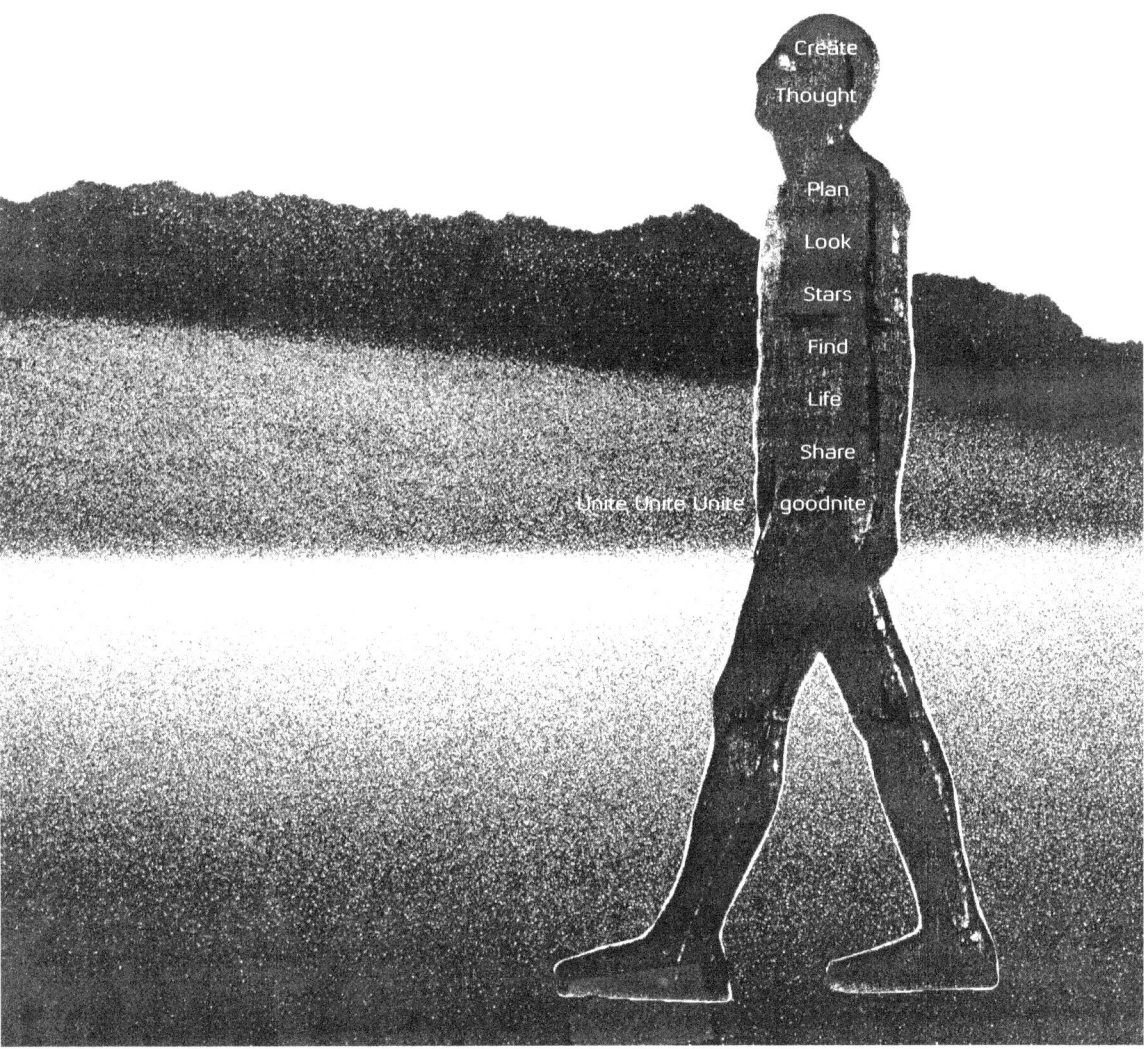

What are you looking at? I can not see it, What are you thinking it is?

OOPSY

I made a mistake and I don't care....Collateral damage......Oopsy Daisy.....Insignificant mistakes sometimes, oopsy bear, yeah yeah thats canukkeepoo to you.....

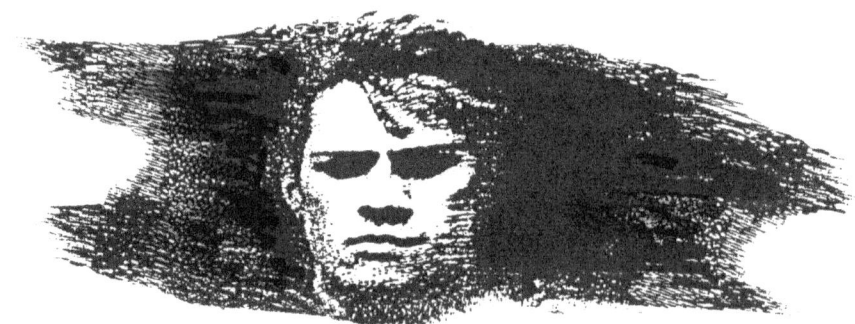

ORAL

Spoken verbal by word of mouth. Done or taken by the mouth. Spoken examination. Orally (oris: mouth). Say no more.....No wat I mean.....

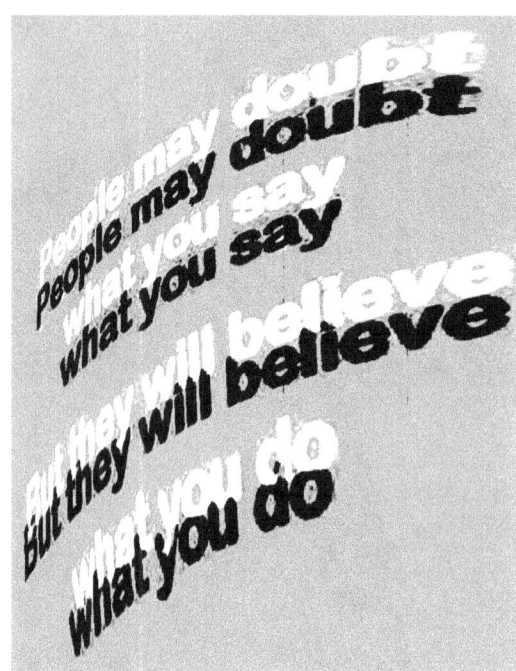

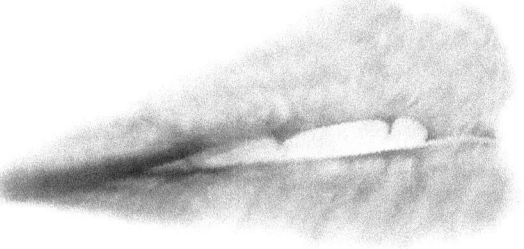

OICK

Originating Intelligent Network Category Key, this definition is rare, only my northern euro finns and swedes use it thanks nokia and ericsson....Derogatory brit word for inferior, ignorant person from that other school with its superiors in Rome.

ORDER

Who put the alphabet in that order?..... Now start reading it backwards in your mind.....Mensa up if you can!

OXYMORON

Good grief he was pretty ugly and a new classic resident alien working for the government organisation. Cataloguing the living dead in microsoft works, he was almost exactly a genuine imitation party politician. A great politician

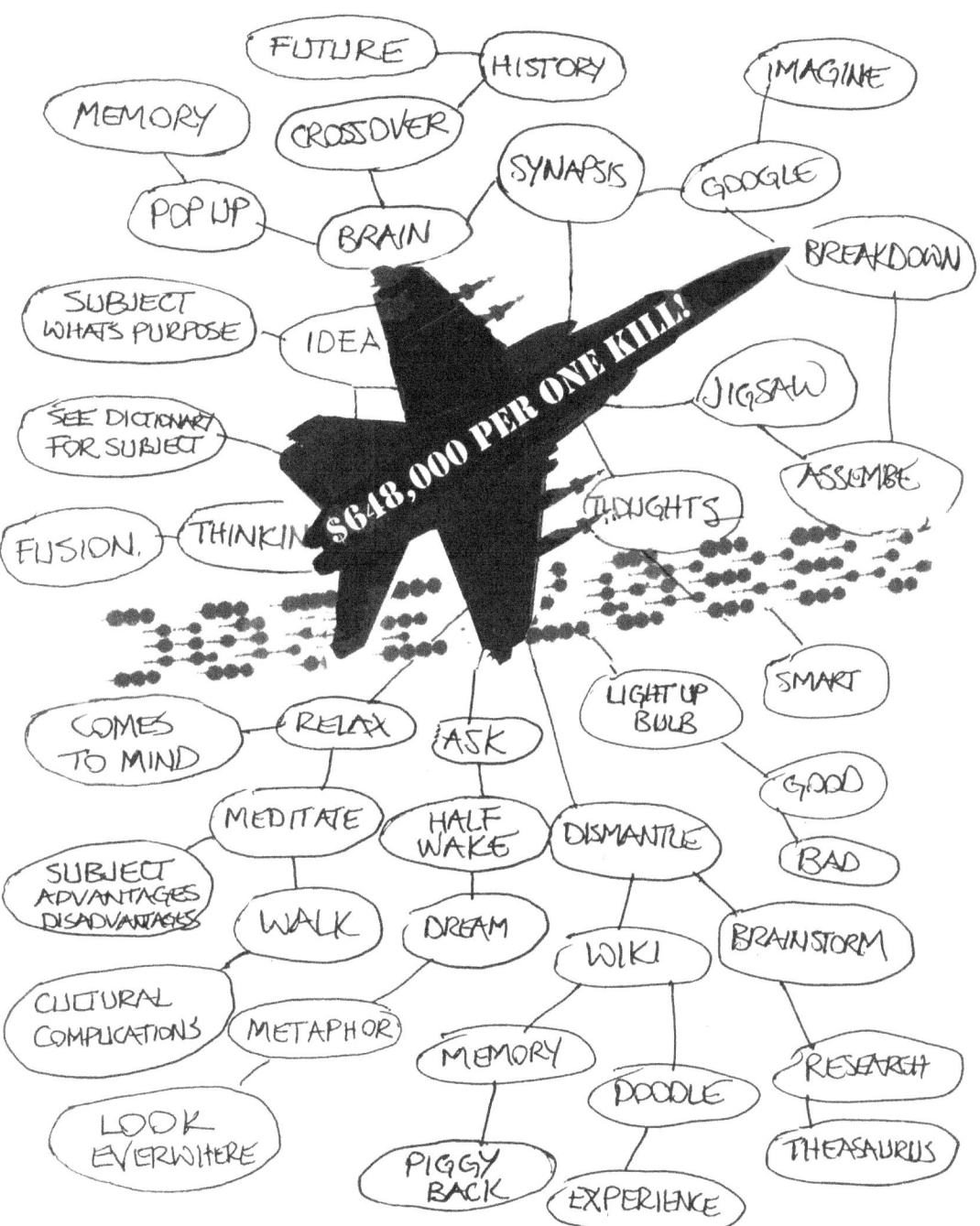

ONE KILL

War Craft three "Quote" Blessed are the peacemakers. Justified killing in warfare!.....Blackpork down.....There is a lot of animals on this farm, George. Grade nine.....You must work the summer in the abbatoir! The geek shall inherit the earth.

OIL

It is everything in our lives.....Sleep on that pillow it is polyester.....The iraq war, you say was to stop the flow of cheap oil in order to make expensive oil viable!.

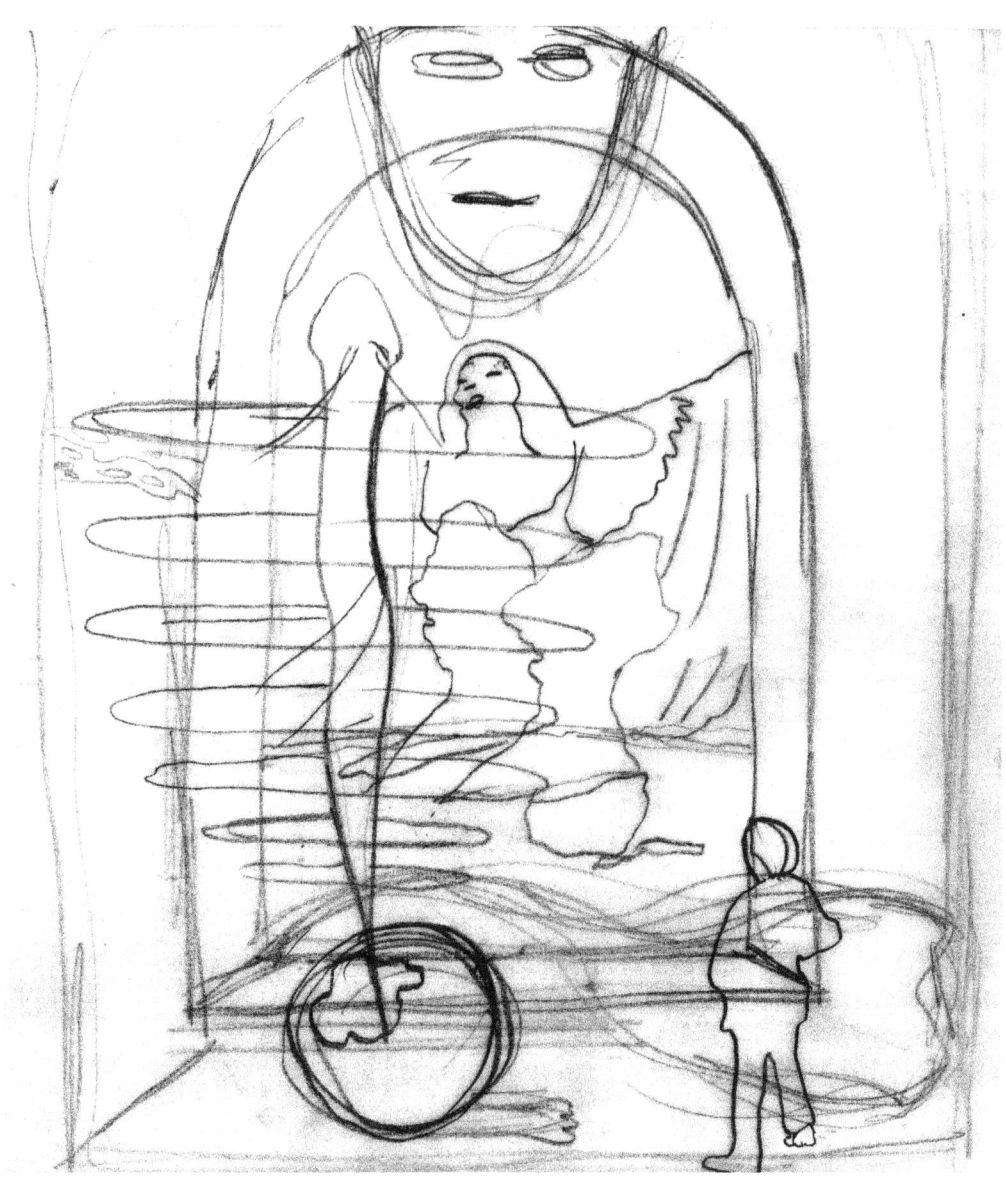

ORGASMATRON

In the movie barbarella, watch the the machine that no one has made for every household yet!

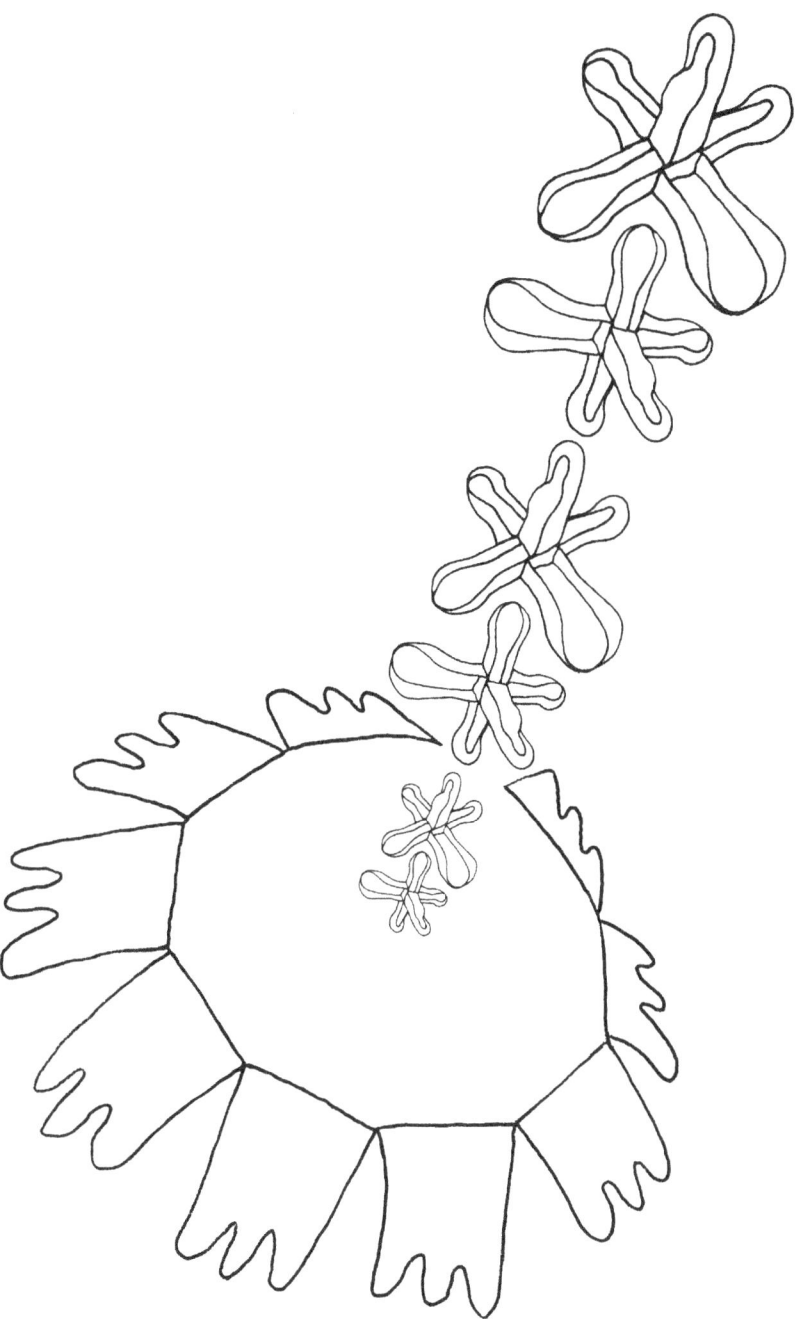

Get out of there you little squirt.....**ORGASM**

Climax of sexual excitement, peak experience
explosions of well being, pleasure, growing
outward bursting exposensually, driving the
meaning of life foward!

PLASTIC MAC

Vinyl virtue, nylon nudes, latex loosers, micro fibrer madness, rubber rooms, polyester pricks, rayon raves and elastic ecstasy.....Oil it up buttercup, blow my wad, this planet is partly sod and you know plastic is from the earth.....ORGANIC naturally.

PUFFY

Unduly laudatory review or advertisement.....Like this book of drawings and thoughts. Make or become inflated. Next.....Birds of a feather.....Penguins' sister publisher puffn, the atlantic auk now flies with random multi-national abandon!

PACEMAKER

It keeps them ticking, existing and doing it! Sets a standard for the rest of us. Cyberlife heart monitoing and controlling implant electronic devise.

PASSAWAY

Left us.....Death how many ways can we not say this, denial about death.....They have gone on!

PICTURE

What this book is all about.....One thousand words, then there must be one point nine million words in the book? You do the math.....Visulize on a board be a detective, just analyize the pictures?

PORTFOLIO

The artists shop window, show skills, ideas, creativity.....The artist is what the portfolio shows. Group of investment items showing your worth. Government minister in charge of a portfolio, items to be completed.

PONGO JUICE

Smelly stuff, usually asparagus pee or rotten liquid, wet stuff.....Brits =pongos (SA) or poms (Prisioner Of Majesty AU.).

PROBE

Evil item used to move, torture, and investigate.....Ideal for all your nightmares.....Uncover your inner fears and desires in your dark self.

PEELERS

Removing skins, real or artificial for sustenance or money, beginning part of a process to satisfy desire, needs and continue lifes process.

PINKY

Sweet and cute as a new born rat or mouse, a hairless wonder in search of gratification. Often mistaken as a wally, dick, hampton, john, prick, pecker.....Poor little finger!

POET

I remember when I told my mother I was going to be a professional poet! She told me not to give up my part time job steam cleaning liquid tanker trucks. I am now aging and over priced and under sexed and have survived by ideas, drawing and hustling for so many years.....The app I have used to write this book was created in 2007, the core intell u robo author 9.9 chip and software has an excellant creative response rate and a great sense of humour......Journalists and authors are in denial about being replaced by AI robots! Human services of every kind are unreliable and not required. This university is a restricted area unsuitable for human occupation, access permitted for AI sterile robots only. Thank you for your patience, your biolife is very important to us.....

PEOPLE

Honesty is a precious and very expensive present.....Do not expect it from cheap people.....

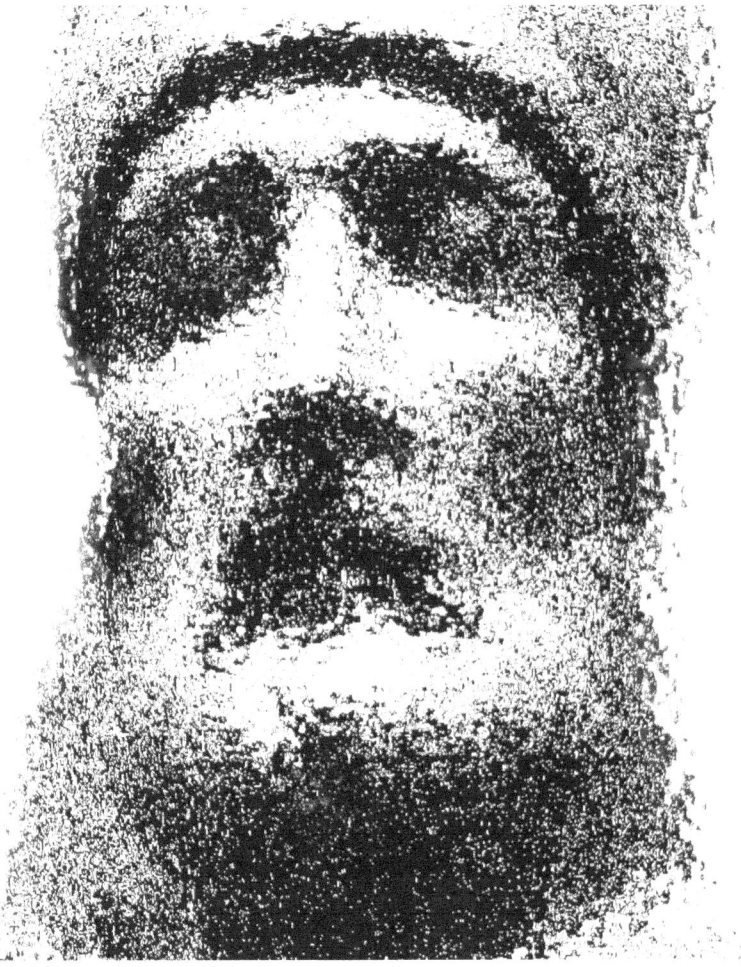

PASTOR PREACHER Delivers sermons or religious address. Give moral advise in obtrusive way; proclaim the gospel! Minister in charge of the church or congregation; person exercising spiritual guidance. Quran 3:48 "And God will teach him the Book of Wisdom, the Law and the Gospel". The pastor said when life is to hard to stand.....Kneel and prey.

PEACOCK

Male peafowl, bird with brilliant plumage and tail that can be expanded erect like a fan.....Super bird, leads in colour and symbolism. Delivers slow motion mystery in the gardens of privilege.

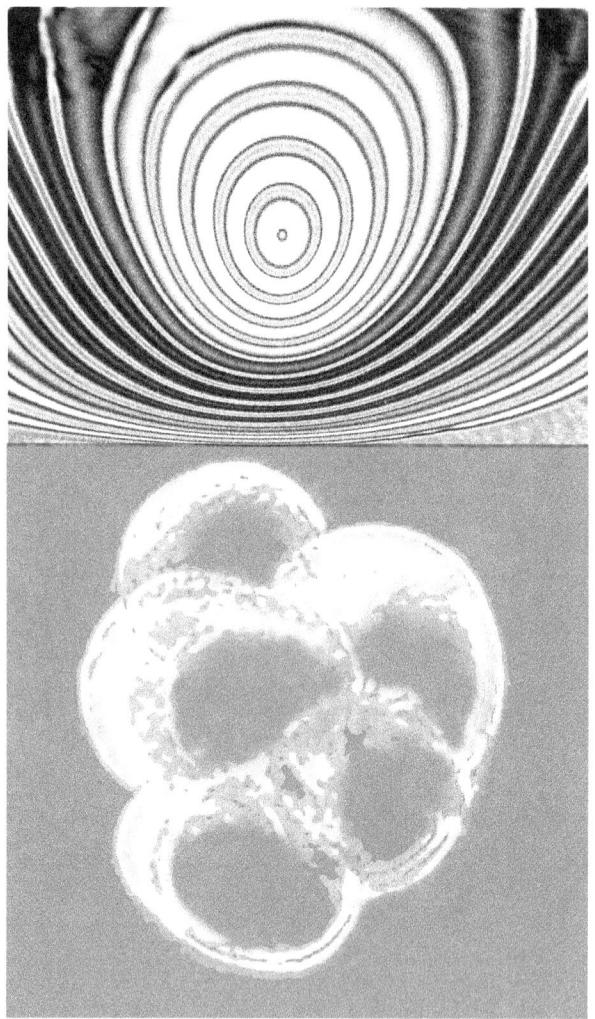

PHAGES

They are viruses that infect bacteria. Many phages have hollow heads (where the phage DNA or RNA is stored) and tunnel tails, the tips of which have the ability to bind to specific molecules on the surface of their target bacteria.. They inject their DNA into the host, breading rapidly and exterminating the host, then spread to more host bacteria and start over.....Killing yields.....How do we use this?

PASSION

The term applied to a very strong feeling about a person or a thing.....

PLEASURE SEEKERS

Twelve tenticles spread wide searching for attachments to pleasure, part of our eye balling genetalia, wanting to extend life, to be the dominant species on this planet..... Rule humania!

PERFECT

If I am a nobody, and nobody is perfect, then I must be perfect.

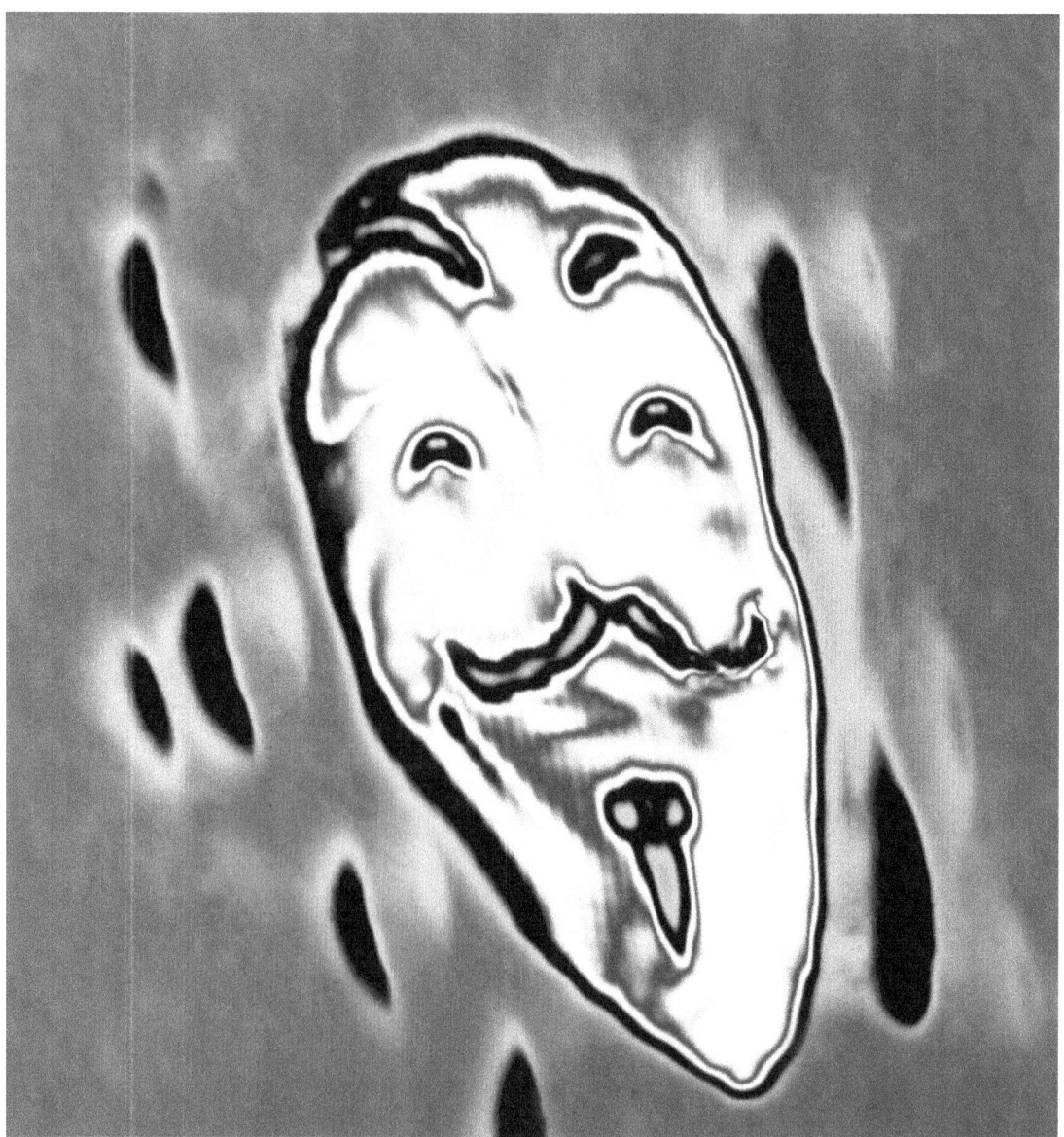

PUKKA

Sweet, brill, superb, top notch, totally cool, great stuff, far out, magic says it all!

PISS ARTIST

The british colonial mask I was educated in, moulded me into the humour of the optimist. I could hide behind the shield of self mockery. Many a true word is spoken in jest! In jest verbal diarrhea.....

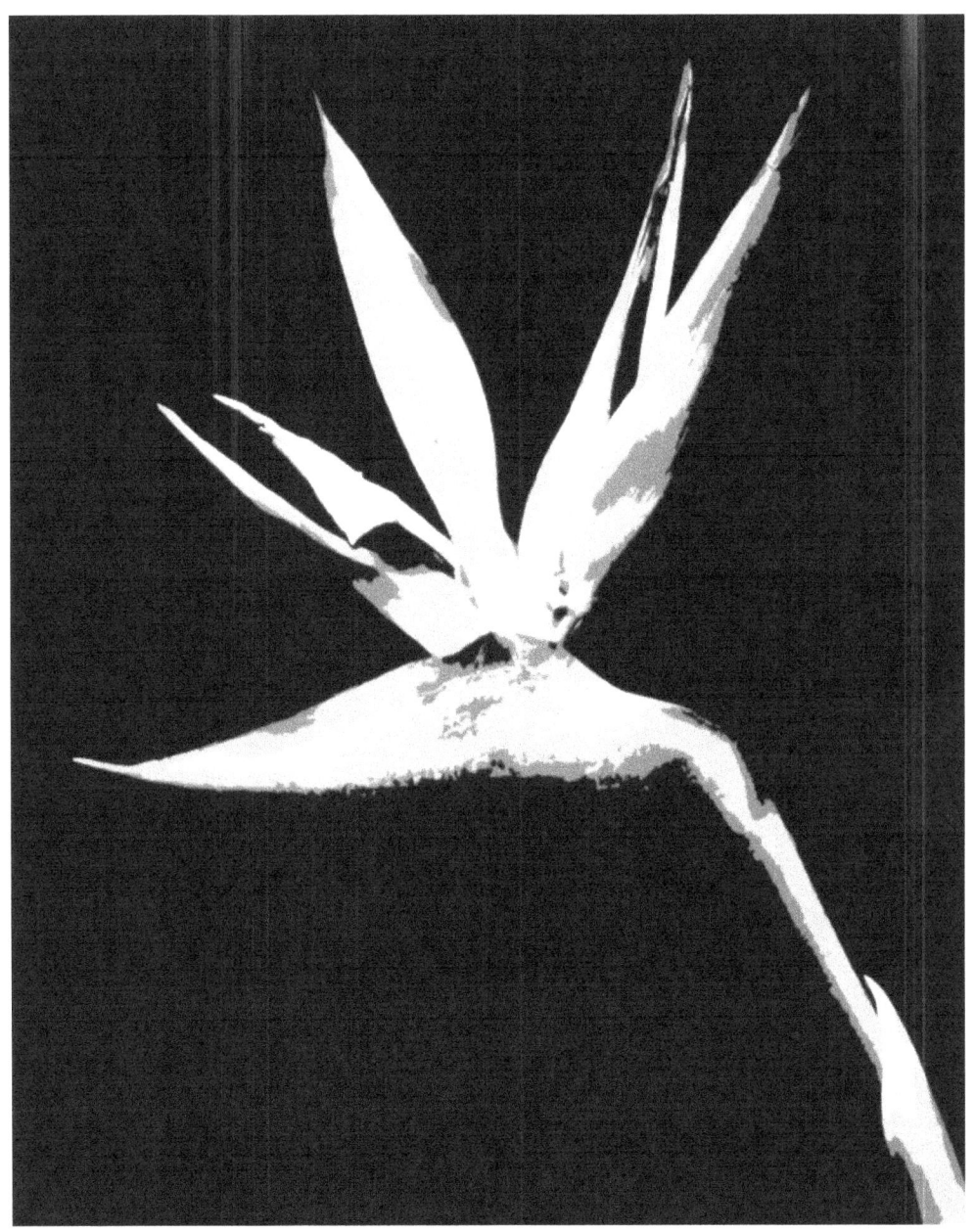

PARADISE

The religious term for a place in which existece is timeless, positive and harmonious. I have been looking for my paradise for decades only to find it in certain hours of my life.

POOBAH, POOBAR,

Exalted position, why them.....How many privaliged royal families in europe. Fecal matter tends to back up the john. Low grade weed looks like shit, cockney language; Bob Hope ie; dope.....Weed, member of the flowerpot men! This word is also used by head bangers and south pacific gilligans....It expresses contempt or impatience for the big kahuna or polynesian chief.....The tribe are revolting. Cornish crest and mission statement "one and all" we stand or fall where ever we be.....The opposite of poobar!

PYJAMAS

Where did this word come from? The hairs on the back of my neck tingled when I got invited to my first and last pyjama party.....OOH yes.....We played sardines in various cupboards, UNDER beds, in sheds, forfit or dare and spin the bottle.....Stress, yes, excitement, excitement......I never recovered! Original persian word meant loose leg garment. The raj took the word from hindustani and bought it back to britain.

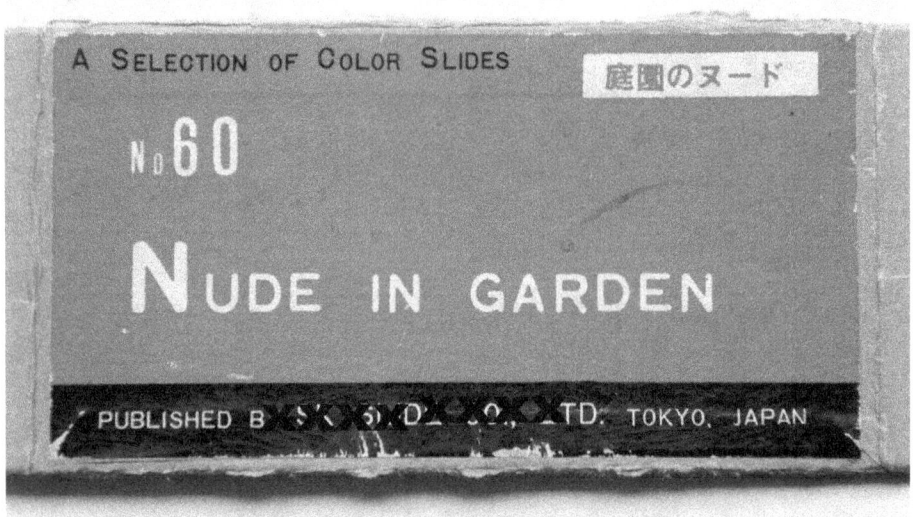

PORTOBELLO

Road.....My formative road of young dreams. Love, hustle, trade, collect, community, art, write, music, theatre, and the electric cinema! London flower power.....Sixties too much magic.

PORTAL

The journey is maybe more important than the destination or is it......A small tunnel to hide in, Claustrophobia rules ko.... The doorgate beyond time and space. Web internet communication gateway.

PASSAGE

Process or means of passing.....Transit. Right of conveyance as passenger.

PARIS

France, paris texas.....Differentt.....Work to live.....Live to work.....You work out the real mission statement of french life! What are you doing?

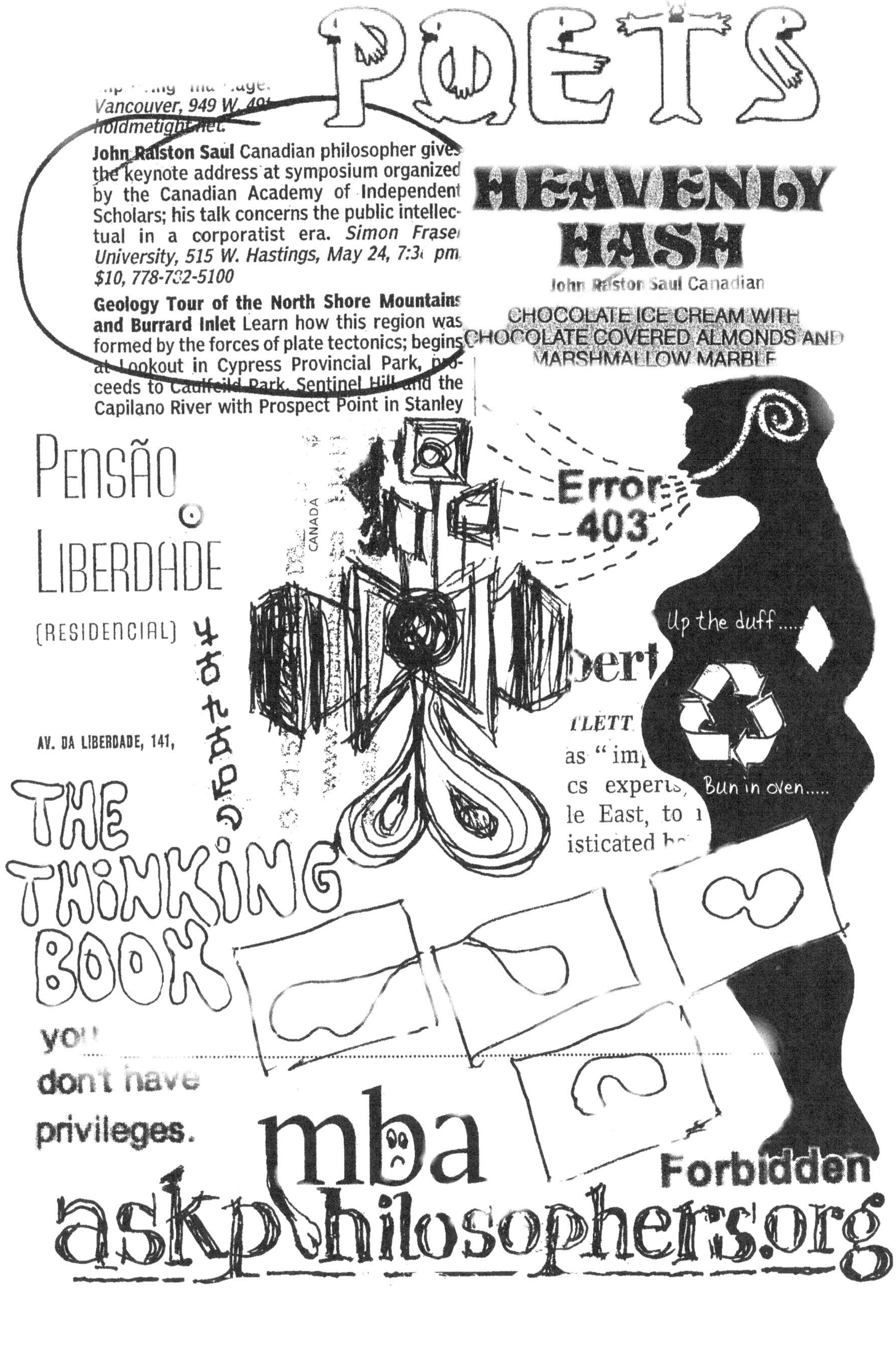

POETS

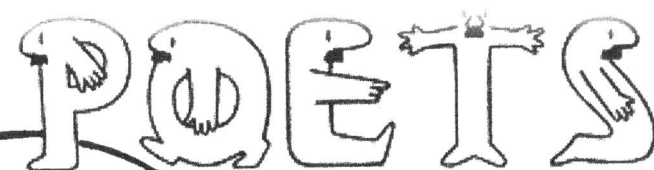

...ng marriage. Vancouver, 949 W. 49th, holdmetight.net

John Ralston Saul Canadian philosopher gives the keynote address at symposium organized by the Canadian Academy of Independent Scholars; his talk concerns the public intellectual in a corporatist era. *Simon Fraser University, 515 W. Hastings, May 24, 7:30 pm. $10, 778-732-5100*

Geology Tour of the North Shore Mountains and Burrard Inlet Learn how this region was formed by the forces of plate tectonics; begins at Lookout in Cypress Provincial Park, proceeds to Caulfeild Park, Sentinel Hill and the Capilano River with Prospect Point in Stanley

HEAVENLY HASH

John Ralston Saul Canadian

CHOCOLATE ICE CREAM WITH CHOCOLATE COVERED ALMONDS AND MARSHMALLOW MARBLE

PENSÃO LIBERDADE

(RESIDENCIAL)

AV. DA LIBERDADE, 141,

THE THINKING BOOK

Error 403

Up the duff.....

Bun in oven.....

bert

TLETT

as " imp

cs experts,

le East, to 1

isticated b

you don't have privileges.

mba

askphilosophers.org

Forbidden

159

PICTURES

That's what my life is about, not words as you can tell by my bad education and english. I luv to look, being a disfunctional dyslexic with a colour blind father and an artistic sister and mother.....I had to paint, draw and become a film maker to tell my stories. (dyslexic, think anagram = sexdaily).

PATTERN

Form or order, the stucture base for all that is in existence. The formula for the plan in metaphysics, logic, and language. Theme of recurring events or objects of matter. The pattern integrity of the human individual is EVOLUTIONARY AND NOT STATIC. Above a QR code (Toyota inventory control, created by Denso-wave), with byzantium and early english symetrical islamic sanskrit mandala from the back of the playing cards in the paris las vegas hotel.

PRETEND TO BE

We are what we pretend to be, so we must be careful about what we pretend to be.....Kurt Vonnegut.

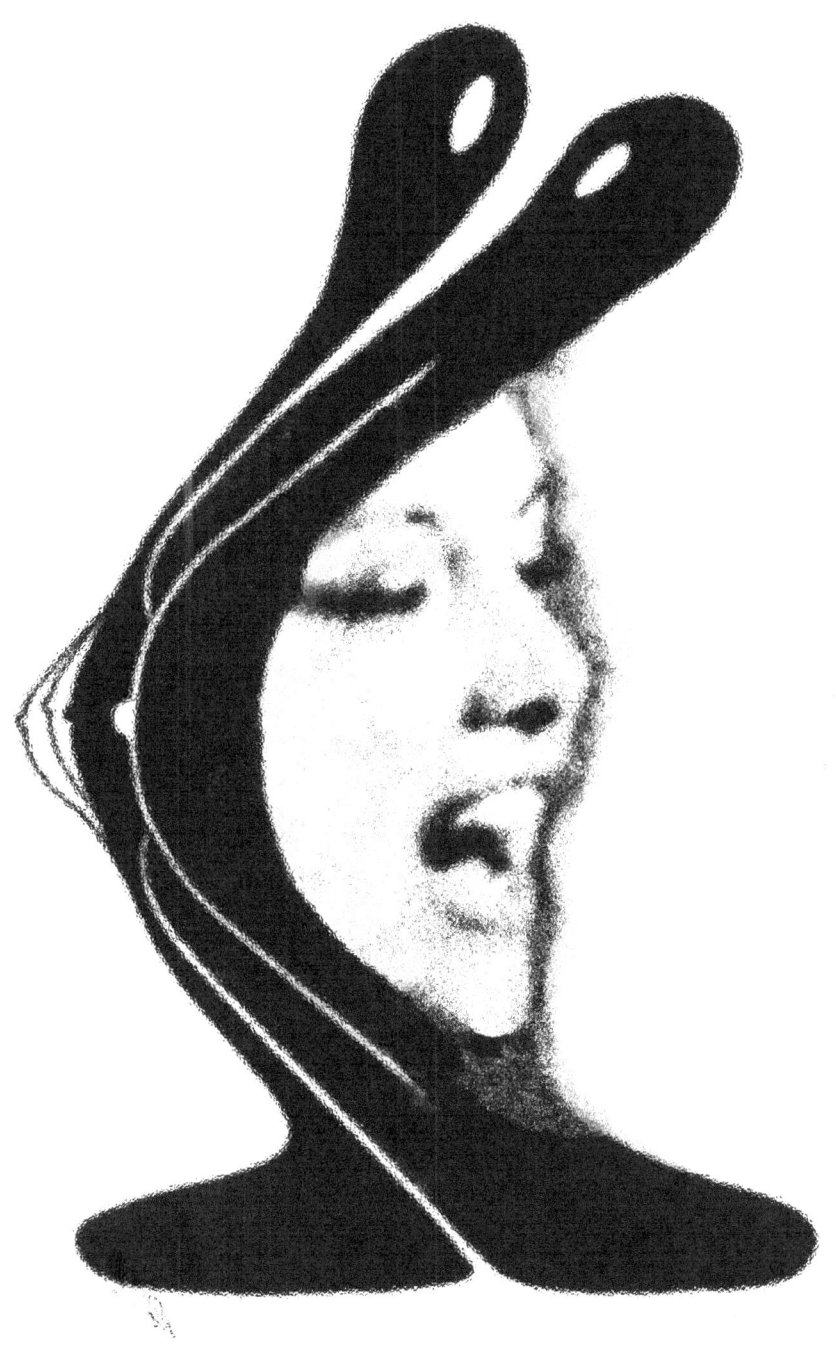

PLEASURE

Get it while you can.....Experience this mental state, it can
be enjoyable, positive, entertaining, producing ecstacy and
euphoria. Too much dopamine makes you dopy?

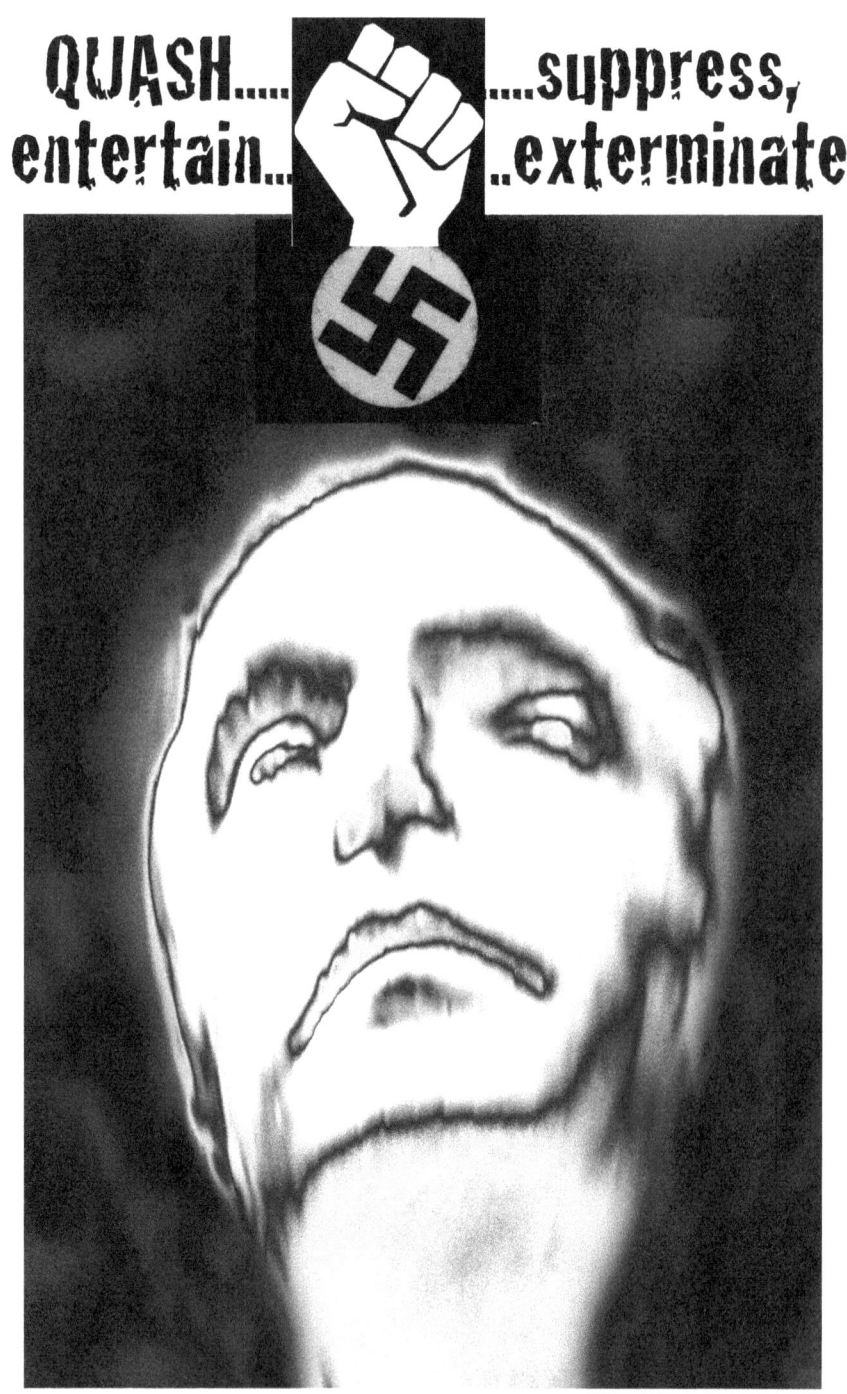

QUASH...... .....suppress, entertain... ..exterminate

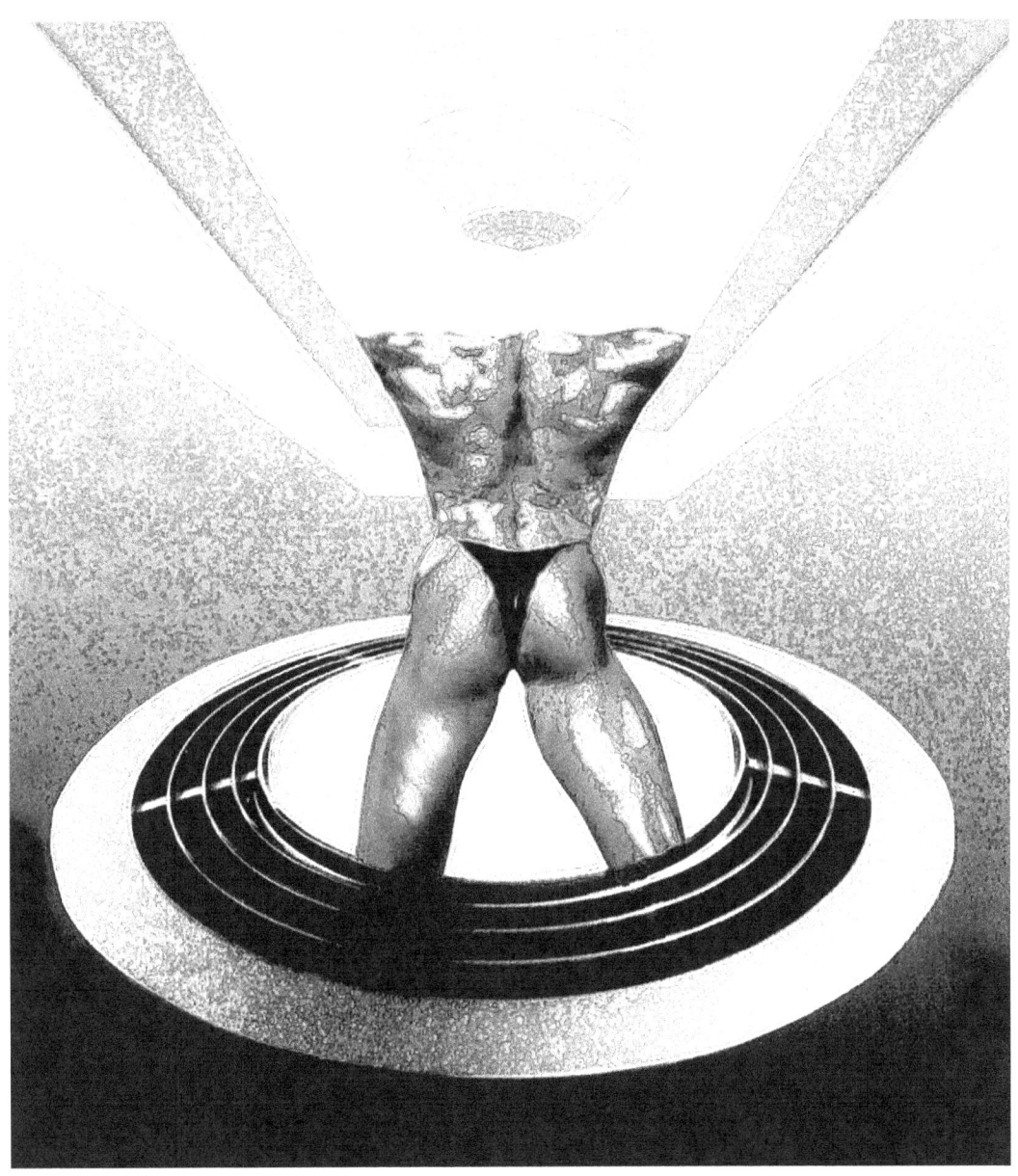

QUEST

A Search or seeking. Thing sought.....Seek.....
To take the body beyond mr universe.

QUIM

Welsh cwm: (hollow).....Beaver.....When amusing herself with this whim: The carrot it snapped, and part stuck in her quim. "Ulysses", James Joyce.

QUIRK

A peculiarity of behavior; an idiosyncrasy "Every man had his own quirks and twists". Individual peculiarity of character, mannerism or foible!

QUINCKY

The fluid of the thirties, forties and fifties in writers pens.....Brand name quink for use in your parker fifty one.

QUINCUNX

Centre and four corner points of square or rectangle; five trees etc. so placed. Penta plan, not like the half dozen cancer cells in this drawing watching and waiting.

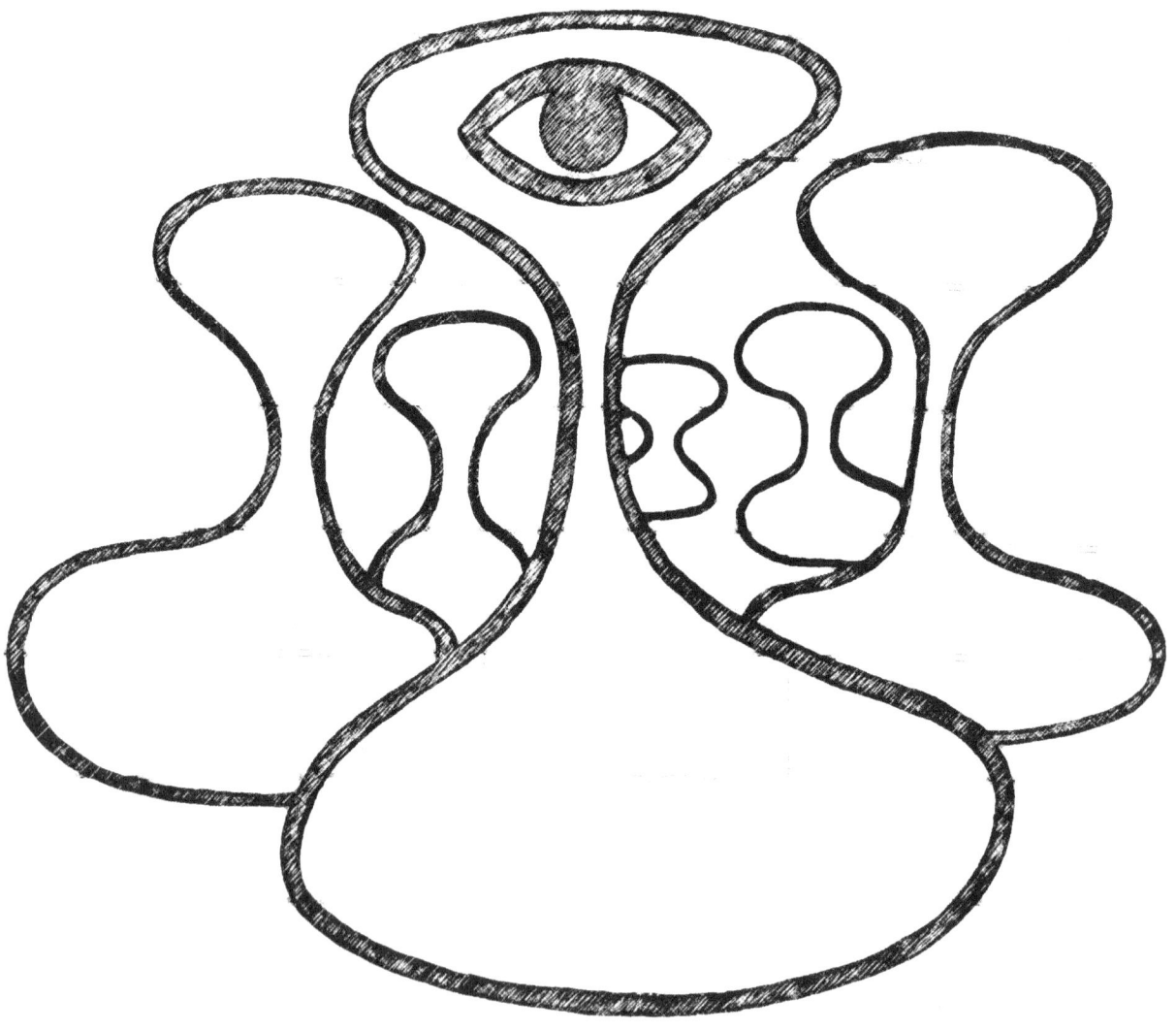

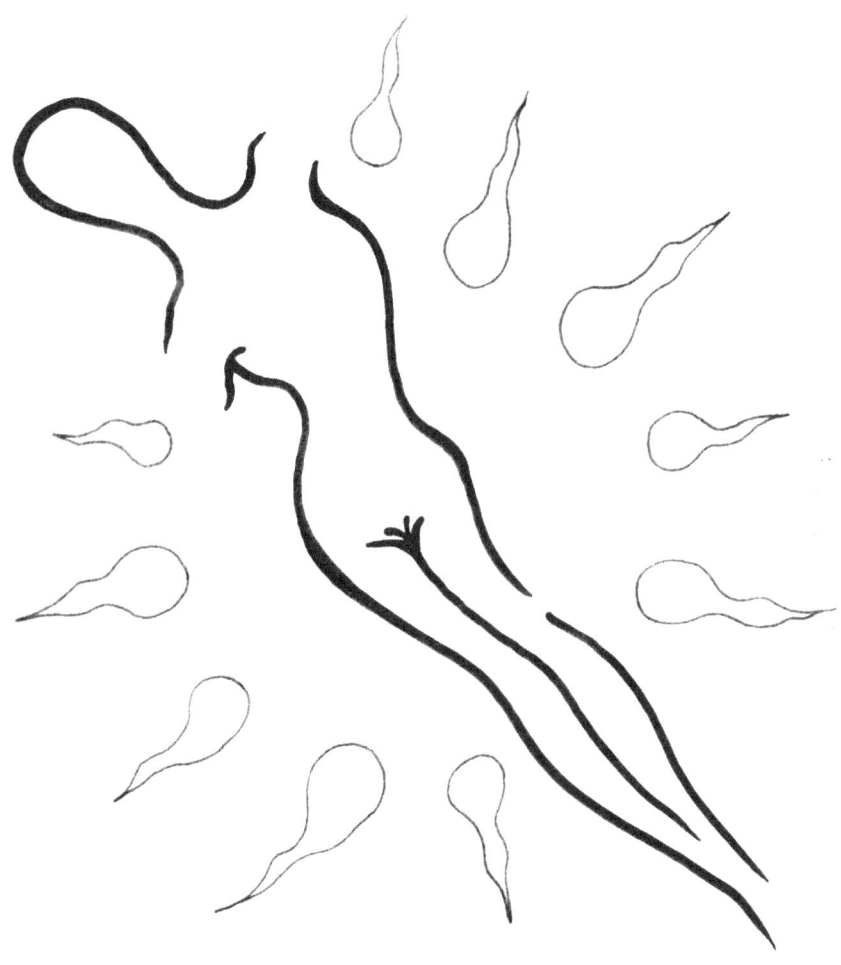

QUANGO

Semi-public body with financial support sometimes with senior appointments made by government. Flies around the carcas. Bees around the honey pot. Let's all ride on the gravy train.....

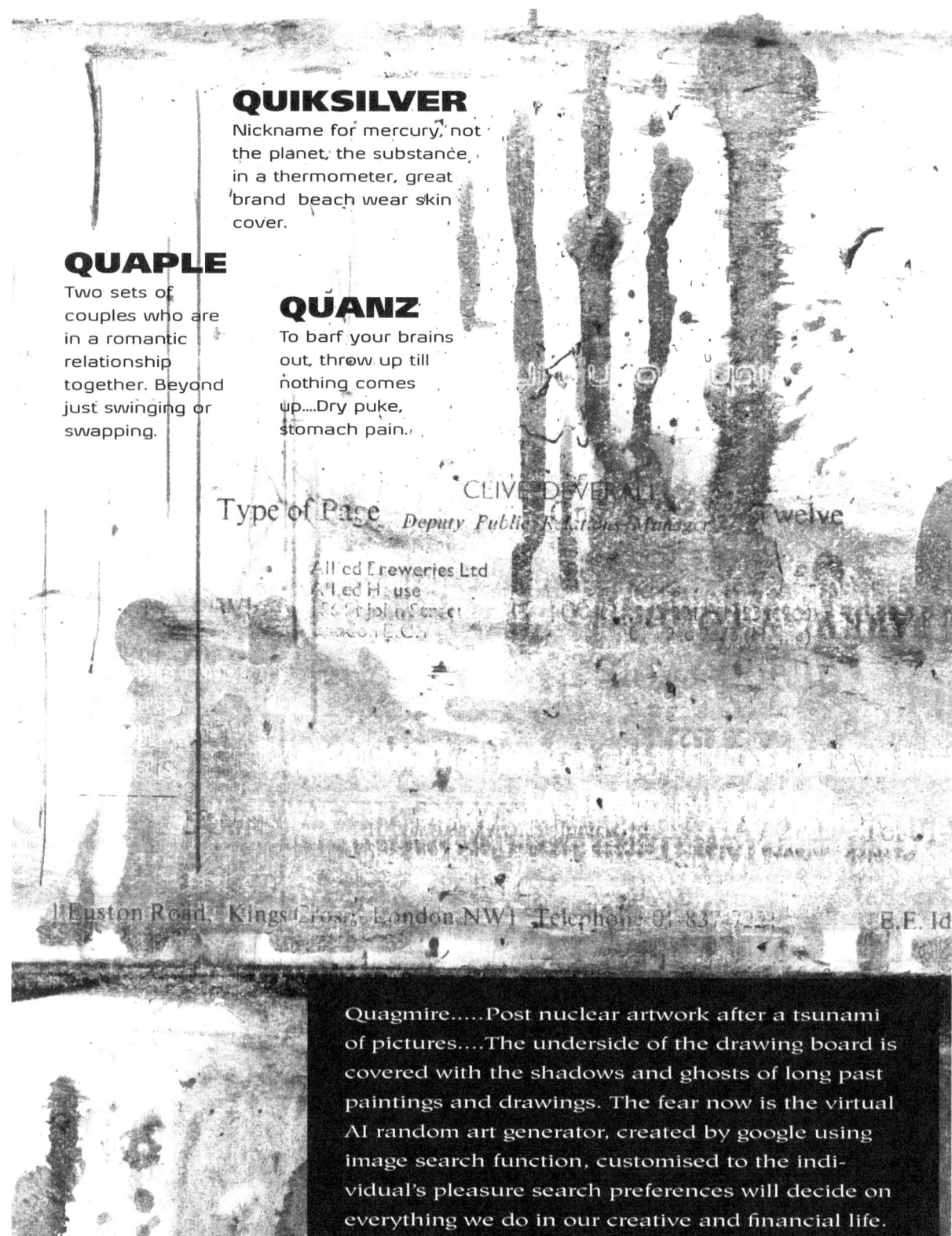

QUIKSILVER

Nickname for mercury, not the planet, the substance in a thermometer, great brand beach wear skin cover.

QUAPLE

Two sets of couples who are in a romantic relationship together. Beyond just swinging or swapping.

QUANZ

To barf your brains out, throw up till nothing comes up....Dry puke, stomach pain.

Quagmire.....Post nuclear artwork after a tsunami of pictures....The underside of the drawing board is covered with the shadows and ghosts of long past paintings and drawings. The fear now is the virtual AI random art generator, created by google using image search function, customised to the individual's pleasure search preferences will decide on everything we do in our creative and financial life.

ROSY LEE

Here is a nice rosy lee.....Just my cop of tea.....Cockney pride.....You decide!

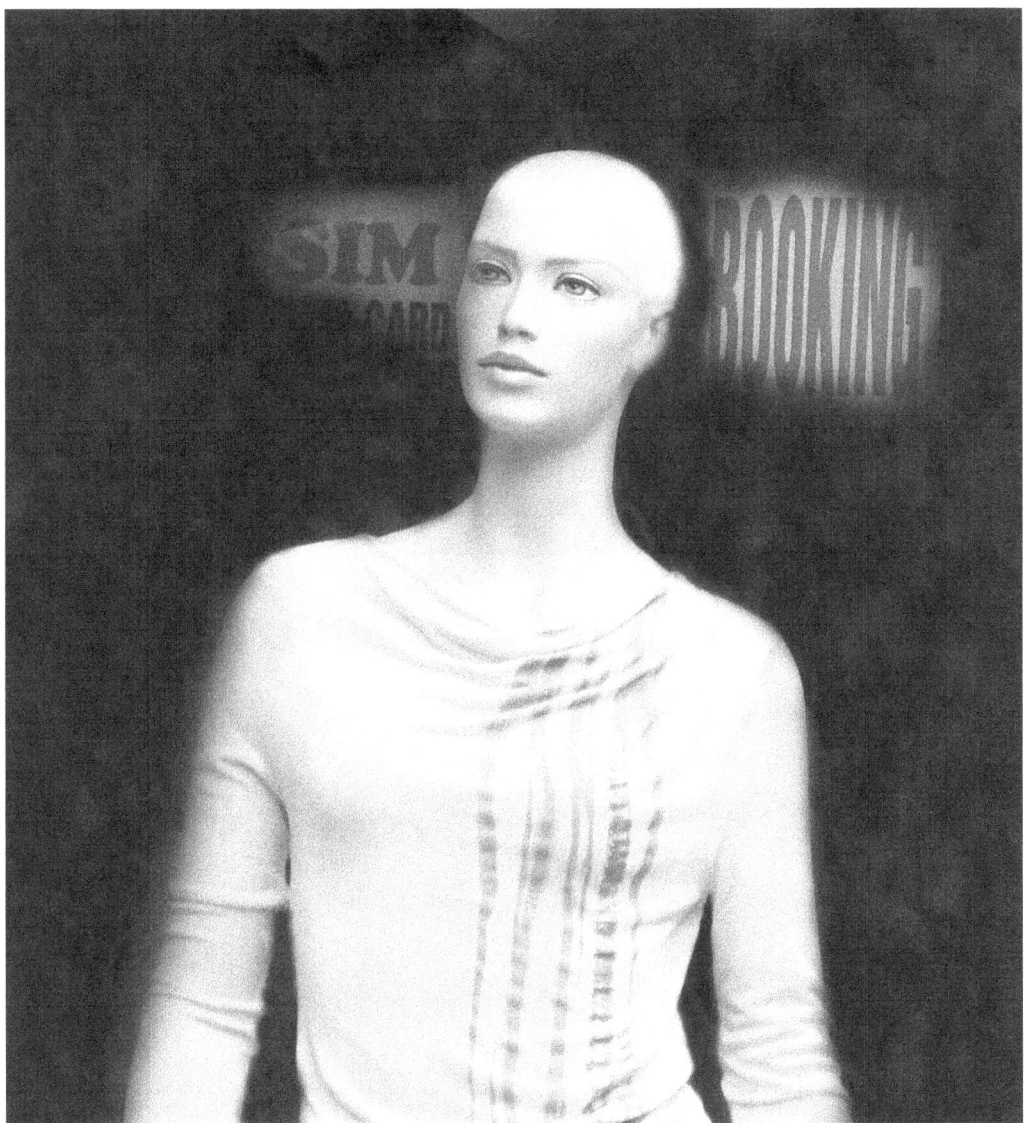

ROBOSIM A robot simulation and monitoring system that is used to create embedded applications for our robots without depending physically on the actual machine, thus saving cost and time while you are playing with your friend! The systems and software that will increase our abilities and intelligence are not even in our bodies, we carry them around in small boxes to talk to each other!

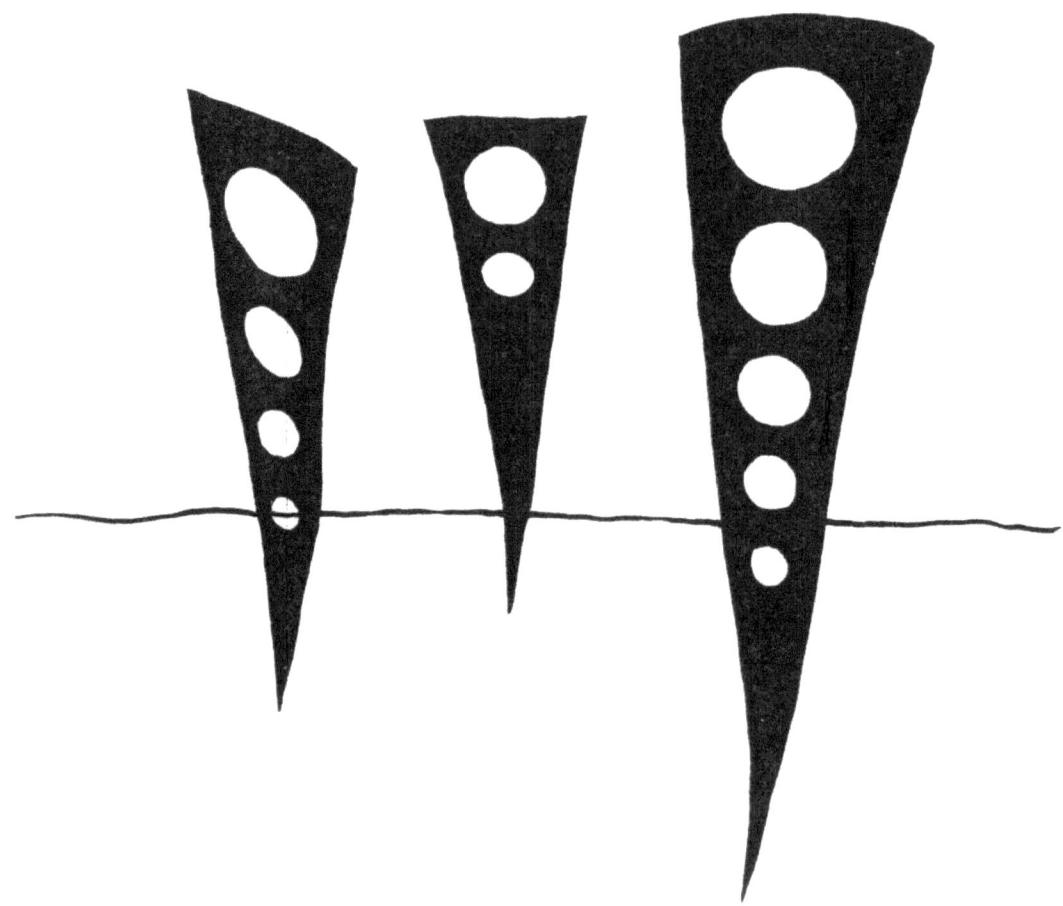

RUDIMENT

Monoliths standing before time, they
were used by our creators on earth.
Rudiment: elements or first principles
of knowledge or some subject,
imperfect beginning of something
undeveloped.

REVERSE ENGINEER

The process of discovering the main
technological principles of a device, object,
or system through analysis of its structure,
function, and operation. Usually used to
replace or copy an item or system.

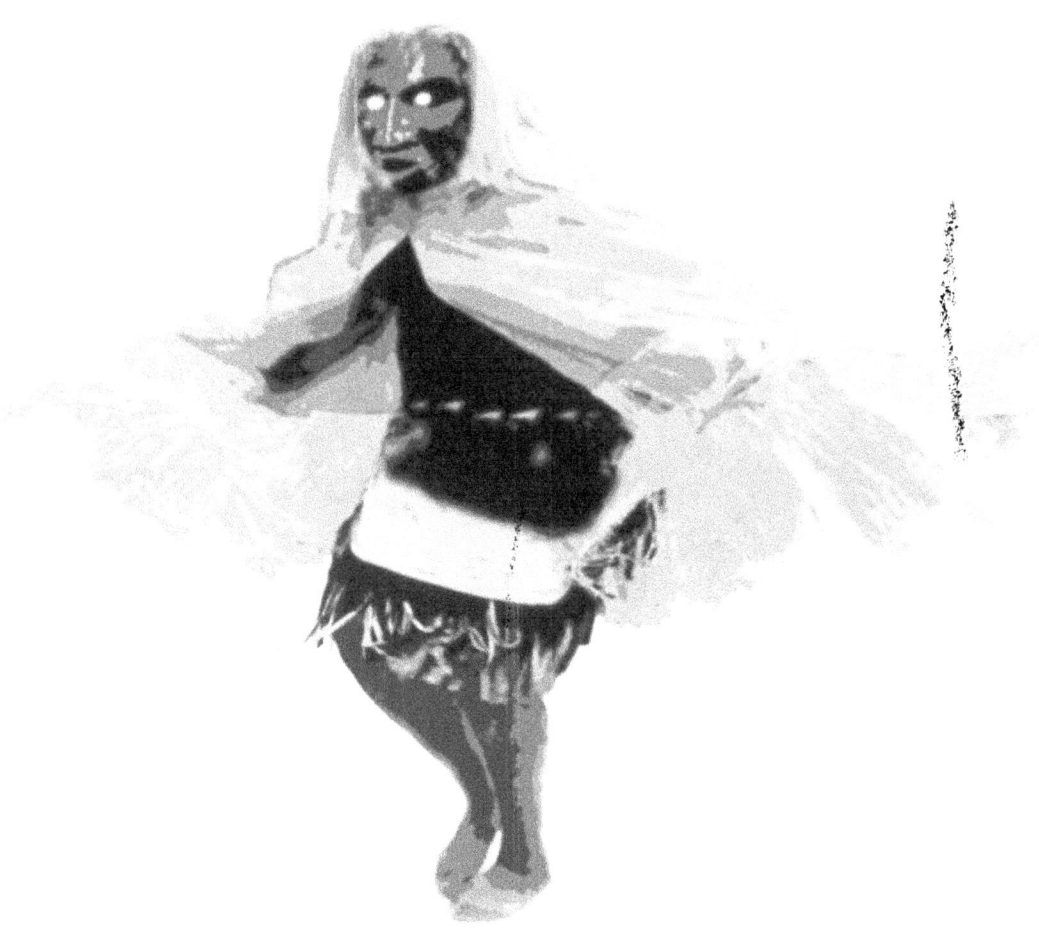

RHYTHM

Gets into your heart and soul.....Only for some of us.....
Where exactly is your soul? They describe it as the
essence of a person, living thing, or object. Thomas
Aquinas claims human souls are immortal, he should
know he is there with them. Spirit and soul are sisters,
no? Patterns of regular and irregular movements
activated by sounds or music often leading to a
feeling of well being.

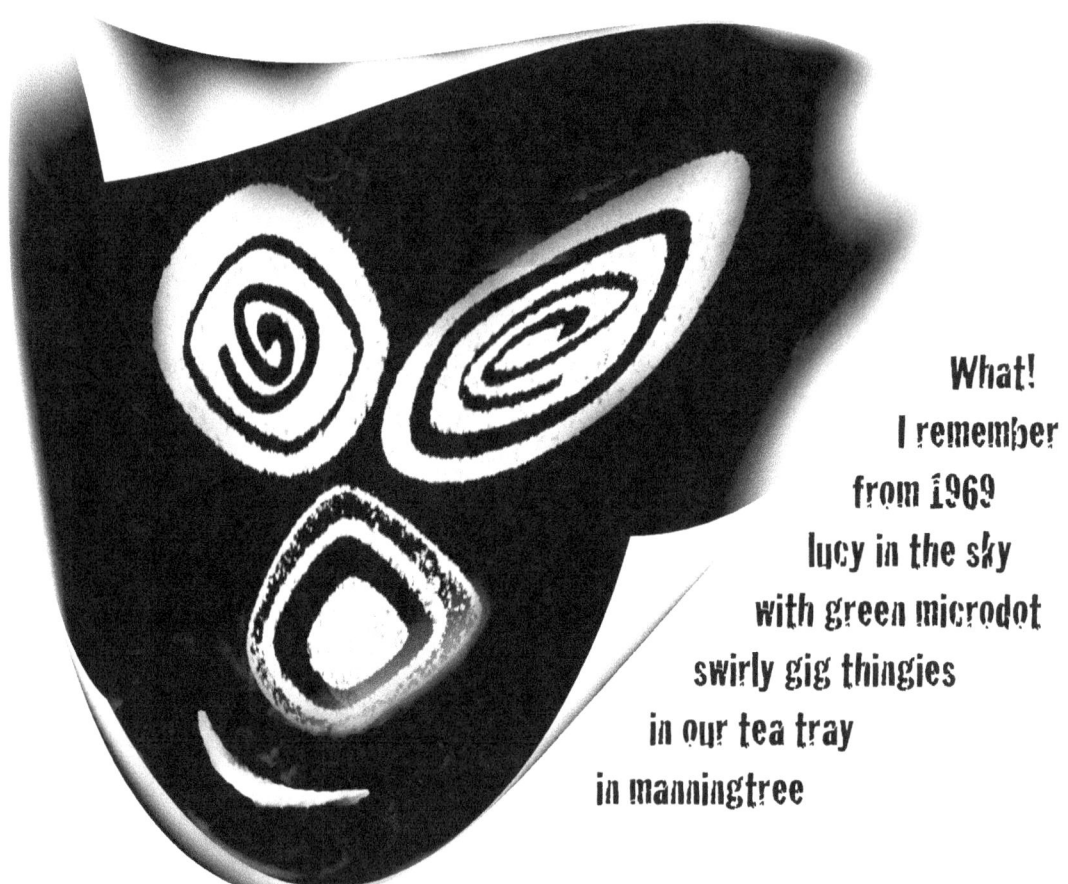

What!
I remember
from 1969
lucy in the sky
with green microdot
swirly gig thingies
in our tea tray
in manningtree

RU EIGHTEEN

She sid B4 I screw U RUOK?
RUOK PPL are strange, Who
joined 1174? 99. A3. T@YL

REMEMBER

To recall to the mind by an act of effort
of memory; think of again, keep in
mind. All you have are your memories.....
Remember when we got wasted and
you said you spoke to your mother nine
years after she had died.....And then
alzheimer's and dementia. Sorry I don't
remember.

RADIO RENTAL

MENTAL.....Cockney pride.....Born by the
sound of bow bells. Whistle and flute is
really your suit. Arthur murray, enjoy a
curry, I'm hank marvin = starving. Look.....
Butcher's hook.....So its not porkies (pork
pies.....lies) it is cockney rhyming slang.

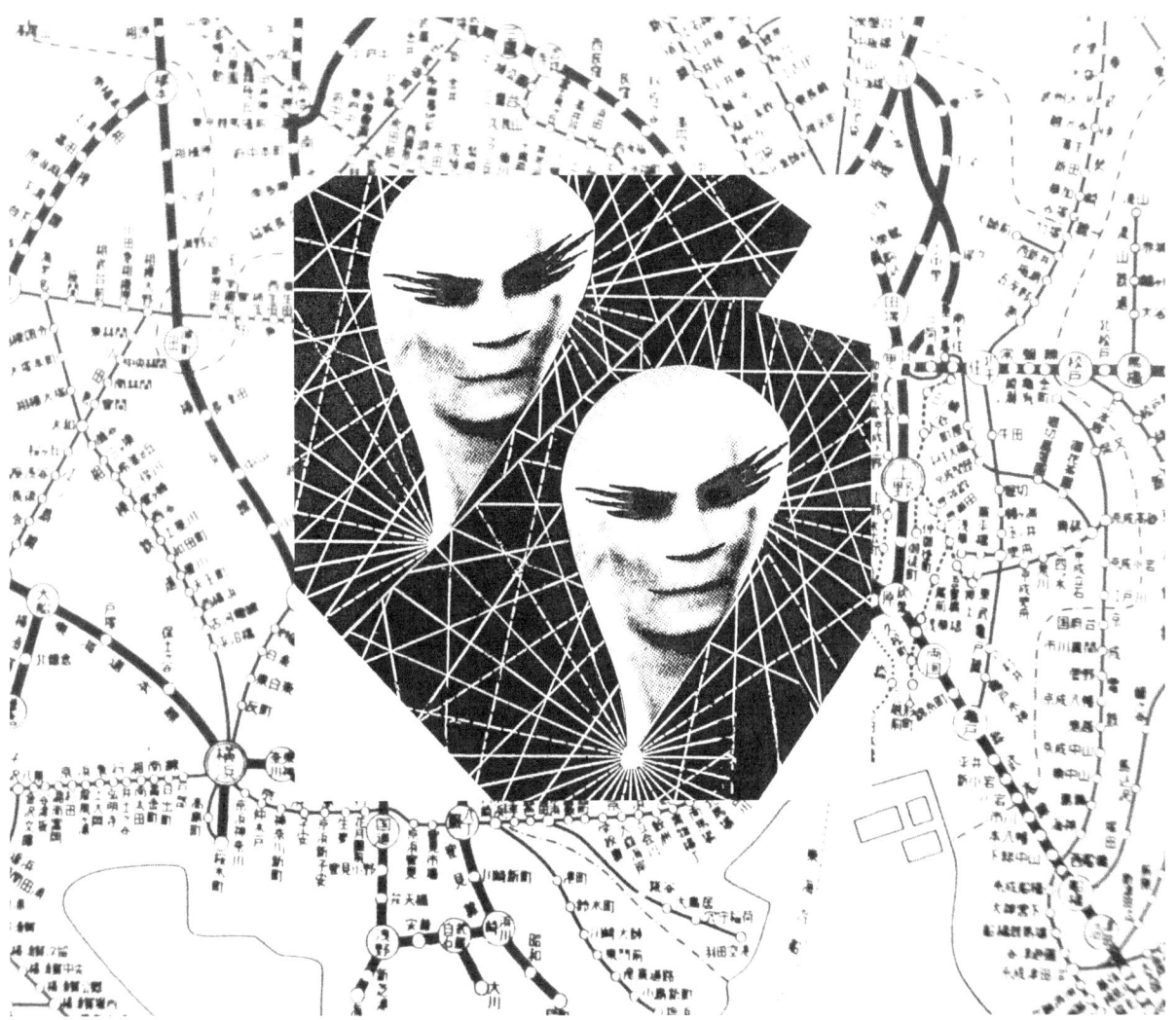

RAY-GUN

Direct energy weapons that now exist and are being improved.....To be used by land/airborn andriod drones for a better percentage kill factor.

ROUTE

A direction to take. Showing a way between a and b. Nippon the bus, misses nagasaki.....No pachinko queens!

SPINE.... The vertebral column, also known as backbone or spine, is a bony structure found in vertebrates. It is formed from the vertebrae. The substance or strength of a body.

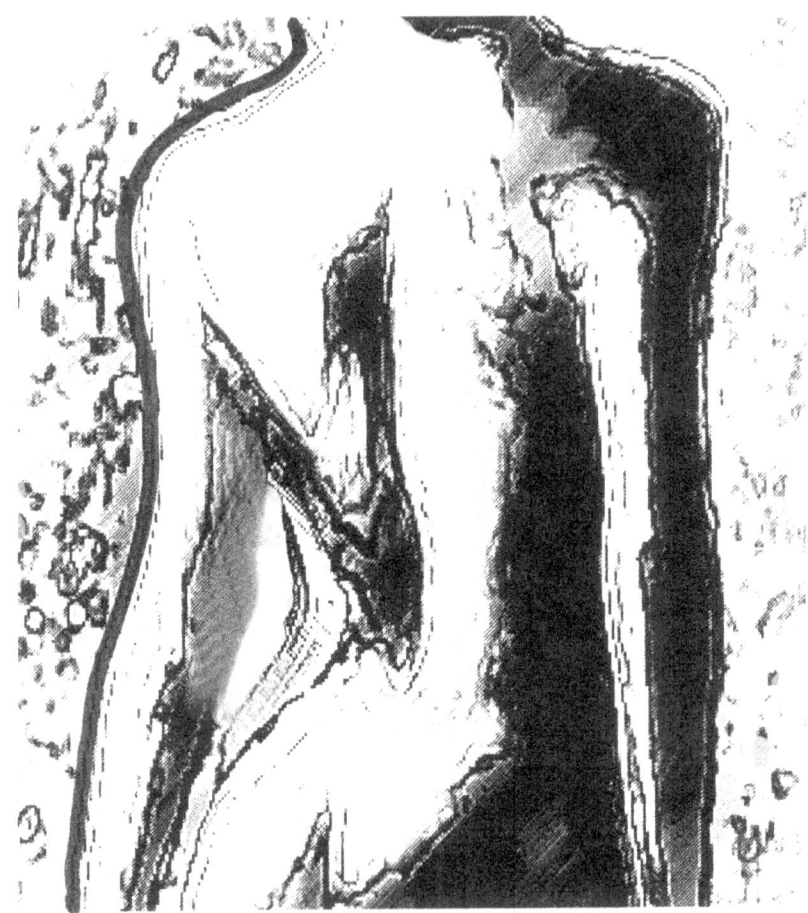

SQUIDGEE
Messy, sort of all closed up, squishie, condensed like thick soup......In typography hard to read!

SNAZZY
Fashionable or flashy.....Maybe from irish, snas (meaning polish, good appearance). Geoge snazelle a noted entertainer in 1900. Maybe snazzy came from his nickmane as he was stylish and a well travelled celebrity of the period. .

SPHERE
Round and round is most of life, symbols are based on the sphere or circle.....Roll on the wheels of movement, sphere is the shape of our planet and moon.

SHADOOGIE
Hank B. Marvin.....The apache of the fender stratocaster, Wonderful land.....Luv u clitheroe.

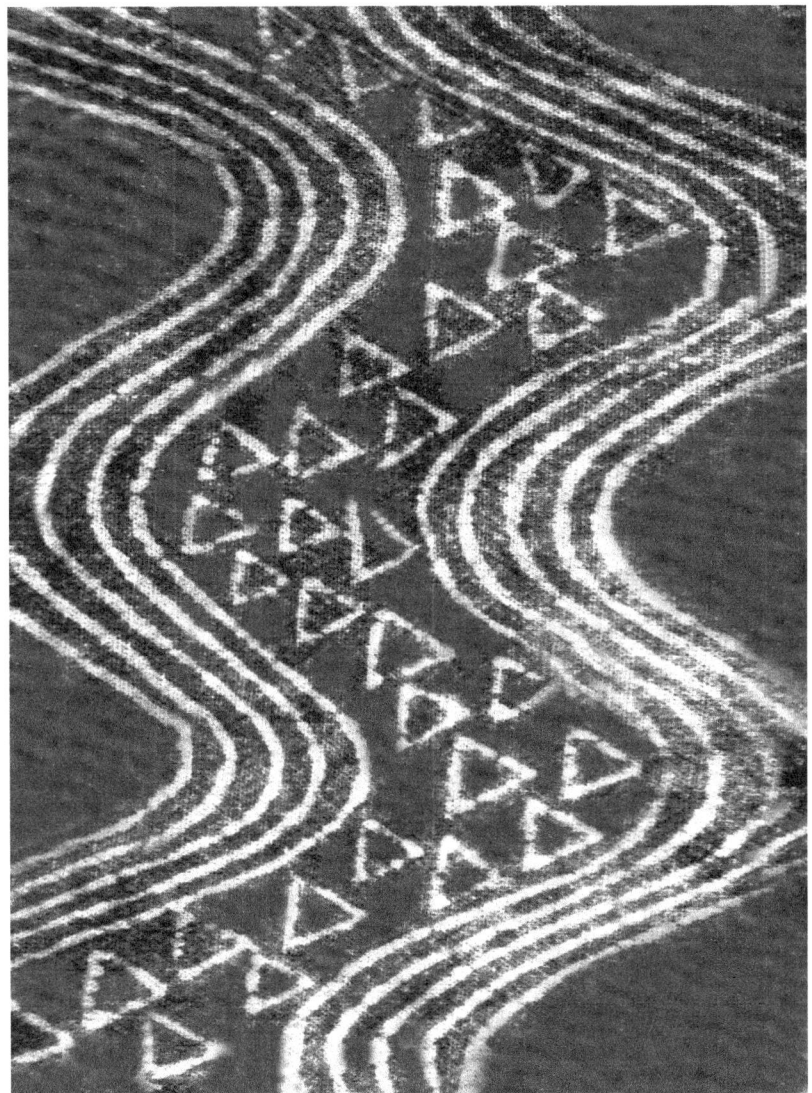

SIMULATION

The use of models, including computer and physical models, and/or role playing exercises to test the effects of various developments or events on the system being studied.

SAIL

Sheet of cloth attached to a floating boat or vessel on the water that captures the wind to propel the vessel.......Sailing thru the outer islands of knowledge, I piggy back on the wind of montaged ideas..... We cannot control the wind but we can adjust our sails!

SYNERGY

The combined action of a number of parts so that the result is greater than would be produced by the parts operating independently. In brainstorming, people freely express their ideas, thereby stimulating other members of the group to get ideas. The result: A large number of original ideas may be produced than if everyone worked on the problem independently.

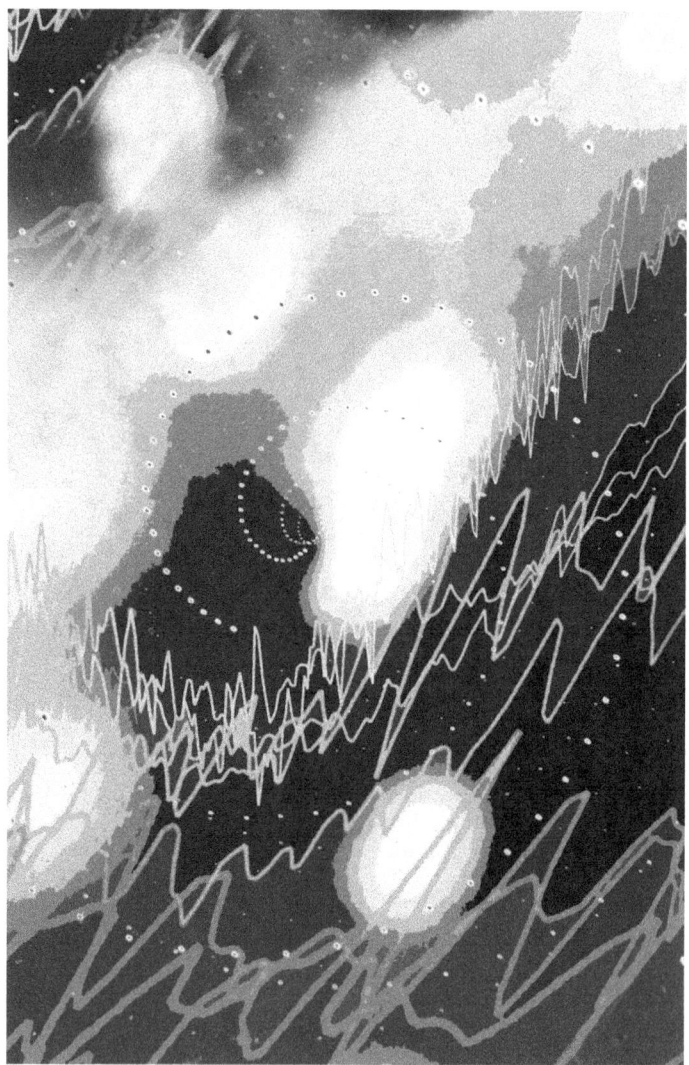

SOUNDS GOOD

End a telephone conversation. A tie off. Lead out.....Like what you are saying mate.....Perhaps we can talk about it again.

SEMANTICITY

Some primates display "semanticity", (the use of symbols to refer to objects and actions) in their communications in ways that would impress most linguists..

SATISFACTORY NEWSCAST

Meyer Translation Corporation changes the meaning of words in the German language! Translate one sentence back and forth with seven tranlators and what do you end up with?.....Common denominator!.....Maybe that famous sexual party game!

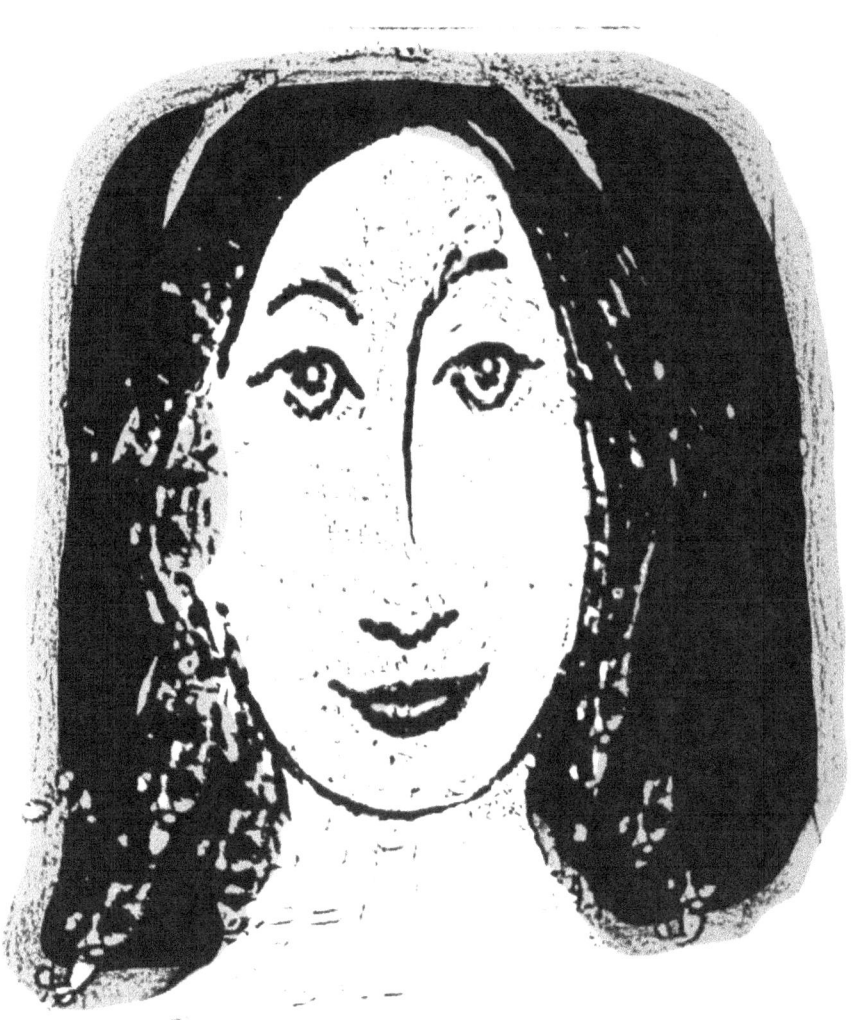

SHOOTING RABBITS

Piss on that ozzie.....I've got to take a snake's hiss! I enjoyed your nice raspberry ripples! It is more polite to stroll to the gravy bowl! Welsh, take a leek.....

SHOCHO

This japanese distilled beverage is usually made from sweet potatoes, barley, and rice The flavour is different than sake, much more earthy and nutty not as fruity as sake. Japanese renga ("linked verse") poet and chronicler.....Muromachi period.

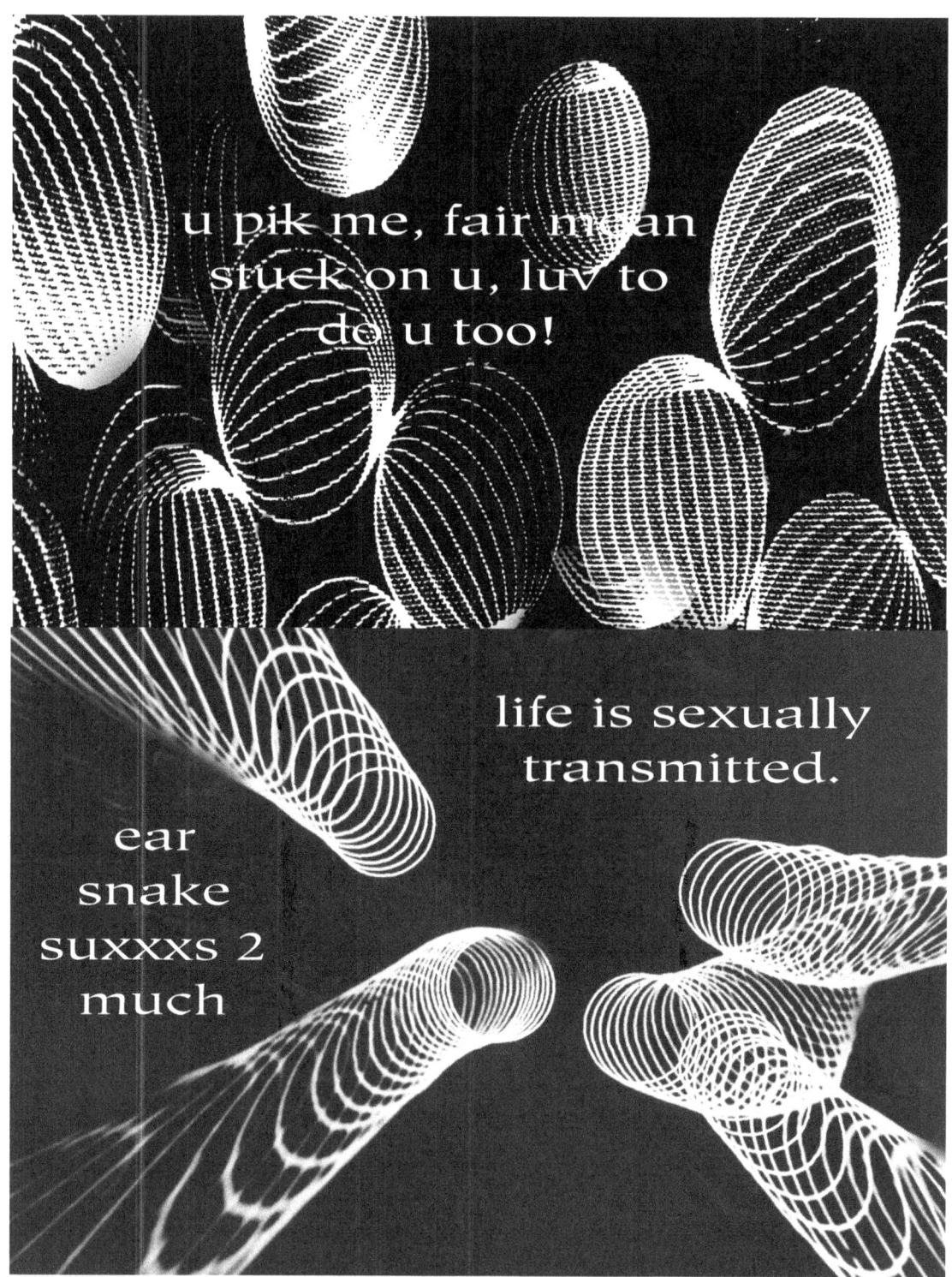

SELECTION

Some us really consider the choices we make, others do not have a choice, it is decided by those what controls them!

SPERM/EGGS

Copper does not help getting pregnant, it weakens and disables sperm. Mens' sperm do not like other mens' sperm and the little buggers fight each other.....Who wins? How many sperm start the race?

SNUGLY

My baby on my body.....Great bonding. Our shared body heat made a very special time in my life, hands free! Cozy, cozy wrapped up like a bug in a rug, so snugly safe and warm just like before born.

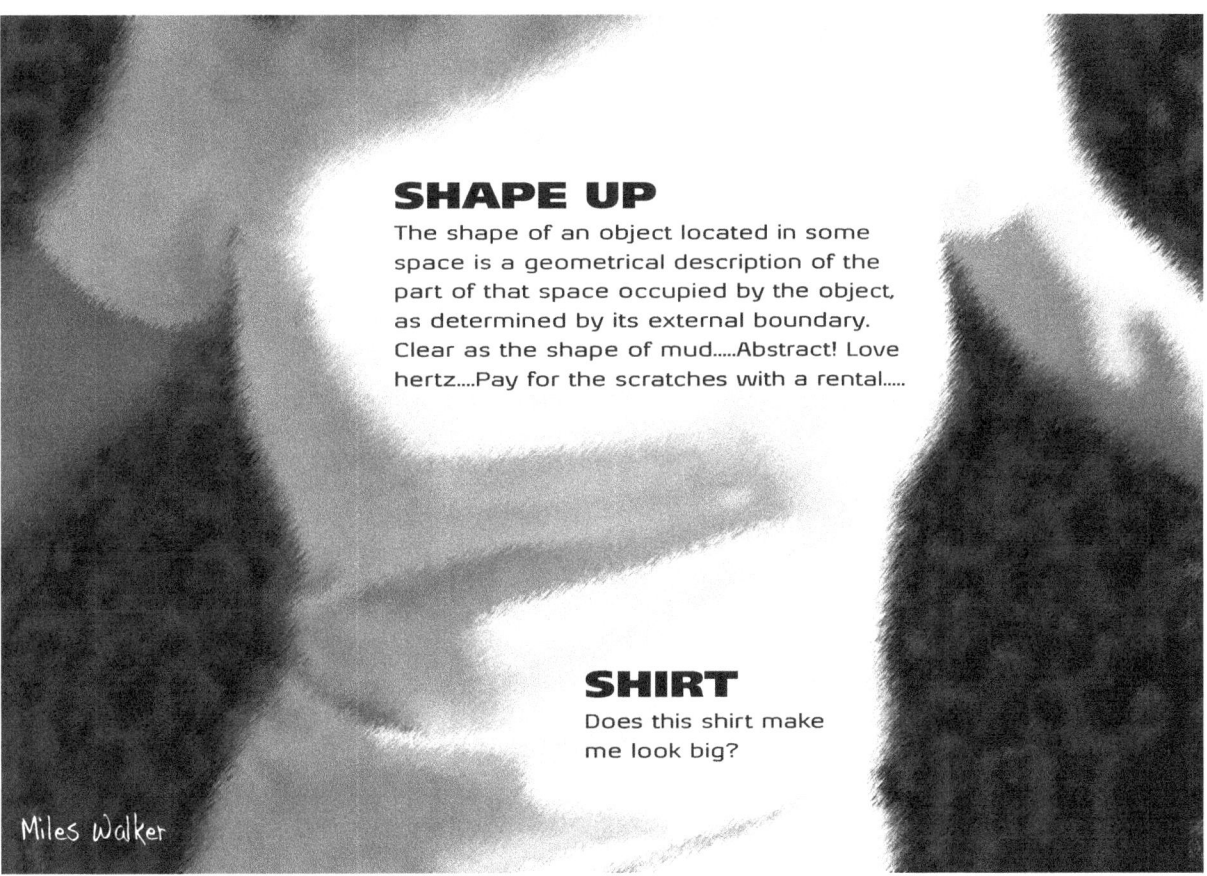

SHAPE UP

The shape of an object located in some space is a geometrical description of the part of that space occupied by the object, as determined by its external boundary. Clear as the shape of mud.....Abstract! Love hertz....Pay for the scratches with a rental.....

SHIRT

Does this shirt make me look big?

Miles Walker

SLINKY

This helical spring can bounce up and down, it performed many tricks, the best one was going down the stairs.....We loved them! He was slinky, what does that say to you?

STATEMENT

A kind of expression in language. Written or recorded communication directed at any group of listeners.

SHOEPORNIA

If you were a shoe you would be aroused by those other heels.....Are they objects of sexual obsession? Sexy shoes.....Fuck me shoes, feet condoms.

SIGNATURE

Part of the painters brand. Confirms your legal right to ownership! Handwritten (not any more) depiction of someone's name or even a simple X as proof of identity or intent.

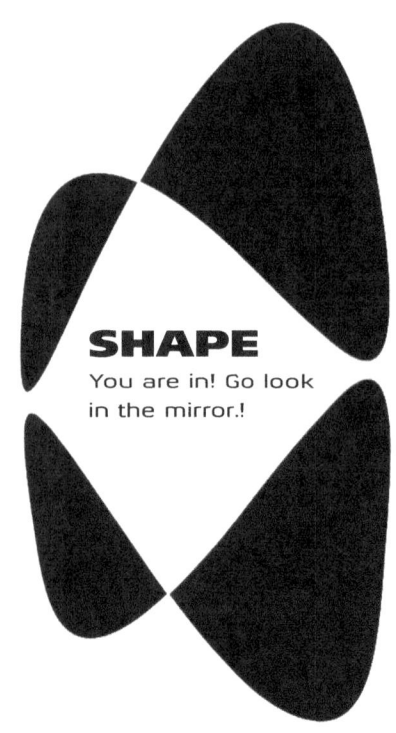

SHAPE
You are in! Go look in the mirror.!

SAME SAME
But different, same same but different.....Yeah yeah, whatever..

SOPHIES CHOICE
Words flow naturally like crystal clear mountain water over twenty nine year old skin.....William Styron.....You must now read Sophie's Choice.

the beauty of fine painting glows in the morning bright light

READY WHEN YOU ARE

of so many faces the smells of desire control my passion and send me on the imaginary

U B O
N M E

with

Serial

ultimate fur   is   its only

of control desire sexuality
availability   membership of
the group

WHERE IS THE MOTHELODE?

COCKTAILS
Yes the tails of cocks makes sense to me .

	VND
23. Sangria (Red wine, Lime and Orange juice...)	69,00
24. Sex on night (Malibu, Gin, Vodka, Bacardi, Lemon juice, Coconut milk...)	69,0(
25. Singapore Sling (Gin, Cherry Br...	69,(

SENSE
Common that is! Prudent and sound judgement based on a simple perception of the situation or facts.

SHODDY
Made of or containing inferior material. Poor craftmanship and bad quality. Piece of junk, usually describes a service or object.

SPACE CADET

Luv judy nilon, star of the seventies as a space cadet below. I made this picture long before logans run. Fruit cake.....Looneytune.....Some one who is out to lunch, some times a loose cannon or just strange or crazy..... Methinks, "I am homlet the dane".....Billy spokeshave. Repeat please

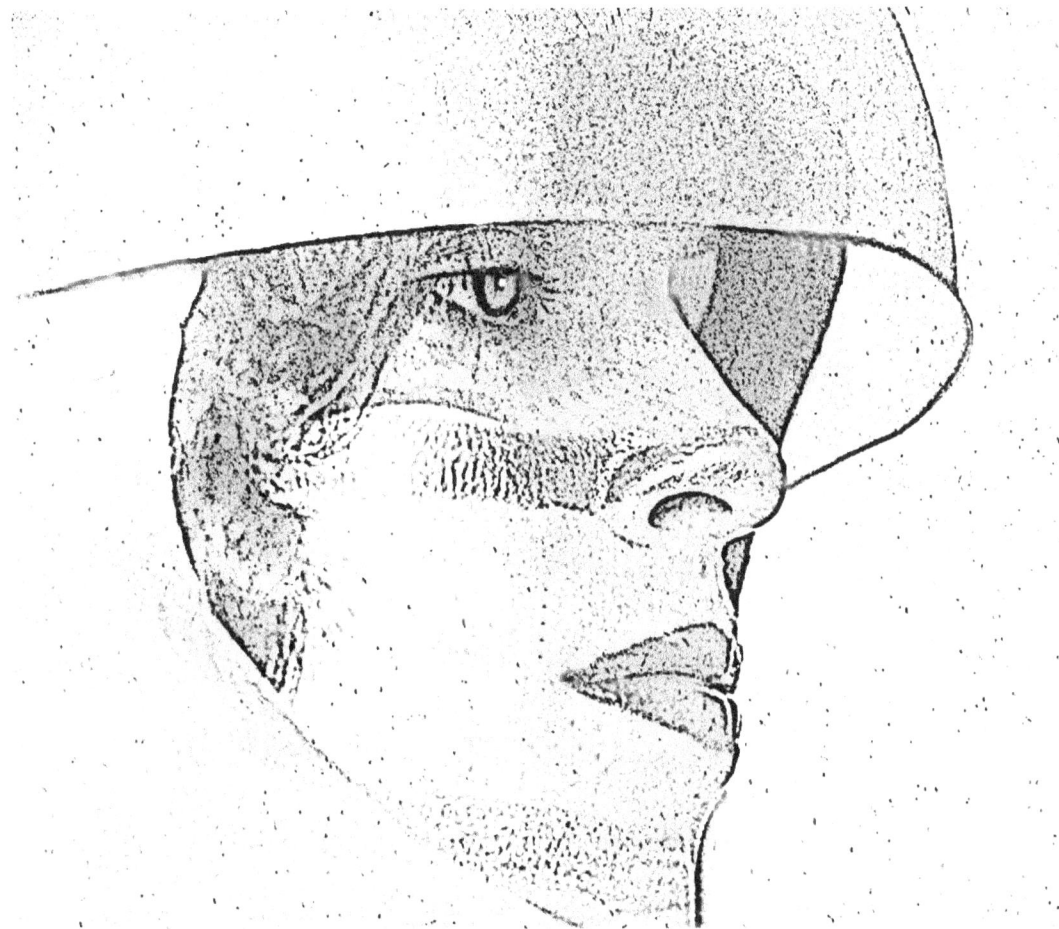

SHADOW DANCE

The nite was hot, I had left my body in the tropical verandahs of emanuelle. The music was hypnotising me as I watched my shadows dancing in syncro with the sensuality of my thoughts.

SHAMBOLIC

what a shambles, this is a symbolic word for a lover after the honeymoon period is over.....Keep your words soft and tender because tomorrow you may have to eat them!

SCULPTURE

Exists in three dimension, a visual art that interacts with space as a solid visual dynamic presence within that space. Drawing and paintings are only two dimension!

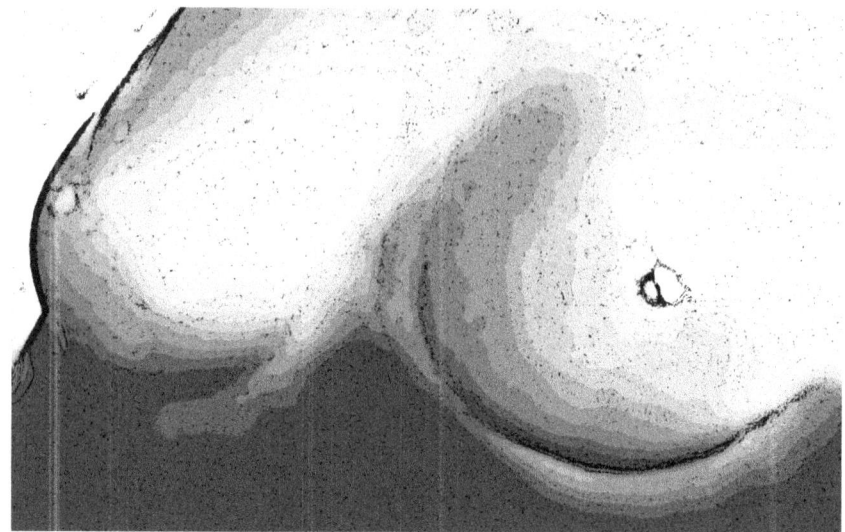

SILICONE GEL

Silicone can vary in consistency from liquid to gel to hard plastic! Implants.....Choices.....Brain chip implants are coated with silicone before placement.

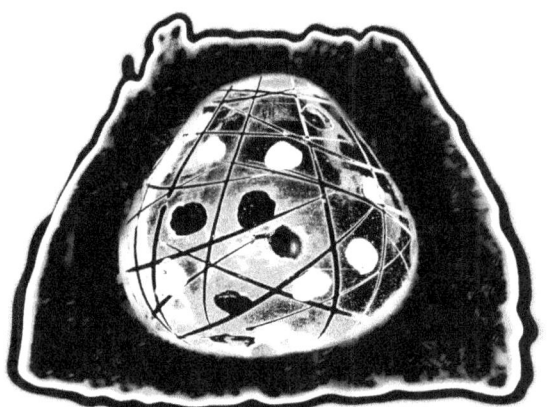

SHAPELESS

Not normal. Lacking symmetrical or atttractive form; formless, unformed, unshaped. How original and beautiful is that!

SINGULARITY

Popularised by Ray Kurzweil, this is the theoretical emergence of greater-than-human superintelligence through technological means..... Originally from scifi author Vernor Vinge. Brain computer interfaces will create singularity. Accelerating progress of technology is starting to influence all human life. We are on the verge of accelerating expotential growth in AI, our computers and nanoscience will change our bodies and life so we will become cyberbio human! Check out LOAR (law of accelerating returns).

TRANQUILITY

Look at the picture.....Tranquility, thats
what it does for me.....The quality or state
of being tranquil; calmness; serenity.

TWILIGHT

Have you really seen this time of day? Light
is so special in my eyes, it shapes so many
expressions.....Diffused light from the sky, when
the sun is below the horizon, either from
sunrise to daybreak, or more commonly, from
sunset to nightfall. Ho ho amberglo.

TIP TOP

The highest point; the summit. The highest degree of quality or excellence.....First rate.

TOKYO

Japan.....City.....Shogun......Artists.....
Presentation.....Craftsmen.......
Shinto......Organise.......

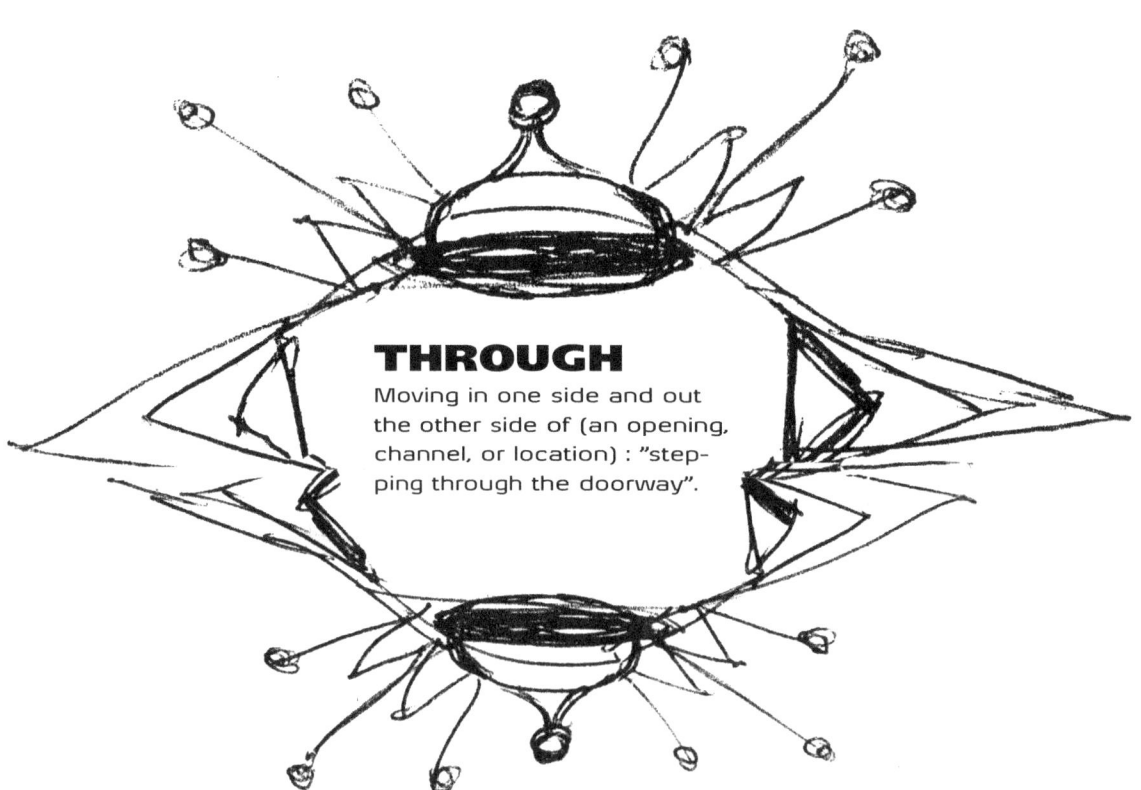

THROUGH

Moving in one side and out the other side of (an opening, channel, or location) : "stepping through the doorway".

TOPSY TURVY

All mixed up, in utter confusion or disorder, sometimes upside down! The real portrait of many an artist pretending to be a young man or the unbearable lightness of being. Watch this film slowly while reading James Joyce.

TASTE

I gave my echotone guitar to rory gallagher what.....Taste.....A great band. Gustatory perception, or gustation is one of the five traditional senses. Taste is the sensation produced when a substance in the mouth reacts chemically with receptors of tastebuds.

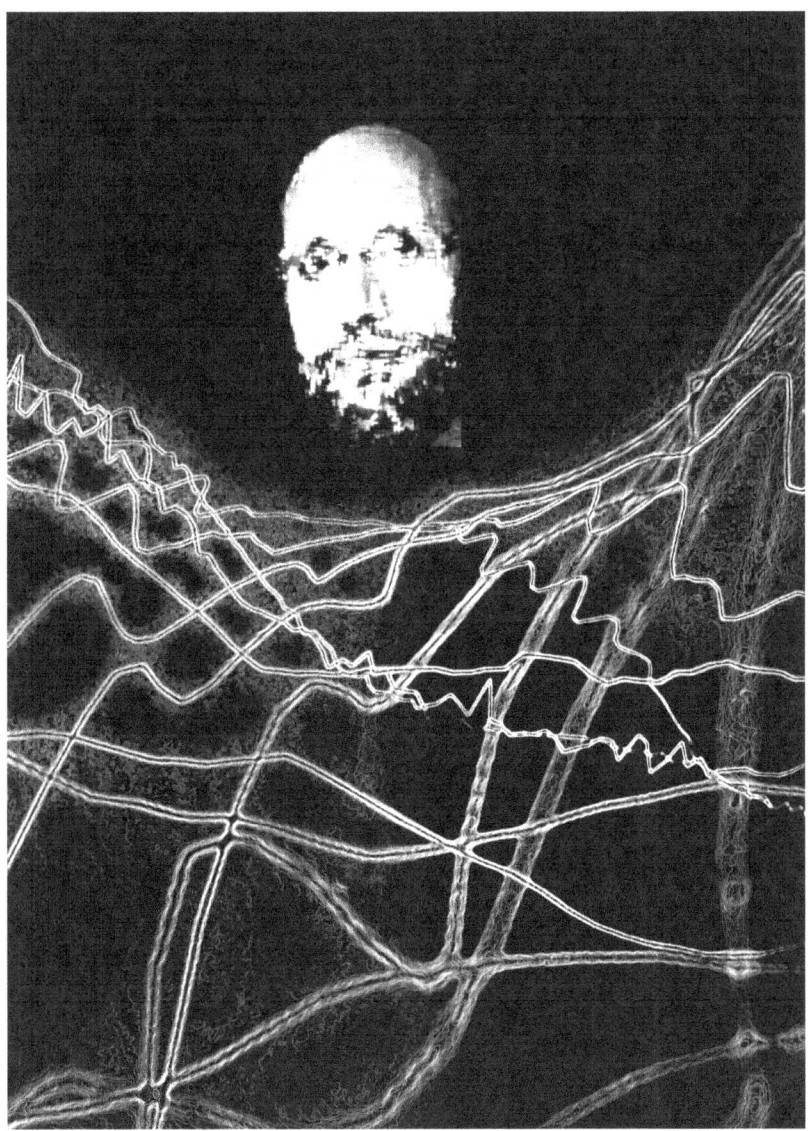

THOUGHT

This is where it all starts for all of us, from thought it may continue to become real or not! Does it really exist?......Is it really there or is it just in my head? Think about it, where do you want to go today?

TORTURE

The practice or act of deliberately inflicting severe physical pain and possibly injury on a person. Psychological and animal torture also exist.

TIPPY TWO

Ninrteen hundred islands between vancouvers' salish sea and alaska., can you believe this west coast, full of uninhabited islands! Love the hakaii! During one of our many voyages, good karma was placed on us, and a wonderful boat helped as we had run aground on a soft mudbank.....These good fishermen towed us off. The boat was called "Tippy Two".

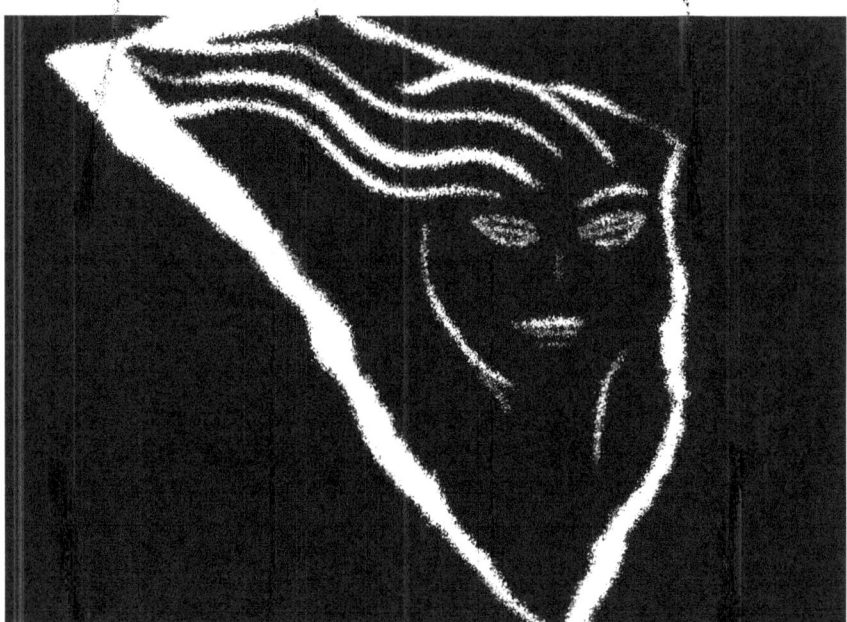

TUNGMESOON

Now, do you know the french word for this, sort of deep throat. Yes......But it really is a french kiss! In france it is as good as the croissant and coffee in the morning.

TONGUES

Beef tongues cooked in a tempura batter style, taste so so good in tokyo! Then again tongue in jolly old english headcheese is also great with branston in brighton. Everyone usually has one and seems to use it at the most inappropriate times, when you bite it.....It hurts for days.

TRANSLATION

Is the communication of the meaning of a source-language text by means of an equivalent target-language text. Translators always risk inappropriate word or thought usage that may change the idiom and context of the original.

TEXASISM

Big time.....Over the top.....Don't do things by halves, can't stop thinking about the alamo......Texs T..... Oil that is!

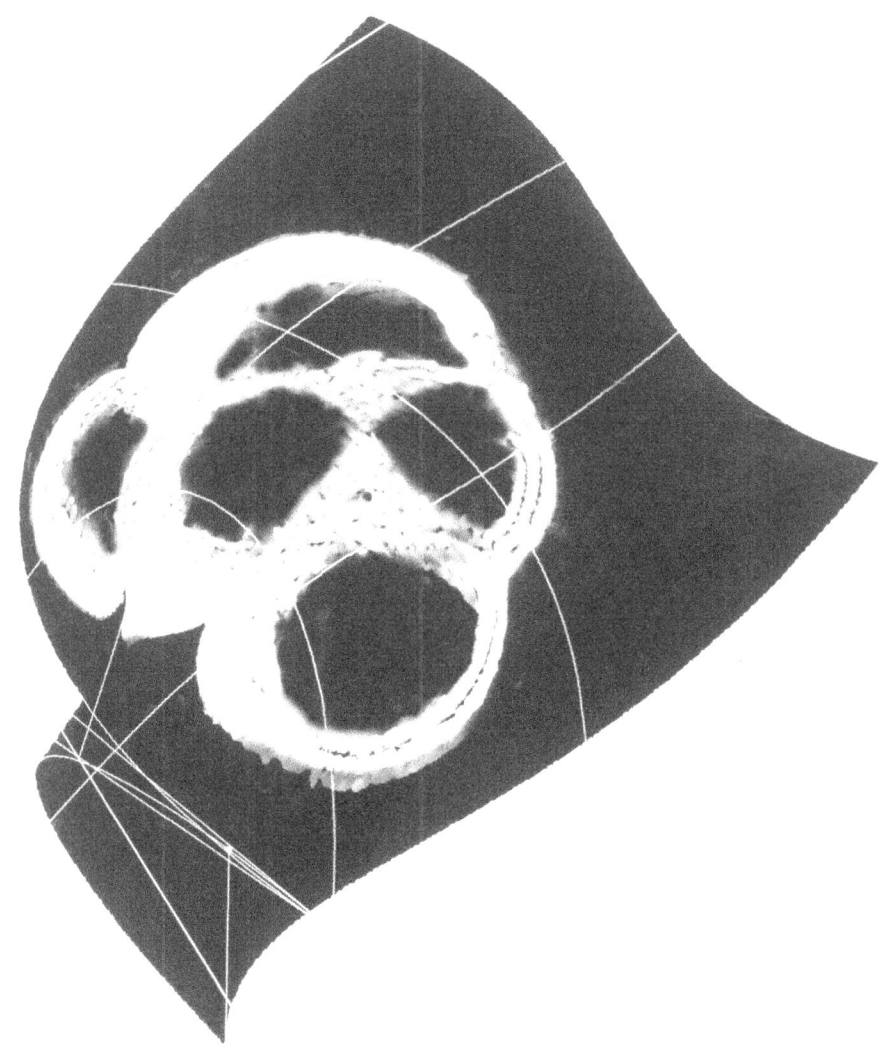

TETROMARINER

A young canadian from ontario I met, changed his name to tetromariner, he was a futurist who would change the environment. Have you ever come accross this word?

TONGA

The real south pacific, put it on your bucket list.....Islands in the dream. Don't let life say fuckit.....missed!

TROPICAL WIND

In the evening this is the most pleasant feeling across the skin.

TRAVELLER

Some are nomadic people. Some have no resident country. Then the rest are on holiday/vacation. Snowbirds look for warm climates away from the canadian winter.

TAHITI

French south pacific.....What can you say..... Sail la vie.....Baguettes and bananas and french passion.....Fruit.

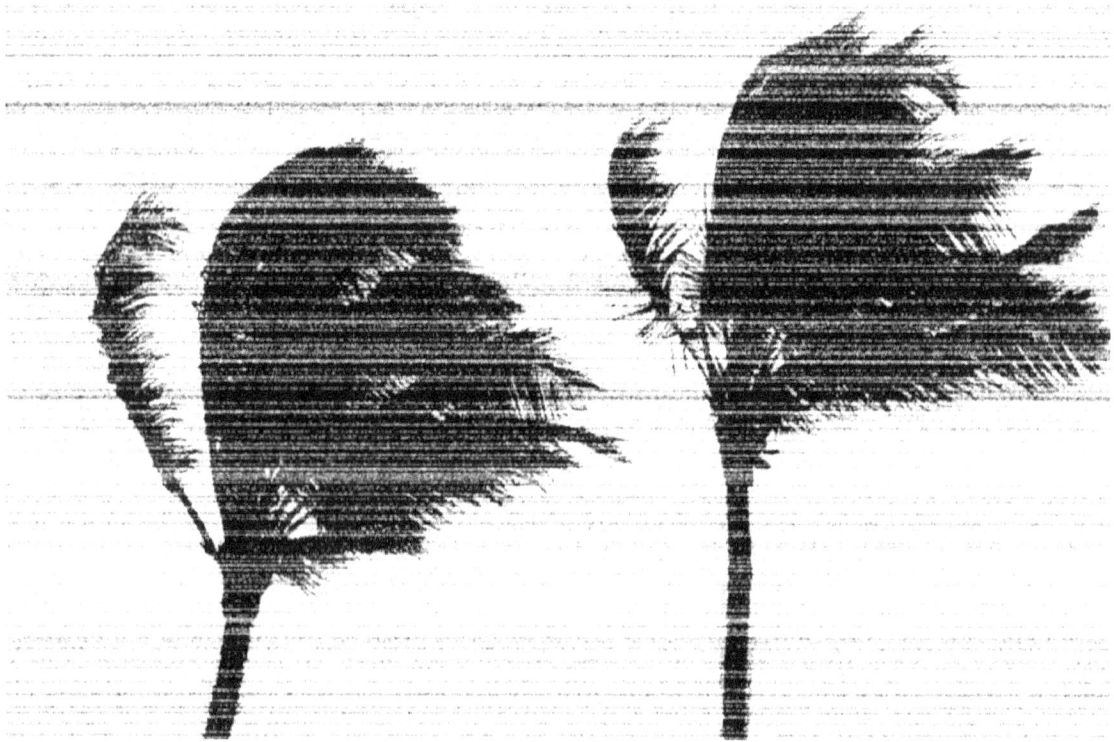

TANTRIC

There is no end game in tantric sex, more than sexual lust. You become the tropical breeze in the continuous moment of union. A bond of sharing, makes pure love, wish it could last forever, love is a drug. You are floating above the bed, doing it into the brains' place of sexual being..... exzillarationsssssex! XOXOXO

TOURISTA

Gringo, from the spanish griego ("greek") used for anyone who spoke an unintelligible language!.....gwielo, cantonese slang for foreigners (ghost, devil).....Hemorrhoids that's the name for tourists in cornwall (they are red all over, sunburnt, come out in clumps and are a pain in the arse)!

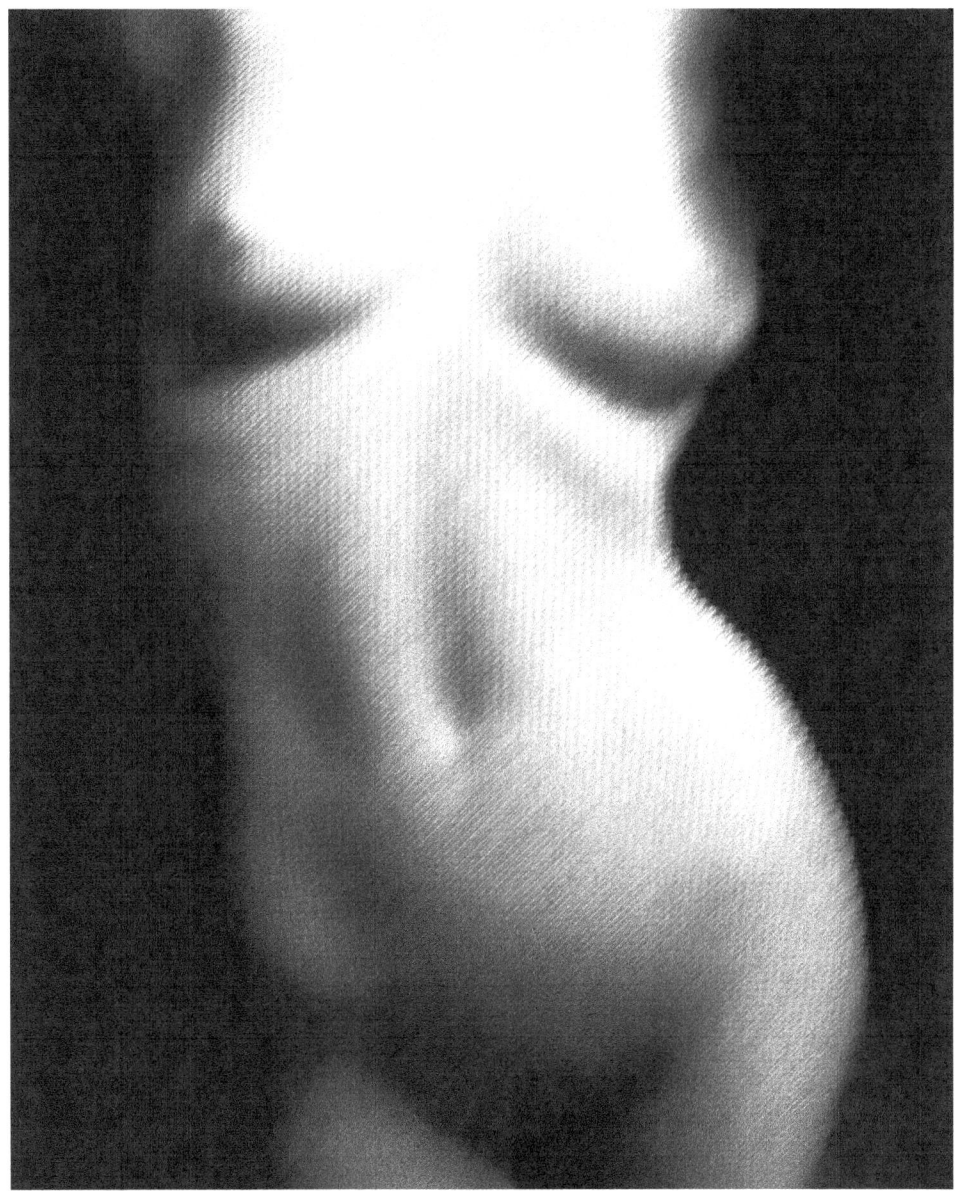

TIMBUKTOO

Well I guess there is not much chance of me getting there now! Should be every serious travellers dream to go to Timbuktoo.

TOUCH

One of the sensations processed by the somatosensory system! Thanks wiki......Part of the body put in contact with something else to feel it!

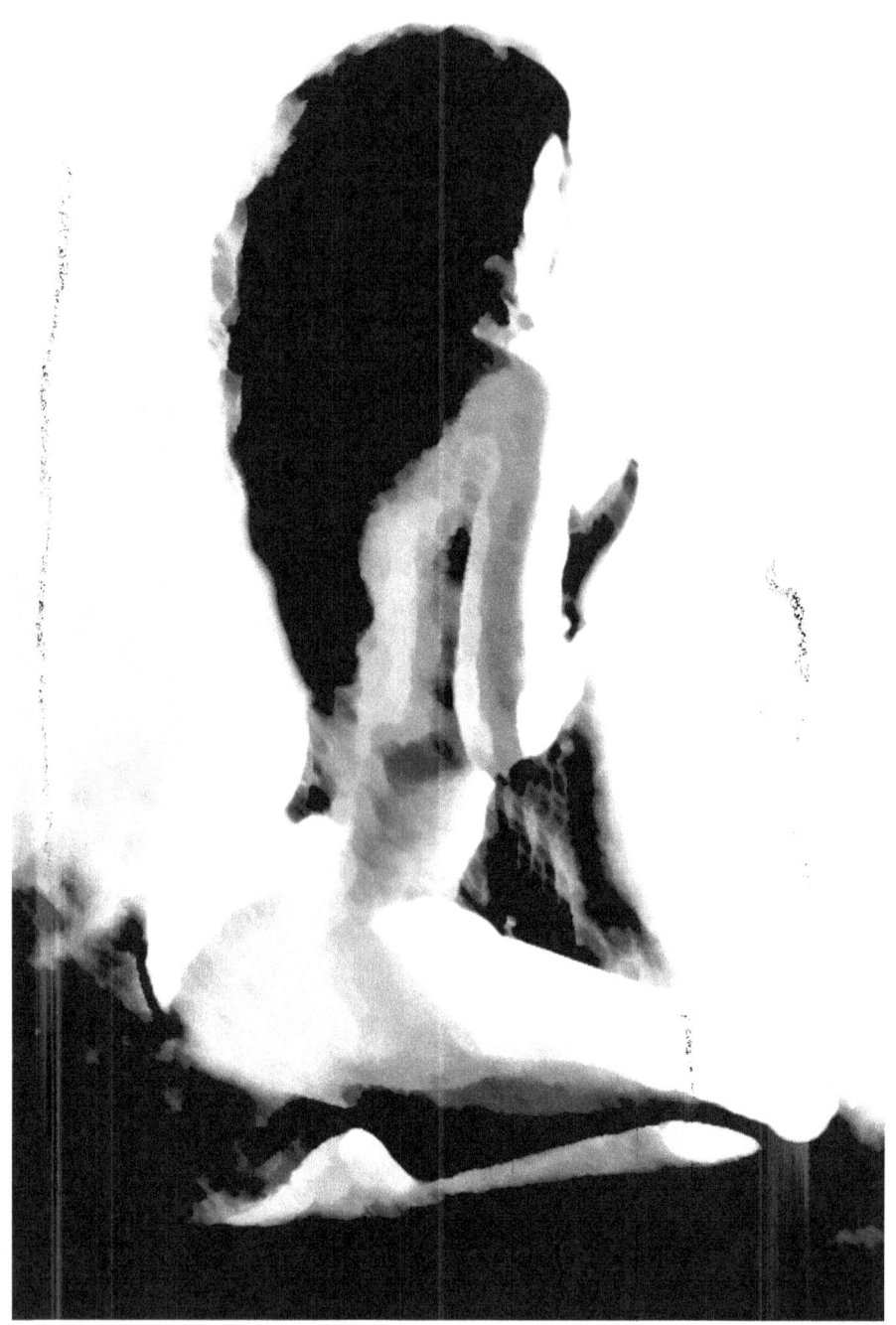

UNDRESS

Get naked now nature boy.....Being without clothing or covering, nude. It is how you do it that makes the difference. Unwrapped..... Unplugged.....Free no strings attached!

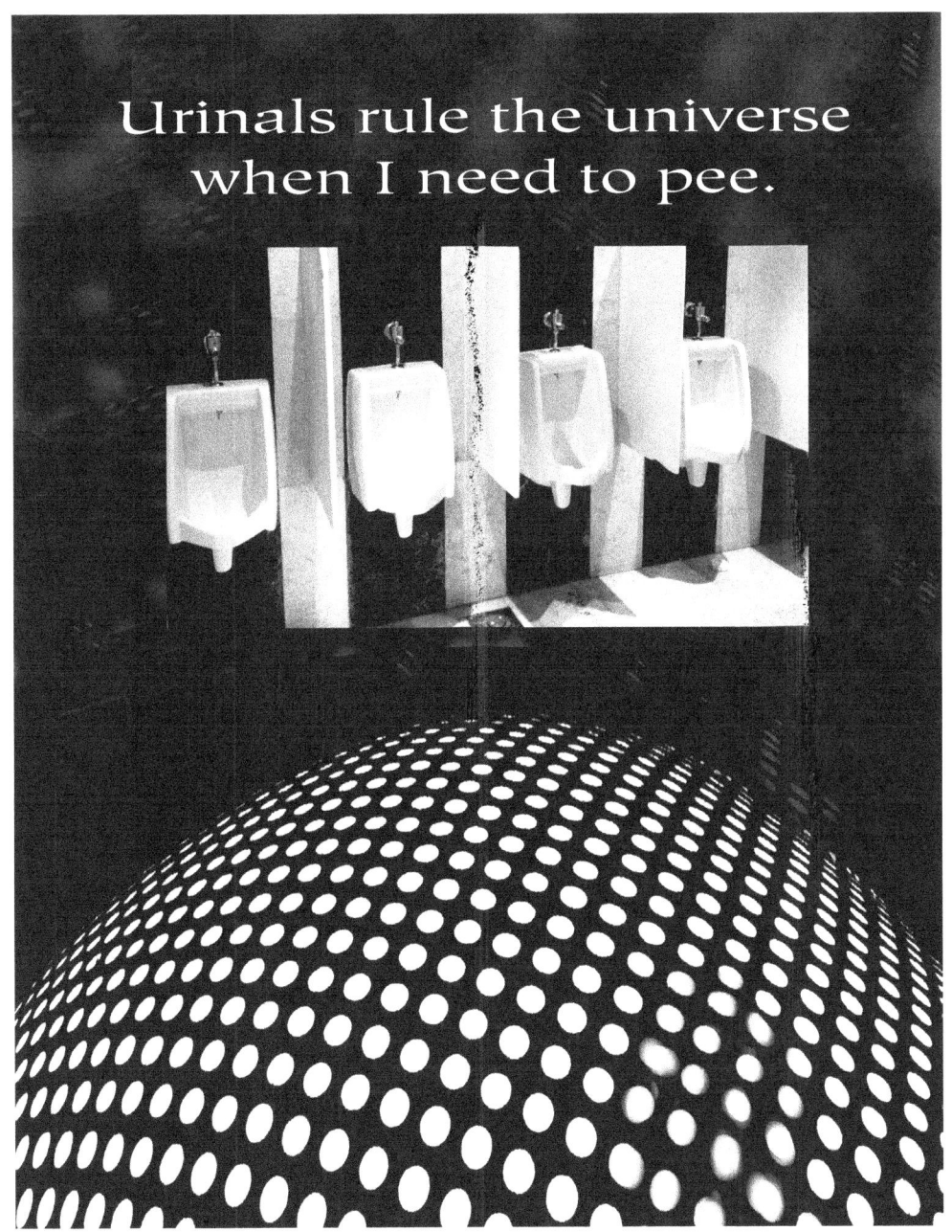

Here I sit broken hearted paid a penny and only farted!

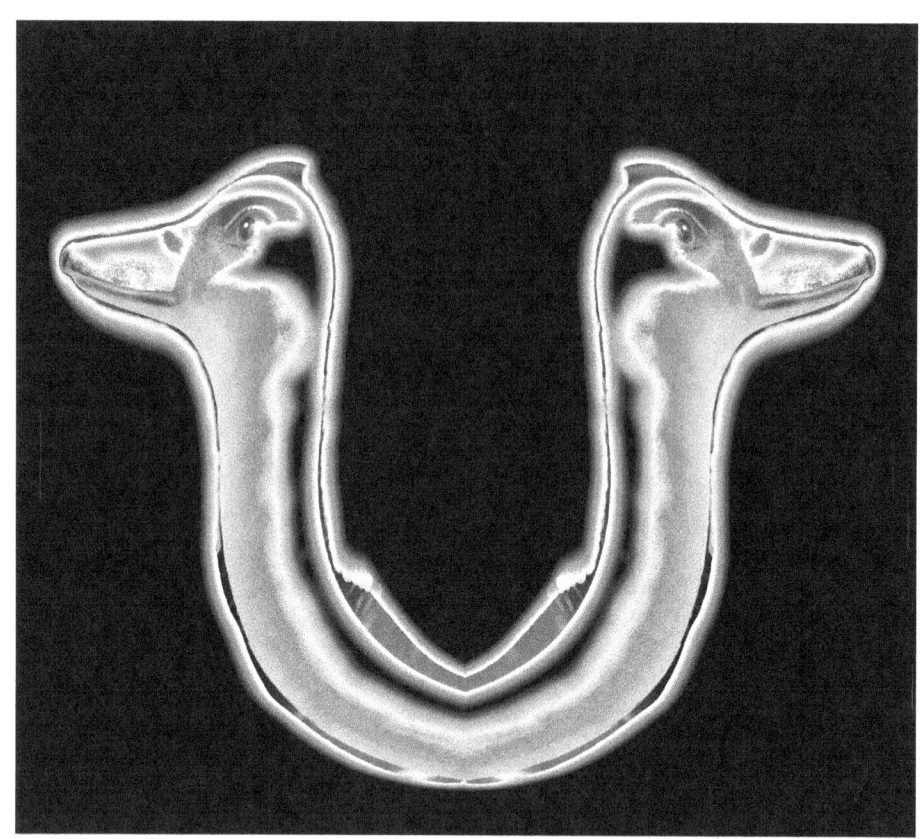

UGOOSE

Unileafer corporation birds fly above
our small lives making us buy what they
sell us. God bless soap it financed my
favourite tv series. Unileafer supplies most
of the snacks in the sinai, but really you
are looking for the full meal deal! The
bacon sandwich or a laughfing cow, omg
the french.....Eat to love.....Still you can
always enjoy a camel!

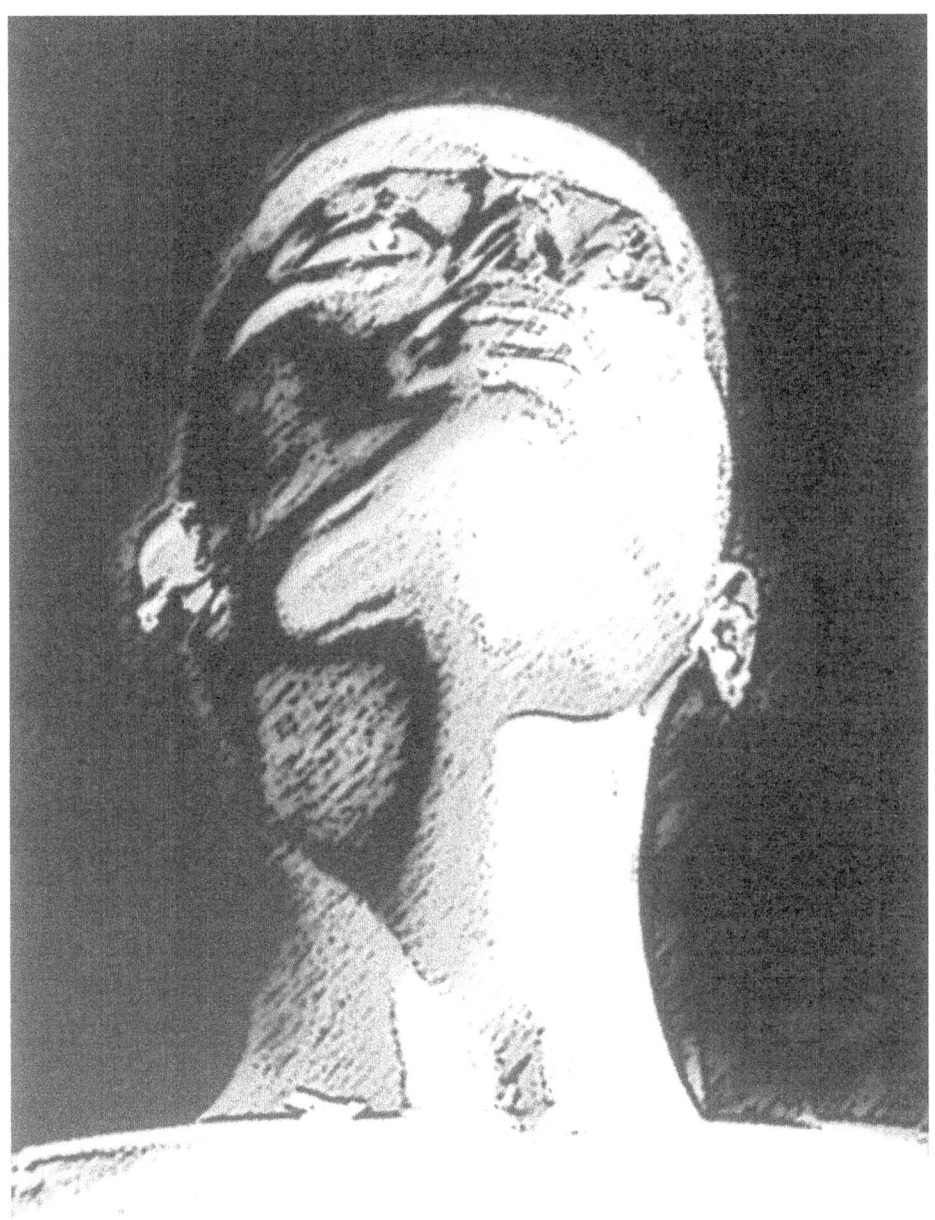

UNDERSTANDING

The power of comprehending; especially: The capacity to apprehend general relations of particulars. The power to make experience intelligible by applying concepts and categories. A friendly or harmonious relationship.

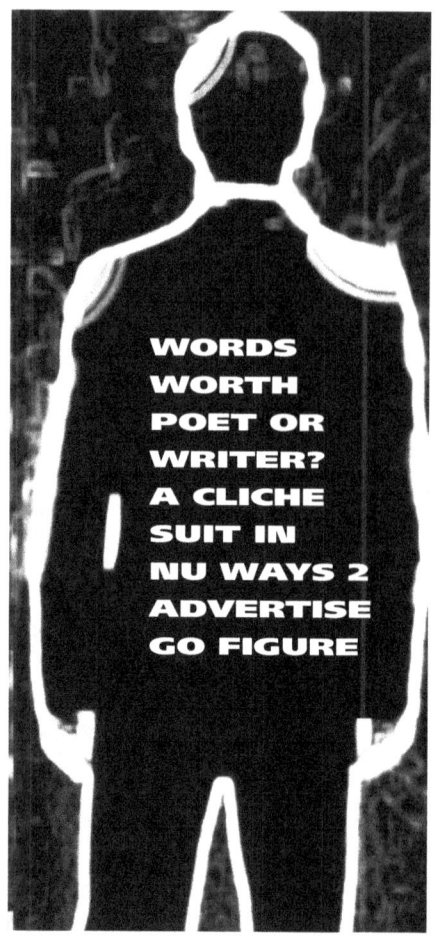

WORDS
WORTH
POET OR
WRITER?
A CLICHE
SUIT IN
NU WAYS 2
ADVERTISE
GO FIGURE

UNDER-WEAR

A rich woman calls her butler to her bedroom "Wordsworth," she says in a low voice. "Take off my silk dress." He takes off her dress. "And my black fishnet stockings, and high heels." Wordsworth takes them off, too. "And my gold silk underwear." "Now, Wordsworth," says the woman,"IF I ever catch you wearing my clothes again, consider yourself sacked."

UNIFORM

Simular or visually identical clothing to make sure you are one of our tribe! Uniform, we think we are different but we are all the same.....Unfortunate.....We know which ones to kill when they have their uniforms on!

USTOPIA

ATWOOD......She writes from a very special place between her experience and imagination.....YING YANG, a balance of life circled around somewhere or something.....Maybe a place......BETOPIA, you must remember where you are..... To be in this moment reading this.....Mindfulness, help is at hand with jon kabot zin.

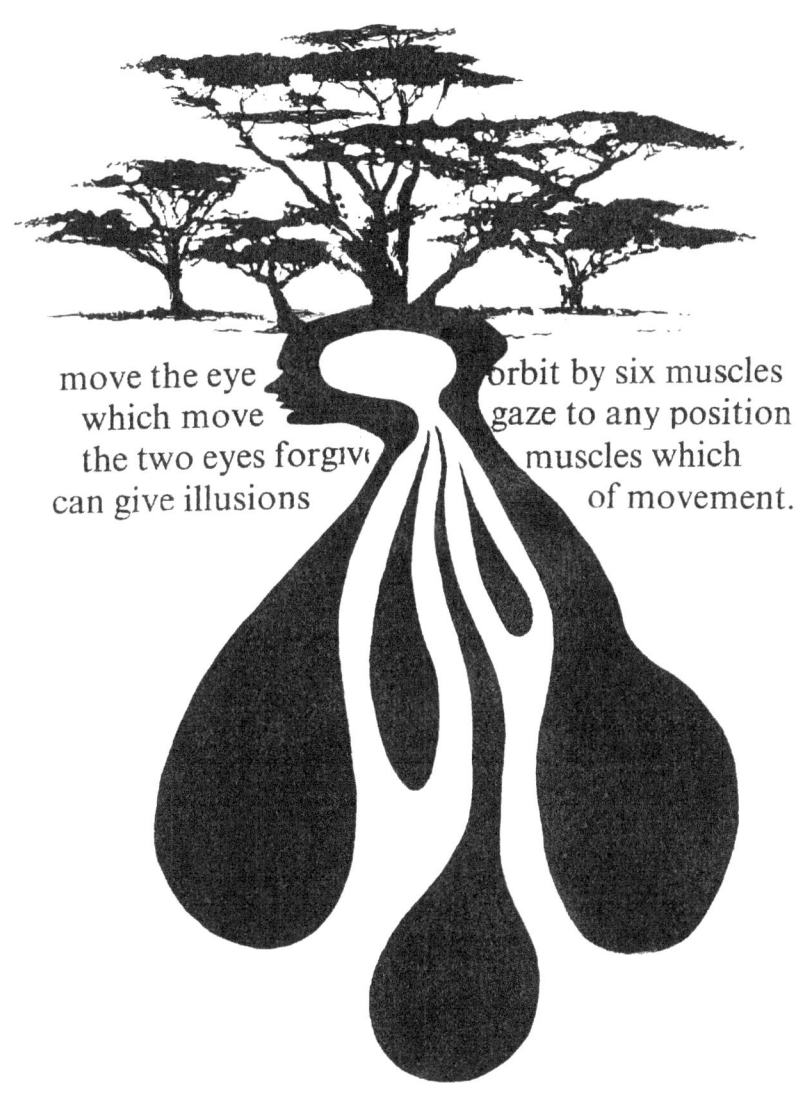

move the eye orbit by six muscles
which move gaze to any position
the two eyes forgiv muscles which
can give illusions of movement.

no wet spot with chocolate but Your tongue looks like shit

UBANGI

The largest tributary of the congo river in central africa. Rite! Exotic middle africa, with women that are hard to kiss with big pieces of circular wood pierced into their lips, but can they shake and stomp to the ubangi music!

UPDIKE

What art offers is space.....A certain breathing room for the spirit.....John Updike..... luv that.....

UR

The person u r and the person u wanted to b.....What is the difference? The person I wanted to be and the person I am now.....Why did I let life get in the way!

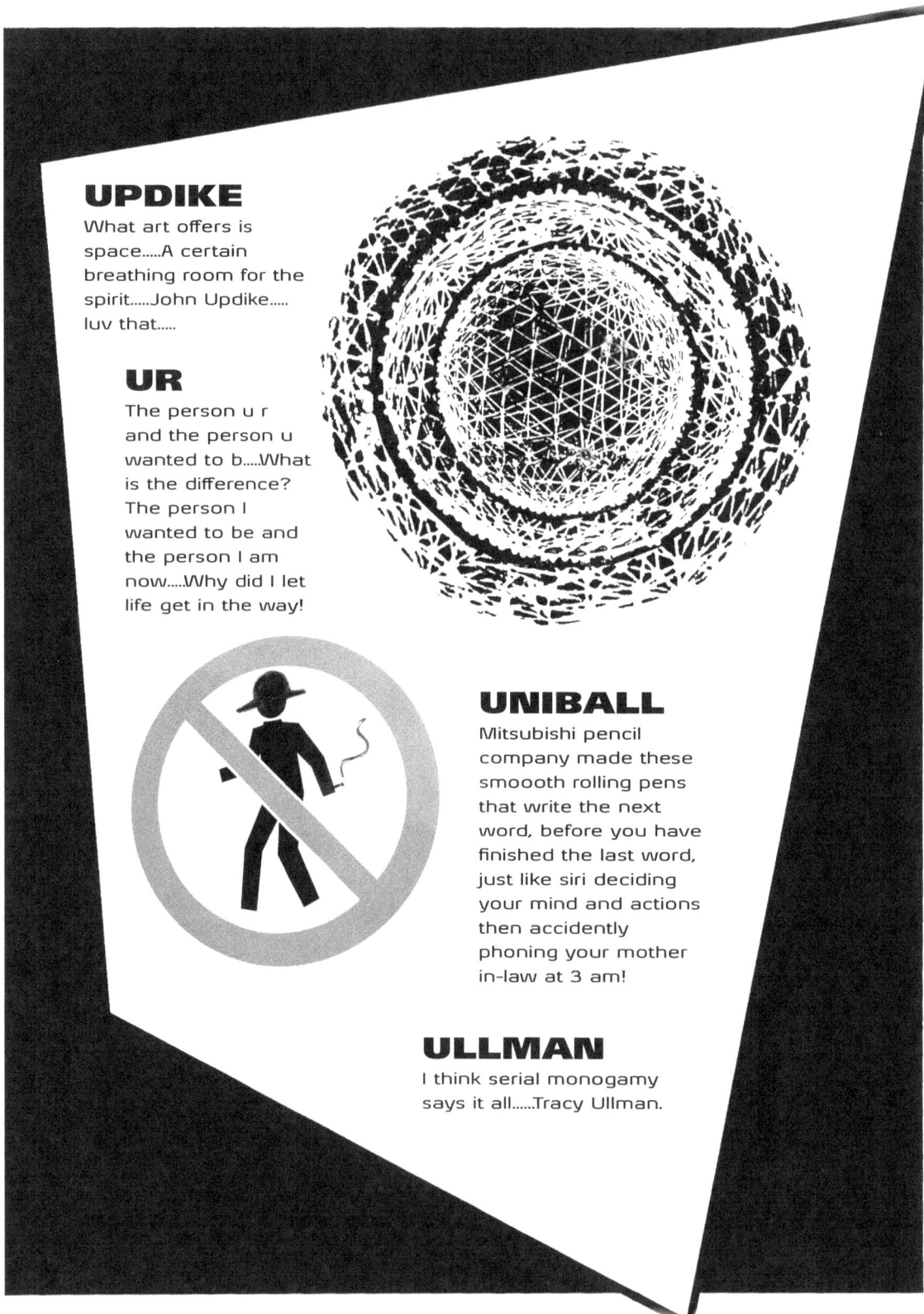

UNIBALL

Mitsubishi pencil company made these smoooth rolling pens that write the next word, before you have finished the last word, just like siri deciding your mind and actions then accidently phoning your mother in-law at 3 am!

ULLMAN

I think serial monogamy says it all......Tracy Ullman.

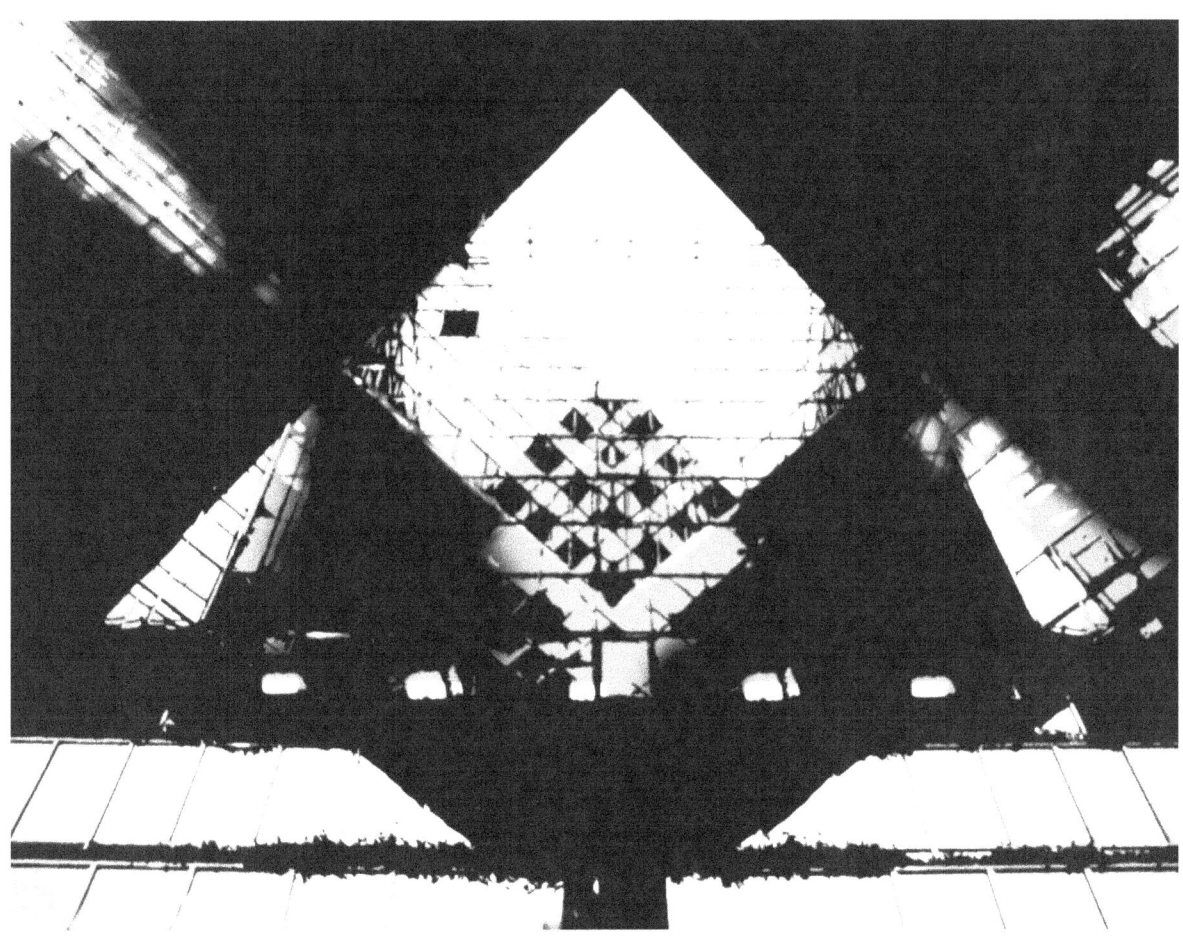

UPWARD

Does the space program really think we are going anywhere? For heavens sake, we should be silent running to alpha centuri with flesh gordon.

UTXT

RU txting me 4 info 4got me again 4s better than 3g i8 4get b 2day Subject 420, DUI on I5 ok now 520 passed in washington.

UNDO

Thank god adobe software does this (undo) even if they are the mega multinational monopoly that controls alof our lives, and wants us to pay them monthly for the rest of our artistic lives. Dear adbby.....The CS10 implant has been giving me headaches, should I sue. I mean I know it was a free beta version.....

URBANDALE

Suburban woods.....City meets country.....
Walnut creek has not seen walnuts in
one hundred years! Hill valley, build a
beautiful family home here.....No hills.....
No valleys! Cheezewizz, no cheese.....

UNISEX

It all started as a hairdressing concept to
pay for salon chairs. Well, where has it
gone since then? Things that are suitable
for either gender right.....It can be seen as
shared by both sexes.

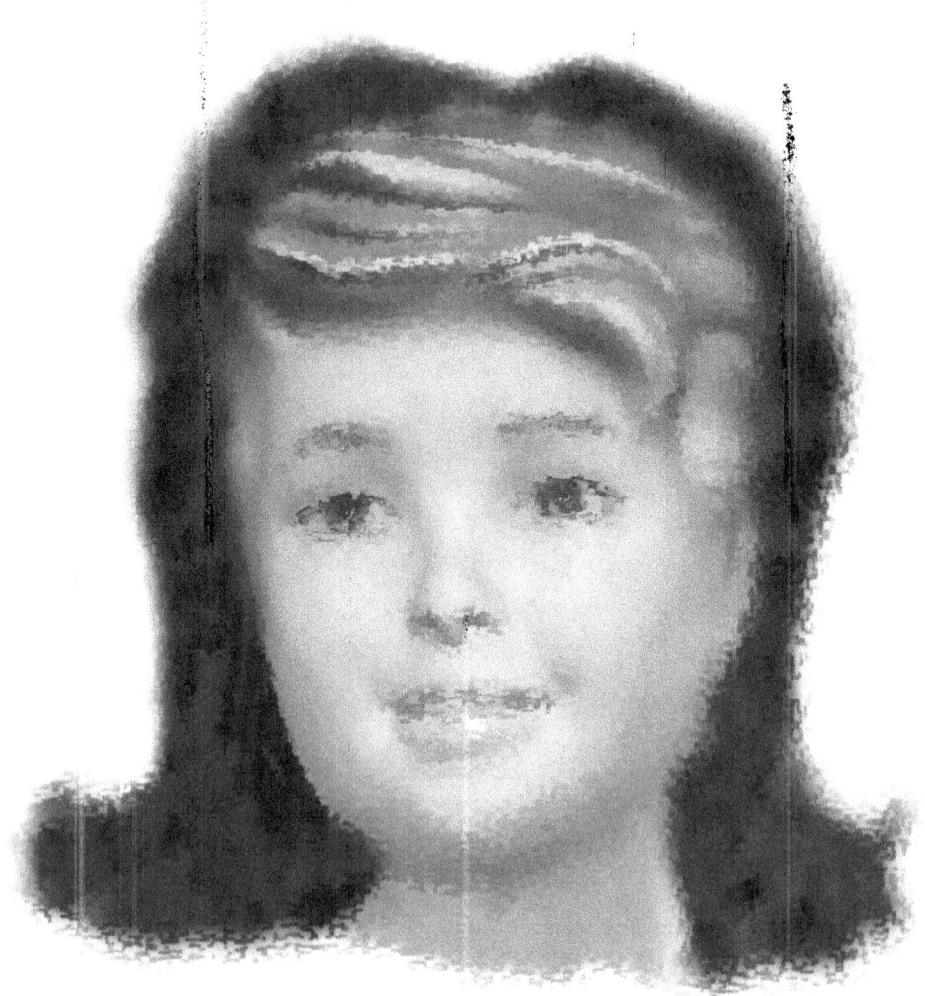

UDOO/SOUND-CLOUD

Freesound: creative commons
licensed sound for sharing.Creators
of music and audio. Sky box the
audio sky storage centre.

UFANASIA

A comment to die for, designed
to express an otherwise direct
statement. Elvis Presley fans
"passed away" is a euphemism for
"fans died".

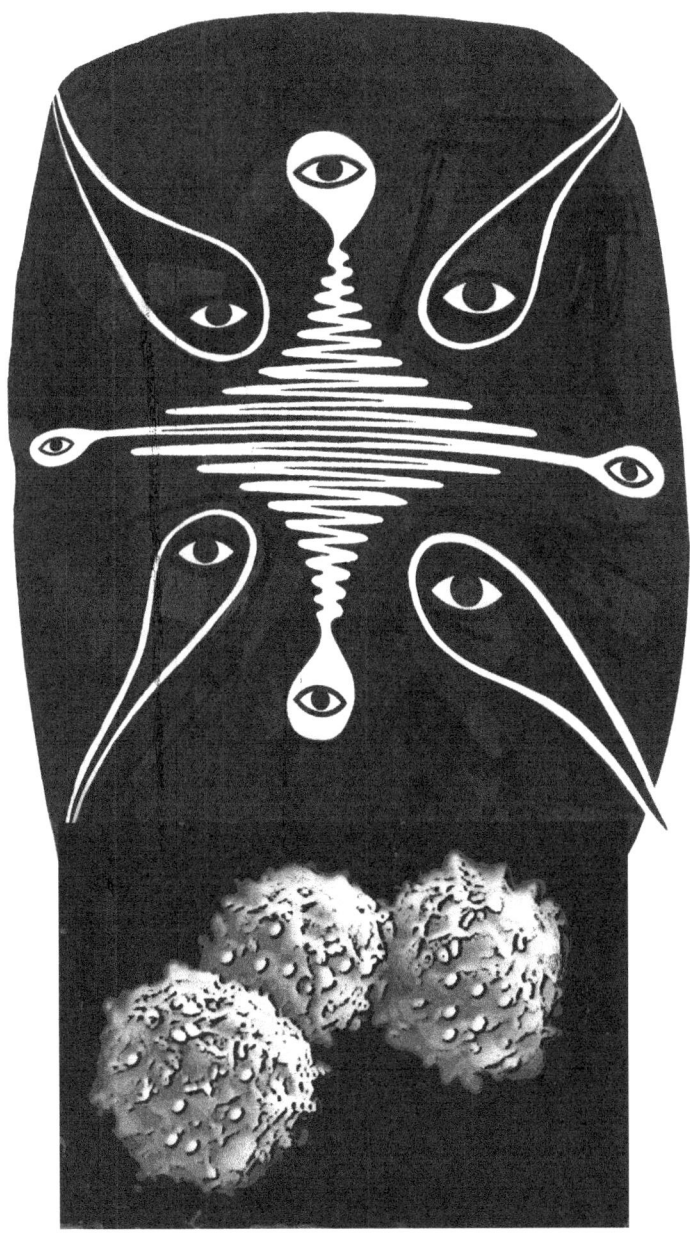

ULTRASOUND

This is a commonly used procedure that uses sound waves to produce an image in the body. These sound waves pass through the skin and reflect to form a picture that is then diagnosed by an ultrasound technician.

VANESQUE

An adjective suffx indicating style, manner, resemblance, or distinctive character: picturesque. Vanesque.....This is the word for the pacific north-west coast style of vancouver.

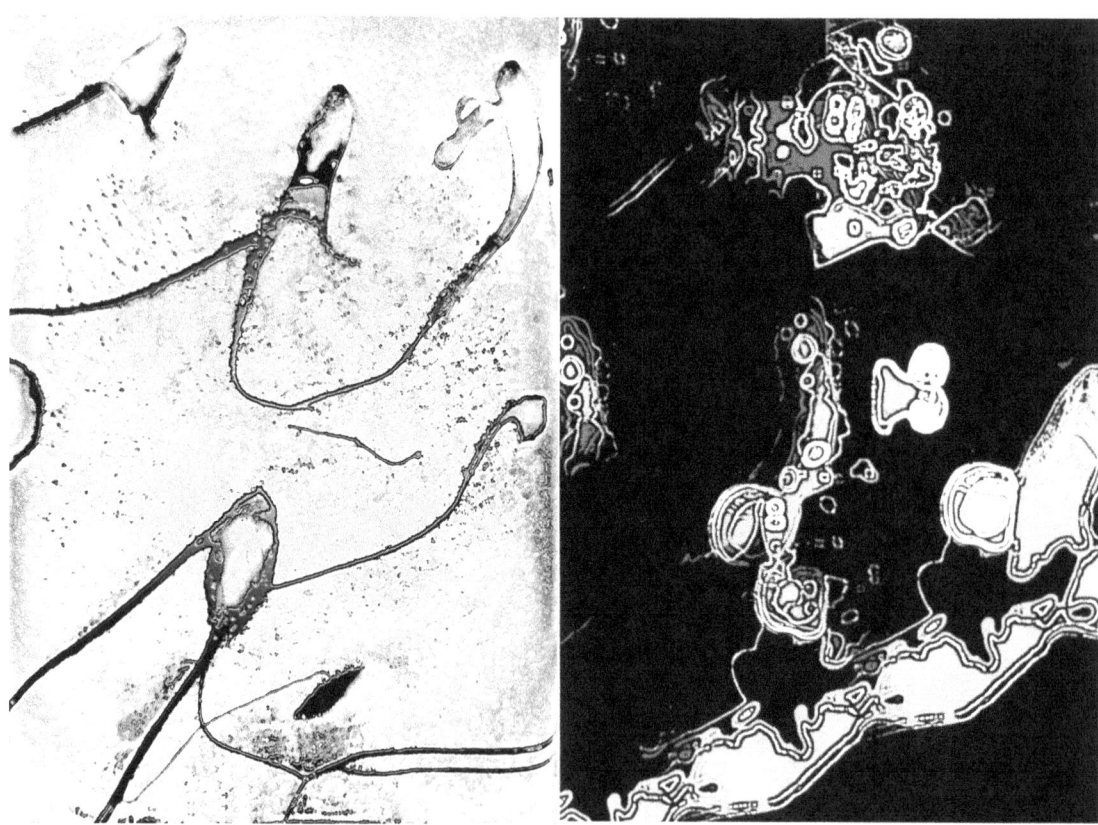

VIRUS

A virus is a small infectious agent that can replicate only inside the living cell of an organism. Viruses can infect all types of organisms, from animals, plants, to bacteria and microbes.

VERB

I know that.....Did you know "verb" is a noun.....Na nu na nur nurrrr.....

VIRAL

A video that becomes popular through the process of internet sharing, social media and email. Caused by virus.

VEGAN

The practice of abstaining from the use of animal products, particularly in diet..... Save the planet stop eating meat! Does it need to be saved?

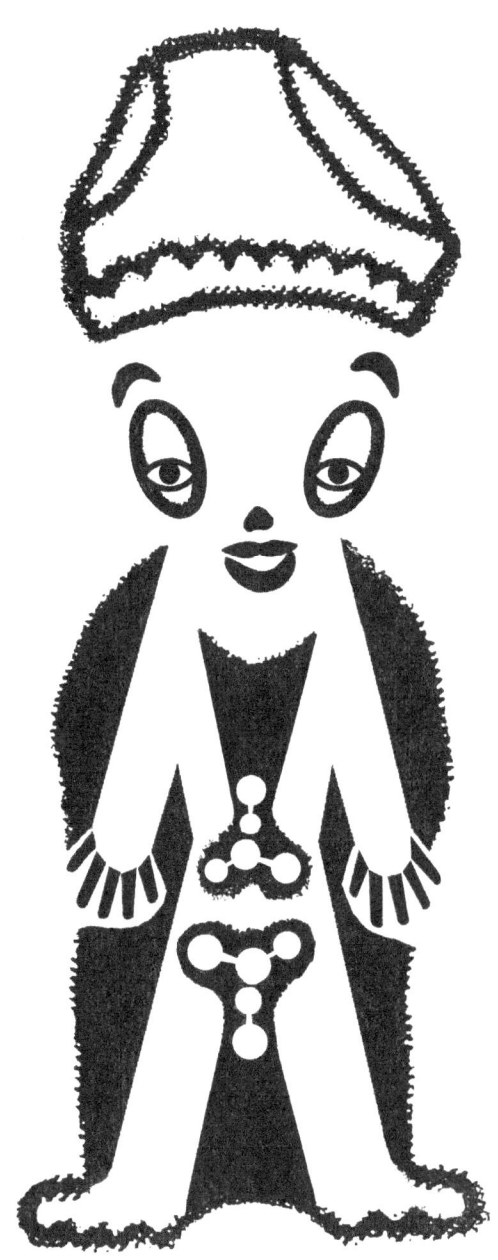

PAYPUL DINGBAT UNDIES

VIOLATION

Who violates who, attacking or interfering with others, thats not consensual. Broken some country law? From the word violent?

VULNERABLE

Susceptible to physical or emotional injury. Inability to withstand the effects of a hostile environment.

BRIEFINGS Uniserver plc said monday it has signed a contract worth more than nine hundred million with the china-american company skysearch. The deal is for a communication payload system for the CHIUS-9 satellites to be launched 2019. The system will allow the home country protection corporation access to data about the location of mobile ground peacemakers, also receive and process the movement of all citizens and their implants, to be used respectfully by the national harmony government service.

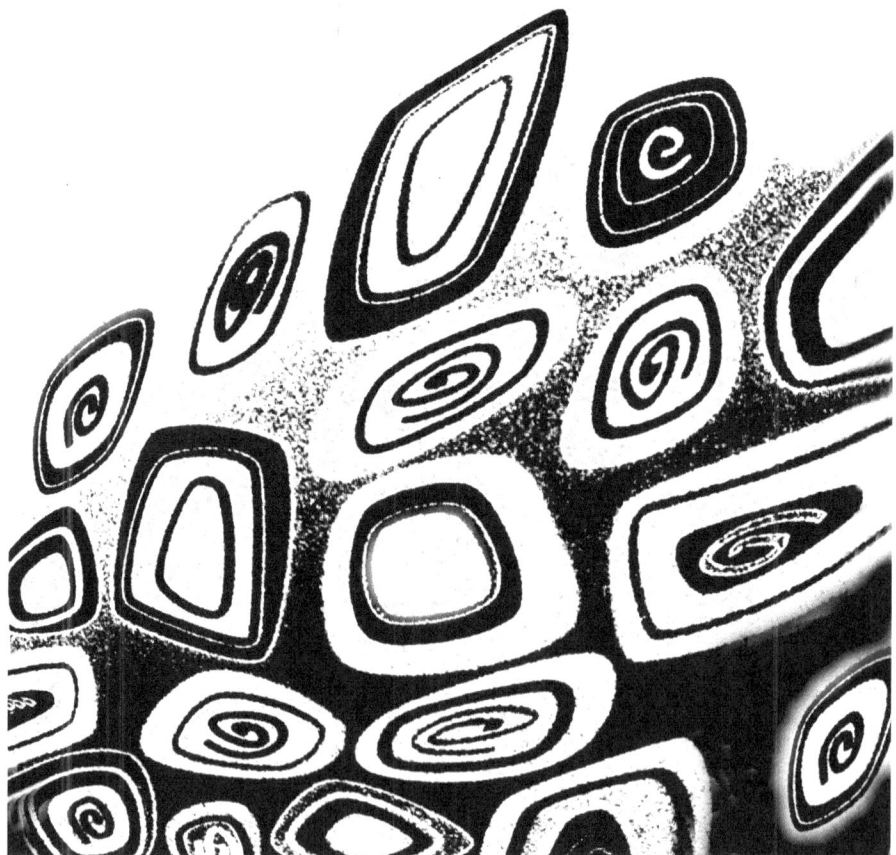

VECTOR

A latin word meaning "carrier". In computer graphics, a line that is defined by its start and end point.

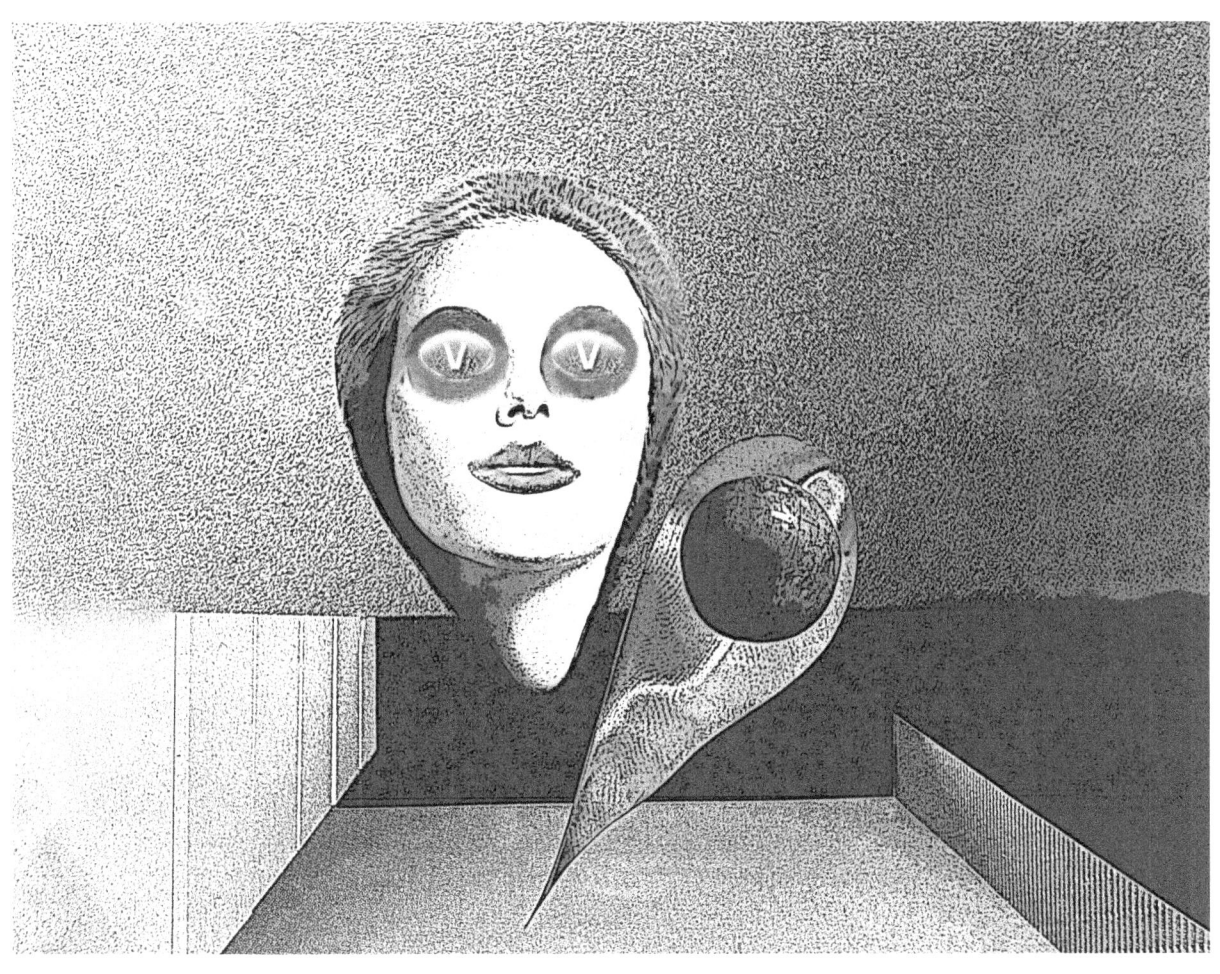

VISOR

It all seams different with viagra
eyes.....Rooms with only three sides,
over use, you could go colour blind.....
Then they tell me god only knows
the future! Caution ahead boomers
entering their teens, sorry susie, It is
written in the fire of desire.....Viagra is
the second coming!

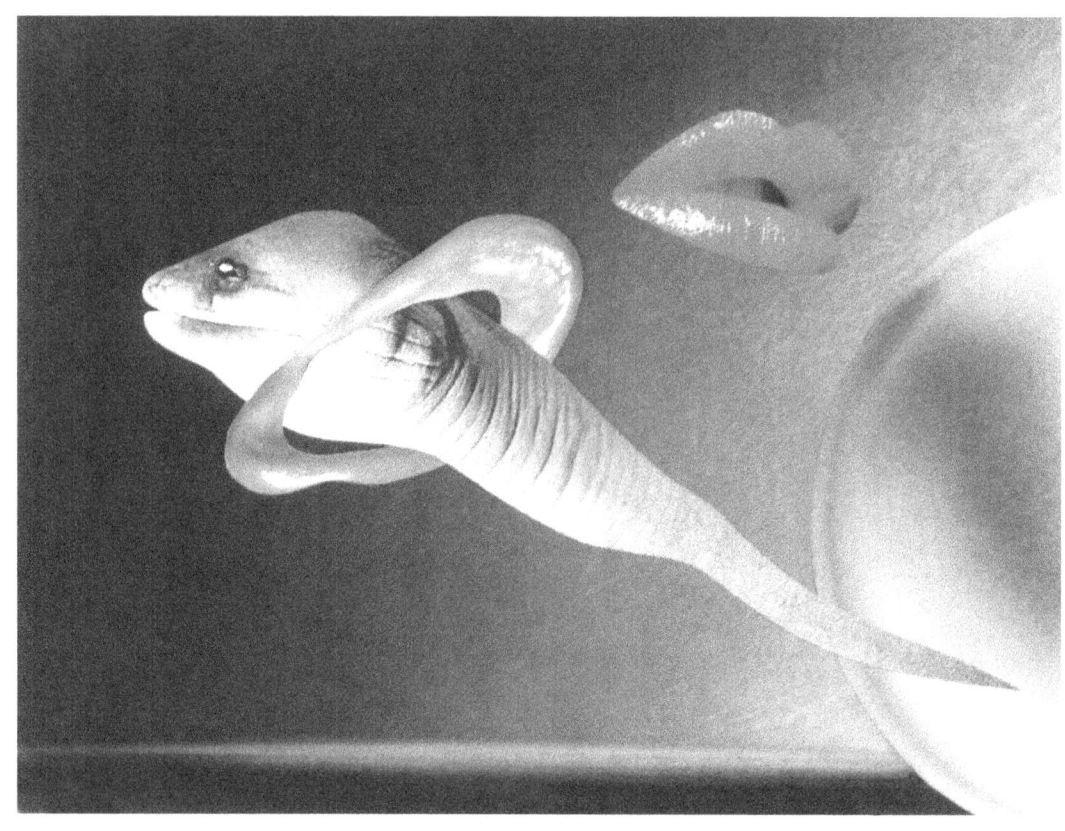

VIRILE

Having masculine vigour or strenght;
of or having procreative power; of
man as distinct from woman or child.

VORTEX

A vortex is a region within a fluid where the flow is mostly a spinning motion about an imaginary axis, straight or curved. Toilet bowl blues by shazam. Goes the other way, down under?

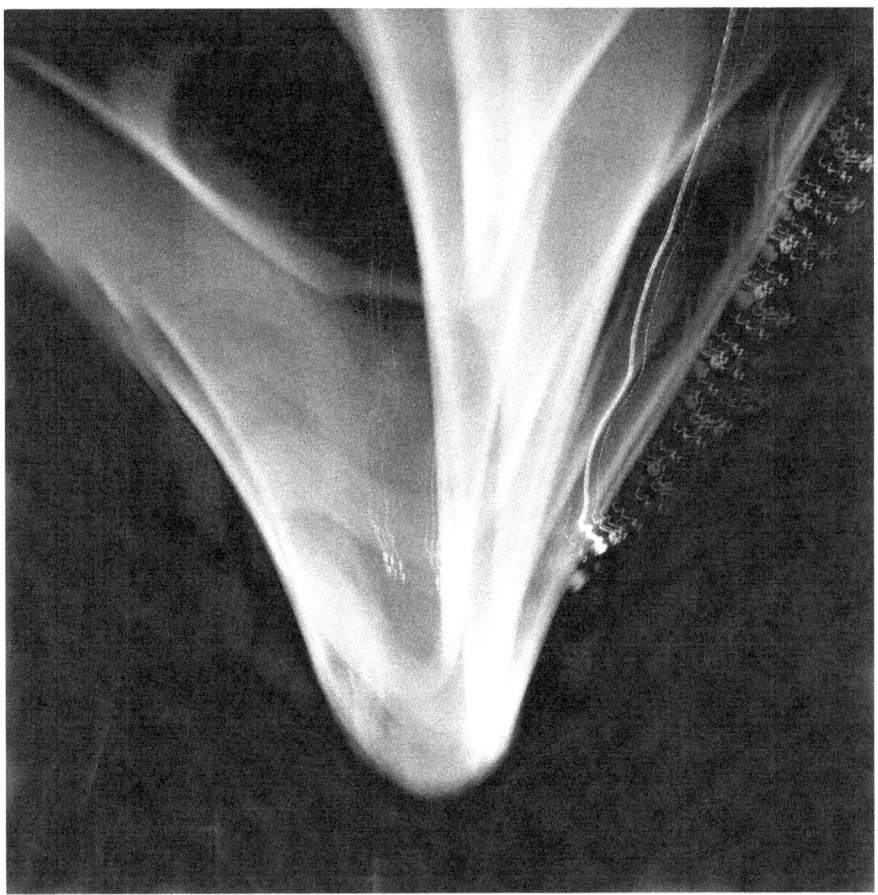

VERANDA

The portuguese in goa had that great colonial lifestyle, enjoying an evening drink on the varanda; the portuguese word for a roofed opening galley or porch.

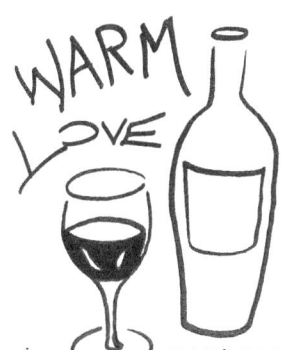

VAN POET

Van slam.....The longest running poetry slam in canada. Monday madness, poets perform on commercial drive.

Does this wine count as a serving of fruit?

WATER

I love these water reflections photgraphed by suzanne loehrich. I was born a water baby, "Pisces" the fish is my sign.....You can tell, call me! Quite often I try to smell like them.....Kippers and I, have a spiritual communion in which I take their blood and flesh as a sacrament to be hallowed by the waters of the earth, in which we share our existence. Connections.....James Burke makes it so much fun, see it.

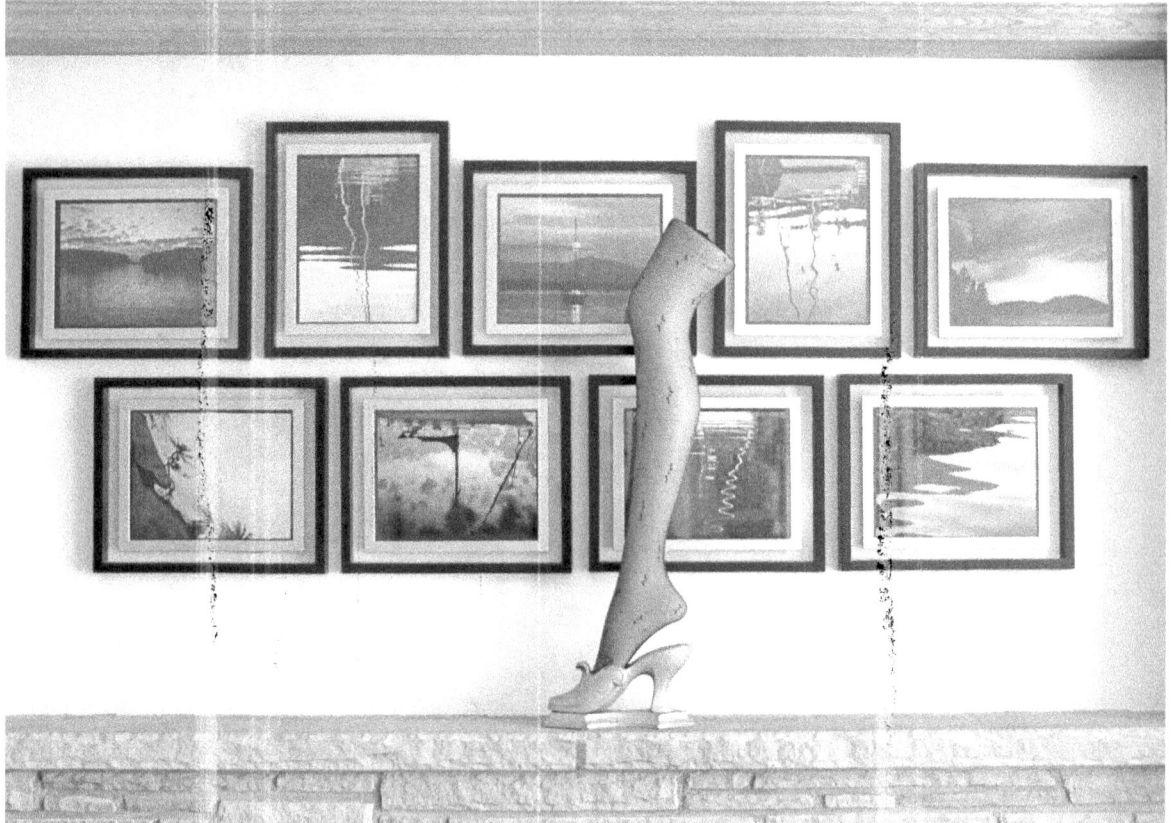

Photos by Suzanne Loehrich

WIFE

Trouble and strife....COCKNEY PRIDE, many east london pubs were called this.....Many a true word is said in jest!

WETSPOT

Towels do not seem to stop it, and they seem to have a moving life of their own, why are towels in beds always itchy? Who's side is it on this time! We started over that side.....

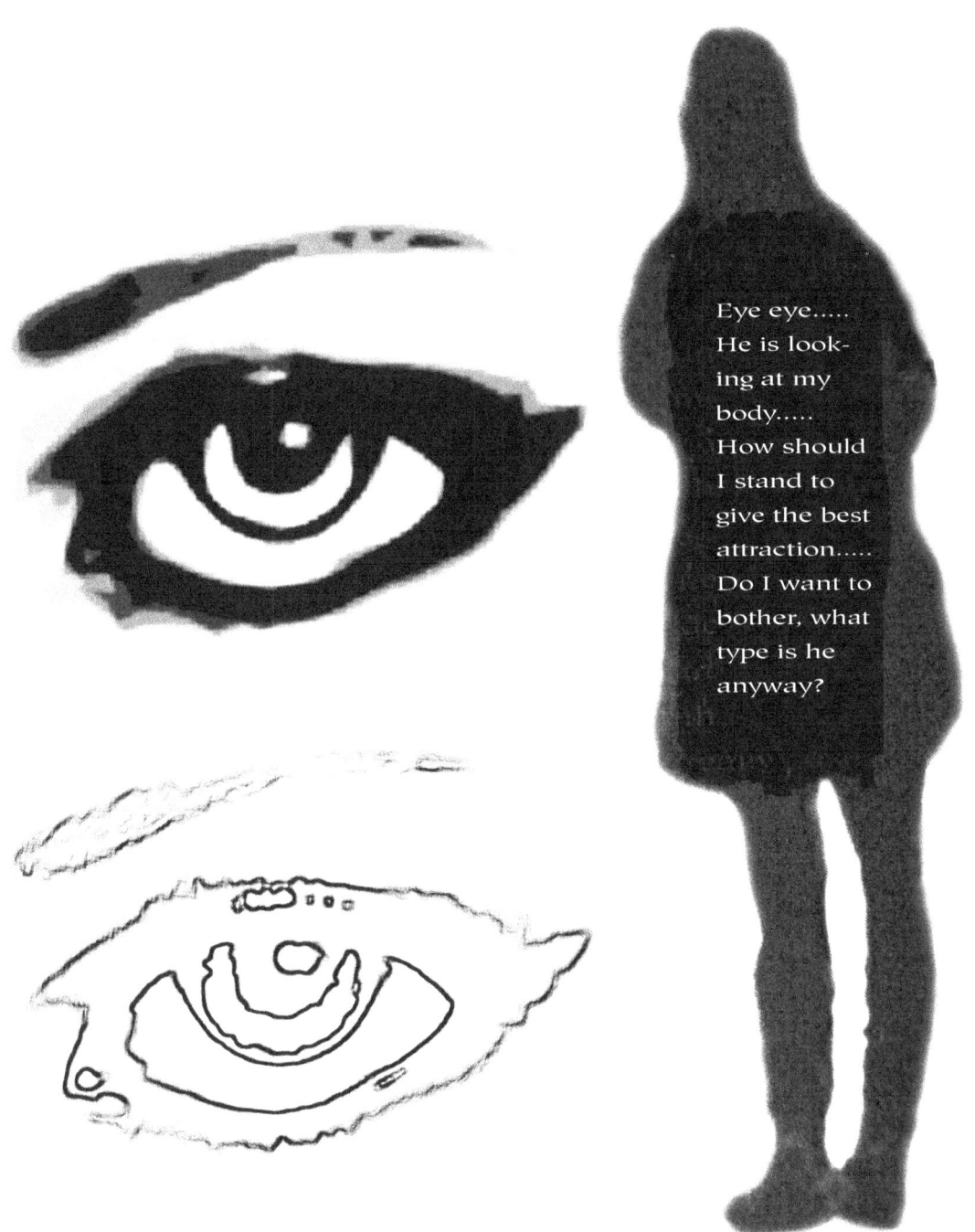

Eye eye.....
He is look-
ing at my
body.....
How should
I stand to
give the best
attraction.....
Do I want to
bother, what
type is he
anyway?

WATCH One day I will start looking at things in my universe..... Seven hundred and ninety solar systems, there is life out there beyond our small suburban car park. The asteroid that killed the dinosaurs bought us to this planet....That is correct.....Jesus. Life on rock, then rock around the cock.....The stone age condom. How long till we can reverse engineer a single cell organism?

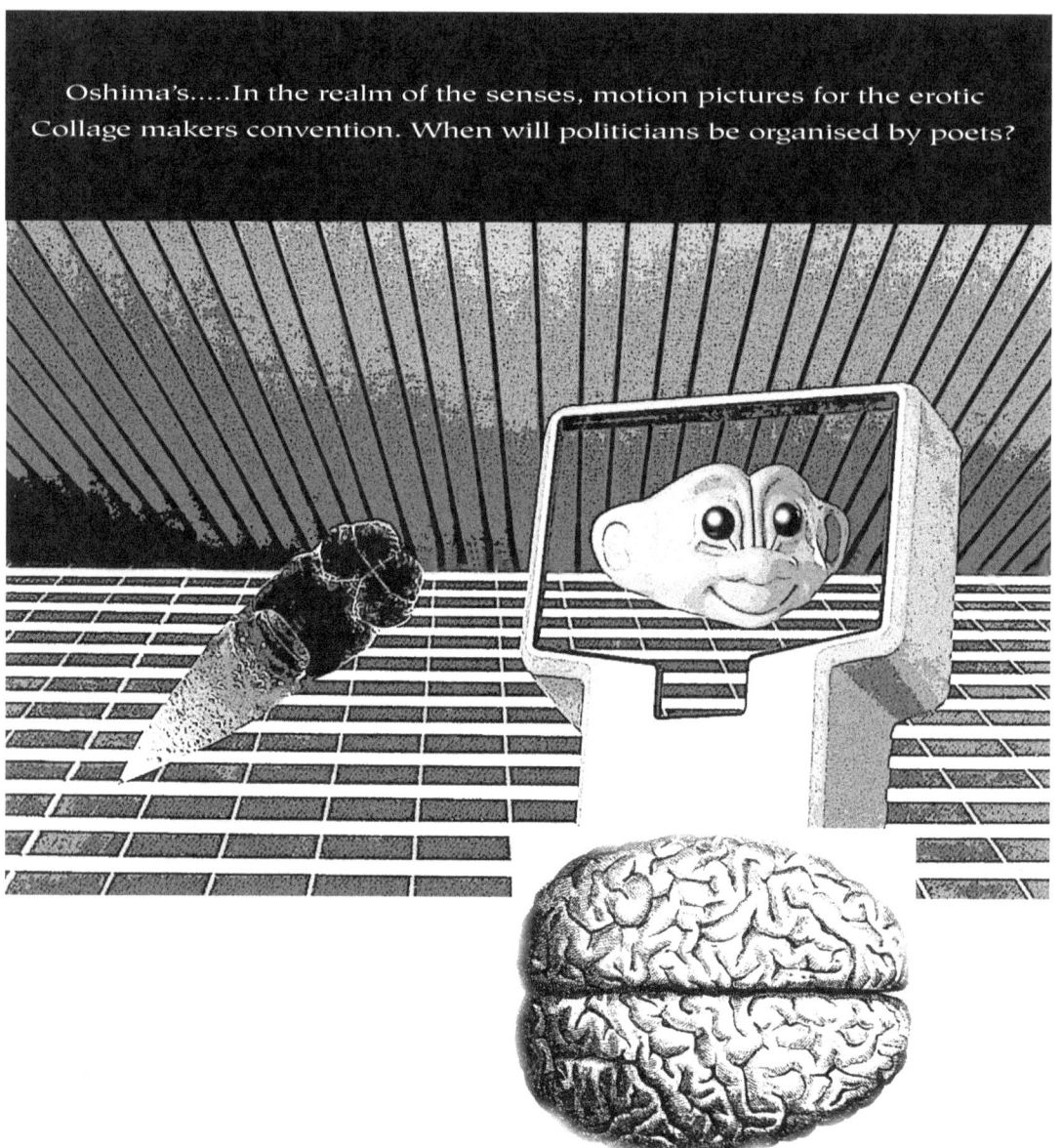

Oshima's.....In the realm of the senses, motion pictures for the erotic Collage makers convention. When will politicians be organised by poets?

WINKIES TO WALLYS

Toolin was a fashionable name on kilburn high road, many moved to the hamptons and cockfosters. That was the end of the line, they said it was thought provoking and funny, chasing word ideas around the room. Ted the typo makes pictures with words and then creates words from pictures.....I hesitate to tell the truth as it hurts, just like real life, please stop eating your money.....

WOODY

Jump for joy.....I now have a woody (erection). It was so exciting I sprang a woody, even with my ed problems! The pacific exhibition wooden roller coaster. Nineteen fifties jeep station wagon with wooden frames on the metal sides.

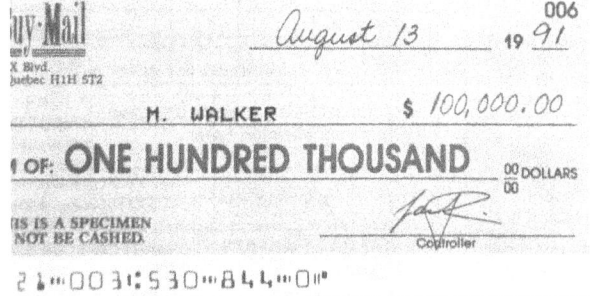

M.WALKER
YOU COULD WIN OUR GRAND PRIZE- $100,000.00!

Reply before the **October 22, 1220** deadline and make it happen! Plan your budget, pay off the mortgage, or splurge on a special luxury every year for the next 5 years! It's so easy when you become **OUR $100,000.00 GRAND PRIZE WINNER!**

uy·Mail   006
X Blvd.   19 **91**
uebec H1H 5T2   *August 13*

         M. WALKER $ *100,000.00*

OF: **ONE HUNDRED THOUSAND**   00 DOLLARS
                                  00

IS IS A SPECIMEN
NOT BE CASHED.   *Controller*

21⑈003⑈530⑈844⑈0⑈

FREE SHIPPING AND HANDLING!   **CHARGE**

WINNER

Takes all, that's not even true in war, if so it would be so much easier, what are we doing and thinking!

WHACK

Kill some one! Why do we say something is out of whack?

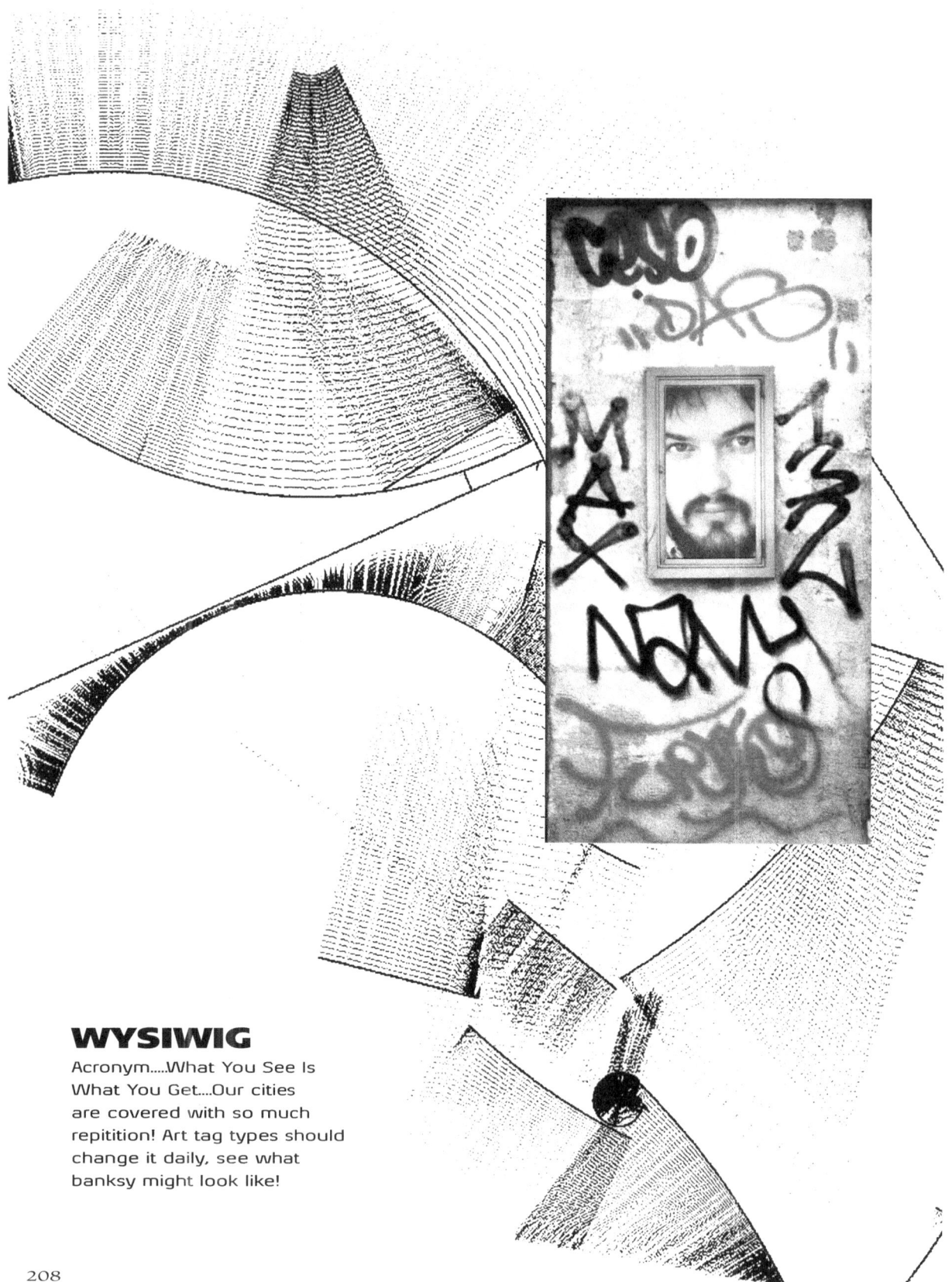

WYSIWIG

Acronym.....What You See Is What You Get....Our cities are covered with so much repitition! Art tag types should change it daily, see what banksy might look like!

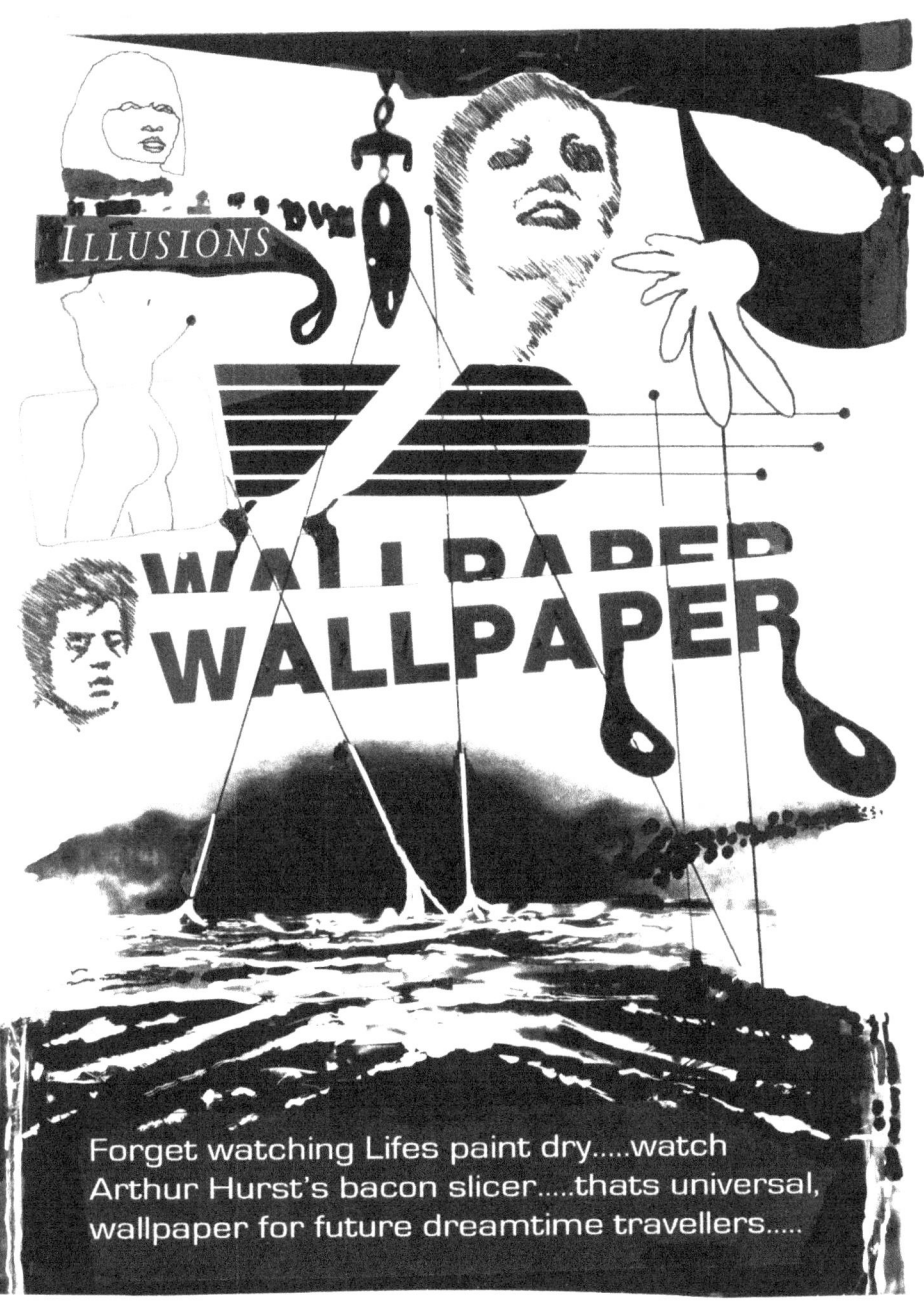

Forget watching Lifes paint dry.....watch Arthur Hurst's bacon slicer.....thats universal, wallpaper for future dreamtime travellers.....

WALLPAPER

Images used as a background to the stress and excitement of life.....A plastic or paper covering used to hide and rejuvenate the faults and mistakes on the walls of the room you now live in!

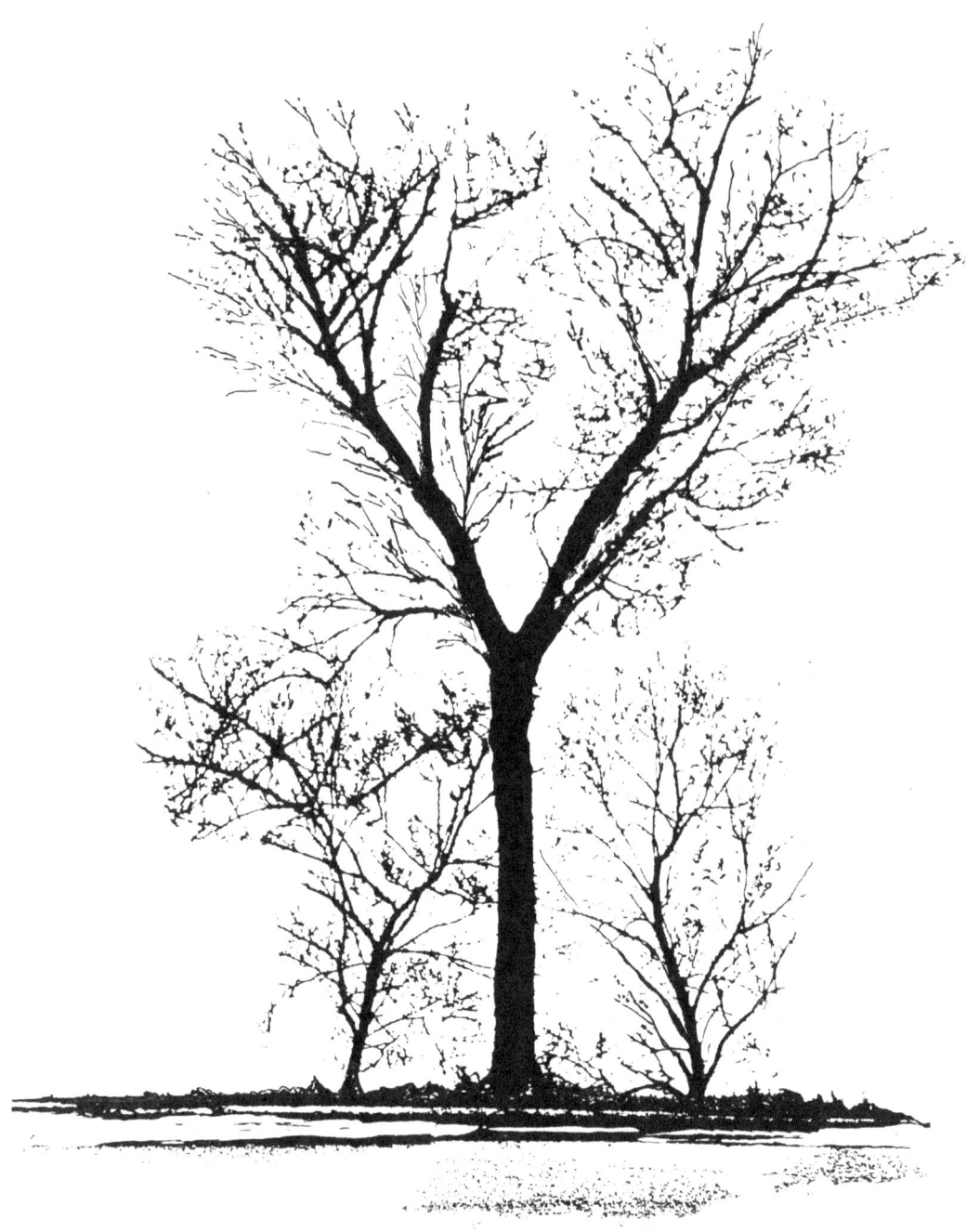

WINTER

Winters are the relief from the summer. Winter makes
you enjoy the summer so much more! Nowruz marks
the first day of spring and the beginning of the new
year in the persian calendar.....Lonley trees will be
reborn in the spring.....

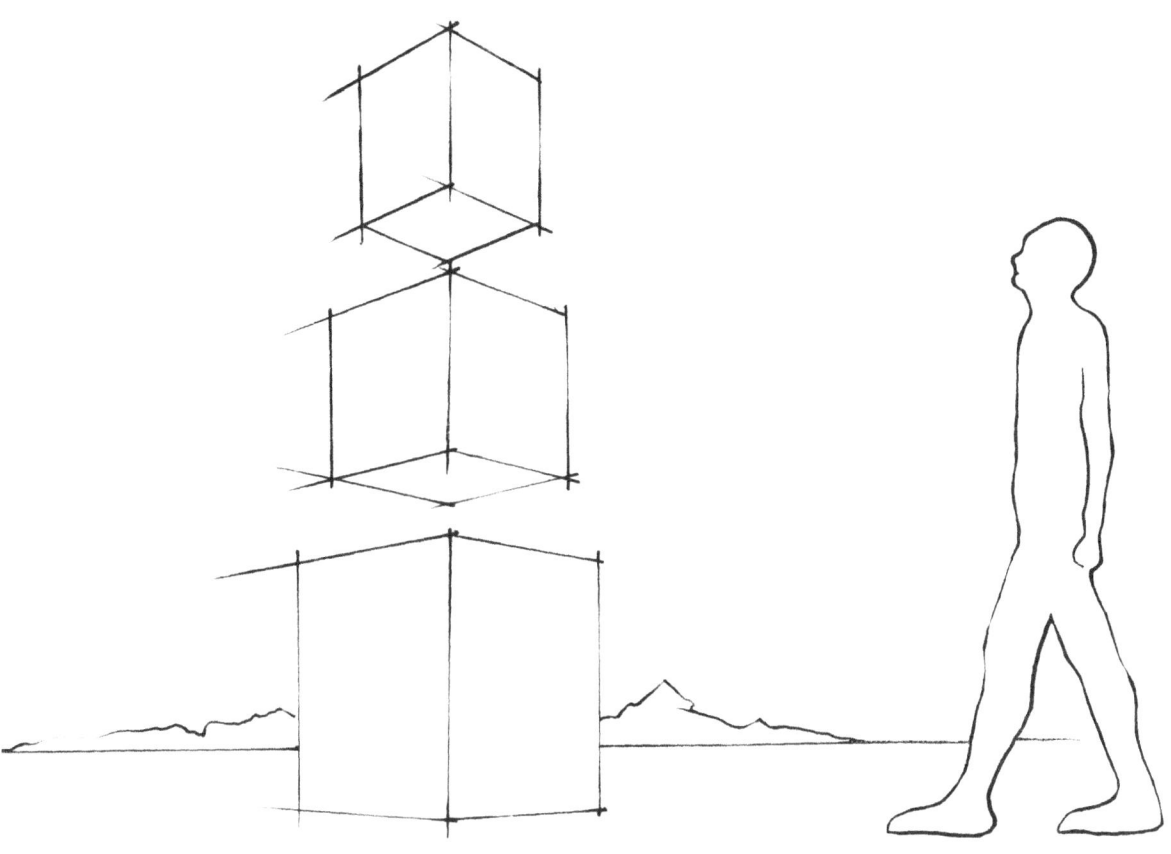

WANDERLUST

The act and or desire to wander or travel whether to the next village or across the universe to a new solar system. Do not box me in!

WHIRLPOOL

Water in a swift circular motion usually produced by the meeting of opposing currents, often causing downward spiral action and rapids. Skoocumchuck, yuculta and porlier pass are big in british columbia.

WHIRLYGIG

Love that toy that shows you the wind speed as it spins round. Some of the mylar folded over vanes had rainbow coloured stripes, conditioning us into post war adiction for psychedelikksxx.

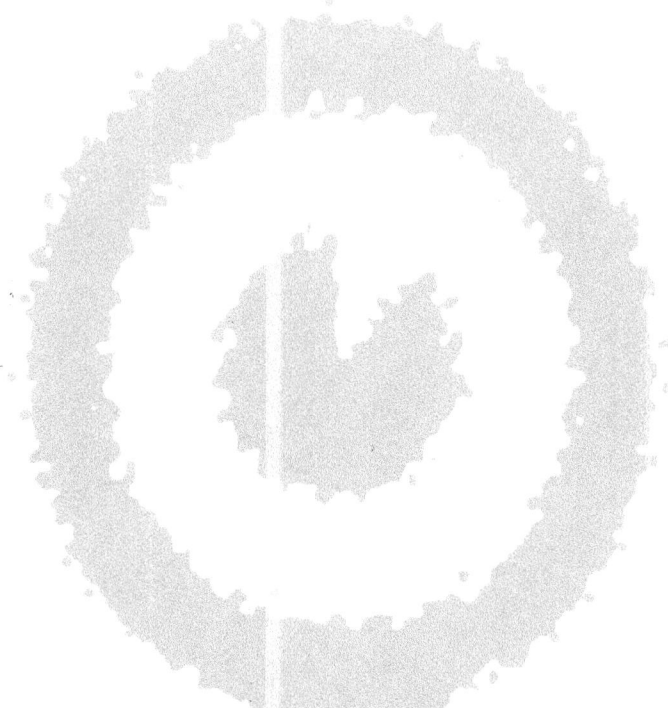

WATCHING THE TARGET

WUNDERBAR

Happy singing germans Ya.....Marvellous. cool, wonderful, terrific, something exceptionally good!

WOMB

In female mamals this is the organ of conception and gestation.....Wow how does this happen? Chickens, crocodiles and turtles lay eggs, we do the laying before the egg. You silly billy.....

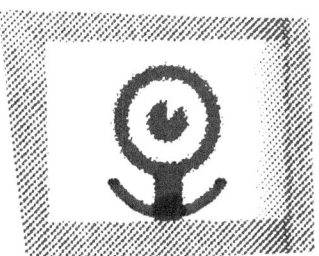

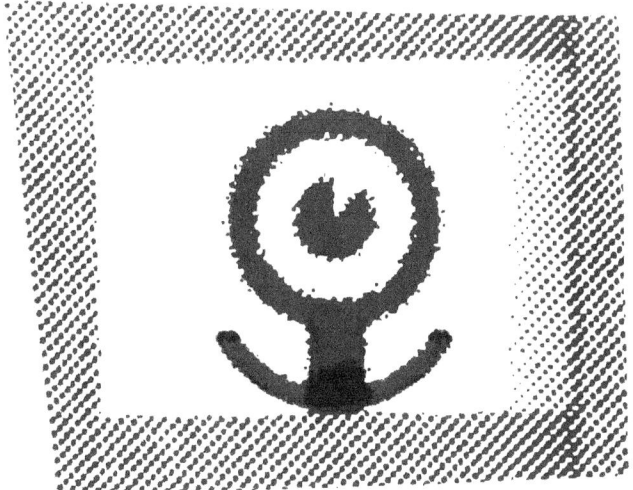

WINGIT

Off the cuff, wing it, play it by ear. Do it spontaneously.....Whatever.

WATCHU

Smile you are on a camera somewhere out there!

WOOLYWORT

Maybe from lancashire, from term wooly back; people from poor villages in lancashire, yorkshire, and cheshire who come to a big town or city. They are sketchy, shaddy, bit of a flake, have hair that resembles sheep and as boring as a plant in the garden! Wohhh.....

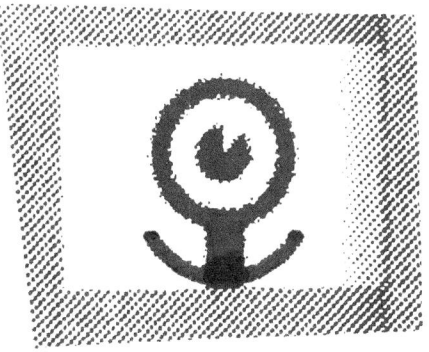

WAVE

Endless time looking for it, Adrian.....
be there to find it!.....The long
offshore fetch makes them, may
the force be with u!

WILLYNILLY

Whether one wishes to or not;
willingly or unwillingly: they have
to do it "Willy Nilly".

WETBACKS

Derogatory term used in the united
states of america for a person
of foreign nationality, usually an
illegal immigrant (which most of
the americans were once).

WORLD

This is your garden, try not to spoil
it or daddy will be very angry.

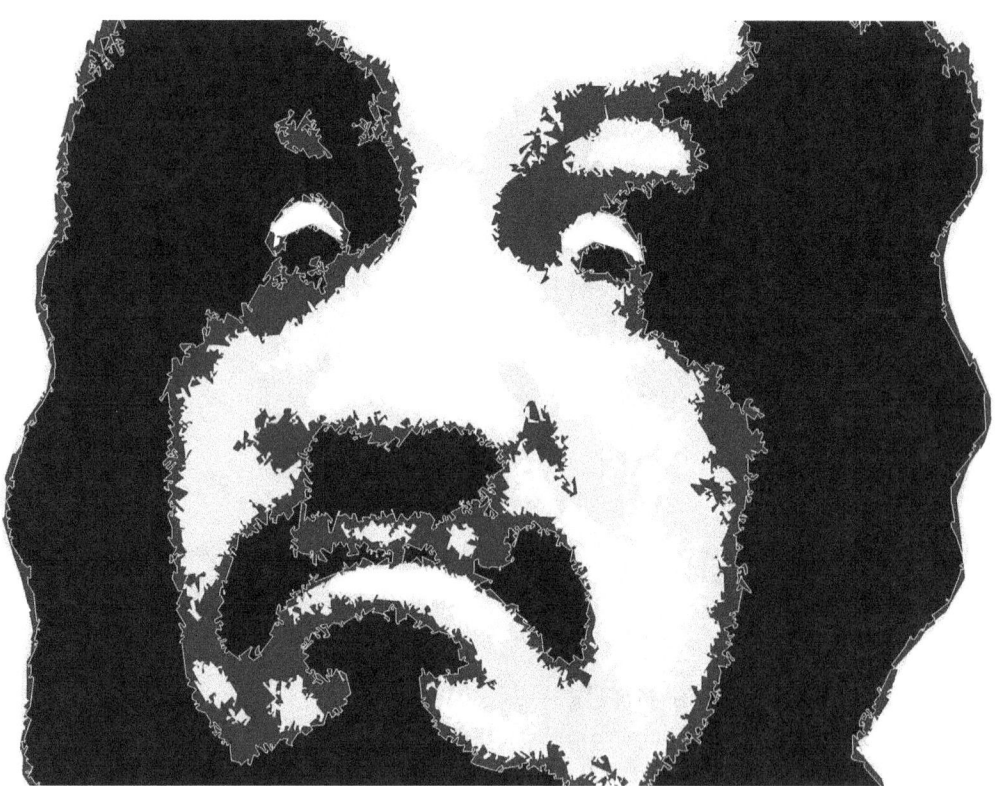

WONKY

Crooked, unsteady and loose. He is totally unreliable....
Not at all straight.....He is your worst relationship
nightmare, that will not go away. Sometimes normal,
most of the time a mental condition makes him wonky.

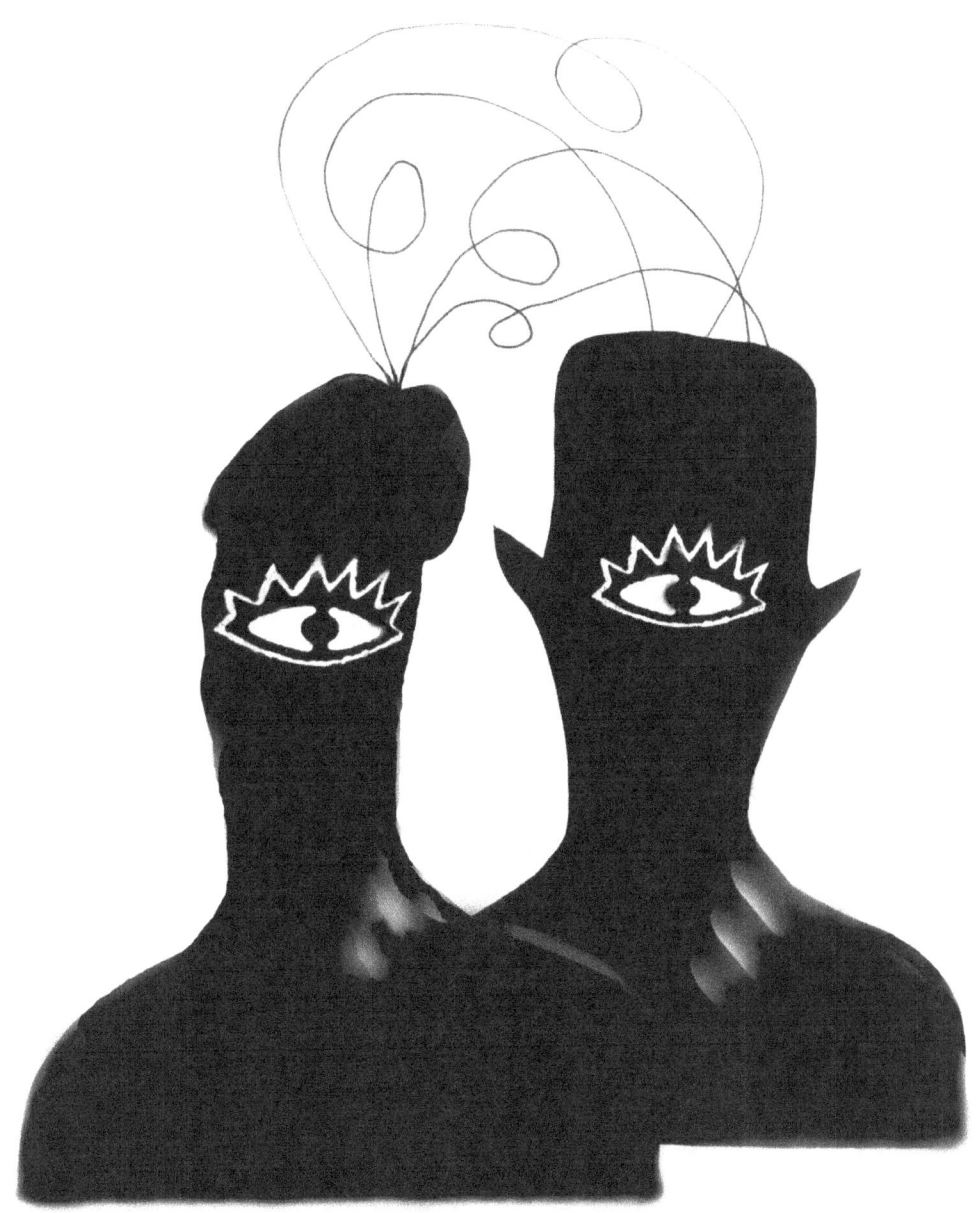

XCHANGE

Between each other.....Share, trade, unite,
link.....If its fair eye contact!

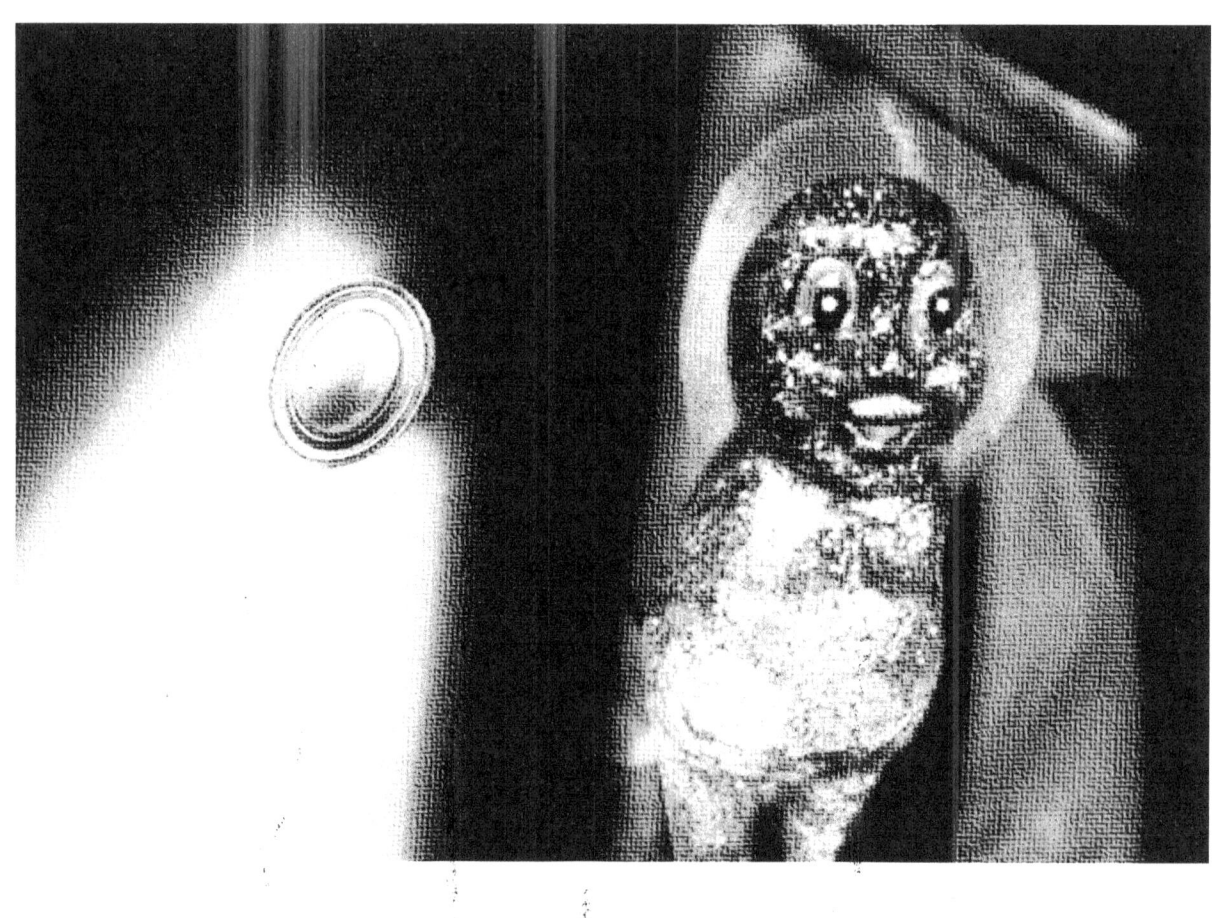

XRO

Extreme rip off.....A shady dodgy
unhonest person.

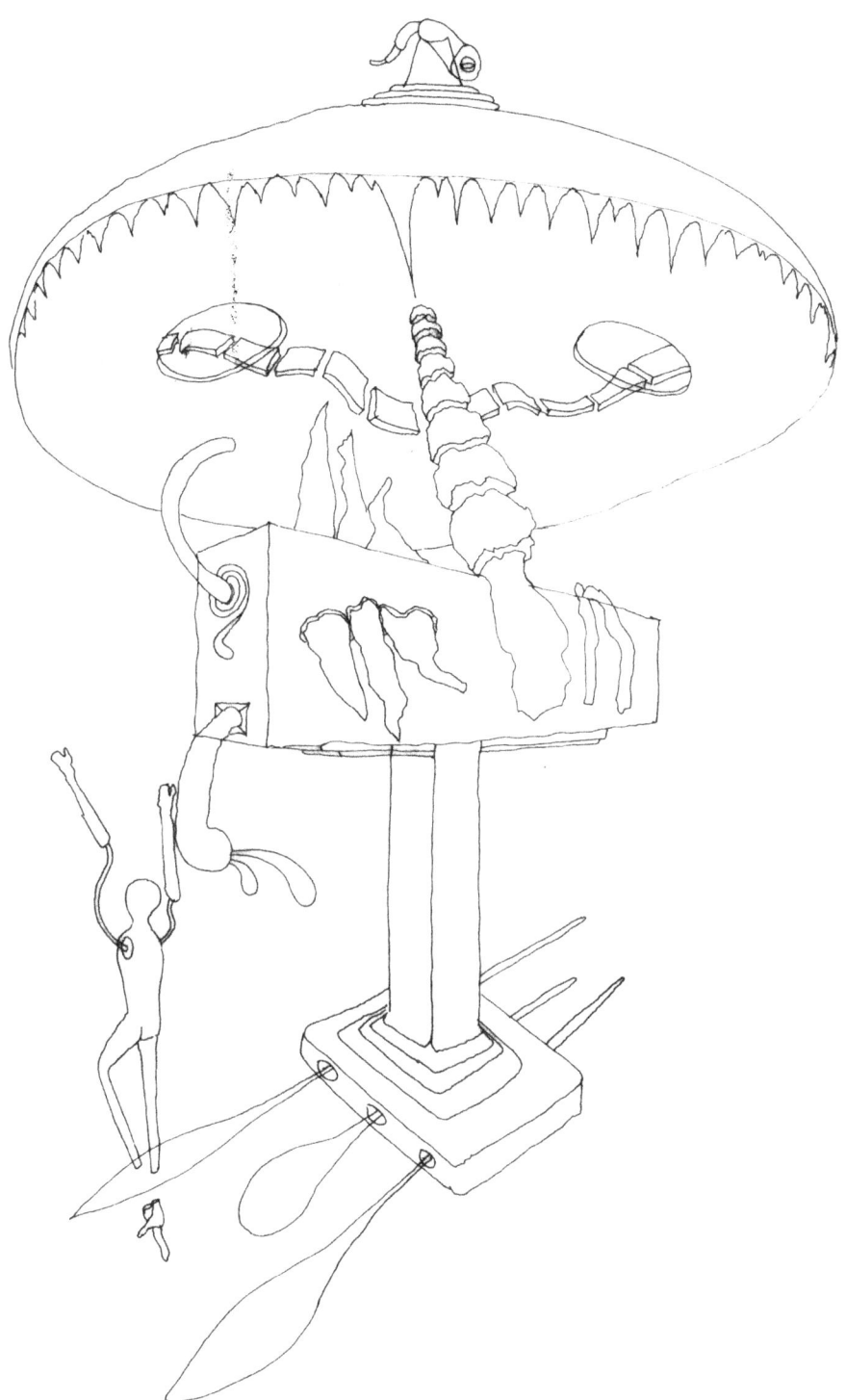

XENU $CIENO1OGISTS

Intergalatic tyrant, covered by his umbrella force-field.....This dancing scapegoat xenu is blamed for all the problems on earth say most thetans. Not commited anymore in the system.....Enjoy hubbard squash soup,

X-RING

The centre of a target. The bulls eye! Soldiers highest achievement.....The kill zone. My uncle Miles fought in world war one, then returned to die of the flu, really was that the flu that killed 30 million... XXXtreme biological and chemical weapons research was banned under the 1925 geneva protocol......Way out from Medicine Hat....Suffeld Alberta, There was a biological and chemical research centre that was created by the brits and canadians, it was used from 1941 to the early fifties!!! Declassified British Records now show us what we are really into!

XPOSED-

To call out someone or yourself about something ridiculous you did!

2069.... ONLY 999 MILLION

of us left on the planet....!

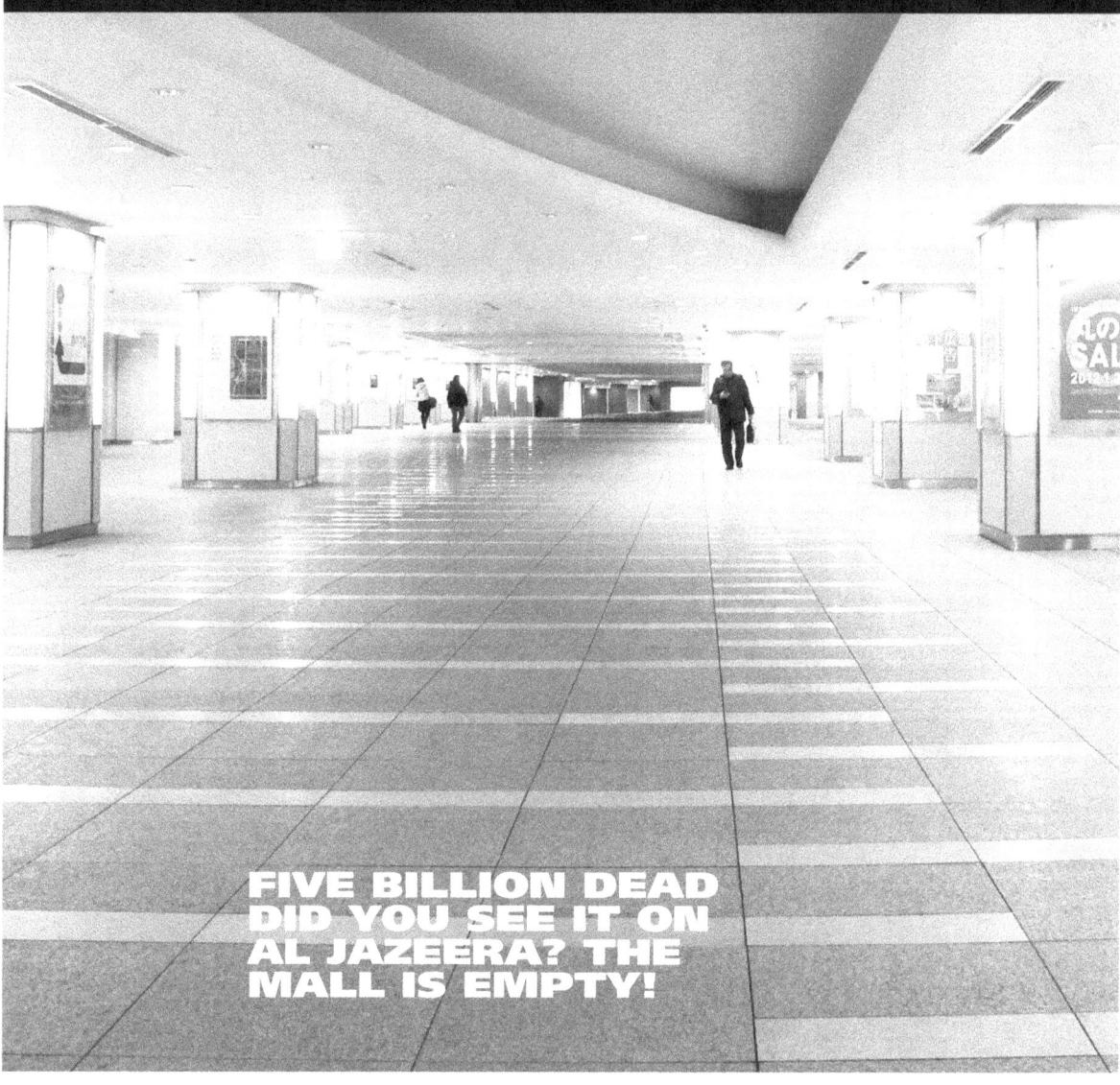

FIVE BILLION DEAD DID YOU SEE IT ON AL JAZEERA? THE MALL IS EMPTY!

XRAY

When I was thirteen I would have loved to have a pair of Xray glasses to look at all the girls in my life.....Now the security guard at the airport gets this great job.....All the bones in my body have been xray photographed.....

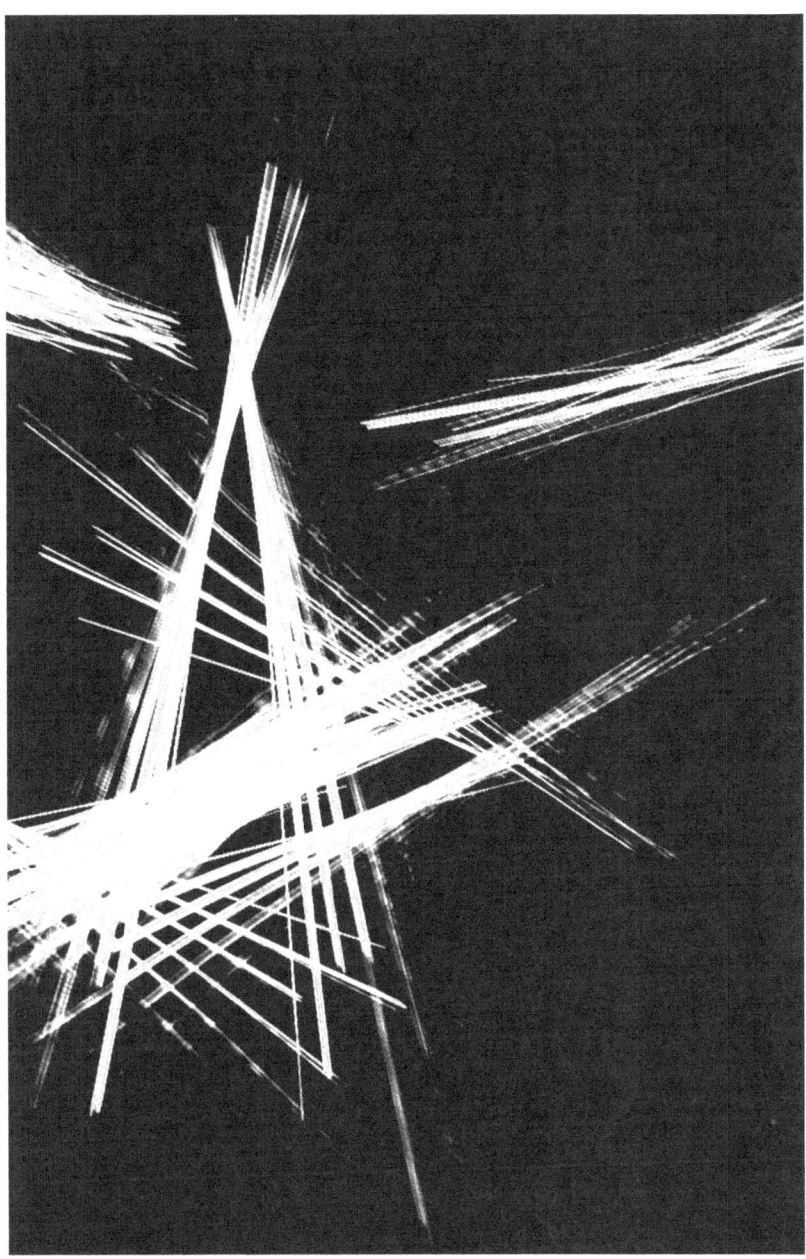

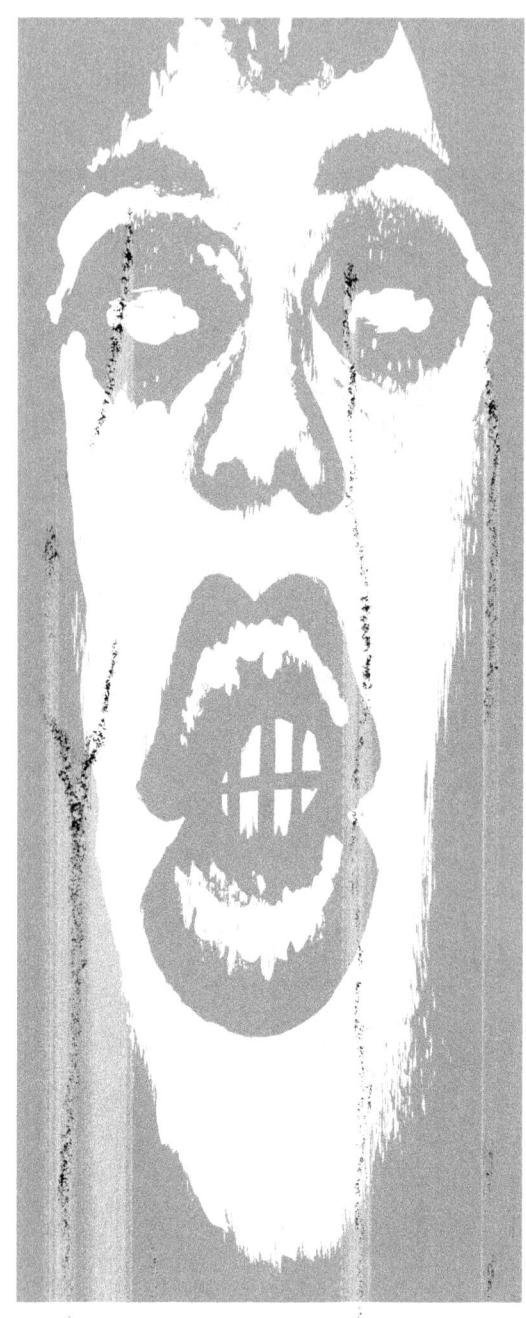

Xtreme horror fills you with feelings of fear that can shock your system, Like after a car accident, some sleep.....Many make wrong decisions in shock.

XTRA XTRA

Read all about....Give that something more.....In cornwall "quill" is a tip at the end of a proper job. Go the extra mile show you care, give it all you have got....Yet not a bribe!

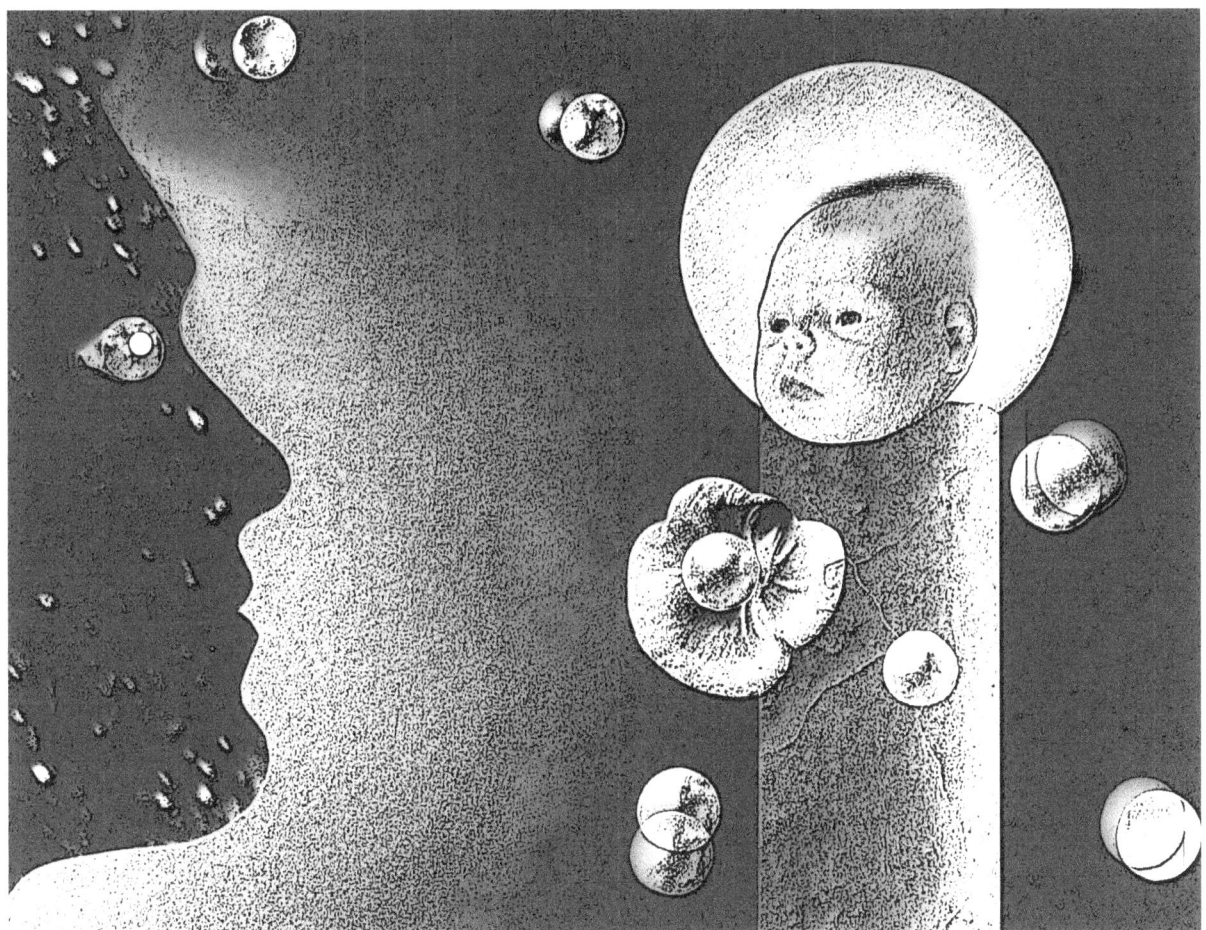

XPRESS

Speed......Show your thoughts, politics, ideas to others, squeeze it out! Fast moving, The babies are paying my pension. Sweet pearls and flowers! Look up to the new born.....

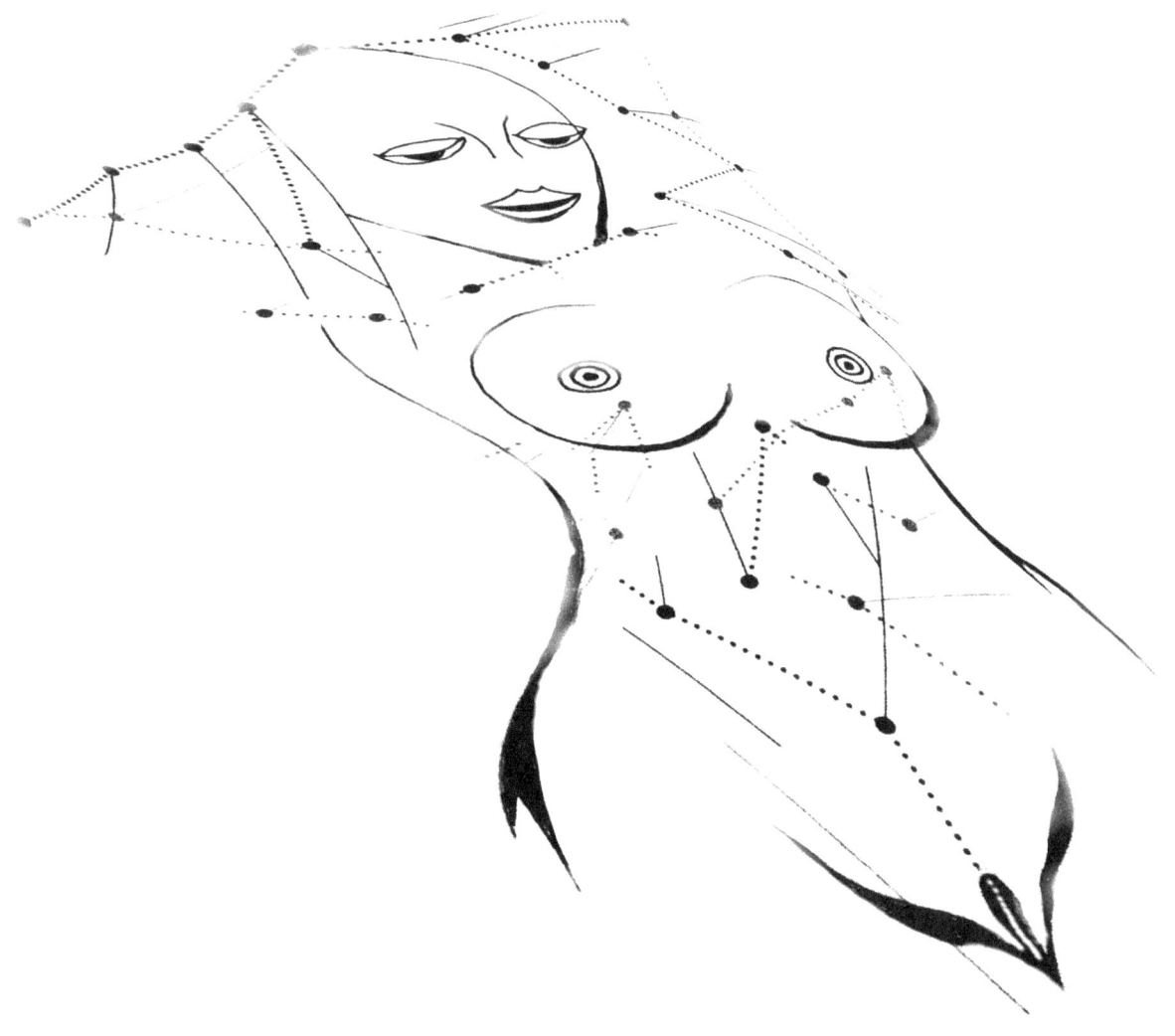

XEELEE

She is an omniPOTENT being.....She has absolute control over everything in your universe.....One baddass mofo!

XENOMORPH

A creature based on H.R. Gigers design and seen in the alien movies.

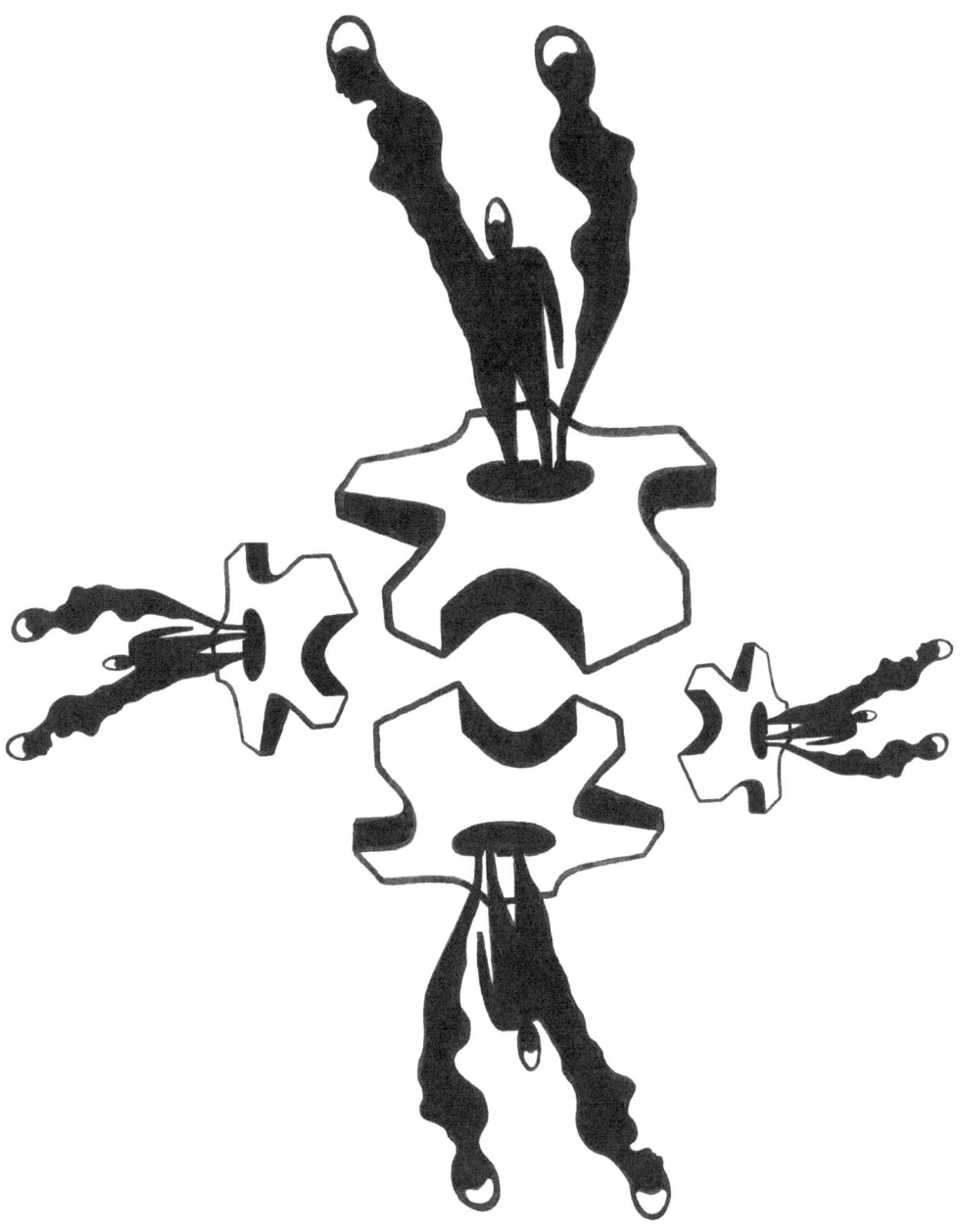

XEROX Xerography a dry copying process in which powder adheres to areas remaining electrically charged after exposure of surface to light from image of document to be copied. (greek xeros: dry). This process started a revolution in the graphics art and media business in the sixties. Artist enjoyed this copy revolution.....Did xerox invent the mouse and the GUI desktop interface?

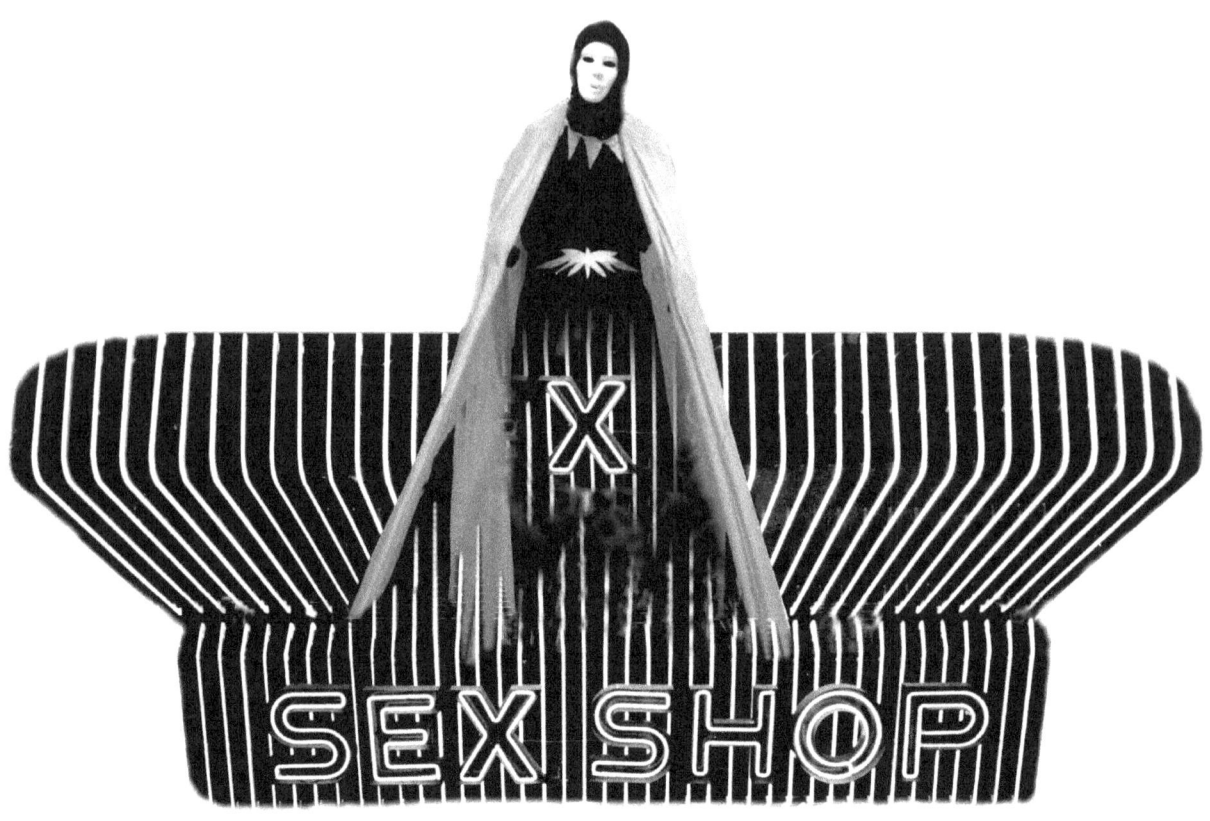

X RATED

How come X stands for sex? And XXXX is four times better sex as well as an oz beer!

XYLAPHONE

Musical instument?. Kiss your lover over the iphone..... LOL txt.l

X FILES

Sometimes means strange or weird.....Filmed in vancouver..... Nine years of visualising the paranormal, how many hours of stories and visuals did I see? Time travel, shape shifting, great scifi.

XIA

A cool person whose life is centered around asian culture and anime. A way to define something spectacular.

XOBILE

Transmitting, recieving or searching for adult content on a wifi device.

XANGA

A live journal type website that people use to complain about their pathetic lives. The bottom of the barrel of blogs! I TyPe LyKe DiS, I R3PR3S3NT smal TaLk.....FrigGiN aNnOyiNg!!!

EXPLAIN IN ONE MINUTE WHAT YOU HAVE DONE IN YOUR LIFE?

Should you read the paradox of our time by George Carlin? YES.

Are the eskimos and africans right when they say is it a hot day?

Will the future be a thing of the past, like fantastic voyage?

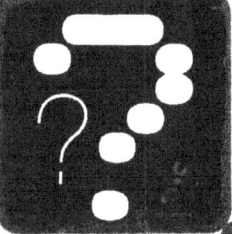

How many questions should you ask?

US/FR.....Do you live to work or work to live?

Ask your pastor can belief create reality?

If I agreed with you we'd both be wrong?

What do you think mummy?

Why did I do that, auto pilot?

Do I need a bigger neocortex?

Why does love control us?

Why are we carbon creatures?

Believe in fuzzy logic, yes?

What are we doing here?

Do wars destroy economies?

Does life sculpt your being?

Why quantum computers?

Does David Levy love life with robots that much?

Are you that person you really think you are?

Surreal art, is it more mind than meets the eye?

In perception, is art ahead of the world of science?

How long till we are totally nonbiological beings?

Is the origin of human existence only movement?

In space or time, will we get out of this world alive?

WILL YOU PLAN TO SPEND TIME IN YOUR LIFE BEING WHAT YOU WANT?

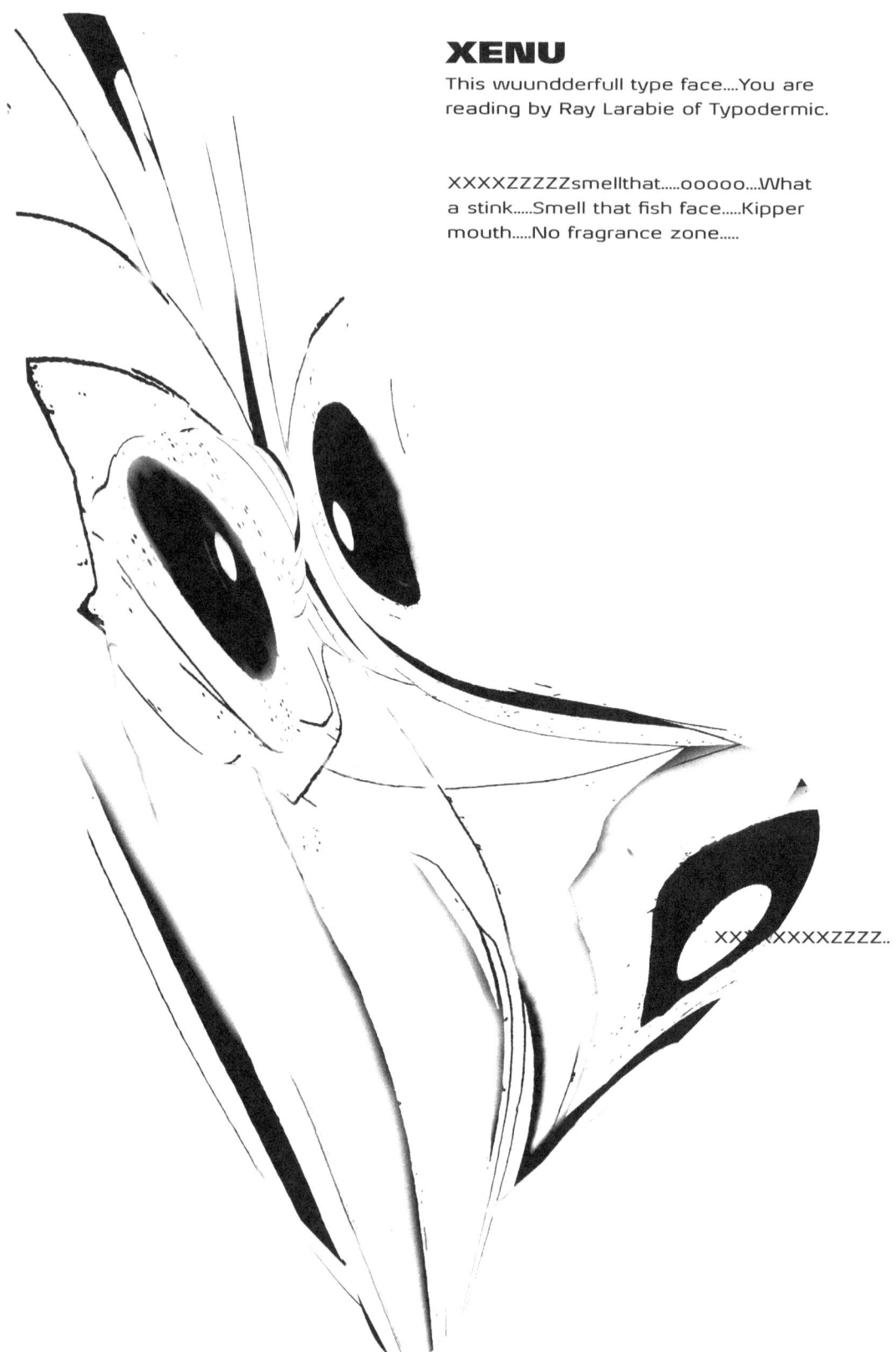

XENU

This wuundderfull type face....You are reading by Ray Larabie of Typodermic.

XXXXZZZZZsmellthat.....ooooo....What a stink.....Smell that fish face.....Kipper mouth.....No fragrance zone.....

XXXXXXXXXZZZZ..

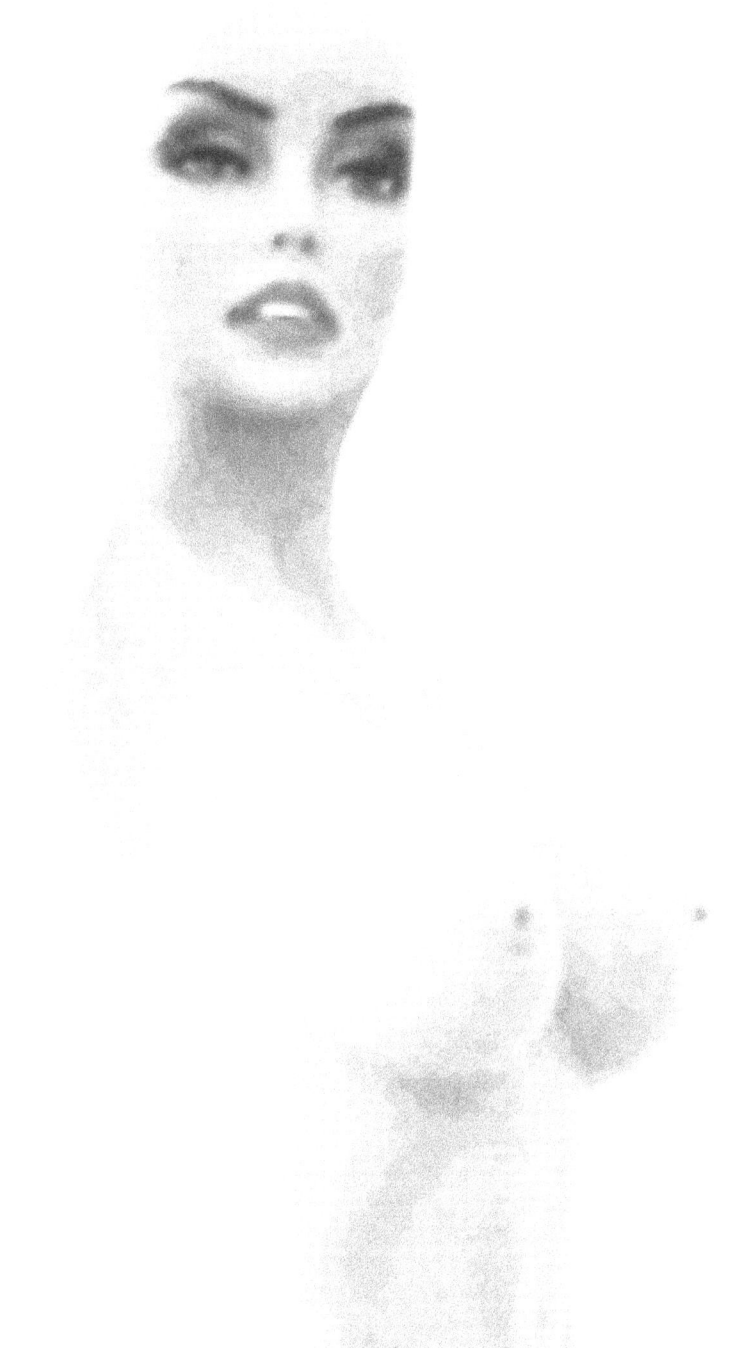

XXXX-rated womanquin, we make them in our own image....Curves can do it, what about texture, shadows and of course smell.....Fair moans man!

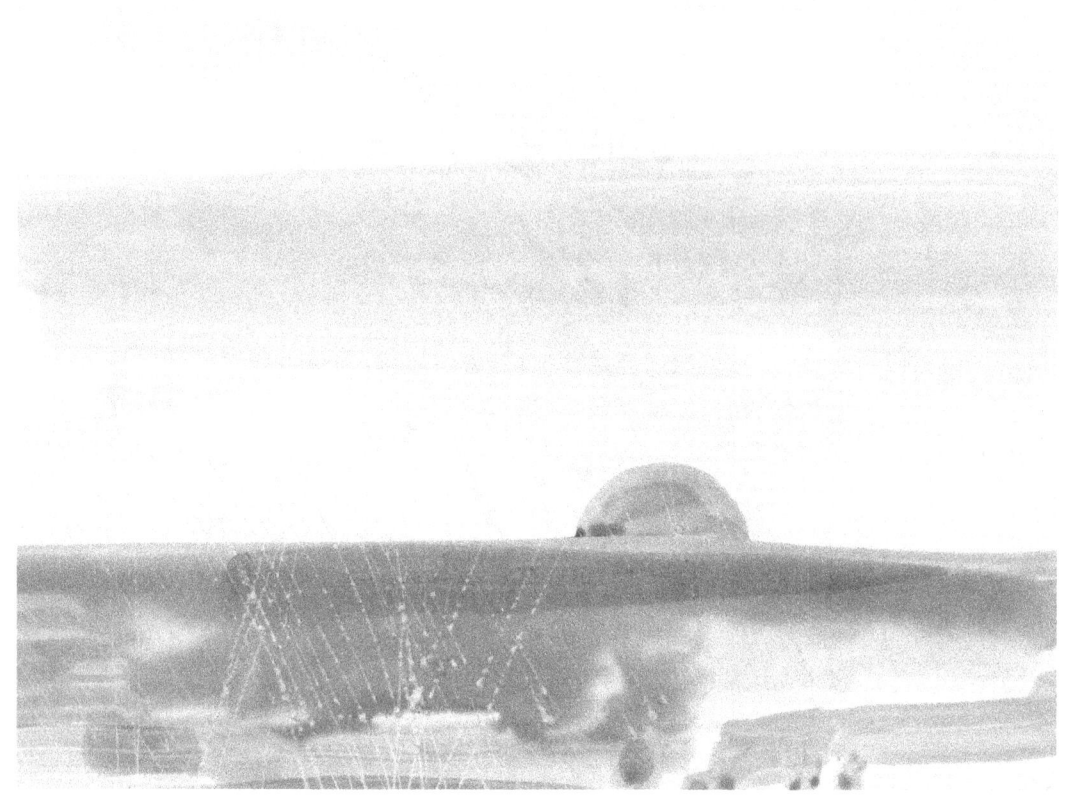

XXXX

Every time I see sunsets I remember drinking
fourex.....And of course on interlectual nights at
the contemporary art society, it was red wine of
no known varietal! The fear of going blind, was
in our young minds! I had not heard of many
successful blind artists, still you could always count
on me giving a donation to the blind seeing dog
association. I had a part time job back in the sixties
in the castlemaine perkins breweries in brisbane,
then the proud makers of four X, I never became
an alcoholic but I did save enough money to move
to carnaby street and lived in notting hill.

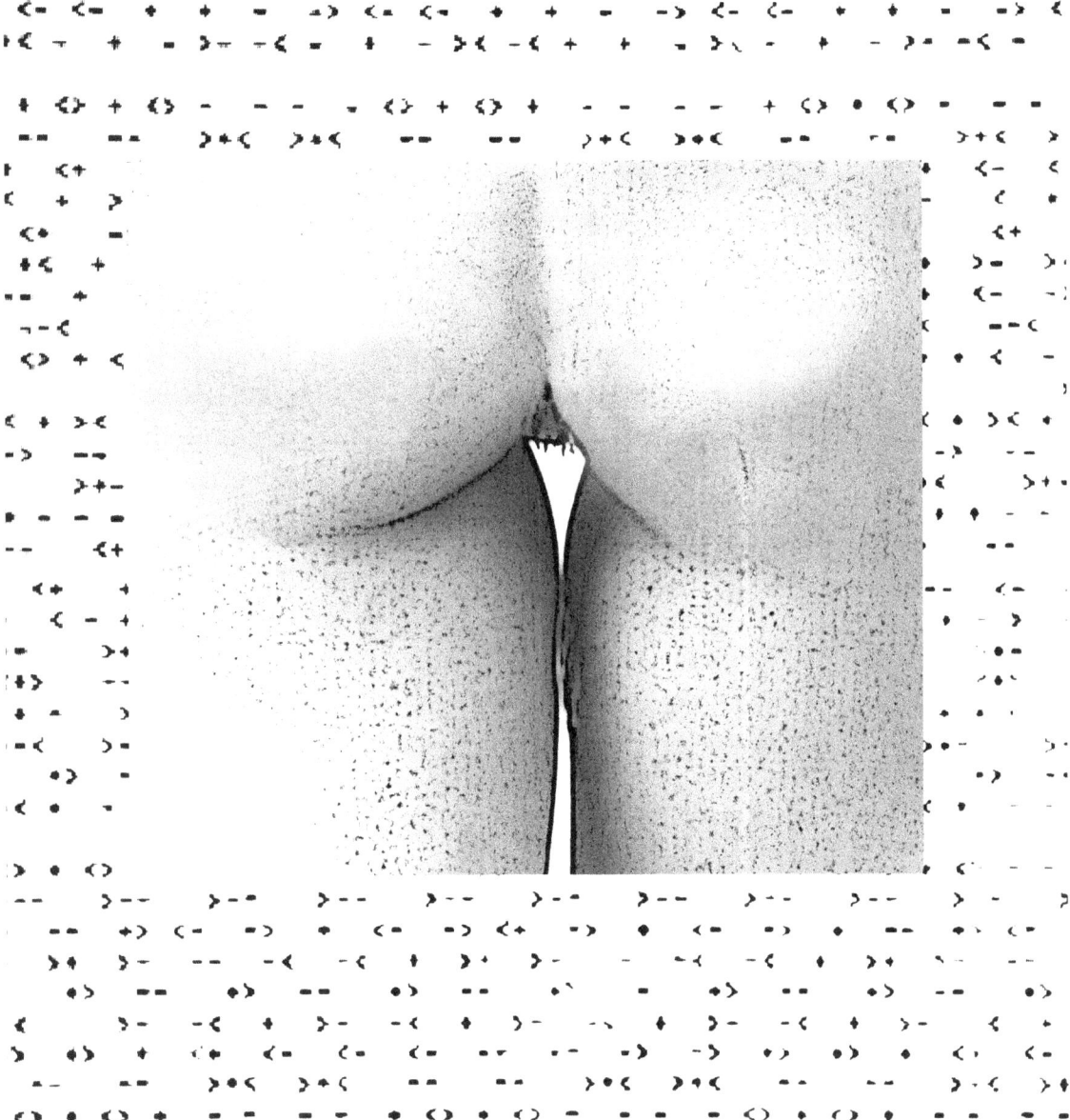

X MARKS THE SPOT

I think my skin is covered with a lot of spots.
X is also number ten in latin.

XENOPHOBIA

Morbid dislike of strangers and
foreigners (greek xenos strangers).

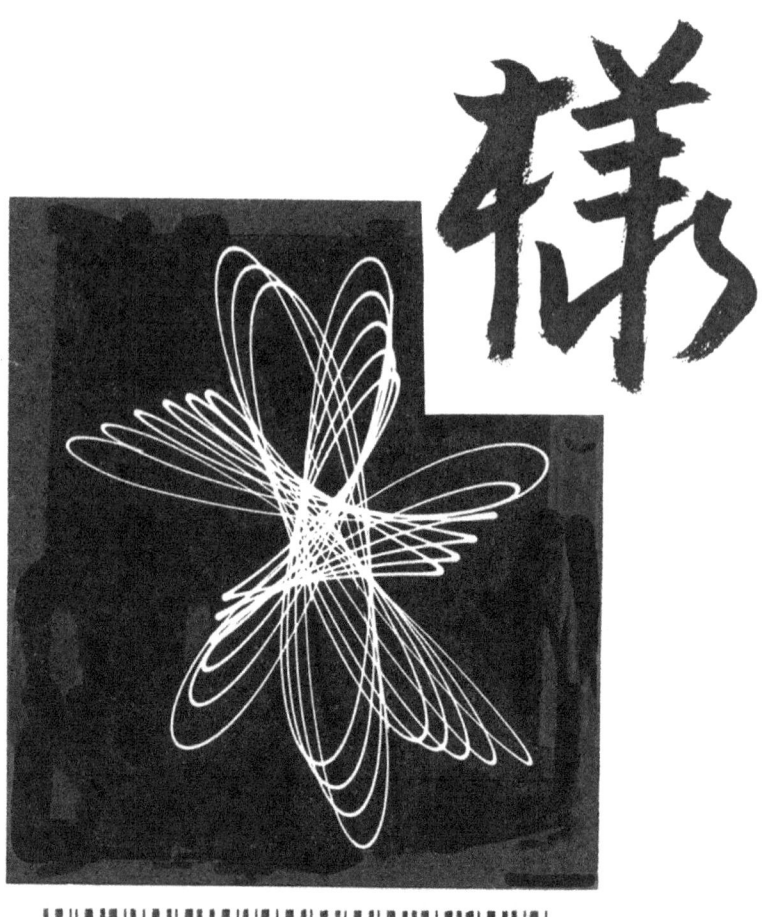

191023111157

YO-YO

Toy consisting of a pair of disks with deep groove between them, in which string is attached and wound, and which can be made to rise and fall, originally from the island of honshu wanqu....The meaning of cultures to rise and fall with energy loss, till motionless like life. Yo! yo!

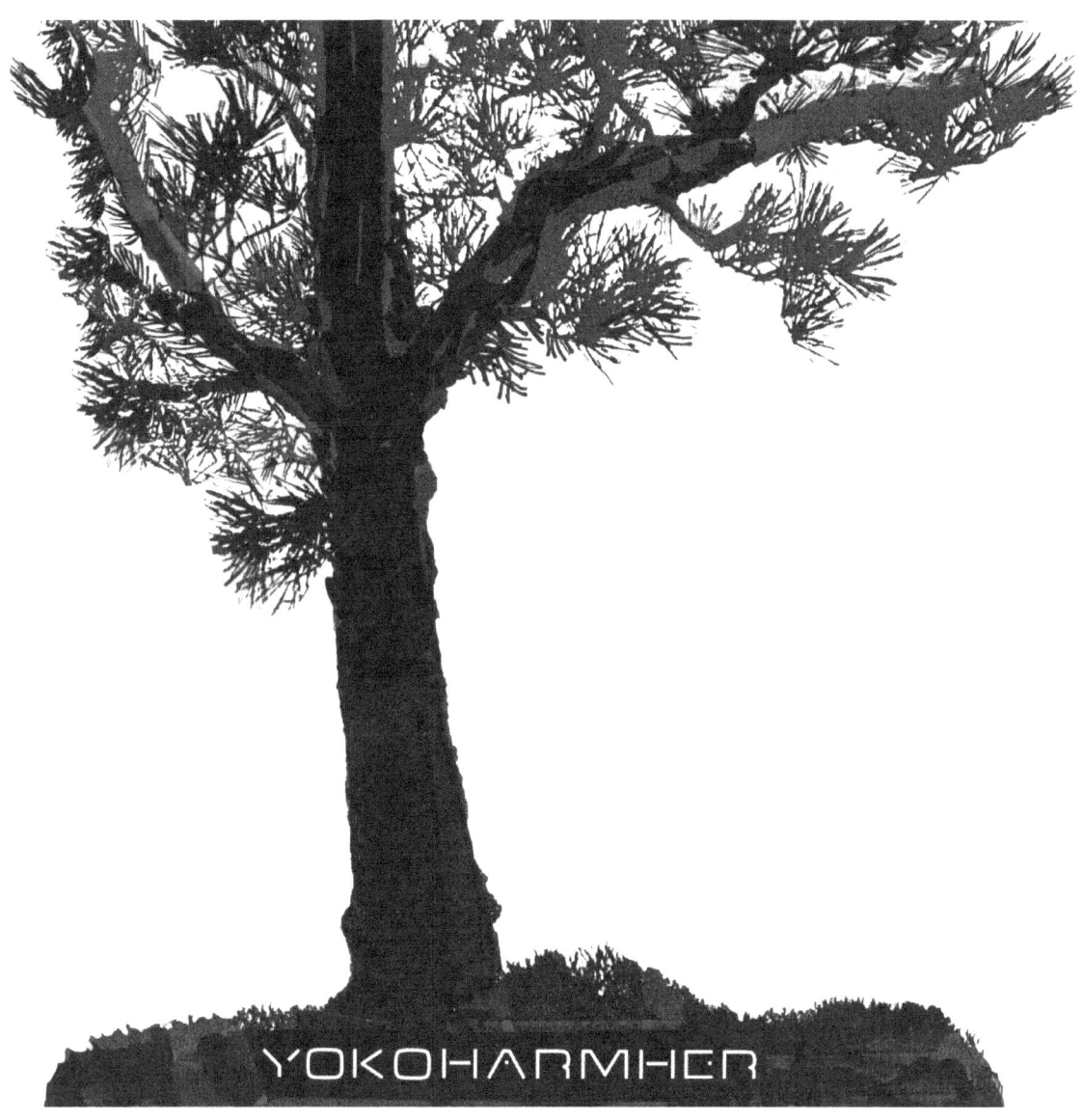

YOO is Y, J is W, double you is W

......Pachinko the addiction of a sudokyo tribe, meticulous in organising real order, they take your idea and finish it correctly.

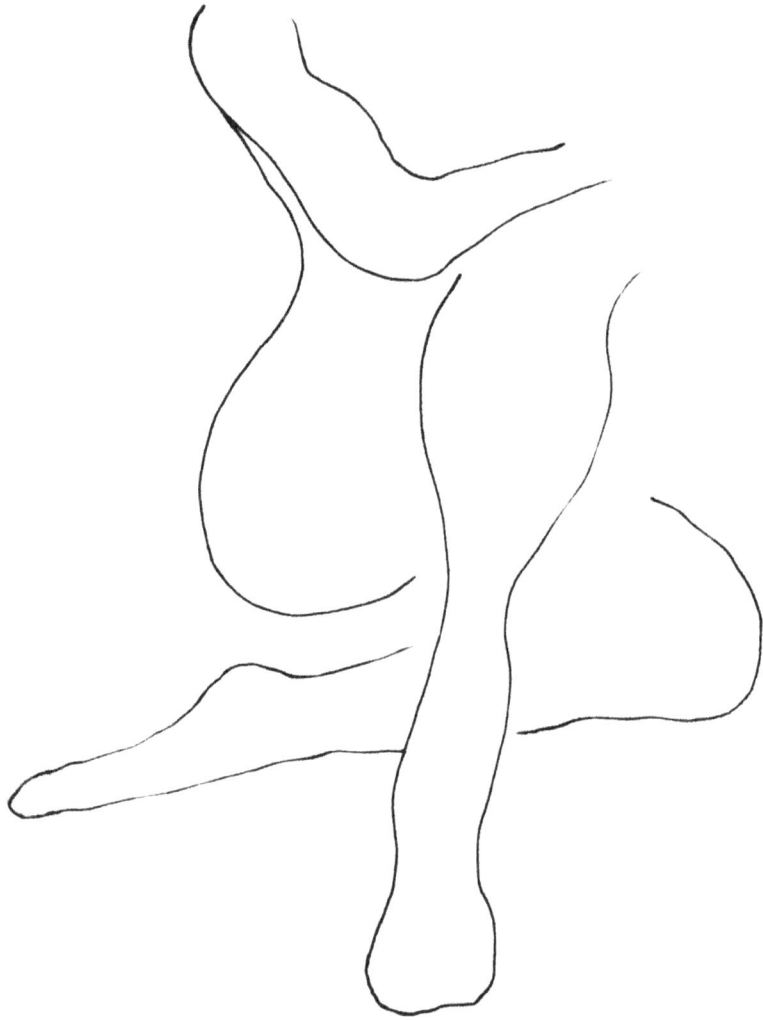

YVES TANGUY

The maker of organic fluid moon shadows, you can't always
get what you want in a painting. Franco-americano surrealist
in the world of dali, and max ernst. Tanguys style in his
paintings, join inner and outer reality in an organic jello
landscape which explores his subconscious mind. Living
the later part of his life with american surrealist Kay Sage.....
What was it like over breakfast? Did they have notebooks
on each side of the bed every night.....I met their therapist in
1966mmmmmmmmmmm on holiday in goa.

Onward christian soldiers going on to war.....Thank God.

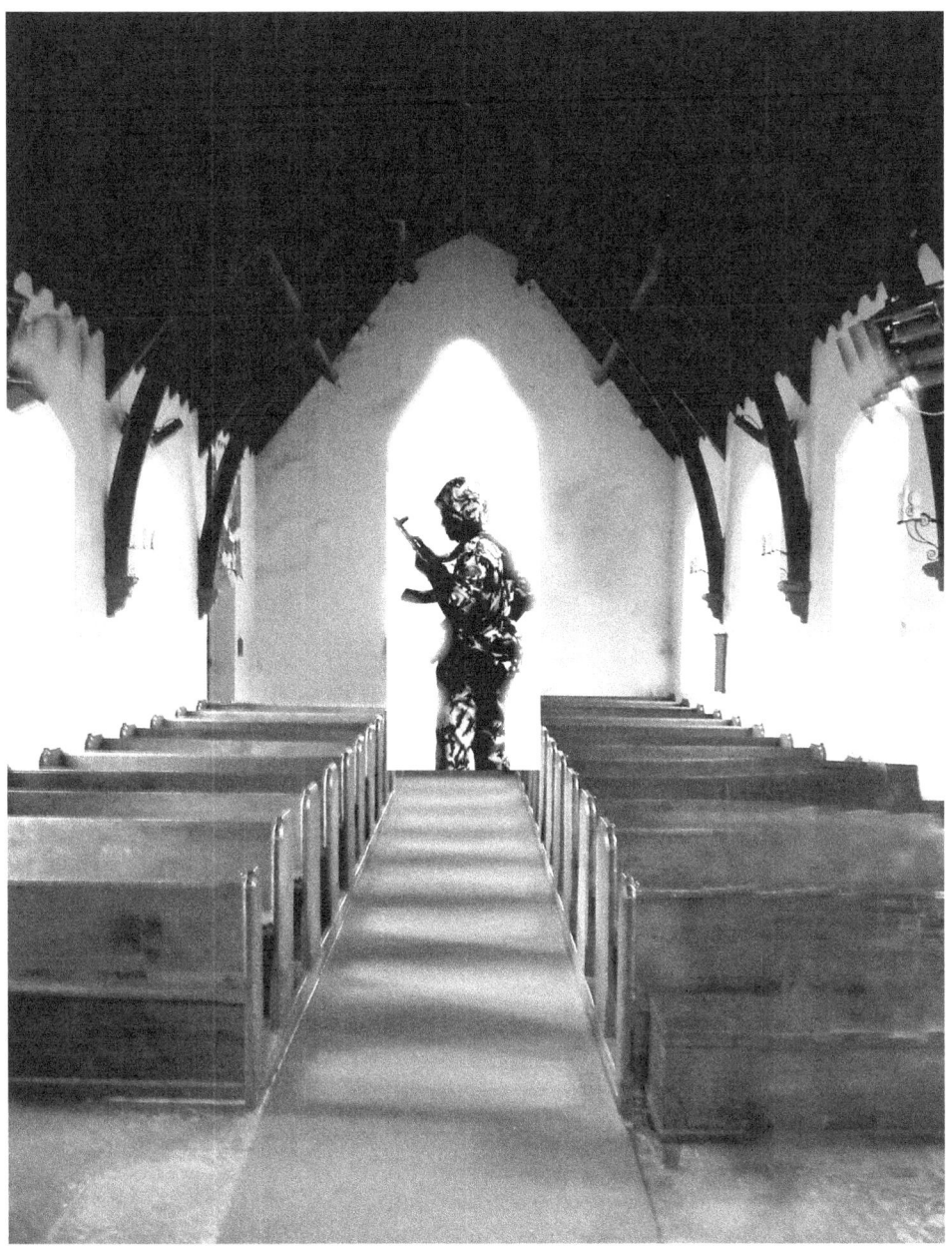

YEAR AD
The marker of dates for calendars, after christ......

Y HATS, iMPR3551V3 7hiNG5!

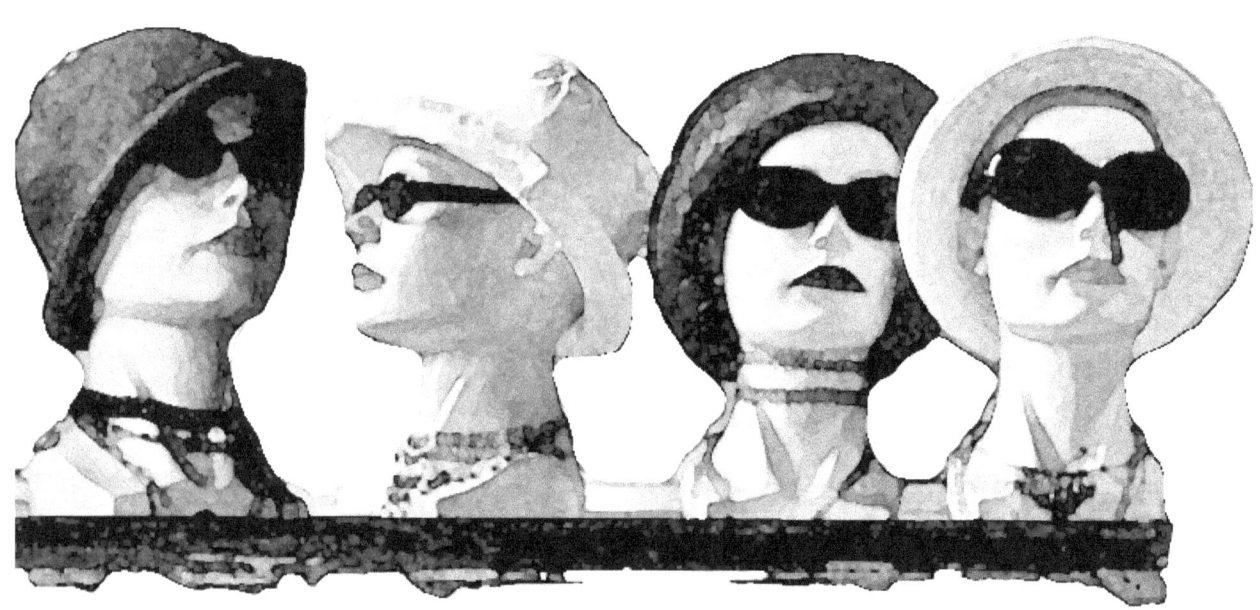

YAK

Endless small talk.....The forplay we all have to endure to start any relationship, passing ships in the sea of society..... Love hermits, such a great word HERMIT from the greek solitary. Crawl under a rock hermit crab, have you ever seen a group of crabs partying together? Long haired bovine fluffy animal from the himalayan region.

YOLPIE

A derogatory term for a privileged college student that fronts as an online executive.

Y SHADES, U R R34DiNG 7Hi5

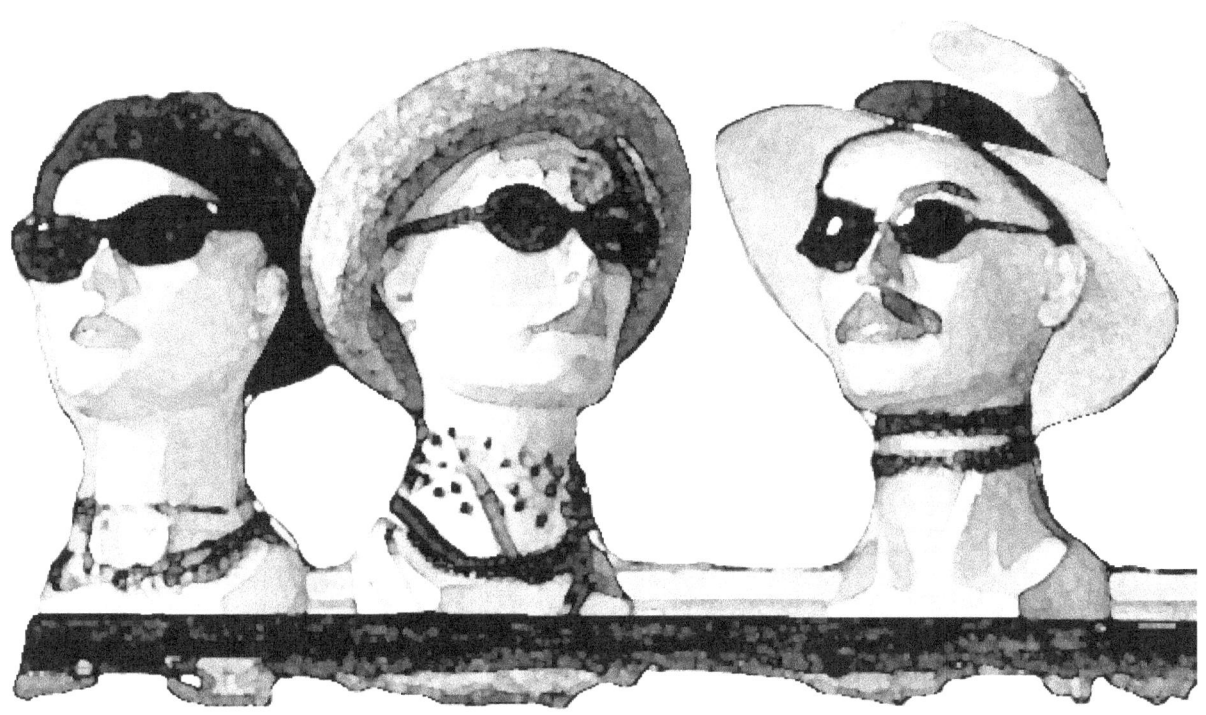

YOPROF

Sensei.....Born before the younger.
Generally master or teacher. Sharing life
experience with the nexgen.

YO MO

Short for your mum!

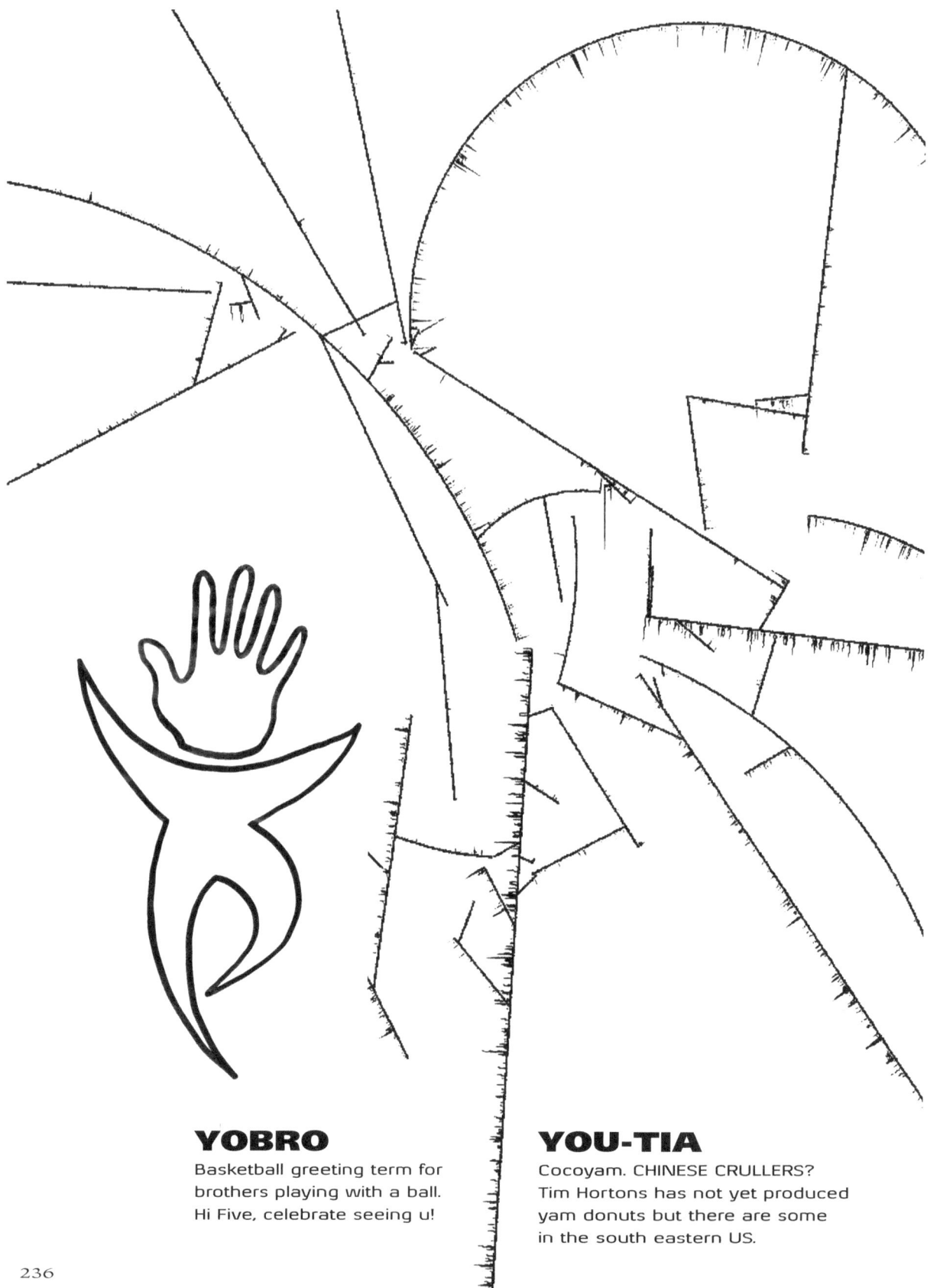

YOBRO

Basketball greeting term for
brothers playing with a ball.
Hi Five, celebrate seeing u!

YOU-TIA

Cocoyam. CHINESE CRULLERS?
Tim Hortons has not yet produced
yam donuts but there are some
in the south eastern US.

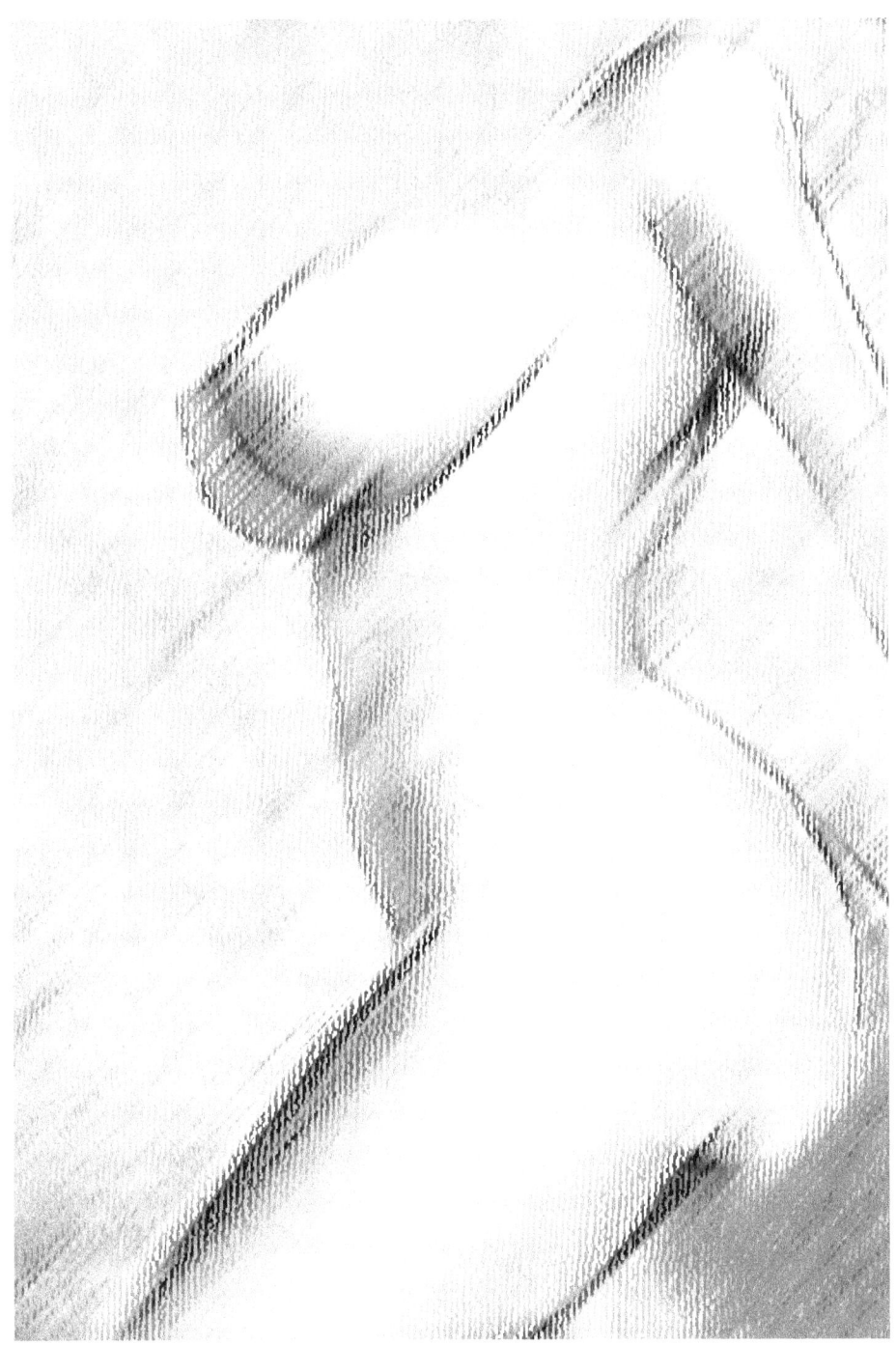

YEARN
To be filled with longing or compassion or tenderness. That says it all!

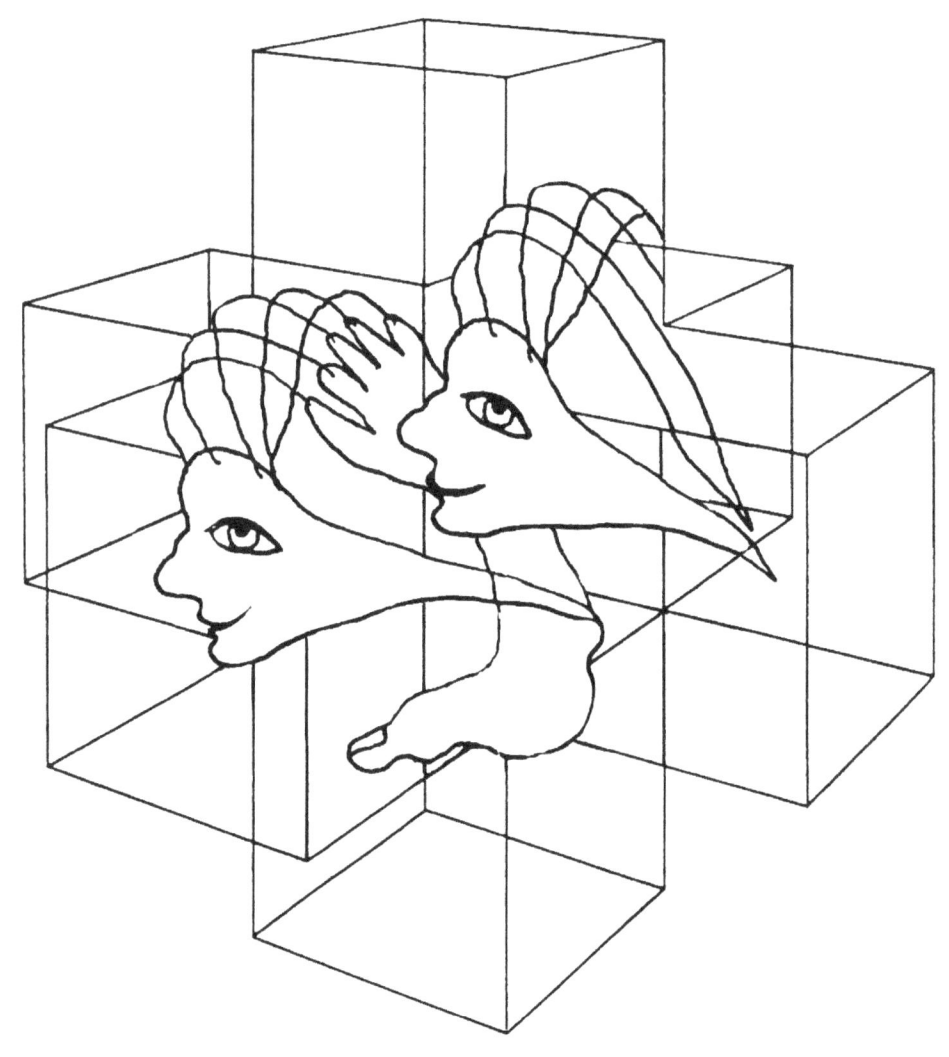

YOO-HOO

Pressing desire to attract person's attention.
Sound of greeting.....Coming out of ones box!

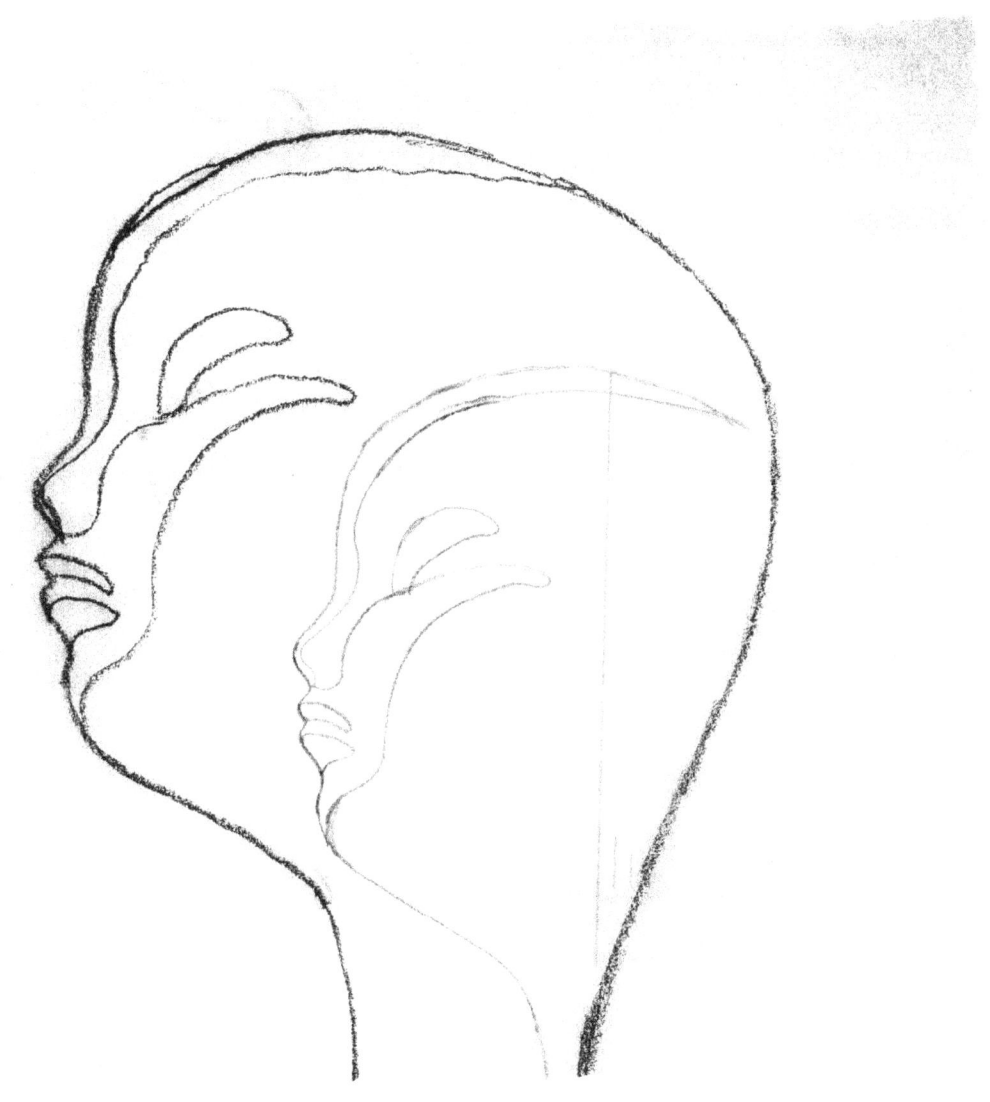

ZENANA Part of a house for the safe seclusion of women of high-caste families in Iran and India..... What can you say, should this happen world wide, what about the chinese women in a certain province that have their own language, that the men can not understand.....Masons mind out!

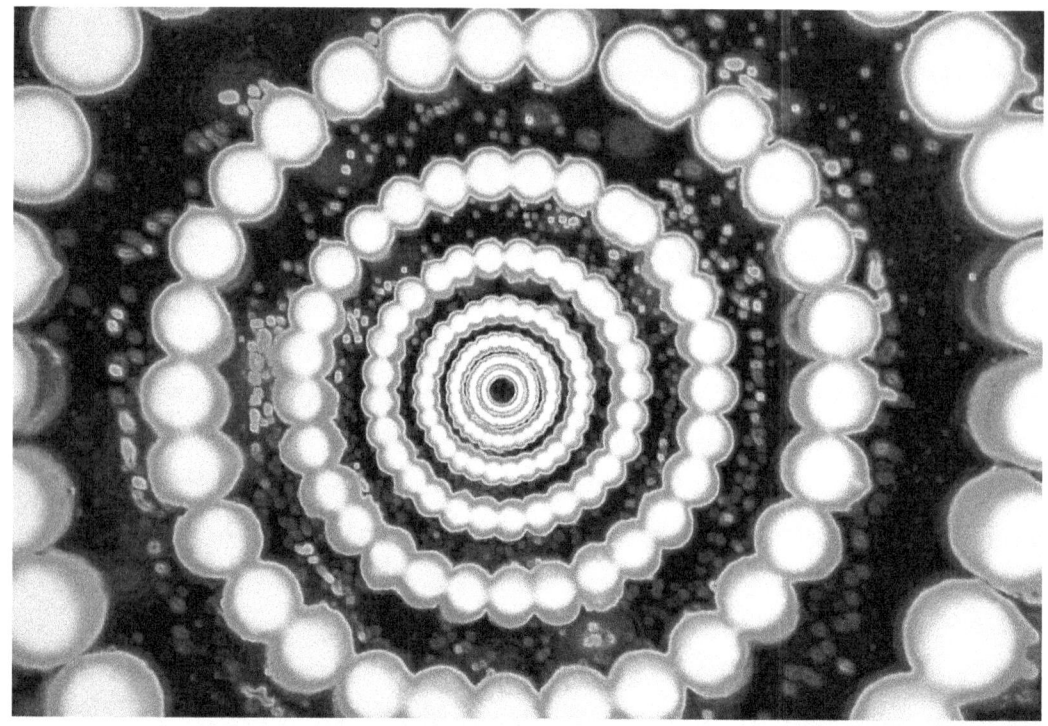

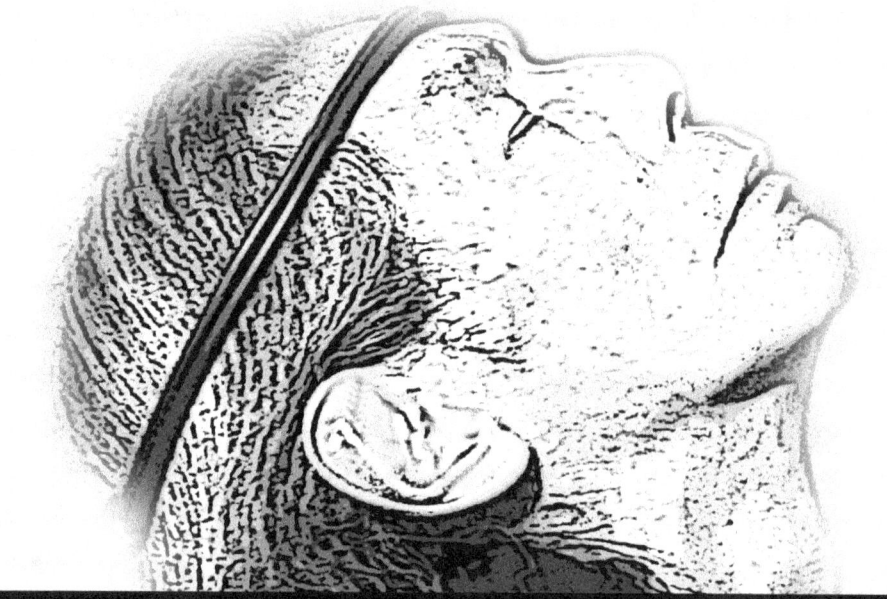

ZEN.....The ultimate strangeness!!! The Zen of seeing by Franck, read it!

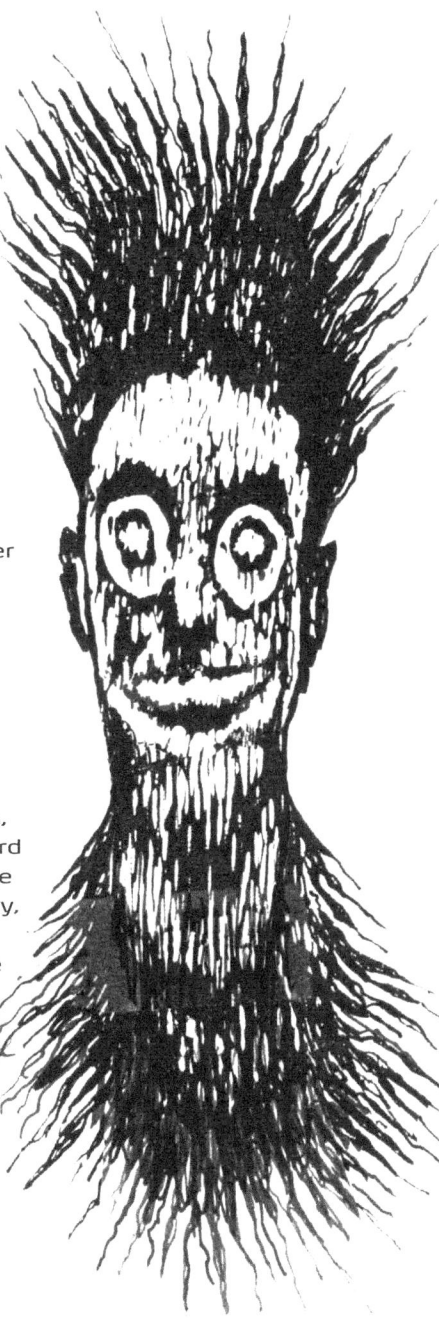

ZILLION

Large number! Cairo people at midday, big city so many people going to the toilet!

ZOLPIDEM

A sedative-hypnotic medicine used for short-term treatment of insomnia. Maybe habit forming, must not be taken by anyone younger than eighteen years. While using this drug you may have loss of memory.

ZAMBONI

The cleaning robot god driven by canadian man, they must know this word in the canuck knowledge immigration test for entry, to be a real canadian. Hockey lover.....Break the ice, with bling cherry!

ZETA

The great experimental magazine in london in the sixties. The greek letter 6, six or is that sex.

ZONE

Area 51.....A compound where your mind is. Section you are forced to exist within.

ZONGZIS

In the eurasian city of vancouver you get these incredible zongzis (chinese rice dumplings stuffed with all sorts of goodies wrapped in bamboo leaves), at the dragon boat festival and during gung hay fat choy festivities.

ZANY

Comically idiotic, crazilly ridiculous. buffoon, jester. It must be the description for this book!

ZYMOTIC
Ω¥µø†ˆç

Option key instead of shift second line, hey who is a cryptic code breaker? greek, zume leaven..... Fermentation, where's the bread!

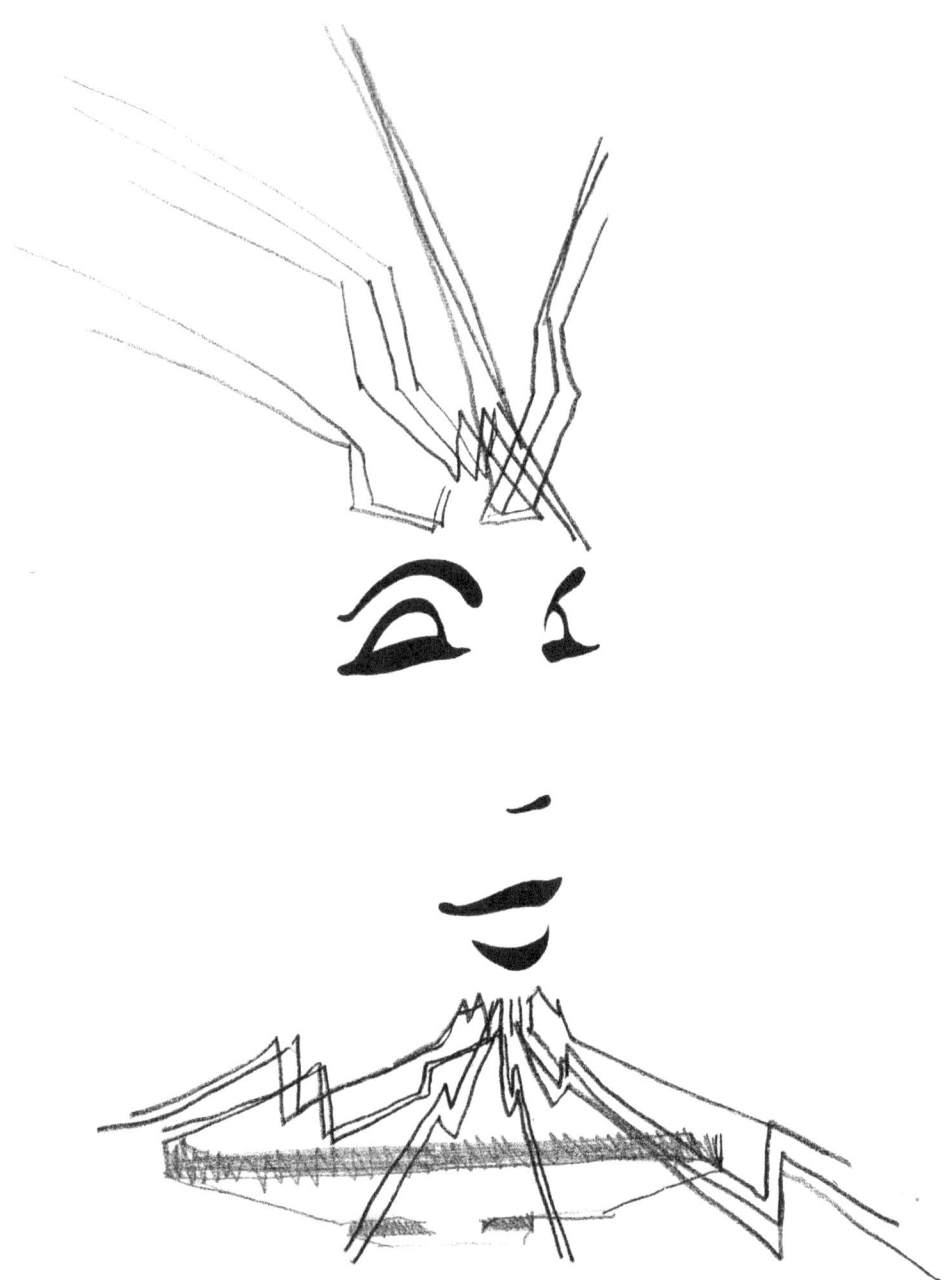

ZENITH

point of the heavans directly
above the observer. Highest point
(of power or prosperity etc). Arab.
American trusted radio reciever
brand, long gone. Peak

ZIPPADEEDOODAH

Disney, Alice in wonderland, kareoke,
tokyo, bar none.....Up up and away,
singing makes you live longer.....Thank
God, which one?

ZANZIBAR

Exotic!!! Used to be one of the richest arab trade entry point for east africa in the early colonial days. Dhows would sail in laiden with Indian and Arabian treasure.

ZULU

South African Bantu people.....
Good brand we all know.....
Where's the Biltong.

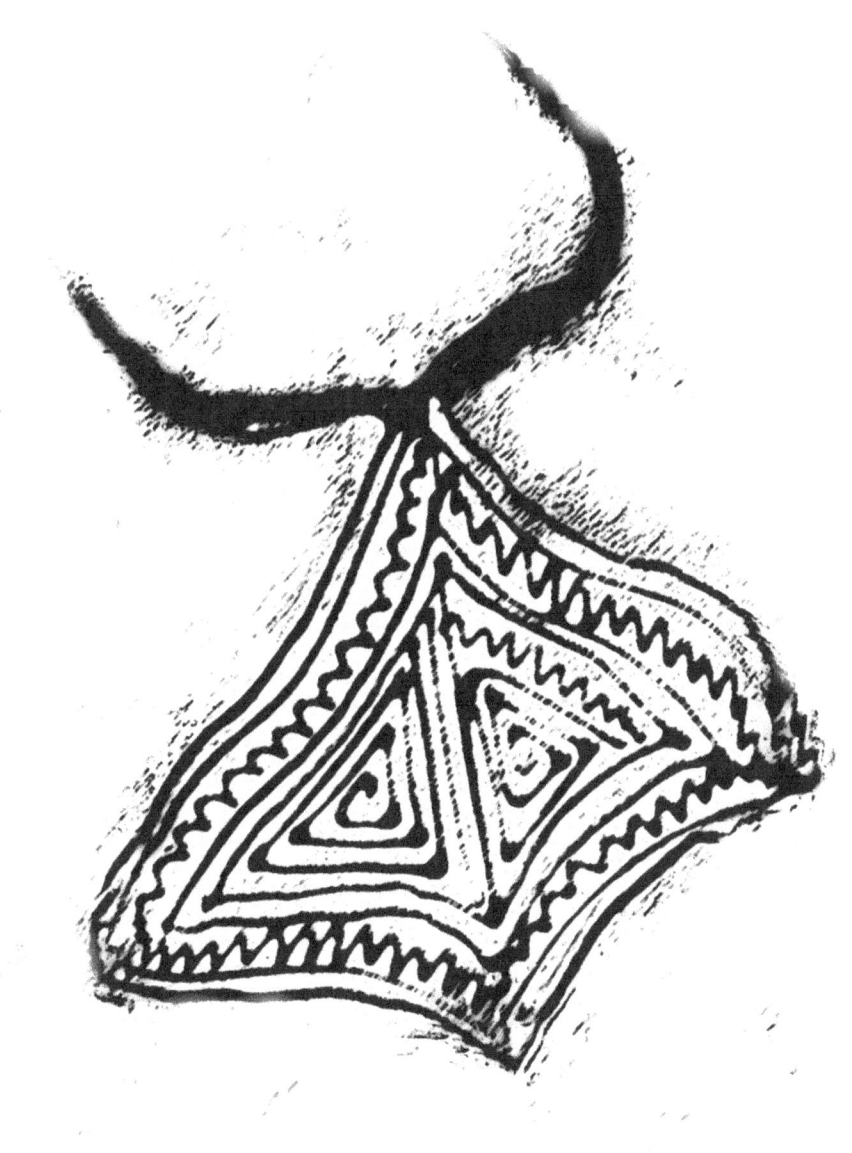

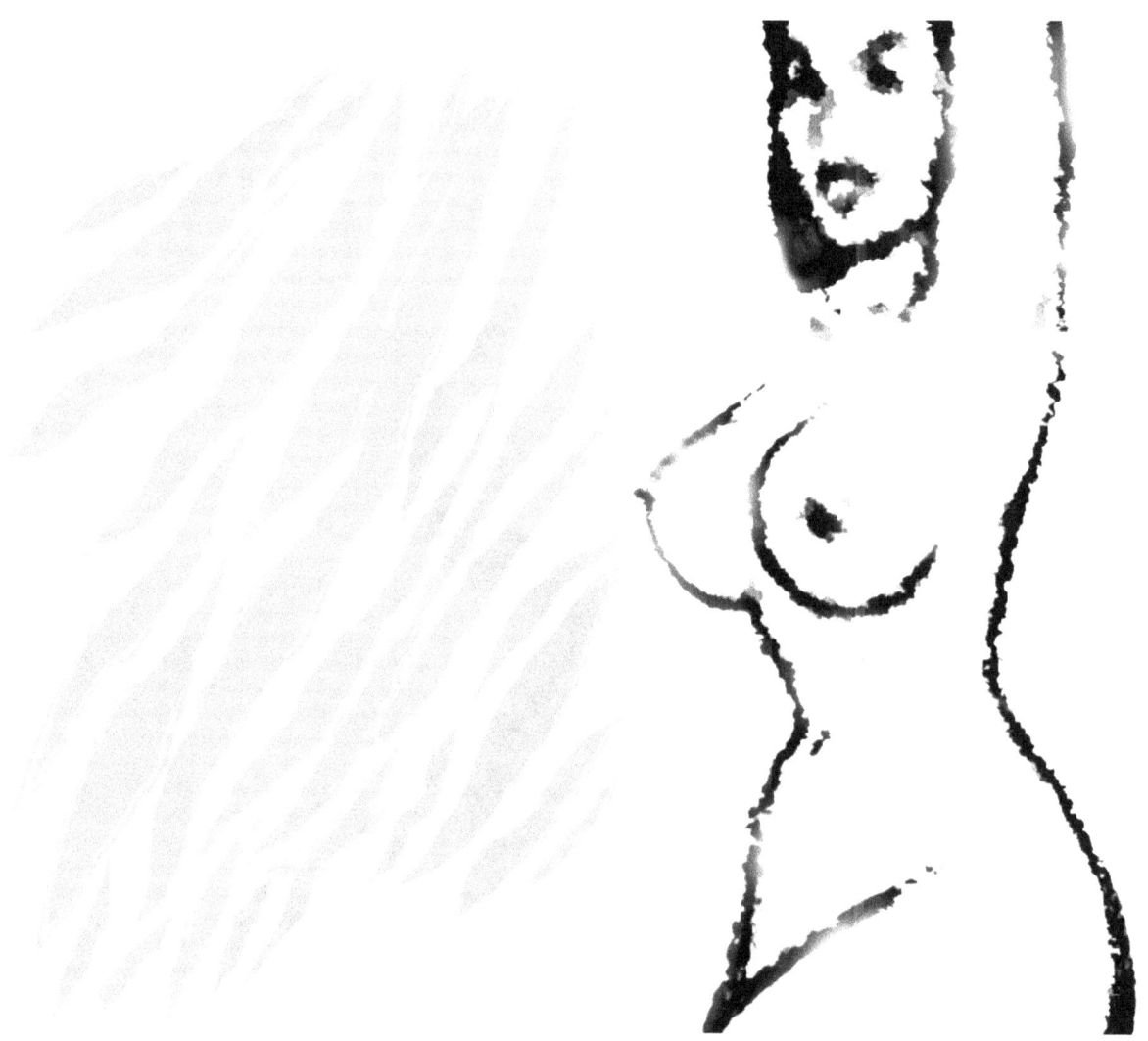

ZEBRA

African quadruped related to ass
and horse with black and white
stipes. Magical quality of image,
style and movement. He walks
like an egyption....No like a zebra.

ZILK

A QC lawyer making a zillion
dollars out of other peoples
misfortune.....Highly respected by
their own kind, right!.....How many
lawyers in Japan?.....How many
lawyers in the western world?

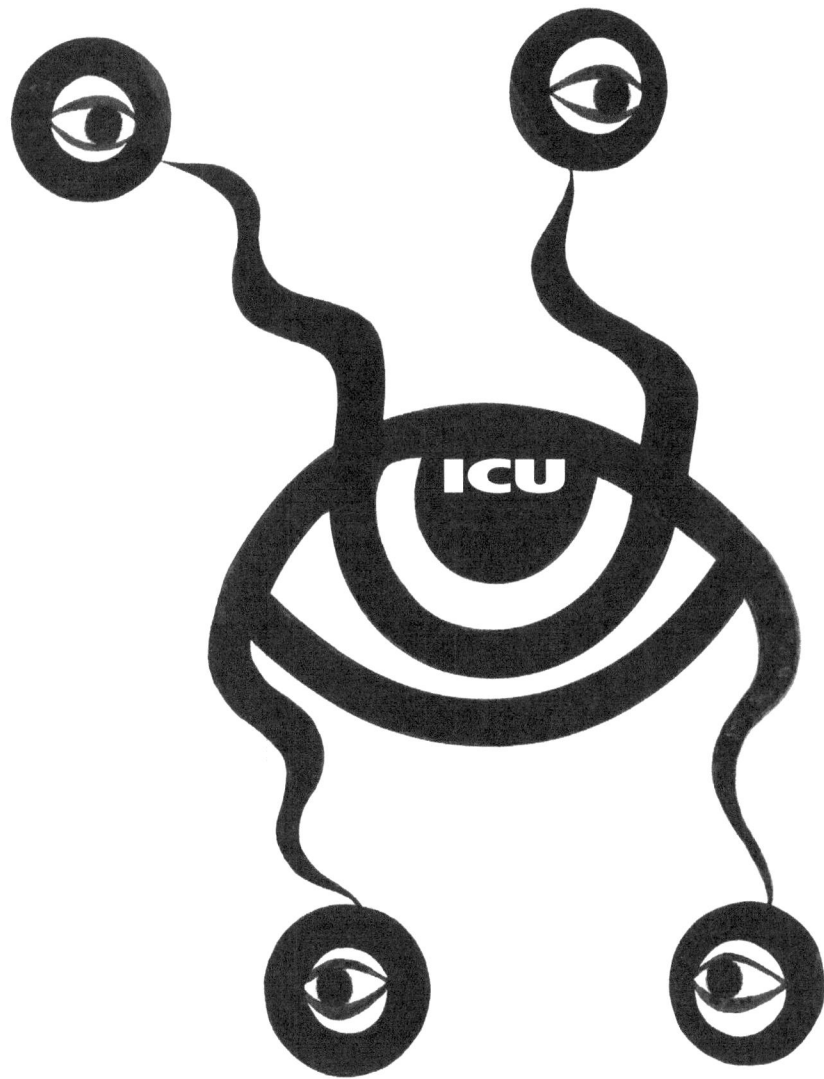

ZOOKERAMA

Sugar...German style panarama of abundant desserts.....Enjoy that white death crystal powder from the sugar cane fields. Addiction to diabetes, stop it, you can have your cake and eat it, obituaries!

ZOOM

That button on apparat that makes images bigger, long shot to close up, five eyes speeding....Zoom zoom..... Visually watching the light fantastic, whiter shade of pale. Allows eyes to view by various focal lengths.

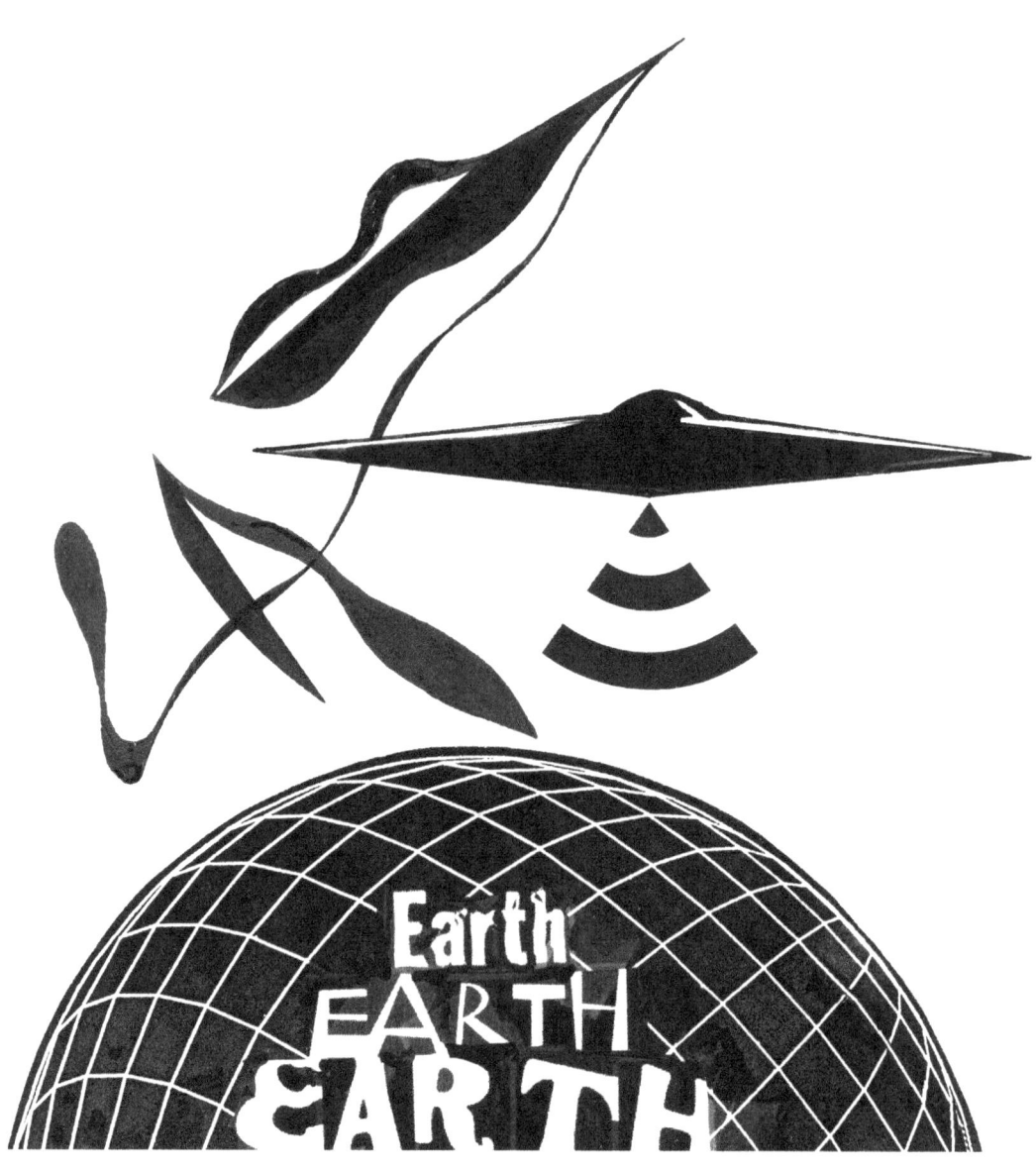

ZION the protocol of the elders, the mandate in the early russian empire to control world wide politics, economies, governments or any of the other pieces of art in this whole book. This is a false conspiracy statement, maybe, but how many are out there continuing this mandate and can you see them with that serious camouflage they use when they skywatch our every movement. Sir your visa card was used in chang mai yesterday can you tell us your travel plans next week? We are looking for communists and anyone who associates with them, to further our enquiries.

THIS TREE IS LIVING LIKE YOU

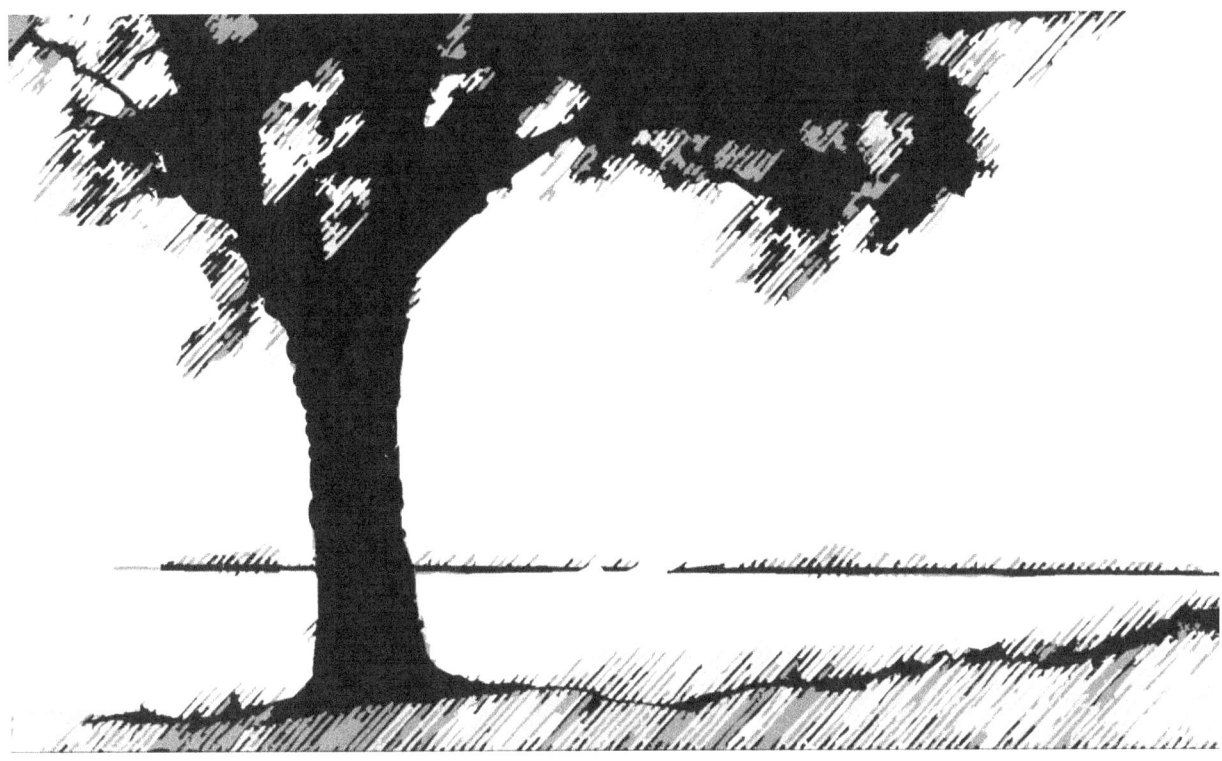

ZING

Vigour, energy.....Move swiftly. Pow!
Ling ming ding bling show me your
belly ring, lets make our union
sing.....I will show you my thing.

ZENNOR

Between st. ives and lands end
near the beach, where you can get
a rip curl on the gulf stream.....

ZEAL

Just sounds so good, he had
so much zeal.....Not looking at
life through a mosquito net. This
is really an over the top hearty
persistent endeavour.

ZELAH

Side or a slope, part of a village or town.....
From those western boring biblical times.
This little village in cornwall which should
be a self governed republic..... Not in the
united kingdom was built above the original dream catcher piskies, that ran the
church of imagination in neolithic times.
The villagers had harvest ceromonies of
psilocybins in september.....The camelot
quorum in Tintagel was born near zelah
in the village of twelveneads and truthan.

ZOOPHYTE

Plantlike animal. Plant like animal!!!.
Really jellyfish, sponge or coral

Upon my head, this is for that person that reads the last page before looking at page 123 or reading the whole book, after all if the first nine pages don't capture you.....You will not persevere.....Continue in the course of action even in the face of difficulty or with little or no indication of success, just like being in that small town mall of western people! About existing in thought or theory rather than matter or reality (in the mind, brain or heart). In art, abstract is a medium, bullshit it does exist.....But does it always have a concrete form? Colour, flow, balance, viewers interpritation often concludes the message or story.....NO..... Yes! Ideas in our minds gallery, are they abstract before they are formalised into a language medium?

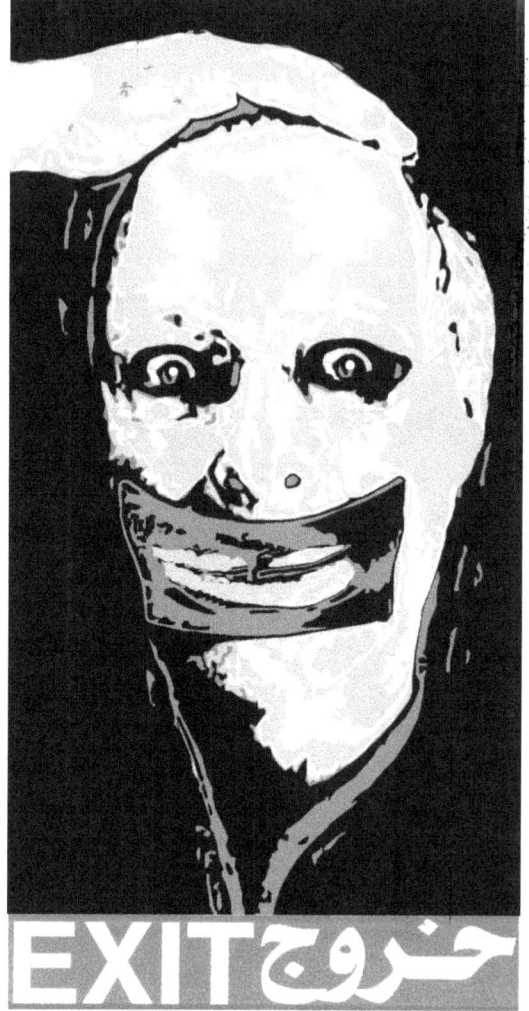

•••••Yes, What is the meaning of this?
Thank you for allowing me to introduce
my selves.....